MAGIC IN HISTORY

The Fortunes of
FAUST

ELIZABETH M. BUTLER

THE PENNSYLVANIA STATE UNIVERSITY PRESS
UNIVERSITY PARK, PENNSYLVANIA

Published in 1998 in the United S tates of America and Canada by
The Pennsylvania State University Press, University Park, PA 16802

First published in 1952 by the Syndics of the Cambridge University
Press

This edition first published in 1998 in the United Kingdon by
Sutton Publishing Limited

ISBN 0 271 01844 5

Library of Congress Cataloging in Publication Data
A CIP catalog record for this book is available from the
Library of Congress

Cover illustration: Dr Faustus *(engraving) by Harmensz van Rijn Rembrandt
(private collection/photograph Bridgeman Art Library, London/New York)*

Printed in Great Britain

The Fortunes of
FAUST

Faust in his Study

CONTENTS

Introduction: FAUST AND DON JUAN   ix

PART I

TRADITIONAL FAUSTS

Chapter I.   LUTHERAN FAUSTS
    (*a*) The original Faust   3
    (*b*) A rhymesters' Faust   13
    (*c*) A fanatic's Faust   22

II.   ENGLISH FAUSTS
    (*a*) An Elizabethan Faustus   31
    (*b*) An immortal Faustus   41
    (*c*) Farcical Fausts   52

III.   HYBRID FAUSTS
    (*a*) Vanished Fausts   69
    (*b*) Miniature Fausts   90

PART II

BRAVE NEW FAUSTS

IV.   ESCAPING FAUSTS
    (*a*) An enlightened Faust, 1759–1784   113
    (*b*) A lucky Faust, 1775   124
    (*c*) Womanizing Fausts, 1772–1778   131

CONTENTS

Chapter V. STORM-TOSSED FAUSTS   *page*

(*a*) A titanic Faust, 1776–1778   141

(*b*) A Faust forlorn, 1777   152

(*c*) Faust in fragments, 1790   154

(*d*) A sombre Faust, 1791   159

VI. FORGOTTEN FAUSTS

(*a*) Faust in Grub Street, 1791–1801   169

(*b*) A quasi-Goethean Faust, 1804   177

VII. POETICAL FAUSTS

(*a*) A romantic Faust, 1804   191

(*b*) An imperishable Faust, 1808   195

PART III

INTERIM FAUSTS

VIII. A MEDLEY OF FAUSTS

(*a*) All sorts and conditions of Fausts, 1809–1823   211

(*b*) Would-be Goethean Fausts, 1811–1833   215

IX. HELENA AND FAUST

(*a*) A histrionic Helen, 1815   228

(*b*) An unearthly Helen, 1827   232

(*c*) A vanquished Helen, 1829   237

X. DON JUAN AND FAUST, 1829   247

XI. THE APOTHEOSIS OF FAUST, 1832   253

PART IV

POST-GOETHEAN FAUSTS

Chapter XII. Non-Goethean Fausts   *page*

    (*a*) Ragtag and bobtail Fausts, 1833–1895   269

    (*b*) An incomprehensible Faust, 1839   276

    (*c*) An ennobled Faust, 1919   280

XIII. Un-Goethean Fausts

    (*a*) A tragic Faust, 1836   284

    (*b*) An irreclaimable Faust, 1842   294

XIV. Anti-Goethean Fausts

    (*a*) *Danse macabre*, 1847   301

    (*b*) 'Schiller's' Faust, 1859–1869   308

    (*c*) A parodied Faust, 1862–1886   311

XV. The First Faust Reborn, 1947   321

Conclusion   339

Bibliography   349

Index   357

FAUST AND DON JUAN

This is the third and concluding volume of a series which has attempted two perhaps incompatible things: to come to rather closer grips with the Faust-legend than has hitherto been done, and also to view it in a wider perspective. *The Myth of the Magus* was chiefly concerned with the place of Faust in the main stream of a tradition deriving from seasonal and kingship rites, stretching back to prehistoric times and reaching forward to the present day. In following the history of the idea through its endless vicissitudes and ravelled ramifications, the loss of status of the magus with the coming of Christianity stood out in strong relief. The god-priest-king of ancient days with his triumphant resurrection became a wicked wizard or shady sorcerer who met a bad end in life and a worse one hereafter unless he repented and forswore magic before his end. This conception which gained ground during the Middle Ages achieved its most categorical statement in the Faust-legend which condemned the hero inexorably to perpetual perdition. In this tragic predicament he remained until the close of the eighteenth century, the deservedly doomed representative of an execrable class. But meanwhile his remote ancestor, the pre-Christian magus, was being rehabilitated by the renascence of occultism and the consequent rise of the secret societies to power from the seventeenth century onwards. Furthered and fostered by them, the sage of antiquity became a super-magus, achieving a curious apotheosis in the Mahatmic doctrine of immortal, omniscient and all-but omnipotent sages and mages, among whom the mysterious Saint-Germain held and still holds a conspicuous position, although he has now fallen from the heights of Theosophical eminence to grace less reputable sects:

You might be interested in knowing that Saint-Germain's mythos is still growing. He was adopted as a patron saint by the I AM cult founded by the Ballards in the U.S. about 1930, whose ideology is a repellent mixture of Theosophy, Rosicrucianism, Spiritualism, Christian Science, etc. In their chapels the Ballardites have a conventional picture of Christ on one side, and on the other a gimlet-eyed bewhiskered character in a white nightgown, allegedly Saint-Germain, but actually as different as can be from the elegant Comte.[1]

Whether or not Saint-Germain will lose caste with the Mahatmas by this and become a spiritually displaced person, his adoption by the Ballardites is at least a sign of his continued posthumous existence.

No such fortune has ever been Faust's, to whom the Himalayan Heavens have remained inflexibly closed. He imposed himself on posterity in a different guise, as was shown in *Ritual Magic*. Humble, if shady and even reprehensible, practitioners of the Black Art in Germany believed in him to the extent of using his name lavishly as the author of magical handbooks warranted to procure for the faithful buried and other treasures galore. The editors of such texts were always at pains to ignore or at least to soften the implications of the pact which, according to the legend-makers, Faust had signed with Mephisto as the price of his immortal soul. The mythologists had in fact invented the pact, basing it on the ritual exorcisms and misinterpreting these in accordance with the Christian belief that magicians were the servants of Satan; whereas mastery over the spirits entailing immunity from physical and spiritual peril was the perennial claim of ritual magic. Faustian legend did violence to ritual; ritual retorted in the Faustian texts by more or less openly pooh-poohing the pact and thus associating the name of Faust with the immemorial traditions of the craft. Interlocked here on the legendary and popular level, the struggle went indecisively on. It then became engaged in the higher altitudes of poetry; and it is this conflict which forms the subject-matter of the present book: the fortunes of Faust in literature. The main duelling-grounds are Germany and England, although the international nature of magic and the world-wide distribution of the myth of the magus would lead one to expect a less circumscribed field. In this respect Faust offers a marked contrast to Don Juan, his great contemporary rival in legendary, literary and musical fame, as a glance at the accompanying chronological sketch will show.

---

[1] From a private letter.

Don Juan and Faust: Chronological Survey

DON JUAN		FAUST	
1350	Don Juan de Tenorio alive	1507–40	Contemporary records of Faust
		1570–87	MS. Collection of tales
	Seville chronicles and oral	1587	First Faustbook
	legends	1592	Dutch Faustbook
		1592	English Faustbook
		c. 1592	MARLOWE
1630	TIRSO DE MOLINA, Spain	1598	French Faustbook
1650	Cicognini, Italy	1608	Marlovian *Faustus* in Graz
1652	Gilberti, Italy	1626	Faust drama in Dresden
1658	Dormion, France	1651	Faust drama in Prague
1659	Villiers, France	1661	Faust drama in Hanover
1662	Cockayn, England	1666	Faust drama in Lüneburg
1665	MOLIÈRE, France	1668	Faust drama in Danzig
1669	Rosimond, France	1679	Faust drama in Munich
1673	Thomas Corneille, France	1684	Mountfort's farce.
1676	Shadwell, England	1688	Faust drama in Bremen
	Puppet-plays in Germany	1696	Faust drama in Basle
1703	Rowe, England	1698	First mention of German
1736	GOLDONI, Italy		puppet-play
1744	Zamora, Spain	1724	Pantomine at Drury Lane
1748	CLARISSA HARLOWE, England	1728	On English puppet-stage
		1730	Ballet in Vienna
c. 1765	GLUCK, Germany		
1777	Regnini, opera, Italy	1759	LESSING's scene
1782	Gluck at Drury Lane	1770	Last popular Faust drama
1787	MOZART and Da Ponte, Germany		(Hamburg)
		1776–8	Müller
		1790	GOETHE's *Fragment*
1817	English tr. of Da Ponte	c. 1790	A Faust drama in the Tirol
1817	Dibdin, burletta, England	1790	Klinger
1817	Moncrieff, farce, England	1808	GOETHE's *Faust I*
1818ff	BYRON, England	1814	Strauss
1829	Grabbe, DON JUAN AND FAUST, Germany	1815	Klingemann
		1817	BYRON's *Manfred*
1834	MÉRIMÉE, France	1829	Grabbe, DON JUAN AND FAUST
1836	DUMAS *père*, France		
1840	Espronceda, Spain	1827	GOETHE's Helena act
1840	Sigismund Wiese, Germany	1832	GOETHE's *Faust II*
1844	ZORILLA, Spain	1836	LENAU
1850	LENAU, Germany	1842	Nürnberger
1887	Campoamor, Spain	1846	Berlioz
		1851	HEINE
1903	BERNARD SHAW, England	1857	Spohr
1923	ARNOLD BENNETT, England	c. 1859	Gounod
		1862–86	Vischer
1925	FLECKER, England		
1937	Humbert Wolfe, England	1919	Avenarius
1938	Sylvia Townsend Warner, England	1946	VALÉRY
		1947	THOMAS MANN

Spain, Italy, France, Germany and England have all been instrumental in furthering the headlong career of Don Juan in Europe. Tirso de Molina and Zorilla in Spain; Goldoni in Italy; Molière, Merimée and Dumas *père* in France; Mozart, Grabbe and Lenau in Germany; Byron, Shaw, Bennett and Flecker in England. Irrespective of the value (often disconcertingly slight) of the various contributions, this is an impressive list; whereas the only non-German names of any eminence associated with the name of Faust are those of Marlowe, Byron and Valéry. They are great names, to be sure; but Don Juan's international status is considerably higher; and not only that—he has been immortalized by music, the most universal of the arts, in a manner which Faust has rather signally failed to achieve.

There are two main reasons, it would seem, for the relatively inconspicuous international and musical triumphs which have fallen to the lot of Faust. The mainspring of Don Juan's actions is passionate love, and the deep desire for knowledge is the mainspring of Faust's. Both are tremendously powerful emotions: the one perpetuates the species; the other has conditioned our history and created our religions; and both are harnessed to the even more fundamental instinct to persist and survive. Yet in the eyes of Western Europe at least, the one has acquired a beauty, a glamour and a mystery to which the other cannot aspire; it has become the poetical theme *par excellence*; the very word love-interest, that parlous parrot-cry, shows how this ubiquitous *motiv*, not content with making the world go round, has also cornered the literary market. Many aesthetic crimes have been committed in its name; many a noble theme handed down from classical antiquity has been trivialized or vulgarized by its inevitable introduction; but it has also created poems, novels and plays of peerless and breath-taking beauty: and the conception of Don Juan, the ruthless, irresistible, conquering male, took Europe by storm; whilst the equally ruthless, titanically aspiring Faust remained caviare to the non-German general public. Moreover music, the language of love, had nothing to say about Faust until he became entangled with Gretchen. For with the entry of the Faust-legend into German literature, love-interest seized upon the theme; first in the plebeian guise of domestic tragedy, then with Goethe in the irresistible form of folk-poetry, and finally with Grabbe, Lenau and Nürnberger in Don Juanesque attire. For Don Juan's personality was stronger than Faust's and at one time overshadowed him. Both Byron and Lenau gravitated from Faust to Don Juan; and few of the Faustian writers after Mozart refrained from inoculating Don Juanism into the magician's veins. Grabbe for his part confronted the two; and lo, not only was Faust a Don Juan *manqué*, but the Spaniard acted the German right off the stage. In a way this was symbolical of what was happening to the two legends in European literature; but it needs some qualification.

The authors of the popular Faust dramas in the seventeenth century in Germany are anonymous and their texts have disappeared. From play-bills, advertisements and the like, the steep descent from Marlowe is evident; but it seems to have been partly compensated by the introduction of genuinely popular and traditional elements. No such compensation is to be found in the contemporary Don Juan dramas. Whether in Italy, France or England, they are, not even excepting Molière, debased literary versions of the great Spanish original and cannot hold a candle to it. When Faust and Don Juan met on the German puppet-stage in Augsburg, Strasbourg and Ulm, there was no comparing them. Don Juan, a criminal and a cad, derived through France from Italy; Faust, an eerie and tragic manikin, was the strange result of a misalliance between Marlowe and the popular mind. Mozart's music rescued Don Juan from the degradation still evident in Da Ponte's text; and Goethe reinstated Faust in the first part of his dramatic poem. The literary current was strongly stirred, but chiefly in Don Juan's favour. Byron, Grabbe and Lenau witness to that. Byron's rather over-wrought *Manfred* cannot be mentioned in the same breath with his incomparable *Don Juan*; make what efforts Grabbe would, his Don Juan outshone his Faust at every turn, combining something of the dynamic power of *El Burlador* with the irresistible appeal of Mozart's music. As for Lenau, the hero of his *Faust* is three parts Don Juan; and his *Don Juan* is drenched in such loveliness and instinct with such poetry and imagination as to throw even his *Faust* into the shade. Neither a Spaniard nor a German, but with the bold bearing of a Magyar and the melting accents of a Slav, Lenau's Don Juan has still, I think, to meet his poetical peer in modern times outside Spain; for the hero of Espronceda's *El estudiante de Salamanca* rivals him there.

Published posthumously in 1850, Lenau's poem must have been completed before 1844, when he lost his reason. It is therefore a product of the same year as saw Zorilla's spectacular rescue of Don Juan from the flames of hell. Goethe had performed the same good office for Faust twelve years earlier; but in both cases the work of salvation had been implemented by others: by Zamora in 1744 and by Lessing before his death in 1781. The spirit of the age demanded it, but it was no easy task in either case. Marlowe's *Tragical History* and Molina's *El Burlador* blocked the way, two wonderfully powerful dramatic organisms, sternly standing for tragic tradition. The phantom of Doña Inez and the spirit of Gretchen were invoked; but technical aid was also sought from frankly spectacular effects. Neither Goethe nor Zorilla was really successful here; but Zorilla's cemetery and his animated and talkative statues were firmly founded on the legendary tradition; they earned universal popular acclamation in Spain as a result; whereas Goethe's final scene in *Faust II* has had to be content with the laboured and at times asthmatic enthusiasm of German aesthetic critics.

The power of tradition, evident everywhere in art, is a vital element in the life of legend in literature, where the collaboration between the popular and the poetical mind is or should be at its closest. And this is the second main reason why Don Juan has on the whole imposed himself more strongly on the European consciousness than Faust. Both legends stretch far back into a mythical past, in which seasonal rites were enacted and also funeral rites; but only the latter still survive in any real sense; adopted and modified by Christianity they are now a permanent feature of the celebrations on All Souls Day in Latin and Catholic countries:

. . . as recently as 1931 the people of Vigo still kept the 2nd of November in memory of those who had died during the past year; and indeed, of all those relations and friends who were no longer alive and whose memory was dear to them. Early on the morning of this day the bells of the churches call the faithful to mass: that service which was instituted ages ago for the souls of all the dead who sleep in Christ. Under the sombre sky, when as yet it is still but a grey twilight, dressed in their holiday attire, the worshippers hurry through the streets to the even gloomier churches. There in the uncertain light of flickering candles they listen with bowed heads while priests and choristers chant the lugubrious service. There, too, they make their offerings of candles before the shrine of Saint or Virgin; even as in immemorial Egypt the worshippers made their offerings at the feet of the dead gods.

Mass over, the congregation return to their homes to prepare the meal for the cemetery feast. Then, laden with their provisions, their simple offering of flowers and the little candle lamps for the tombs, they make their way to the graveyards on the outskirts of the town. . . . In the cemetery they separate, each family grouping themselves around the graves of their own dead, decorating them with flowers and lamps, making them neat and tidy for the great occasion; eating and drinking in company with the departed ones. . . . Then, as the daylight fades, and the little lamps glow pale through the grey dusk, they gather up their belongings and, taking farewell of the silent sleepers, they return slowly to the life of the town. Here all the theatres, even the cinemas, present the great treat of the day: José Zorrilla's *Don Juan Tenorio* [which has replaced Zamora's], staged for this special occasion year after year as a fitting end to so great a festival. . . . It is the climax of their festive day. Thus, in Spain at least, Don Juan is, in very fact, the hero of this immemorial custom; and by the strange chances of time, the last representative of Osiris, first god and guardian of the dead.[1]

No such 'strange chance of time' has operated in favour of Faust and no day in the Christian calendar could be connected by the wildest stretch of imagination with this pariah-god, who will never regain his lost status, in spite of all that Goethe has done for him. His connection with the popular mind, as far as ritual observance goes, has been confined exclusively to Black Books used in the service of the gentle art of money-grubbing. This is poetic justice, for the dim historical figure who gave his name to the legend was precisely the sort of person to whom his supposed magical hand-books appealed: a shady specimen of the sorcerer class; whereas the real Don Juan de Tenorio belonged to a more prepossessing category in whom courage and cruelty, ruthlessness and gallantry, audacity and arrogance were on the heroic scale. 'Es un Tenorio.' Such was the young hero-villain of legendary exploits who was finally cast for the rôle of protagonist in Molina's version of those grim and macabre tales of invitations to the dead which were told orally all over Spain and beyond from time immemorial, and were still being told on the Peninsula in 1905.[2] There is no denying that Molina's Don Juan shone in his double rôle:

> Great lord, within those royal hands of thine
> Lives all my life. For all that lives in me

[1] J. Austen, *The Story of Don Juan*, London, 1939, pp. 100 ff.
[2] Cf. Austen, op. cit., pp. 113 ff.

Lives in the life of that rebellious son,
Who yet is valiant, young and gallant too;
So brave, they call him Hector, his young peers:
Hector of Seville, for his valiant feats,
Many and signal, daring deeds of youth.[1]

In this guise he achieved literary status at one bound; whereas Faust fought his way through the folkbooks into Marlowe's drama, which irradiated him with a tragic glory only Marlowe could have bestowed:

For, falling to a devilish exercise,
And glutted now with learning's golden gifts,
He surfeits upon cursed necromancy;
Nothing so sweet as magic is to him,
Which he prefers before his chiefest bliss:
And this the man that in his study sits.[2]

Thereafter Faustus bore a charmed life in popular literature, whether in ballads or farces or pantomimes; whether as a barn-stormer or in the puppet-booths: the rudest and roughest handling could not destroy him. But when the day of rationalism dawned he was threatened with extinction at the hands of enlightenment and might have succumbed had Goethe not saved him in *Faust I* by leading him back to the fount of folk-songs and folk-poetry. Almost simultaneously Mozart revived Don Juan, who was withering away in sophisticated literature, by the magic of his music:

After Molière comes the artist-enchanter, the master of masters, Mozart, who reveals the hero's spirit in magical harmonies, elfin tones, and elate darting rhythms as of summer lightning made audible. Here you have freedom in love and in morality mocking exquisitely at slavery to them, and interesting you, attracting you, tempting you, inexplicably forcing you to range the hero with his enemy the statue on a transcendant plane. . . .[3]

Perhaps only Shaw himself, that merciless *raisonneur*, could have disenchanted and undone the work of Mozart. Juan has not recovered yet from the deadening effect of the sermon on the Life

[1] Tirso de Molina [Gabriel Tellez], *Obras*, Madrid, 1922, Vol. I, p. 225.
[2] C. Marlowe, *The Tragical History of Doctor Faustus*, ed. Boas, London, 1932, p. 57.
[3] G. B. Shaw, *Man and Superman*, London, 1928, p. x.

Force in *Man and Superman*. Bennett and Flecker, following in the footsteps of Merimée and Dumas (to whom Zorilla also owed a debt), moved on from Don Juan to Don Miguel de Mañara, 'the worst man in the world', who, after crimes unspeakable, repented as violently as he had sinned and made a saint-like end.

And Faust? Has he disappeared from sight in the Goethean empyrean, as Don Juan vanished into Shavian skies? Far from it. There is a marked difference between the fortunes of Don Juan and Faust in literature. The first has had a much wider distribution in Europe; the second has generated a much more numerous progeny in Germany than has fallen to the lot of Juan in Spain. The present book contains a more or less detailed study of nearly fifty specimens, mentions more and lists still others in the bibliography; and there are also the countless traditional versions produced anonymously. It is symptomatic of the extreme tenacity of the Faust-legend over educated German minds that there are upward of fifty *Fausts* of one sort or another after Goethe's *Faust II*. Exercising a rigorous selection here, I have given some account of seventeen. Among them are those of Lenau, Heine and Thomas Mann, all three of whom were intent on rescuing Faust from the rarefied regions to which Goethe had finally relegated him. They were bravely aided and abetted in this by that brilliant parodist Theodore Vischer. The proportion of success which has attended their efforts is part of the story of the fortunes of Faust.

PART I. TRADITIONAL FAUSTS

Chapter I. LUTHERAN FAUSTS
      (*a*) The original Faust
      (*b*) A rhymesters' Faust
      (*c*) A fanatic's Faust

II. ENGLISH FAUSTS
      (*a*) An Elizabethan Faustus
      (*b*) An immortal Faustus
      (*c*) Farcical Fausts

III. HYBRID FAUSTS
      (*a*) Vanished Fausts
      (*b*) Miniature Fausts

LUTHERAN FAUSTS

(a) *The original Faust*

The Spiess Faustbook of 1587, which has proved itself to be one of the greatest inspirational books of modern times, is surrounded by a massive wall of belief abutting on to the rock of faith. One cannot get over and one cannot get round; one can only get in by using the key to the gate of entrance, the text quoted on the title-page:

'Submit yourselves therefore to God. Resist the devil, and he will flee from you.' James, iv, 7.

And one can only get out again by the door of exit, to which the key is found at the end of the book:

'Be sober, be vigilant; because your adversary the devil, as a roaring lion, walketh about, seeking whom he may devour.' I Peter, v, 8.

The reader has been in very strange company and has taken part in terrifying, grotesque, preposterous and incredible incidents. Emperors and dukes, devils and wraiths, peasants and boors, students and monks have surged round him; palaces, market-squares, cellars and inns have flashed past; he has travelled far and wide over the earth, he has visited hell and journeyed through the air. It was all like a dream, a nightmare-dream, distorting life and humanity. But there was reality too behind the shifting phantas-magoria: the grim reality of an aspiring mind goaded to the desperate step of concluding a pact with the powers of evil; the torments, the terrors and unavailing remorse; the fearful question-ings, the vain efforts to repent, and the final horror of the taking off.

The first coherent account of Faust's life and death boasts one characteristic not to be found, or only embryonically present, in previous narratives of medieval magicians and sorcerers. These on the whole confined themselves to telling the story and stressing the miracles and feats. 'Spiess'[1] in the still living and vital parts of his biography emphasized the psychology of the situation. It is true that the spiritual pride of Simon Magus and the hectic lust of Cyprian adequately account for their implicit or explicit bondage to Satan. It is also true that the external facts which led Theophilus to league himself with the prince of darkness are made abundantly clear, and that much space is given to his rather stereotyped outbursts of repentance and remorse. But 'Spiess', dealing with a man not long since dead, attempted and indeed succeeded in representing the type of darkly questioning mind which James I delineated in his *Daemonologie* ten years later, the eternally unsatisfied spirit of scientific enquiry, the incurable thirst for knowledge which drives its victims to transgress human limitations:

For divers men having attained to a great perfection in learning, and yet remaining overbare (alas) of the spirit of regeneration and frutes thereof: finding all naturall thinges common, aswell to the stupide pedants as vnto them, they assaie to vendicate vnto them a greater name, by not onlie knowing the course of things heavenlie, but likewise to clim to the knowledge of things to come thereby. Which, at the first face appearing lawfull vnto them, in respect the ground thereof seemeth to proceed of naturall causes onlie: they are so allured thereby, that finding their practize to prooue true in sundry things, they studie to know the cause thereof: and so mounting from degree to degree, vpon the slipperie and vncertain scale of curiositie; they are at last entised, that where lawfull artes or sciences failes, to satisfie their restles mindes, even to seeke to that black and vnlawfull science of *Magie*.[2]

This might almost be a description of the hero of the Faustbook, and may even have been inspired by it, since it had been translated into English in 1592 and contains passages which harmonize with the above:

As announced above the mind of Dr. Faustus was fain to love forbidden things, after which he hankered night and day, taking unto himself the wings of an eagle in order to search out the uttermost parts of heaven and earth; for his frowardness, lawlessness and wantonness pricked and goaded him to such a degree, that the time came when he

[1] Spiess was the name of the publisher of the first Faustbook, published in Frankfurt am Main in 1587 with a preamble by him. I use his name in inverted commas when referring to the anonymous author, and I use Scheible's edition in *Das Kloster*. I also refer *passim* to the first edition of 'Spiess' as the Urfaustbook.

[2] King James I, *Daemonologie* (1597), London, 1924, p. 10.

4

decided to try out and put into action certain magic words, figures, characters and conjurations in order to summon up the devil before him.[1]

And this apostasy was nothing more nor less than his pride and arrogance, despair, audacity and insolence, like unto those giants of whom the poets sing that they carried the mountains together and were fain to make war on God, yea like unto that evil angel who opposed God, and was cast off by God on account of his arrogance and presumption.[2]

Moreover the text of the pact, which I have given elsewhere[3], fully bears out the ruthless nature of Faust's insatiable desire for knowledge. There was no stopping him; he must have truthful answers to all his questions, even if it meant renouncing God, the whole heavenly host and all human beings; and even though the blood with which he was about to engross the deed formed the words *O Homo fuge* in the palm of his left hand. Yet it cannot be said that he was reckless of the consequences. Invincible obstinacy and a conscience at once hardened to crime and most prone to remorse and fear (two of the criteria mentioned by Eliphas Lévi as marking out black magicians) are in evidence throughout. And it is the desperate heart made manifest even more than the horror of the biographer which gives emotional value to the tale. The conjuration-scene, the cohorts of Infernus, Faust's supernatural and terrestrial journeys, his magical tricks, even the feats of necromancy, even the evocation of Helen of Troy and the sprite (Justus Faustus) she bare to Faust, are incidental to that; though the fearful explosion of Satan's wrath and his direful warnings when Faust broke the spirit of the agreement by hankering after the married state show to what a powerful and malignant spirit the magician had surrendered his soul. But the recurrent uneasy questions always circling round the dread subjects of hell, the fallen angels and the torments of the damned; the devil's evasive answers finally yielding to plain and brutal speech; the categorical denial that the lost can ever be saved; Faust's heavy melancholy and fruitless remorse, so near and yet so far from repentance—all this is darkly impressive and sombrely sorrowful:

[1] J. Scheible, *Das Kloster*, Stuttgart and Leipzig, 1846, Vol. II, p. 943.
[2] Scheible, op. cit. Vol. II, p. 950.
[3] *Ritual Magic*, pp. 187 f; cf. also in the present study p. 330.

If you were in my place [Faust demanded of Mephistopheles], a human being created by God, what would you do to be pleasing to God and man?

Were I like you [answered his dreadful familiar], I would bow myself before God as long as the breath of life was in me; and I would take thought not to provoke the wrath of God against me, but to obey as far as in me lay his teachings, laws and commandments, and call upon him alone, praise, honour and glorify him alone, that I might be pleasing and acceptable to God, and might know that after my death, I would attain to eternal joy, glory and splendour. Doctor Faustus answered thereto: But this I have not done. Indeed no, answered the spirit: you have not done this. On the contrary, you have denied your creator, who created you, and gave you speech, sight and hearing in order that you might comprehend his will and strive after eternal salvation; you have abused the glorious gift of your understanding, you have rejected God and all mankind, for which you have none to blame, but only your own proud and arrogant spirit, through which you have thus lost your best treasure and jewel, the refuge in God. Yes, alas, that is true, said Doctor Faustus; but tell me, Mephostophiles, would you fain be a man instead of me? Yes, replied the spirit with a sigh; and here there is no need of much argument with you; for even if I had thus sinned against God, I would nevertheless yet restore myself to his grace. To whom Doctor Faustus made answer: So then for me there is still time if I should amend. Yes, said the spirit, if you could but come to the grace of God with such gross sins; but now it is too late, and the wrath of God is heavy upon you. Leave me in peace, said Doctor Faustus to the spirit. And the spirit made answer: Then leave me in peace henceforward with your questions.[1]

Mephisto's answers, including the blasphemous lie 'too late', give the real truth of the situation, a psychological rather than a theological dilemma. It was not then, nor ever would be, 'too late' to repent and achieve the grace of God; but the hero of this tragic tale was incapable of real repentance:

For his remorse was the remorse and repentance of Cain and Judas, for though he felt remorse in his heart, he despaired of the grace of God. . . . He was haunted by thoughts of the devil and hell, and he realised what he had done, and ceased not to believe that through many and oft times disputing, questioning and talking with the spirit, he

[1] Scheible, op. cit. Vol. II, pp. 973 f. Although the early form of the spirit's name was Mephostophiles, I use the now familiar modern Mephistopheles throughout except in quotations.

6

would finally attain to betterment, remorse and abstinence. But it was all in vain, for the devil had too strong a hold over him.[1]

In striking contrast to the spiritual tragedy illuminated in the beginning and again towards the end of the biography are the grotesque descriptions of the supernatural journeys undertaken by Faust, the pedestrian chronicle of his terrestrial wanderings lifted bodily for the most part from a contemporary geographical compilation,[2] and the collection of tales of the magic feats he achieved. This forms the really popular part of the book, the nucleus round which the cosmic drama crystallized. These stories were all traditional, and it has often been pointed out that by concentrating them in this manner and attributing them to Faust, he was made heir to the feats of a long and famous line of magi, magicians and sorcerers, whose deeds if not whose names still lived on in popular esteem. But he was a degraded heir, and the magical tradition had deteriorated greatly. The tales are devoid of glory and glamour; there is nothing weird, strange, sinister or imaginative about them. Yet great names, and interesting ones, have been discovered by those who have investigated the remote or contemporary sources of the Faustian feats: Moses and Aaron countering the magic of Pharaoh's sorcerers Jamnes and Jambres; the Witch of Endor raising Samuel's spirit at the bidding of Saul; Numa Pompilius and his Egeria (? 714–671 B.C.); a master-magician of the North called Othin (probably Odin); Virgil (70–1 B.C.), who had a second existence in medieval Europe as an extremely powerful sorcerer; the notorious and ill-starred Simon Magus; Merlin, half fiend, half mortal; Nero's dreaded necromancer Teridates (A.D. 54–68); the Jew Zedechias attached to the court of Louis the Pious (814–849); the far-famed Albertus Magus (1193–1280); the brilliant Roger Bacon (1214–94); Johannes Teutonicus, Canon of Halberstadt in 1271; a certain Magister Theodo, a Prince Baian and a much talked-of Wildfire, who were roughly Roger Bacon's contemporaries; the mischievous and malicious but wonderfully clever Bohemian Zyto at the court of King Wenceslas IV at the end of the fourteenth century; Faust's famous contemporaries, Tritheim, Agrippa and Paracelsus—all these and several anonymous sorcerers whose feats were published by the demonologists Bodin, Wierus, Reginald Scot and Lercheimer some years before 'Spiess' brought

[1] Scheible, op. cit. Vol. II, p. 965.   [2] Schedel's *Nürnberger Chronik*.

out his Faustbook contributed their quota to the stories now told about the hero of that biography. There were borrowings also from *The Gesta Romanorum*, *The Golden Legend*, from Ariosto and Boccaccio. It sounds impressive enough: a whole body of oral and written tradition, much of it of great antiquity, some of it pre-historic, swarming round and settling on the figure of a sixteenth-century charlatan and transforming him into a myth.

It *sounds* impressive, but an examination of the text destroys the conception. It was not the bizarre or boisterous, the ugly, cruel, spiteful or paltry, the shop-soiled collection of tricks which effected this miraculous transformation. It was the vision of a despairing soul in torment, it was the deep religious feeling of the biographer (certainly no *raconteur*) which produced such immortality as mortals can bestow upon the name of Faustus, who also covered himself with honour and glory in the eyes of Marlowe and later of Goethe and Heine by conceiving a fatal passion for Helen of Troy. In the years to come Helen was to disappear and reappear again and again in subsequent versions of the legend as befits a bewildering wraith. She was there from the beginning, and could and often did play an important, indeed decisive, part, but she was never really vital to the action; and if to-day the name of Faustus were given in a thought-association test, the overwhelming majority of responses would be divided between Mephistopheles and Gretchen, that lovely and lovelorn late-comer. The great adversary to the hero of the Urfaustbook, the evil spirit with the arresting name, the fiend so deeply versed in the knowledge of good and evil, with his black despair, his fearful ruthlessness and sinister immunity from pity, is the real and efficient cause for the hold which the sixteenth-century tale of damnation and doom had over the minds of the readers. His effect upon Faust is represented indirectly and perhaps not even consciously by the fact that something latently noble or more precisely titanic in the hero's mind diminishes as the tale goes on. The author may have been merely losing grip as he weltered amongst the anecdotes of magic; but he probably wished to portray the progress of the moral degradation of the hero. This is further indicated by the vain attempt made by Faust's neighbour, a good old man, to persuade him to repent and to throw himself on the mercy of God. Faust half-heartedly promised to mend his ways, and went home to reflect on repentance and atonement. But his better self was soon put to flight by the angry

8

menaces of Mephistopheles to tear him limb from limb. Terrified by this threat, Faust signed a second and even more binding oath of allegiance, whilst Lucifer for his part promised that his servant

The Death of Faust

should suffer no physical torments in hell. Years of soft and lewd living had taken their toll of the man who at the outset of his career sinned from spiritual pride. The venomous hatred he experienced against the would-be saviour of his soul and the cynical complaisance with which he sped his graceless servant Wagner along the same road to eternal perdition do not dispose one to listen very sympathetically to those maudlin laments he began to pour forth when the fearful day of reckoning was at hand. Here again, the author may have exhausted the vein of sombre eloquence with which Faust had earlier searched his heart; or he may have intended to show that the spiritual ruin was real. Certainly the contemptuous, utterly merciless and highly moral answer of the spirit expresses the views of the author, at times literally in the language of Luther. It is like a bracing if bitter blast of fresh air sweeping through the craven turpitude of the laments.

9

This cathartic outburst was followed by a last wild plaint, and then came the violent and terrible end of the unhappy magician. In a little village inn about half a mile from Wittenberg he prepared himself for what was coming by making a plenary confession of his tragic and hopeless situation to the students he had invited to sup with him, begging that it might serve them as a warning. This can be interpreted as a travesty of the Last Supper, and it probably was intended to evoke a comparison, but without any blasphemous intent; or it may have been merely an automatic adherence to a pattern which had become traditional. The deeply religious author was probably well aware of the emotional effect of the parallel and the weight it gave to Faust's utterance that he would gladly surrender his body to the devil if his soul might in that way escape. Shaken to the core, his audience reiterated that forlorn and desperate hope:

When they had heard what he had to say, they answered: Since now nothing else was to be hoped for, he must call upon God and pray for forgiveness for the sake of his beloved son Jesus Christ, and say: Be merciful to me a sinner, and enter not into judgment with me, for I cannot be justified in Thy sight. Although I must surrender my body to the devil, nevertheless consent to save my soul. He agreed to do that, but like Cain he could not be convinced, who also said that his sins were too great to be forgiven. For he perpetually told himself that he had offended too grossly with the pact.[1]

As the pact had expressly included the soul of the magician, one can sympathize with Faust's despair of forgiveness; but this did not preclude him from clutching at the straw as he felt himself sinking into the depths of the ocean of damnation. He bade farewell to the students and wished them a peaceful night, expressly hoping that he for his part might have a vexed, bad and terrible one; that is to say he was offering his body as a ransom for his soul; whereas in the second pact he had signed his soul away for immunity from bodily torment. His injunction to the students not to watch with him but to seek their rest once more points a moral: the immeasurable abyss between the agony in Gethsemane and the anguish here. How did that anguish ultimately end? It is not really possible to say; for though Faust's body was torn limb from limb during the night to the sound of his terrified cries, this was no

---

[1] Scheible, op. cit. Vol. II, p. 1067.

earnest of salvation, which indeed the penultimate words of the story seem to deny:

> Thereafter it became so uncanny in his house, that no one could live in it. And Doctor Faustus appeared bodily to his Famulus by night and revealed many secret things to him. And those too who went by his house at night saw him looking out of the window.[1]

So frail, indeed so flimsy, is the hope twice uncertainly held out in the text that it is not to be wondered at if neither the contemporaries of 'Spiess' nor succeeding generations paid any heed to it. Overwhelmed, overpowered, overridden by the Lutheran belief in the malignant might of the devil and in the numberless hosts of the damned, the salvation of an arch-sinner such as Faust had no chance to prevail, though it existed as a possibility in his own tormented mind. But the inspiration behind the biographical portions of the book is so Lutheran that one almost seems to hear the clarion tones of the great Reformer proclaiming his disastrous conviction that the whole of human life is entangled beyond disentangling in the wiles and snares of the devil. Nevertheless the ghost of a glimmer of a doubt has crept into the text about the ultimate fate of Faust. It may have been a verbal survival or reminiscence of the more merciful Catholic tradition, according to which another famous pact-maker, Pope Sylvester II (Gerbert), drew down the divine grace by a genuine eleventh-hour repentance, vouched for by the command that his body should be mutilated before and after his death. Characteristically enough Hans Sachs, whether before or after his Lutheranization, adopted this version of the tale, though subsequent Protestant writers insisted that Sylvester had been damned. Not so the humane and laughter-loving cobbler, who ended the story of Gerbert with the following reassuring reflection:

> Now from this story mark and see
> That no sinner of any degree
> Of God's great mercy need despair.[2]

Wherever the ambiguity in the Urfaustbook may have come from, and whether the author were fully aware of it or not, it is

---

[1] Scheible, op. cit. Vol. II, pp. 1068f.

[2] Hans Sachs, *Dichtungen*, ed. Goedeke and Titmann, in *Deutsche Dichter des XVI Jahrhunderts*, Leipzig, 1870, Vol. II, p. 175.

there: a faint, wavering question-mark at the end of an otherwise unequivocal statement that Faust was damned to all eternity in hell. It is like a minute fissure in an impregnable fortress of faith; coming ages were to widen it into a breach and thus take the tragic citadel by storm. In view of the future history of the legend the significance of this infinitesimal loop-hole needs no pointing out.

Another aspect of the Urfaustbook also claims attention: the extreme discrepancy both in content and style between the biographical and anecdotal portions of this arresting and unequal work. It was the direct outcome of a mystery which has plagued the minds of men almost since the beginning of time, the strange and unpalatable fact that religion and magic came into the world as Siamese twins, linked together by a supernatural affinity, a bond which no amount of spiritual incompatibility could sever. Medieval theology had recourse to the desperate remedy of cutting them asunder, and thereby dealt a fearful injury to magic, the left-hand and weaker twin, in whose arteries nevertheless the blood of religion still circulated, whilst magic still coursed through the veins of the stronger; but, in both cases sundered from the living source, the alien element was harmful. And yet one cannot blame the theological surgeons; for the sight of those two distinct and separate entities coupled together by an inscrutable fate was barely tolerable. Moreover the widely differing expressions on their strangely similar features seemed to prove that the left-hand twin belonged to Satan and the right-hand twin to God, an assumption which did not clarify the baffling relationship, nor explain why magic and religion were perpetually gravitating together again after they had been disjoined. It is claimed that religion was purified and ennobled by the separation; it is certain that magic was debased; and on the countenance of its sixteenth-century representative, Doctor Faustus, was such a piteous blending of soaring aspiration and grovelling lust, of reckless resolution and abject fear, of grandiose dreams and ignoble desires, of rollicking humour and malignant glee, of tragic despair and maudlin remorse, of paltriness, seediness and titanism combined as only a mutilated figure could exhibit.

The first Faustbook came to life with this wound, and the legend has ever since been seeking along the highways and byways of literature for a poet to make it whole. This was the challenge inherent in the very imperfections of an uncouth and anguished organism demanding aesthetic liberation, an irresistible appeal to poets and artists to lift the treasure it contained but which was almost buried beneath the mound of rubble to which the sixteenth century had reduced magic. The intense emotional truth vibrating in the situation itself was to prove the salvation of a legend which as far as magic was concerned seemed hardly fit to survive its first literary presentation.

(b) *A rhymesters' Faust*

Probably only Luther, who dominates the Urfaustbook spiritually, could have produced anything greater than 'Spiess' in the Germany of that day. A version of the Faust-legend by Luther is one of those ghost-masterpieces which sometimes haunt the mind with the sense of an opportunity wasted or lost. But perhaps it is something quite different, a situation saved. For had the Reformer bent his mind to describing the fate of Faust, one can hardly imagine him leaving one stone unturned to make his rendering completely and utterly final. Nor would the horror-stricken sympathy of 'Spiess' have found an echo in that devil-haunted mind. He might have damned Faust so irretrievably with such a wealth of lurid and vivid invective that the chapter would have been closed; there would have been nothing more to be said. Faust's poetical life might have been cut off before it had really begun, that is to say before the Renaissance could speak through the mouth of Marlowe. The latent titanism of the hero might have been crushed beneath the weight of Luther's antagonism. Moreover any version on which he set the seal of his genius would have discouraged the further development of the legend in Germany. There would have been a formidable finality about it; whereas, from 'Spiess' onwards down through Marlowe and Goethe to the present day, it is the lack of finality, the manifest imperfections of all the versions, which have caused so many strange and beautiful variations on a theme which is not exhausted yet.

The tendency of the Urfaustbook to become great poetry remained latent in the country of its origin for a century and more; but it put out feelers in that direction almost at once; for it was translated into verse during the year 1587, and published in that form on 1 January 1588. Skilful, spirited and readable, this version performed one undoubted service for the original. The anecdotes which make such a jaded impression in prose take on something of the gaiety of Hans Sachs when rendered in the light and artless doggerel which the genial shoe-maker stamped with the imprint of his own racy humour. To versify the many and various tricks and feats in this way was greatly to improve them, as even a rough and ready translation into English shows:

DOCTOR FAUSTUS DECEIVES A HORSE-COPER

He treated a horse-coper at a fair in the same way; for he made himself a fine steed on which he rode to market in a place called Pfeiffering, where he had many offers for it. Finally he sold it to a horse-coper for forty florins, warning him not to ride it into water. The dealer, curious to see what he meant by that, rode it into a pond, whereupon the horse disappeared, and he found himself bestriding a bundle of straw, and was all but drowned. Knowing where the man who sold it was lodging, he went there in his wrath and found Doctor Faustus lying on a bed, sleeping and snoring. The horse-coper seized hold of his foot, intending to pull him off the bed, whereupon the leg came away in his hand and he fell to the ground with it. Then Doctor Faustus began to yell blue murder, the horse-coper much affrighted took to flight and made himself scarce, believing that he had really torn the leg from Faustus' body. So the Doctor made a profit by these means.[1]

> Thereafter he himself bethought
> And a horse-coper made his sport
> In this wise at a village-mart.
> But first he made with wondrous art
> As proud and mettlesome a gee
> As on this earth you'll ever see.
> He rode it long and rode it well
> To market with intent to sell;
> And Pfeiffering was the market-town.
> Many a buyer and many a clown
> Stood round the horse to have a look;
> But Faustus forty florins took
> From a horse-coper who had got
> The ready money on the spot.
> At the same time he bade him take heed
> And not into water ride the steed.
> The dealer rode off in a trice
> Pondering this strange advice

[1] Scheible, op. cit. Vol. II, p. 1035.

And what the meaning might well be.
He rode into a pond to see,
And when he reached the deepest part,
The horse he'd purchased at the mart
Was lost to sight; the rider saw
Himself astride a bunch of straw.
Upon this bundle he sank down
And in the water thought to drown.
The dealer knew the inn full well
Wherein the cozener did dwell,
And thither wrathfully he sped
To find the Doctor on his bed,
Sleeping and snoring at his ease.
The angry dupe made haste to seize
Faust by the foot, for he was fain
To drag him out with might and main;
Which Faustus, spying his intent,
Did make as if his leg were rent
And in the grasp of the horse-coper
Who tumbled down and came a cropper,
As if he had been struck by hail.
Whereat the Doctor gan to wail:
Oh murder, help, oh woe is me,
What have you done? Oh let me be!
The dealer, now half dead with fright,
Rushed from the room and took to flight,
Firmly convinced the leg was off,
Nor did he hear the devil scoff.
If only Faust keeps mum, thought he,
I'll let the other matter be.
And thus the Doctor kept his loot
And terrified his butt to boot.[1]

The rather clod-hopping humour of the tale sounds a good deal livelier in verse than in prose, and this goes for all the other anecdotes in the book, that is to say for the hard core of magic which made it so popular at the time. It is even possible, I think, to prefer the description of Helen in rhyme to the enumeration of her beauties in prose:

This Helen appeared in a sumptuous dark purple dress, and her hair,

[1] Scheible, op. cit. Vol. XI, pp. 124ff.

which was of a beautiful golden colour, fell down to her knees. She had lovely coal-black eyes, and a charming countenance, with a small round head, cherry red lips, and a little mouth, a swan-white neck, cheeks as pink as little roses, and a shining and resplendent countenance. She was tall and upright of stature, and in a word there was no blemish on her. She looked all round the room with a bold and wanton air.[1]

In the original German she sounds even more like a doll than in English, because of the liberal use of diminutives; and although the rhymesters faithfully reproduced these caressing terms, they approximate to folk-poetry in the medium of verse and produce an agreeable jingle:

> Fair Helen in this guise was seen:
> Clad in a gown of purple sheen,
> And moving with a stately air.
> Hanging unbraided was her hair,
> All bright and lovely, a wealth untold,
> It had the glitter of purest gold;
> And was so long, it fell below
> Her waist, for she did wear it so.
> Her coal-black eyes did glance with grace;
> She had a lovely, charming face,
> She had a little rounded head;
> Her lips were cherry-ripe and red.
> Her tender cheeks were like the rose,
> Her tiny mouth sweetness disclosed;
> Her countenance with beauty shone,
> Her little neck was like the swan.
> In stature tall, she walked upright
> And was without a blemish quite.
> All round the room her eyes she rolled,
> With wanton gaze and glances bold.[2]

Any faint feeling one may have on comparing these two passages that the rhymed version is a poetical improvement on the original does not survive the perusal of both works in their entirety. On the contrary the poetry latent in the tragic passages of the Urfaust-book is utterly to seek in the quaint doggerel, which softens the situation with its facile rhymes, and slackens the tenseness and tautness of the original with metrical padding, leavening and lightening the tragic lump:

---

[1] Scheible, op. cit. Vol. II, p. 1029.   [2] Ibid. Vol. XI, p. 150.

But it happened between twelve and one o'clock in the night, that a great wild wind blew against the house from all sides, as if wishful to destroy everything and to raze the house to the ground; upon which the students felt their hearts quaking, sprang out of bed and began to speak cheer to each other; nor would they leave their chamber. The host of the inn forsook his house for another. The students lay near the room in which Doctor Faustus was, and they heard a horrible whistling and hissing, as if the house were full of snakes, adders and noxious worms, and then suddenly Doctor Faustus' door flew open, and he began to scream for help and to cry murder, but in a weak voice, and soon after that he was heard no more.[1]

> And now, while Faustus in this plight
> Sat betwixt twelve and one that night,
> A fearful tumult rose and raged
> Against the house, nor would be 'suaged,
> With heavy storms and violence grim,
> And all the house encompassed round
> As if to tear it to the ground.
> Whereat the students, loudly wailing,
> Felt that their very souls were quailing;
> Out of their beds in haste they leapt
> And very close together kept,
> Talking of comfort what they could;
> But leave the chamber no one would.
> As for the host he rushed away
> And sought another house that day.
> The students for their part did lie
> Near Faustus' room which was hard by.
> They heard a fearful sound of whistling,
> Of rushing, roaring and of hissing,
> As if great snakes the house did fill,
> And noxious worms, and worse things still.
> And then the door of Faustus' room
> Did open like the crack of doom,
> And he began to call out: Help!
> And Murder! 'twas a strangled yelp
> And faint, as if his voice were failing;
> Then silence fell, and stilled the wailing.[2]

One hardly needs this example to remind one of the fact that doggerel metre, like its most famous exponent Hans Sachs, is in-

---

[1] Scheible, op. cit. Vol. II, p. 1067.   [2] Ibid. Vol. XI, pp. 208f.

capable of expressing tragedy; on the contrary it is always fringing comedy. The fearful Lutheran views about hell and everlasting damnation, which are capable of evoking horror in the mind of a twentieth-century reader of the Urfaustbook, sound like mere cautionary tales in the Sachsian medium. Yet even in the original version the style is too blunt and brutal to be tragic; for Germany had not yet evolved the language which could lift the legend into poetry, whether in verse or prose. Nevertheless it is nearer its ultimate transformation in the Urfaustbook than in those essentially heartless, pattering rhymes. And this is probably the reason why the versified rendering never really caught on. The anecdotes were greatly improved, but the legend as a whole was not.

The authors, two students of Tübingen University, stated in their preface that they brought the whole 'into a proper order'; it would therefore seem as if they should be credited with certain formal improvements which are also present and practically identical in the 1588 prose edition of the 'Spiess' Faustbook. The improvements consist firstly in the omission of eight of the magical tricks in the original version; and, although any curtailment of the anecdotal third part would be to its advantage, the choice of the ones to discard was on the whole a happy one. Five of them were trivial: *Faustus embroiling two peasants*, in which mere mischief and no magic was involved; *Faustus depriving a priest of his breviary*, by deluding the eyesight of the victim, who took the breviary to be a pack of cards and threw it away; *Faustus eating a hake which he had not cooked*, one of the many banquets provided by the magician from other men's tables with the spirits' aid; and not only a feebler version than most, but lifted bodily from Lercheimer's book on sorcery, where it was attributed to Tritheim; *Doctor Faustus' marksmanship*, a dullish account of his magical prowess with shot and with shell; and *Doctor Faustus shaves a priest's beard*. Here again mischief and not magic was the *leitmotiv* of a spiteful and cruel trick, for which Wierus was the authority. It is therefore probably true; but it does the perpetrator of the practical joke little honour and can well be spared.

The remaining three are on a higher level. *Doctor Faustus' guests are fain to cut off their noses*, which has become immortal in *Auerbach's Cellar*. Lercheimer told it in 1585 about an anonymous sorcerer; Phillip Camerarius attributed it to Faust and gave a very lively Latin version of it in 1591 in *Operae Horarum Subcisivarum*;

Auerbach's Cellar (Are Noses Grapes?)

but this was after the Urfaustbook had copied it from Lercheimer. It is the tale of yet another magical banquet at which the guests implored Faust to show them some specimen of his magical art. He finally agreed, and then bewitched them into taking their noses for bunches of grapes, which they were just about to cut off, when he disillusioned them at the last moment. The second tale (already recounted by Lercheimer about Faust) is more exciting. Exasperated by the impertinence of a young Boots at an inn, Faustus opened his mouth and swallowed him whole; then he took a long drink, and the wretched youth was discovered under the stairs drenched to the skin and trembling like an aspen-leaf (*Doctor Faustus eats a servant*). This may have been left out because there were several other gargantuan meals to Faust's credit in the Urfaustbook, such as the swallowing of a load of hay, and of a horse, cart and wagon; or it may have been in order to reduce the considerable debt to Lercheimer, four of whose anecdotes altogether were blue-pencilled by the rhymesters. The fourth, *Doctor Faustus beheads someone*, had been taken over word for word from that authority by 'Spiess', the only difference being that Lercheimer had told it about a certain A.v.Th. It is a very good story in itself, but less sensational than the one on very similar lines which the rhymesters kept and which followed the first immediately in the Urfaustbook. Both deal with magical decapitation and restoration; in both a lily-flower figures as a symbol of life; and in both a rival magician is destroyed by cutting off the bloom at the psychological moment. In the first tale this was done because he was thwarting the restoration of the original patient; in the second case it was done because Faust could not bear to witness the prowess of his rival. The second version shows the hero in a much darker light than the first, and may have been kept for that reason. The general tendency of the omissions seems to have been on the whole to avoid the paltry and the repetitious, and to concentrate interest by means of selection. It was therefore partly aesthetic; but in so far as such tales were left out which Lercheimer had attributed to others (the hake tale, the first decapitation story and the business with the noses and grapes), it may have also been an effort in the direction of what the editors took to be 'historical truth'.

The second improvement, the 'better order', led to the re-arrangement of the anecdotes in the third part. It seems likely that a stricter chronological sequence was the aim, for there are occasional mentions of the dates at which various feats were performed, the year being reckoned after the signing of the pact; so that verisimilitude and not art was probably the deciding factor. Nevertheless both the omissions and the regrouping resulted in a perceptible aesthetic improvement. The impassioned warnings of Faust's neighbour, the good old man, to repent and be saved now follow straight after the worst and wickedest of all the tricks, the murder in the decapitation scene, which shows Faust at his moral nadir and therefore desperately in need of spiritual exhortation. This scene leads as in the original to the menaces of Mephisto and the signing of the second pact, and the juxtaposition of the murder and the old man intensifies the drama of that situation. But it seems unlikely that the editors had such a purpose in mind. Otherwise they would not have inserted between the second pact and Faust's cohabitation with Helen of Troy four anecdotes which came before the intervention of the old man in the Urfaustbook; this gave only two tales after the second pact (the beard story and the noses and grapes). Had the rhyming editors not replaced these two cancelled episodes by four others equally irrelevant, one would have argued some real feeling for form and, what is more, for the emotional value of the final scenes. As it is, one can only say that it was a happy accident which brought the murderous deed of Faust and the intervention of the good old man into such close proximity. It is almost as if the Urfaustbook itself were feeling its way towards drama.

The prose edition of 1588, still under the auspices of 'Spiess', is practically identical with the verse rendering, and may have been first in the field, though in view of the rhymesters' claim to have brought the whole 'into a better order' this seems rather improbable. Oddly enough, the two students with their publisher suffered a severe reprimand and incarceration for producing their version, which evidently seemed more dangerous to the authorities than the sombre prose of 'Spiess'.

The revised 'Spiess' of 1588 was used for the Low German version by the piratical and evidently incompetent Balhorn which appeared in the same year; it was also the text of which P.F. gave an English rendering in 1592; but the Dutch translation (1592) and the French version (1598) by Victor Palmer Cayet were based on the Urfaustbook. In 1589 a cycle of new tales was added to 'Spiess' from the Erfurt tradition, written and oral: the summoning up of the heroes of Homer for the benefit of an undergraduate audience; the challenge made by Faust to the Senate of Erfurt that he could restore the lost comedies of Plautus and Terence for a period sufficiently long to allow of their being copied (the offer was not accepted); the appearance of Faustus on a magic horse to partake of a banquet to which he contributed magic wine by boring holes in the table (again this feat was made memorable by Goethe); the choice of a (possibly supernatural) servant to wait at a meal, who claimed that he was 'as fast as the thoughts of man'; the unsuccessful pleadings of the barefoot monk Doctor Klinge, that Faust should renounce his evil ways. Although Faust shows himself very hardened and reckless in this conversation, whereas he was brought to remorse for a time by the old man in the Urfaustbook, the two tales are practically identical. There was further added to the 1589 edition the Leipzig legend of the magician bestriding a barrel of wine and riding it out of Auerbach's Cellar. And so the development went quietly on until the year 1599, the original accumulating fresh material as the years went by, but otherwise unaltered.

(c) A fanatic's Faust

Many and varied although the editions of the Urfaustbook were which kept on appearing until 1598, they did not differ fundamentally from the original in tone, in content or in form; and the canon was indeed so firmly fixed in the popular mind that, rather than meddle with it, the gentry who catered for the sensation-loving public produced a sequel to it, the Wagnerbook, recounting the fortunes and the fate of Faust's erstwhile Famulus. This appeared first in 1593 and ended with the promise of another sequel, the life-story of Wagner's crony and partner in guilt, Johannes de Luna. Although following the main lines of the Faustbook, it introduced a good deal of new matter, and was clearly designed to go one better than the original in sensationalism and in esoteric learning. Moreover a voyage to the New World replaced Faust's journeys through Europe and the Near East. In spite of all this, and though it ran through several editions down to 1717, the Wagnerbook never succeeded in throwing the story of Faust into the shade, and has no literary merit.

In 1599 an almost deadly blow was dealt to the legend by Georg Rudolf Widman, a blow from which the folkbook Faust never really recovered, and which might have arrested its literary progress altogether, had it not already achieved an imperishable form in England. Widman flung himself upon the German organism and dissected—worse—vivisected it, limb from limb, joint from joint, filament from filament and nerve from nerve. Using the 1589 edition of 'Spiess', or possibly a later one, and supplementing it with details from the Wagnerbook as well as from oral tradition of various kinds, he took it to pieces chapter by chapter with that inexorable German thoroughness one has learnt to dread, using each short chapter as a peg on which to hang a lengthy disquisition of a moral, or a religious, or a learned or an informative nature. Whilst mercilessly cutting the original text down by about a third, he produced a work of 522 pages in Scheible's edition, whereas the Urfaustbook has a modest 135. Apart from condensing many passages, he explicitly omitted the disputations about the heavens, winter and summer, the comets and stars, thunder, lightning, etc., as too childish to repeat. Whilst not altogether disagreeing with him here, one could nevertheless spare the lengthy lectures on astronomy and astrology which Widman put in their place in order to display his learning. He also refused to give the text of the second pact for 'various impelling reasons'; and Christian modesty forbade him to enumerate Faust's amours or to reproduce the personal description of Helen of Troy, although he did not scruple to add the ugly detail that she bore the magician a monster before giving birth to Justus Faustus. He further considered the journey to the stars and round the world as 'too offensive to modest ears and hearts', which is pious nonsense; and he not unnaturally omitted the dream journey down to hell, though oddly enough he omitted to say so. On this mangled and truncated text he then proceeded to comment.

Widman's Faustbook is essentially a work of education, religion, learning and research, although admittedly on no very high level; and it is instructive to see what effect those elements have when applied to a living structure deriving from folklore and progressing imperceptibly towards art. The educational aspect is devoted to teaching Widman's readers what and how to think. A moral purpose of an extremely serious kind obviously underlay the Urfaustbook and occasionally became explicit in horrified comments by the author. Widman supplemented these by weighty sermons appended to the chapters: on drunkenness, on idleness, on parental responsibility, on evil communications corrupting good manners, on marriage and the like. Platitudinous and tedious, they are mere ballast and their place is overboard. The learning is less oppressive. No student of the period will take exception to the references to Thales, Plato, Ovid, Origen, Democritus, Dionysius Areopagita, Epicurus, Metrodorus, Pythagoras, Aristotle, Actaeon and Orpheus, for they were almost *de rigueur* at the time; and disquisitions on predestination, on the creation of the world, on the fall of the angels, on paradise, on devils and the infernal hierarchy, on the nature of spirits, on ghosts, on witches, on the Wild Hunt, on buried treasure, on white and black magic, on astrology, on astronomy, on cheiromancy and auguries, on giants and heroes—after all, these subjects are not altogether out of place in a book about a black magician. All this part is in fact a popular demonology (there are similar chapters in the Wagnerbook), and has at least a historical interest since it gives the generally accepted views of the period. But it will not do to remember the 'Digression on Spirits' in Burton's *Anatomy of Melancholy* whilst ploughing through Widman's treatise. The two men agree on many things, they appeal to the same authorities, they sometimes use the same illustrations; but what a world of difference between the lively curiosity and wide sympathy of the Englishman, and the dull dogmatic rancour of the German! Their styles are also poles apart, since the authors were on different levels of civilization; but in temperament too they are utterly dissimilar. And Burton was within his rights in introducing such a digression into the framework of his book; Widman would have been better advised to leave the learning out of the story and keep it for another occasion.

Although his learning did not extend beyond what any reasonably educated and well-read person could pick up at the time, it must be allowed that he showed aptitude for research. Painstaking and thorough, he set out to discover all the similar or parallel instances he could find to the anecdotes told about Faust. He did not quote many authorities, and probably never went back to the sources, but the list of magicians and of persons practising magic before Faust which he composed is certainly impressive. At one time or another he instanced the following names: Zoroaster, Zarmocenide the Assyrian, Circe, Heliogabalus, Thales, Hermogene, Macarius the Hermit, Paletes, Numa Pompilius, Simon Magus, Virgil, Merlin, Mosca, Robert the Devil, Gormo of Denmark, the Abbot Erloffus of Fulda, Antonius Morus, Johannes Teutonicus, Tritheim, Cornelius Agrippa, Scotus, Johannes von Bar, Baian the Bulgar, Wildfire, Laurentius, Peter of Apono, and Faust's Famulus Wagner. This list is far from being exhaustive, as will be seen directly; but it gives some idea of the weight of evidence brought to bear, which makes of Widman a pioneer of Faustian scholarship. Directly or indirectly later scholars are indebted to Widman, both as regards matter and method. For it was he who began to unearth the predecessors and parallels to the hero, and by analysing the legend in this way destroyed it as a living and independent creation, whereas the Urfaustbook had severed it from the seething mass of legend and story from which it ultimately derived, and had made it unique and individual. This method of dismemberment (the decomposition into sources) deflowers works of literature during the process, and Lowes has demonstrated in *The Road to Xanadu* that the only fruitful approach to a work of art is the opposite method, the observation of its growth. But works of art are resilient and survive the blundering and bungling hands too often laid upon them. It is a different story with an

Faust und Mephistophiles.

embryo like the Faust-legend in Germany in the year 1599. Widman hacked it into little pieces; and it seemed doubtful, to say the least, whether anyone who came after him could ever put it together again.

But the worst has not yet been said. Burdened with moral questionings, swamped with learning, dislocated by research, Widman's *Faust* was hideously disfigured by religious fanaticism as well. There was a certain anti-Catholic element in the Urfaustbook; but there is nothing obtrusive or violent about it; it is rather in the nature of hints. Mephisto waits upon Faust in the habit of a monk;

there are sneers at the celibacy of the monks and nuns, and when Faust wants to marry he is wrathfully forbidden to break the spirit of his contract, in which marriage is not explicitly mentioned. This has always been interpreted, and I think rightly, as a criticism of Catholic views on celibacy, together with Mephisto's cynical advocacy of concubinage without limit. Furthermore, Faust befools the Pope during his sojourn in Rome, and His Holiness is not shown up in a good light; but both these remarks apply even more strongly to the Sultan in Constantinople. Finally in Mephisto's wrathful outburst against Faust towards the end, he concludes a speech of a crushingly moral nature with the dictum that God is the Lord, and that the devil is only an abbot or a monk. These are all fairly broad hints that the author was a Lutheran; but they are not nearly so obvious as the positive inspiration, the terrible spiritual climate in which the legend took root and grew: the fear of hell, the terror of the devil, and the horror of everlasting damnation. Here embryonically is the poetry of Marlowe.

If Luther at his tragic best inspired those emotions in 'Spiess', Luther at his tragic worst collaborated with the fanatical Widman. He is quoted at every turn in the Commentaries, and although words were very often put into his mouth, or reported from hearsay, still the general violence which informed his anti-Catholic utterances rings all too true. Luther's polemical writings with their sledge-hammer invectives, like cudgels studded with murderous nails, served Widman for a model, even when he did not actually quote from them. Although the ultimate responsibility rests with the Reformer, yet those traits which in him seem tragic appear intolerably offensive in a disciple like Widman. One could pass by the statement that witches are only to be found in Catholic countries with a smile; and merely think *Legendenbuch-Lugendenbuch* a very bad pun; and though one's taste is offended by the contention that the devil created monks by saying 'fuat' instead of 'fiat', these are only trifles. But nothing can be said in extenuation of the venom and piety combined with which Widman besmirched the Holy See at every conceivable and inconceivable opportunity. Too squeamish and too fearful of corrupting youth (or so he said) to describe the beauty of Helen of Troy, he wallowed in the reputed blasphemies, obscenities, incests, murders and other nauseating crimes of the Popes Sylvester II, Benedict IX, John XII, John XIX, John XX, John XXI, Gregory VII, Gregory XI, Clement II,

Damasus II, Leo IX, Victor II, Paul II and (inevitably) Alexander VI. The only wonder is that Honorius III escaped mention; for he was believed to be the author of a famous (and infamous) *grimoire* which became popular in the early seventeenth century. One can only deduce from this that it was not then known in Germany. All the other popes I have mentioned were accused by Widman (sometimes on the authority of Cardinal Benno, sometimes on Luther's and often, one suspects, on his own) of having concluded pacts with Satan; and he gloats over their horrible deaths with malignant glee after describing Faust's. This deprives the hero of the tale of his sombre prerogative and reduces him to an insignificant member of a highly conspicuous crowd. But it is the same all the way through. The wicked papal sorcerers (those figments of Widman's heated brain) keep on bobbing up in the commentaries, throwing Zoroaster and Circe, Virgil and Merlin, Simon Magus and Robert the Devil, let alone Doctor Faustus, quite into the shade. There is also a strong anti-Semitic element in the book; so that, sickened by necromantic popes and Jews stained with the blood of Christian babes, one can only condemn it as a peculiarly unpleasing monument to intolerance and fanaticism without one redeeming feature; for Widman is so dull that his treatise on Faust even lacks the saving grace of sensationalism. The shape, rough-hewn but arresting, of the Urfaustbook has been obliterated beneath the tidal wave of commentaries; the tragic sympathy of 'Spiess' has been lost in sanctimoniousness; the latent beauty has resolved itself into its opposite, although oddly enough just a flicker is seen for a second in the farewell speech to Wayger (Wagner) made by Justus Faustus before he and Helen vanish away on Faust's death:

Now bless thee, my servant [said Justus], I must hasten away, for my father is dead, and therefore my mother can have no abiding-place here, and must hie away too. . . .[1]

One learns to be thankful for very small mercies with Widman; and though small enough, one is grateful for this innocuous little speech, to which Widman for once appended no lurid comment.

One particularly interesting feature in the anti-Catholic propaganda is the inclusion of the marriage-bar in the terms of the contract. This was in line with the attitude of the Urfaustbook;

---

[1] Scheible, op. cit. Vol. II, p. 793.

but the explicit clause in the pact was introduced by Widman, who never stopped railing against the Catholic hatred of marriage and the consequent immorality. Luther, it will be remembered, took the same line. The conspicuous position given to the prohibition by Widman was probably responsible for a later development which in its turn almost certainly influenced Goethe. This therefore may be tentatively put down to the credit of the author.

Otherwise it seems impossible to say anything in his favour. He embodies everything that is least admirable in the German make-up: dullness, heaviness, unscrupulousness in propaganda, vindictiveness, unctuousness, credulity, and the destruction of beauty simply by handling it. Widman is the typical blundering, aggressive, insensitive German at his worst. But it would surely be too much to hope that Faustus, during the course of his long peregrination through the centuries, should never have fallen into the hands of a man such as this? Actually it is hardly Faust who suffers most in this dreary compilation; for the chorus deflects attention from the hero, that hideous chorus of damned and howling popes.

Manner and not matter is the deciding factor in poetry. Both the Wagnerbook and Widman's Faustbook illustrate this truism; for both recount a tale similar in all essentials to that told in the Urfaustbook, yet both are intrinsically valueless and neither proved capable of inspiring better things. On the contrary Widman's version of the Faust-legend seemed almost to have given it the *coup de grâce*; there was no demand at the time for a second edition, and this appears natural enough. But, what is less comprehensible, there were also no further editions of 'Spiess', who fell into complete oblivion and was not rediscovered until the nineteenth century. This lack of enthusiasm for the Faust folkbook in the seventeenth century was no doubt partly attributable to the vogue for Faust dramas, but must also, I think, have been a direct result of Widman's daunting and deadening version.

Such as it was, a physician called Pfitzer saw fit to bring out another edition of it in 1674, omitting some episodes and adding some others. He partly reinstated Helen, whom Mephisto procured as a concubine for Faust to compensate him for the ban on marriage; but the invocation-scene in the original, when Faust summoned her up on White Sunday before an audience of students, was still left out. In its place a real girl of flesh and blood was introduced with whom Faust was represented as being violently in love:

At that time however he caught sight of a rather pretty but poor young girl who had come to the town from the country and had taken service with a tradesman. Faust was so violently attracted to her, that he sought by every means in his power to make her his mistress. But in spite of all his promises she never consented to his sinful desires, but defended her virtue, so that, do what he would, he could neither bend her nor break her, nor achieve his purpose save through marriage, which his good friends and comrades therefore urged upon him. . . .[1]

Faust himself was nothing loth; but Mephisto terrified him into desisting from the project, and then rewarded him with fair Helen. Here in embryo is the figure of Gretchen, adumbrating that tragic love-story which was to achieve the highest pinnacle of poetry, and bringing into an ironical relationship one of the greatest dullards who have ever put pen to paper and one of the greatest poets in the world. For although Pfitzer invented the peasant-girl, she was enshrined in that ponderous tome of Widman's, which otherwise remained substantially unaltered by Pfitzer, who religiously kept the commentaries.

These were thrown overboard with much other ballast by the self-styled Christlich Meynender in 1726. Basing himself on Pfitzer he cut and condensed, curtailed and abridged and produced a truly popular folkbook which takes a bare thirty pages in Scheible's edition, and became the basis of the chapbooks circulating in Goethe's time. In this form it was readable at least; but how thin and flabby, how utterly devoid of grandeur, when compared with the Urfaustbook from which it ultimately derived! It might have some value as a source-book for curious tales about Faust, it might even suggest the notion of bringing love-interest into his life; but the fount of inspiration had dried up. As far as the Faust-legend was concerned, that was flowing in the eighteenth century through another channel.

The Christlich Meynender said at the beginning of his booklet that he had at first intended to try to solve the vexed question of whether the story he was about to tell was true or false. But he had found this such a complicated and intricate matter, with so many writings for and against, that he had finally abandoned the attempt. It had been made a quarter of a century previously by

[1] N. Pfitzer's edition of Widman's Faustbook, Nürnberg, 1674; reprinted in *Bibliothek des literarischen Vereins in Stuttgart*, Tübingen, 1880, p. 511.

Johann Georg Neumann, first in Latin, which he then translated into German in 1702. Neumann knew only Widman and Pfitzer, and was ignorant of 'Spiess'. He was very severe on Widman (whom he called an obscure writer), and mocked at his 'curious zeal for godliness' as well as at his superstitiousness. He finally came to the conclusion that there was such a person as Faust, but that his life was a mere legend and hardly worth a second thought:

So that this sorcerer led a rather obscure life; and one would know even less about him than one does, if he had not been brought on to the stage so often by the comedians. . . . As for the rest, the fellow is certainly not worth making such a fuss about.[1]

Sic transit gloria Fausti!

[1] Scheible, op. cit. Vol. v, pp. 479, 482. J. G. Neumann, *Curieuse Betrachtungen des sogenannten D. Faustens*, Dresden and Leipzig, 1702.

CHAPTER II

ENGLISH FAUSTS

(a) An Elizabethan Faustus

The possibilities of a poetical and tragic nature latent in the Urfaustbook had not been (and at that period could not be) thoroughly exploited in Germany. On the contrary, in spite of the pruning and regrouping in the 1588 editions, and the comparatively lively tales added in 1589, no further progress was made after that. Mauled and mangled by Widman in 1599, the folkbook raised up a diminished head in the eighteenth century and deteriorated into a chapbook. Long before that, however, the situation had been saved in England by the translation of P. F. *Gent.*, which appeared in 1592 under the title of *The Historie of the damnable life, and deserued death of Doctor Iohn Faustus.* Although this bore the legend 'newly imprinted', modern opinion (whilst postulating an earlier edition in May) tends to accept the year 1592 as the date of the first appearance of the English Faustbook in print. Internal evidence makes it seem possible that the manuscript was completed as early as August 1590; and since the arrangement and grouping are those adopted in Germany in 1588, a claim that P.F. was responsible for these in the first instance has been put forward and not very convincingly argued. This would mean that his version was then translated into German prose and versified as well, the whole within the space of a bare year after the appearance of the Urfaustbook in 1587. To put it mildly this seems highly unlikely; the modest honour of the alterations belongs in my opinion to Germany, either to the editor of the 1588 'Spiess', or more probably to the Tübingen students who versified the Faustbook. But the question is not one of fundamental importance. P.F. almost certainly had the slightly handier prose version of 1588 at his disposal; but he would have impressed his personality quite as deeply on the original Faustbook, and would have made any alterations he thought fit. For his part, he cut out one of two almost precisely similar stories which the 1588

'Spiess' edition had kept: 'How Faustus ate a Horse, Wagon and Load of Hay', and 'How Faustus ate a Load of Hay'. And strangely enough, since the Elizabethans were no niggards of strong effects, it was the first more sensational feat which he omitted. He also excluded the devil's savage answer to Faust's laments at the latter end of his life, possibly because the idioms and proverbs with which it abounds were too irksome to 'English'; but possibly for another reason; and he either paraphrased or ignored the occasional telling doggerel verse in the text. But this by no means exhausts the list of his manifold alterations.

A certain high-handed carelessness is one of P.F.'s most obvious characteristics, not unmixed with intellectual arrogance; and although a mere translator, his personality emerges more vividly than that of the original author. The latter impresses one as a fervently religious man, a good Lutheran, and one not devoid of learning. But P.F. is a *Gent.* with a personal point of view, a more unshackled mind, a livelier curiosity and a perhaps more haphazard but wider education. One obvious sign of this is his ability to translate the Faustbook, and in a manner too which shows that it was a labour of love. The vigorous style puts that beyond doubt; and it is this same dash and vigour which makes it impossible to accept Rohde's attractive and ingenious theory that the author was John Dee. The latter was in Germany and Bohemia during the years 1583–1589, and might well have become acquainted with the first or second edition of the book. Considering his occult experiments and his association with Edward Kelley, he might also have taken a lively interest in it. Yet it is never once mentioned in his *Spirituall Diary* or elsewhere in his voluminous writings. Moreover Dee's ponderous style and his complete lack of humour rule out the attribution. He was far too solemn and too deadly in earnest ever to have added the inconsequent flourish to a description of Lucifer manifesting as a squirrel: 'I thinke hee could cracke nuts too like a Squirrel'[1]; or to have appended the following conceit to the German simile of the Roman 'swine' fatted and ready to be cooked in hell:

Let him [the devil] summon the Nunnes to turne the spits: for as none must confesse the Nunne but the Frier, so none should turne the rosting Frier but the Nunne.[2]

[1] P. M. Palmer and R. P. More, *The Sources of the Faust Tradition,* New York, 1936, p. 164.   [2] Ibid. p. 178.

Nor can one imagine this learned scholar, whose life was then given up to alchemical and spiritualistic experiments, applying himself to the task of rendering 'Spiess' into English.

On the other hand, Rohde is probably right in believing that P.F. (whoever he may have been) was a travelled man. He may or he may not have obtained the details he added to the geographical data of the original from first-hand observation; but he gives the impression of having been to Germany; for he had certainly acquired a very respectable knowledge of the language, and sometimes commented on the manners of the country in a way which sounds as if he were speaking from personal experience; as for instance when he calls it a land of sots 'where it is counted no feast except all the bidden guests be drunke'.[1] This remark betrays the swaggering Elizabethan; and P.F. obviously prided himself on being a man of polite manners. Recounting the story of three young noblemen transported on Faustus' magic cloak to the wedding festivities of the Duke of Bavaria on condition that they kept silent throughout, he gave the following reason why one of them broke this promise and began to speak when they were about to wash their hands before the feast:

One of the three had enough manners to desire his friend to wash first.[2]

Characteristically enough, Widman gave a different reason:

One of them forgot the fair warning and began to speak to those who were offering him hand-water, saying that he didn't need it and refusing it.[3]

Quite apart from interpolations of various kinds, P.F. according to the general admirable practice of the time was intent on rendering the whole into English rather than on literal translation. He could be accurate enough when it so pleased him, although he sometimes misunderstood his text and made an occasional howler; but on the whole his attitude to the original was anything but slavish. He took any amount of liberties with 'Spiess': expanding, condensing, diverging and interpolating whenever the spirit moved him. The effect is extraordinarily happy, owing in the first instance to the language itself. To compare the German and English Faust-

---

[1] Palmer and More, op. cit. p. 206.   [2] Ibid. pp. 198f.
[3] Scheible, op. cit. Vol. II, p. 484.

books is to become acutely aware of the disadvantage under which German prose then laboured. Sixteenth-century English was a rich, lusty and flexible medium: overflowing with *joie-de-vivre*, imaginative, adventurous, creative. German prose, hardly out of its swaddling-clothes, was uncouth, wooden, blunt and crude, except in the masterly though homely idiom of Luther. His language ennobled the style of the 'Spiess' Faustbook in its grander moments, but did not transfuse the whole with that indefinable spaciousness which the English version has. Even the anecdotes are transformed by it. A man who could ring the changes on 'Clown, dolt, buzzard, buzzardly asse, clownish dolt', had a very unfair advantage over a man who had only '*Tölpel*' to fall back on. And a writer who spontaneously rendered 'sighing' by 'fetcht a great sigh' could clearly outdo his original when it came to emotional intensity. So that, even had P.F. been strictly faithful to his text, he could not have failed to improve on it. Again and again on reading P.F. after 'Spiess' one has the impression that whole passages are new; only to find on comparing them with the German that (at least as often as not) they are almost literal translations. This is the fundamental reason why the whole strikes one as grander, loftier, more intense and tragic than the by no means paltry original. The horizon has widened and the atmosphere has changed: all the proportions are greater. And the magic has been effected by Elizabethan prose.

But P.F. *Gent.* had individual contributions to make in addition to the medium which he handled with slapdash ease. There was, for instance, the description of hell and its horrors to be rendered. Few could outdo, or wish to outdo, the long, ghastly and harrowing account given by 'Spiess'; and the Englishman slightly toned down some of the more hair-raising tortures. On the other hand, his spiritual vision extended further:

. . . ours is a perpetuall darknesse, cleane exempt from the face of God. . . . We haue also with vs in hell a ladder, reaching of an exceeding height, as though it would touch the heauens, on which the damned ascend to seeke the blessing of God; but through their infedilitie, when they are at the very highest degree, they fall down againe into their former miseries, complayning of the heate of that vnquenchable fire . . .[1]

As a make-weight to this almost Dantesque vision were the intoxicating promises of far-flung glory and power which the English

---

[1] Palmer and More, op. cit. p. 155.

Mephisto made to the English Faust, the very stuff of Renaissance dreams, altogether beyond the compass of the Lutheran 'Spiess'.

... learne now of me to make thunder, lightening, hayle, snow, and raine: the cloudes to rent, the earth and craggie rockes to shake and split in sunder, the Seas to swell, and rore, and ouer-run their markes ... so, the more thy Arte is famous whilest thou art here, the greater shall be thy name when thou art gone. ... Yea, *Faustus*, so must thy heart bee enflamed lik the fire to mount on high: learne, *Faustus*, to flie like my selfe, as swift as thought from one kingdome to another, to sit at princes tables, to eate their daintiest fare, to haue thy pleasure of their fayre Ladies, wiues and concubines, to vse their jewels, and costly robes as things belonging to thee, and not vnto them: learne of mee, *Faustus*, to runne through wals, doores, and gates of stone and yron, to creepe into the earth like a worme, to swimme in the water like a fish, to flie in the ayre like a bird, and to liue and nourish thy selfe in the fire like a Salamander: so shalt thou be famous, renowned, far-spoken of, and extolled for thy skill: going on kniues, not hurting thy feete; carrying fire in thy bosome, and not burning thy shirt; seeing through the heauuens as through a Christall. ... Come on my *Faustus*, I will make thée as perfect in these things as myselfe, I will learne thee to goe inuisible, to finde out the mines of golde and siluer, the fodines of precious stones, as the Carbuncle, the Diamond, Saphir, Emerald, Rubie, Topas, Iacinct, Granat, Iaspis, Amathist, vse all these at thy pleasure, take thy hearts desire: thy time *Faustus* weareth away, then why wilt thou not take thy pleasure of the worlde: Come vp, we will goe visite Kings at their owne courtes. ...[1]

Not only is this heady stuff with a species of magical compulsion in the reiterated invocations to Faustus, but it also shows more knowledge of the reputed powers of magicians than the god-fearing author of the Urfaustbook ever betrayed; and represents an almost irresistible temptation to put fear and remorse aside and to cease from fruitless questionings. Moreover some feeling for drama informs the psychological linking together of two separate though contiguous events in the original. Faust having put a question about the creation to Mephisto, the latter gave him a lying answer to the effect that God had not created the world nor mankind, but that both had existed since all eternity. Faust, remembering Genesis, was not entirely convinced, but did not argue. In the next chapter he was not a little startled to receive a state-visit from

<hr />

[1] Palmer and More, op. cit. pp. 161 f.

the whole infernal hierarchy in their true bestial shapes. P.F. turned this visitation into one of warning, first showing Mephisto's anger at being questioned in this wise, and then making Lucifer appear incontinently with the satanic host, addressing him thus:

Faustus, I haue seene thy thoughtes, which are not as thou hast vowed vnto me by vertue of this letter, and shewed him the Obligation that hee had written with his owne blood, wherefore I am come to visite thee and to shewe thee some of our hellish pastimes, in hope that will drawe and confirme thy minde a little more stedfast vnto vs.[1]

This at least gives the whole grotesque and ugly masquerade some kind of *raison d'être*.

Intellectually superior and better informed than his author, as P.F. conceived himself to be, he was not the man to suppress that opinion from any feelings of false modesty. Impatiently interrupting a description of a voyage through the firmament which Faustus was describing in a letter, he boldly announced in the first person:

Yea, Christian Reader, to the glory of God, and for the profite of thy soule, I will open vnto thee the diuine opinion touching the ruling of this confused Chaos, farre more than any rude Germane Author, being possessed with the diuell, was able to vtter. . . .[2]

This certainly looks as if P.F. took the letter to be a genuine document: and indeed there is no sign anywhere that he was writing ironically. On the contrary, his interest in magic was stronger if anything than that of 'Spiess'; and the additions he made to the account of Faust's voyage round the world (derived either from fuller sources than Schedel's *Nürnberger Chronik* or from personal information and observation) deal largely with legend, magic, folklore and ritual, illustrating not only Elizabethan interest in the curious and the occult but his own personal predilections. The geographical section is certainly enlivened by P.F.'s inquiring and retentive mind.

Mephisto's figure gains in stature, it must be owned, by that impressive outburst about the powers he could give from which I have quoted above; then too the omission of the mocking proverbs towards the end of the book and of an earlier passage where he was represented as laughing at Faust up his sleeve favours the impression that diabolic pity rather than fiendish scorn animated

---

[1] Palmer and More, op. cit. p. 163.   [2] Ibid. pp. 172f.

his breast in his relation with Faust, an impression which the Urfaustbook does not convey. Moreover when sent by Faust to frighten the old man who had vainly attempted to reform the sorcerer, he was mocked at by that stalwart, and confessed this humiliation to Faust in the original. P.F. stated on the contrary that the spirit could not bring himself to do this, which shows satanic pride.

It is, however, Faustus himself whose latent titanism is most strongly disengaged and comes into bolder relief in the English version. Many slight omissions and alterations contribute to a total effect of greater spiritual proportions. There is less emphasis placed on the hero's sexual debaucheries and less interest shown in the material benefits accruing to him from the pact, so that the squalid side of the situation is rather less in evidence; whereas the burning desire for knowledge is given greater prominence:

. . . for his frowardness, lawlessness and wantonness goaded him on
. . . for his Speculation was so wonderfull. . . .[1]

. . . when we saw your heart and the thoughts that were in it . . .
for so soone as we saw thy heart, how thou didst despise thy degree taken in Diuinitie, and didst study to search and know the secrets of our kingdome. . . .[2]

Doctor Faustus said: But I will know or I will not live; you must tell me.
Quoth *Faustus* ragingly, I will know, or I will not liue, wherefore dispatch and tell me.[3]

. . . had I but had godly thoughts. . . .
. . . had not I desired to know so much. . . .[4]

The cumulative effect of these slight verbal alterations here and there is concentrated in the statement made by P.F. that Faustus entered his name at the University of Padua as 'Doctor *Faustus*

[1] Cf. Scheible, op. cit. Vol. II, p. 943 with Palmer and More, op. cit. p. 137.
[2] Cf. Scheible, op. cit. Vol. II, p. 964 with Palmer and More, op. cit. p. 153.
[3] Cf. Scheible, op. cit. Vol. II, p. 966 with Palmer and More, op. cit. p. 154.
[4] Cf. Scheible, op. cit. Vol. II, p. 964 with Palmer and More, op. cit. p. 153.

the vnsatiable Speculator';[1] moreover when Mephisto told the hero that he would learn the secrets of hell only after damnation and death, the German magician began to falter:

Doctor Faustus was terrified at that and said: I will not be damned on that account and to gratify you.[2]

The English Faustus reacted differently:

Doctor *Faustus* vpon this arose where he sate, & said, I wil haue my request, and yet I wil not be damned.[3]

'Arose where he sate' is probably meant to be a literal translation of '*entsetzt*' from a confusion with '*sitzen*'; but the mistake itself is revealing, since it presents the hero in a dynamic as well as a resolute attitude. The German Faustus, before encompassing the death of his rival in the decapitation scene, indulged in sanctimonious reflections on the roguery, impiety and blasphemy of the successful practitioner; not so the Englishman, whose straightforward jealousy and undisguised malignancy are at least free from hypocrisy; nor did he keep the craven clause in his predecessor's second pact, conditioning (how vainly) that the signatory should not suffer physical torments in hell. Both of them instructed Wagner to publish an account of their lives after their death; Faust for the simple and sufficient reason that people would want to read it; Faustus, more grandiosely, thinking of his posthumous fame:

So shall the greate actes that I haue done be manifested vnto the world.[4]

The hero's prolonged and piteous laments as the end drew near sound slightly less lily-livered in Elizabethan English than in German prose. In one of the sections, however, P.F. misunderstood and rather mangled the original, possibly because he had less patience with the magician at this juncture than 'Spiess', preferring his titanic aspect. And yet, although he stressed the darkly heroic side, he was even more aware of the desperate wickedness and the fearful price to be paid for it, the irretrievable nature of the pact, and the loss to all eternity of the doomed and wayward

[1] Palmer and More, op. cit. p. 176.   [2] Scheible, op. cit. Vol. II, p. 947.
[3] Palmer and More, op. cit. p. 139.   [4] Ibid. p. 223.

soul. At the very beginning a more inexorable note was struck on this subject by P.F.:

... and without doubt he was eloquent and well grounded in Holy Writ. He knew the commandments of Christ full well. But he who knows the will of God and does it not, he is twice chastised. Moreover, no one can serve two masters. Likewise, thou shalt not tempt the Lord thy God. All this he threw to the winds and took no heed of his soul at that time. Therefore there shall be no excuse for him.

And without doubt he was passing wise, and excellent perfect in the holy scriptures: hee that knoweth his masters will and doth it not, is worthy to be beaten with many stripes. It is written, no man can serue two masters: and, thou shalt not tempt the Lord thy God: but *Faustus* threw all this in the winde, & made his soule of no estimation, regarding more his worldly pleasure than ye ioyes to come: therfore at ye day of judgement there is no hope of his redemptiō.[1]

The theme of eternal damnation, which exercised the minds of both writers, was affirmed again and yet again more emphatically to be the future lot of Faust by P.F. than by 'Spiess':

And this I proclaim as a warning and example to all good Christians, so that they shall not ... injure their souls and bodies like Doctor Faustus did. ...
... as did this vnhappie Faustus, in giuing his Soule to the Diuell.[2]
... therefore I have submitted myself to MEPHOSTOPHILES, the spirit here present, messenger and servant of the hellish prince of Orient. ...
... now haue I Doctor *Iohn Faustus*, vnto the hellish prince of Orient and his messenger *Mephostophiles*, giuven both bodie & soule. ...[3]

If you continue to serve me like this, you may expect good treatment from me.
... thou shalt win my heart and soule, yea and haue it.[4]

In a word it was all stolen and misappropriated wares, and was therefore a fine and godless way of life, as Christ the Lord through the mouth

---

[1] Cf. Scheible, op. cit. Vol. II, pp. 942 f. with Palmer and More, op. cit. p. 136.
[2] Cf. Scheible, op. cit. Vol. II, p. 950 with Palmer and More, op. cit. p. 142.
[3] Cf. Scheible, op. cit. Vol. II, p. 951 with Palmer and More, op. cit. p. 142.
[4] Cf. Scheible, op. cit. Vol. II, p. 954 with Palmer and More, op. cit. p. 144.

of John also calls the devil a thief and murderer, which he is. Besides this, the devil promised him a weekly allowance of twenty-five crowns, which makes thirteen hundred a year: that was his annual income.

All their maintenance was but stolne & borrowed ware: and thus they liued an odious life in the sight of God . . . as Christ saith through *Iohn*, where hee calls the diuell a theefe, and a murderer: and that found *Faustus*, for hée stole him away both bodie and soule.[1]

Then, during a moment of remorse:

. . . the devil attired himself in the form of a beautiful woman, came to him, bussed him and did all kinds of lewdness with him, so that he soon forgot the Word of God, whistled it down the wind, and continued in his wicked practices.

. . . straightwaies the diuel . . . thrust him a fayre Lady into his chamber, which fell to kissing and dalliance with him, through which meanes, he threw his godly motions in the wind, going forward stil in his wicked practises, to the vtter ruine both of his body and soule.[2]

This fearful insistence on the hopelessness of the situation intensifies the sombre gloom prevailing in both versions to a pitch that induces tragic emotions and makes the final clause in the second pact strike home to the very heart of pity and fear:

And hereupon [wrote the German Faust after the stipulation that he should suffer no torments] I promise for my part never again to listen and take heed of any man who may come whether with warnings or persuasion, with counsels or threats, or with the Word of God, or whether he speak of temporal or spiritual matters.

. . . and herevpon [wrote Faustus] I renounce all perswaders that seeke to withdrawe mee from my purpose by the Word of God, either ghostly or bodily. And further, I will neuer giue eare vnto any man, be he spirituall or temporall, that moueth any matter for the saluation of my soule.[3]

It is quite in keeping with P.F.'s greater emotional certainty about his hero's ultimate fate that the loop-hole in 'Spiess', which

[1] Cf. Scheible, op. cit. Vol. II, p. 956 with Palmer and More, op. cit. pp. 145 f.

[2] Cf. Scheible, op. cit. Vol. II, p. 972 with Palmer and More, op. cit. pp. 157 f.

[3] Cf. Scheible, op. cit. Vol. II, p. 1051 with Palmer and More, op. cit. p. 216.

even Widman retained, little knowing that it was there, was stopped up in the English version. 'I will gladly give him my body' was altered to 'would'; and the piteous wish of the German magician that he might have a bad and terrible night was not echoed by his English namesake. He merely stated that such a night lay before him when wishing a quiet one for his friends. The frail hope had vanished, the last ambiguity was gone; the tragedy of Doctor Faustus was ready for a master's hand.

P.F. had transformed the work of the 'rude Germane author' by waving the magic wand of Elizabethan prose, releasing the inspirational power from the stranglehold of an unyielding and at times ungainly language. He had also added those flashes of vision and those moments of stress which arrest and hold the imagination. It had been a smouldering, it was now an inflammatory, book.

(b) An immortal Faustus

If the history of the Faust-legend is a typical instance, then it must be granted that legends travel fast and far. The speed with which Faust got to England, Holland, Poland and France is impressive, although doubtless parallel cases could be found. But there is something almost uncanny in the way the whole complex of events (Faust's real life, its posthumous legendary accretions, the manuscript accounts, the first printed biography, and the English translation) followed hard on each other's heels with the minimum delay, as if to ensure that the German magician should be immortalized by that 'prophetical spirit of Merlin's race', the one poet above all others

> Fit to write passions for the souls below,
> If any wretched souls in passion speak.[1]

And if it is true that the English Faustbook made its first appearance in May 1592, then the race was run and the goal attained only just in time; for twelve months later Marlowe was stabbed to death.

All the biographers and critics of the dramatist are struck, as one cannot fail to be, with the spiritual affinity between the 'vnsatiable Speculator' and the poet who cried out through the lips of Tamburlaine:

[1] G. Peele, *The Honour of the Garter* in *Works*, ed. Dyce, London, 1828, Vol. II, p. 141. Written 26 June 1593.

Our souls whose faculties can comprehend
The wondrous architecture of the world,
And measure every wandering planet's course,
Still climbing after knowledge infinite,
And always moving as the restless spheres,
Wills us to wear ourselves and never rest.[1]

Moreover, as Boas has pointed out, there is a strange similarity, almost an identity, between the lives and fates of the hero of the Faust-legend and the poet who immortalized him:

And in more specific ways Marlowe must have recognized in Faustus his own counterpart. The Canterbury boy through the bounty of Archbishop Parker had reached Cambridge to qualify himself there for the clerical career. His studies had earned him the Bachelor's and the Master's degrees, but he had turned his back on the Church, and on arrival in London had gained a reputation for atheism. Similarly, Faustus through the bounty of a rich uncle had been sent to Wittenberg to study divinity, and had obtained with credit his doctorate in the subject. But his interests lay elsewhere, and he had turned secretly to the study of necromancy and conjuration.[2]

The resemblance goes deeper: we know next to nothing about the real Faust; we know very little more about Marlowe; both men remain enigmatic; legend has been busy with both; both enjoyed an evil reputation during their life-times; both were tarred with the brush of black magic; and both came to a violent end, Faust perhaps only in legend, but Christopher Marlowe in life. The mysterious affray which led to the stabbing may have been the result of a brawl about 'le recknynge' or (more probably) of a conspiracy to kill. No adequate reason of a political nature can be found; but neither is there a shadow of proof for Tannenbaum's more acceptable suggestion, that Marlowe was murdered for fear he should make damaging disclosures about Raleigh's so-called School of Atheism before the Privy Council, whither he had been summoned to answer personally to the charge of atheistical views. There is, however, no reliable evidence that this problematical School was of so sinister a nature as to call for such violent measures, and hardly a shred of proof that Marlowe was one of

---

[1] C. Marlowe, *Tamburlaine*, ed. Ellis-Fermor, London, 1930, p. 113.
[2] F. S. Boas, *Christopher Marlowe*, Oxford, 1940, p. 208.

its members. Its unsavoury reputation now rests upon the assertion of one Robert Parsons, a Jesuit pamphleteer; and if Widman has taught one nothing else, he has at least made one very wary of believing charges of magical and suchlike practices made by religious fanatics:

Of Sir Walter Rawleys school of Atheisme by the waye, & of the Conjurer that is M[aster] therof, and of the diligence vsed to get yong gentlemen of this schoole, where in both Moyses, & our Sauio^r, the olde, and the new Testaments are iested at, and the schollers taughte, amonge other thinges, to spell God backwarde.[1]

It sounds uncomfortably like a Satanist's Lodge; but when one learns that the Master was the famous mathematician and astronomer Harriott, a member of Raleigh's household, one takes heart of grace; for outstanding abilities of that nature were apt to be attributed to evil causes. And even if Harriott did indeed preside over a 'School of Night', Marlowe's link with it seems to have been tenuous and dependent on the testimony of ill-wishers or shady customers, such as Richard Baines and Richard Cholmeley:

. . . almost into every Company he cometh he perswades men to Atheism willing them not to be afeard of bugbears and hobgoblins . . . that the first beginning of Religion was only to keep men in awe . . . that Moyses was but a Jugler and that one Heriots [Harriott] being Sir W. Raleigh's man Can do more than he. . . .[2]

Hee [Cholmeley] saieth & verely beleueth that one Marlowe is able to shewe more sounde reasons for Atheisme then any devine in Englande is able to geue to proue devinitie & that Marloe tolde him that hee hath read the Atheist lecture to Sr Walter Raleigh & others.[3]

It is all very inconclusive; moreover Marlowe's conversation seems to have been of the caustically sceptical kind; whereas Satanists and black magicians are fervent if perverted believers; also, as I have shown elsewhere,[4] it seems clear that his knowledge of infernal

[1] English summary of Robert Parsons, *Responsio ad Elizabethae edictum*, 1592; quoted by Boas, op. cit. p. 113.
[2] Richard Baines, *A Note Containing the opinion of one Christopher Marly . . .*; quoted by Boas, op. cit. pp. 250f.
[3] *Remembraunces of wordes and matter against Richard Cholmeley;* quoted by Boas, op. cit. p. 255. The 'School of Night' in *Love's Labour's Lost* is identified by modern Shakespeare scholars with Raleigh's School of Atheism. [4] *Ritual Magic*, pp. 305 ff.

invocations (more extensive than that of 'Spiess' or P.F.) was limited to the kind of handbook circulating everywhere at the time. Even Greene's solemn warning to his brother-dramatist on his death-bed is more consistent with the view that Marlowe was a notorious atheist than with the notion that he frequented 'Schools of Night':

> I knowe the least of my demerits merits this miserable death, but wilfull striuing against knowne truth exceedeth al the terrors of my soule. Defer not (with me) till this last point of extremitie; for little knowest thou how in the end thou shalt be visited.[1]

And could Marlowe, however much of an 'atheist'; could Marlowe with his beauty-loving mind, and with that superb vision of God he gave in *Tamburlaine*:

> . . . he that sits on high and never sleeps,
> Nor in one place is circumscriptible,
> But everywhere fills every continent
> With strange infusion of his sacred vigour;[2]

could Marlowe ever have fallen as low as magic-mongering, devil-worship, and such ugly infantilism as 'spelling God backwarde'?

The answer to that question involves the power of magic altogether, which certainly attracts the noblest as well as the basest among mankind; it involves too the close, the fraternal relationship between the sinner and the saint, the ambiguity surrounding mysticism and vision, the danger of aspiring minds; in a word it involves the tragedy of Doctor Faustus as comprehended by Marlowe; and comprehended so deeply, probably not because he had ever himself drawn ceremonial circles and summoned up fiends, but because in those reckless atheistical conversations he had been 'striuing against knowne truth'. This is the very pith of the play; and only a man who had undergone that soul-searing experience could have found those accents of terror and despair which were wrung from the magician's heart.

It is clear from the conjuration-scene and from other slighter signs and tokens that Marlowe knew something about black magic, and that he must have seen one or other of the ritual texts in use,

---

[1] R. Greene, *Groats-worth of witte, bought with a million of Repentance*, London, 1592, f. 1 recto.

[2] Marlowe, *Tamburlaine*, ed. cit. p. 210.

of which Reginald Scot had given several examples in the *Discouerie of Witchcraft* in 1584. The invocation and the description of the magic circle, although handled with poetical licence, follow orthodox lines, and were not to be found either in the Urfaustbook nor yet in P.F.'s translation. 'Spiess' omitted these details on purpose, he maintained, in order that they should not be abused, and P.F. was content to follow his example. But no dramatist worthy of the name could scamp this scene; and no tragic dramatist but must darken and deepen the tone and the content of the superficially pious and fundamentally sordid manuals of magic, whose technique consisted in an attempt to obtain power over the fiends by invoking the aid of the Trinity. Marlowe adopted that formula in the invocation (if indeed *valeat* means prevail and not avaunt); but the sombre shadow of Satanism enveloping the legend of Faustus cast a retrospective gloom over the performance:

> *Meph.* For, when we hear one rack the name of God,
> Abjure the Scriptures and his Saviour Christ,
> We fly, in hope to get his glorious soul;
> Nor will we come, unless he use such means
> Whereby he is danger to be damn'd.
> Therefore the shortest cut for conjuring
> Is stoutly to abjure the Trinity,
> And pray devoutly to the prince of hell.
> *Faust.* So Faustus hath
> Already done. . . .[1]

Now it is true that Faustus represented himself as having prayed and sacrificed to the devils before undertaking the conjuration; but the protective circle, containing kabbalistic anagrams for Jehovah's name, and the names of holy saints as well; the sprinkling of holy water during the ceremony and the making of the sign of the cross, together with the invocation of Jehovah, all show that the source which Marlowe used for the conjuration was not a Satanist production, but merely one of those comparatively harmless ritual texts which are called black, because they invoke fiends to bully or cajole them into obedience with the aid and support of God. Marlowe's attempt to fuse the two diametrically opposite conceptions of Satanism in the legend and so-called black magic (in

---

[1] Marlowe, *The Tragical History of Doctor Faustus*, ed. Boas, London, 1932, p. 71. Cf. my *Ritual Magic*, pp. 305 ff. for a closer discussion of this subject.

reality a dirty grey) in the ritual texts was not entirely successful; it goes far to prove that, though he understood Satanism emotionally, he was ignorant of its practices.

These and other borrowings from magical sources, slight enough in themselves, and even cumulatively not very outstanding, are nevertheless conspicuous because Marlowe clung so closely in other respects to the text of the English Faustbook, condensing, selecting and transmuting it, but adding very little to it. The content, the structure and even the shape of *The Tragical History* differ very slightly indeed from the folkbook, allowing for the fact that it was now in dramatic form. Part I of the original (the decision of the hero to devote himself to magic, the conjuration, the pact, the spiritual questionings and the distress of soul) occupies Acts I and II of the tragedy. Part II (the journeys through heaven and hell and round the world, with the sojourn in Rome), all this, either recounted or represented, forms the matter of the third act, to which was later added the queer Saxon Bruno episode at the papal court. Part III fell naturally into two acts. Act IV concentrated on the magical feats: the raising of Alexander the Great and his consort at the request of the Emperor Charles V; the affair of the knight and the stag's horns; the episode of the horse-courser, the bundle of straw, and the luckless leg-pull of the dupe; the scenes at the court of the Duke of Anhalt, rudely interrupted by the appearance of the horse-courser, the carter whose load of hay Faustus had devoured and others, all determined on revenge. Faustus thereupon strikes one after another dumb, and another anecdote in the Faustbook finds a dramatic form. Act V, leaving all this tomfoolery behind, gives the scenes with Helen, the intervention of the old man, the anger of Mephisto, the second pact, the tragic revelations to the scholars, rising through a crescendo of remorse to the final monologue during which the clock strikes thrice and Faustus is haled off to perdition. The horrified comments of the students and the epilogue then repeat in poetry what 'Spiess' and P.F. had said in prose.

Analysed in this way, it becomes apparent that Marlowe, and whoever may have collaborated with him at the time or have added scenes later, kept almost pedantically to the framework of the English Faustbook. In particular the balance of power between the serious and the comic as 'Spiess' had established it remained quantitatively at least *in statu quo*. Emotionally, tragedy predominated, even though someone (who may or may not have been Marlowe) was trying to tip the balance towards farce.

The rather boisterous dramatic divinity who shaped the rough-hewn outline of the English Faustbook in the third and fourth acts was not content with adding a plot of some moment to the tricks Faustus played upon the pope; nor with adumbrating a conflict between Benvolio and the magician to account for the jest with the horns; nor with kaleidoscoping the battle-scenes between Faustus and the offended knight; nor with insinuating the behead-ing-trick into this series of events; nor with bringing dramatic coherence and movement into the tales of the sorcerer and his dupes; he (and this may well have been Marlowe) interpolated a comic sub-plot which travestied, in true Elizabethan style, the deeds of the hero himself. This was not only to alter slightly but signi-ficantly the structure of the whole; it introduced a farcical element into the assumptions of the legend as such. However comic, in a rude and artless way, some of the stories in the Faustbook may be, they never by any chance throw a comic light upon the magician let alone on the fearful subject of the pact with the powers of evil. This is treated throughout with the utmost seriousness; such humour as is to be found in the third part is always of Faust's making, and the laugh is against his dupes. In *The Tragical History*, although the hero is not ridiculed directly, his magical practices are implicitly held up to scorn, first by Wagner and the hireling clown travestying the pact-scene, later by Robin and Dick (or Ralph) attempting conjurations and suffering violence from Mephistopheles. In exactly the same way, Miles in Greene's *Friar Bacon and Friar Bungay* imitates and thereby parodies his master; for the sub-plot was a stock feature of Elizabethan drama: a con-cession to the groundlings, an aesthetic device and a philosophical comment all in one. Applied to magic, its ironical and philosophical force could be annihilating; this element is only rudimentary in Marlowe's drama; but it had been introduced and was to have far-reaching and unforeseen results.

To return to the tragic action: apart from introducing a ritual conjuration, there was the whole problem of manipulating epic into drama to be faced, with the added difficulty that it was a drama of a spiritual kind which must be visibly represented. The prologue, introducing 'the man that in his study sits', and the various choruses connecting the acts evade that difficulty, and seem wonderfully appropriate in a drama embracing heaven and hell, the firmament and the physical world. The good and bad angels are theoretically more questionable; but they are so well managed that Faustus seems to be listening to the promptings of his own divided heart; they concentrate and intensify those terrible inner wrestlings about which the Faustbook is so eloquent in a manner subtly different from the great monologues, as if they were the direct projections of Faustus's subconscious self. As a stage device they are full of dangers; but dramatically they could ill be spared. Valdes and Cornelius for their part make the sinister influence of those 'diuers that were séene in those diuelish Arts' as real and convincing as their promises seem to be; and the anxious scholars, mistrustful of Faustus's association with them and determining to seek counsel of the Rector of the University in order to reclaim him, not only pave the way for the scene with the old man, but also set the stage for the presence of the students at the summoning up of Helen of Troy and during Faustus's last hours on earth. It was also in the interests of dramatic art that the spectactular effects following upon the invocation of Mephistopheles were reduced to a minimum, and that the sinister spirit in person answered almost at once. Although Marlowe did not radically alter this character as found in his source, yet Mephisto's awareness of his own eternal damnation brought the first and indeed subsequent dialogues between the magician and his control to the very summit of tragic art, whilst dispensing with those moral preachifyings 'Spiess' had delighted in and P.F. had not cut short. As for the interlude of the Seven Deadly Sins (whether due to Marlowe or Rowley), it was at least an improvement on the state-visit by the grotesque cohorts of Infernus which it replaced. In these ways, and in others like them, Marlowe disengaged the essentially dramatic nature of the story of Faust.

He did far more than that: he laid bare the tragic aspect, that unresolved discord which made the tale told by 'Spiess' so questionable, the fearful discrepancy between the motives impelling the hero towards the crime and the appalling price exacted. In the authentic tragic style Faust provokes a nemesis far beyond his deserts: punishment in *eternity* for a sin committed in *time*. This was the dreadful doom brooding over the whole of Christendom, and Marlowe made of Faustus the great protagonist, the supreme hero-villain of an action which concentrated, intensified and sym-

bolized the dark mythological drama engrossing the thoughts of
the age. The tragic hero of Satanism was now fully revealed with
the whole enormity of the desperate, irremediable, fatal false step,
involving a destiny so greatly in excess of even that iniquity as to
arouse a passion of pity and fear as one sees the transcendental
guilt inevitably attracting to itself the inexorable transcendental
response. All this, latent in the legend recounted by 'Spiess', was
developed by Marlowe with tragic intensity and power.

By presenting it as a drama, he made it ten times more vivid and
real; any dramatization would have done that. But only Marlowe
with that extraordinary feeling for titanism, whether soaring upwards or plunging into the abyss, could have represented in so
moving and heart-piercing a way the passions of his hero. The
Miltonic grandeur of Satan in *Paradise Lost* almost dares one to
pity him; and Dante's attitude towards the damned hardly admits
of sympathy:

> Qui vive la pietà quando è ben morta.

Thus Virgil rebuked Dante when he wept to behold the fearful
fate of the diviners, augurs and sorcerers in hell:

> Chi è piu scellerato che colui
> che al giudicio divin compassion porta?[1]

But it is just this compassion and understanding which have
rendered Marlowe's *Faustus* the greatest of all the tragic versions
the legend has inspired. 'Spiess' had been markedly receptive to
the ideas of spiritual aspiration, despair and downfall inherent in
the tale. P.F. had stressed this aspect and dignified it by his style.
Marlowe in the monologues gave those emotions an expression
unsurpassable and unsurpassed, the supreme utterance of a tortured recreant soul.

In the opening monologue, which thereafter figured in almost
every dramatization known, he not only illuminated the motives
of the magician from within, whereas hitherto the fierce light of
religious horror had beaten upon him from without; but apart
from the actual content of the monologue, it had so personal and
individual a character and rang so true as to attract poet after poet
down the ages, whether they were dramatists or not. A vent for
expressing every conceivable kind of aspiration, disillusionment,

---

[1] Dante, *Inferno*, Canto xx.

despair and discontent had been found at the dawn of the age of individualism; something that could and would carry the legend on through centuries in which the belief in its very basis and its very core was completely extinguished. Paradoxical though it may sound, the close spiritual kinship between the hero of the Faust-book and Marlowe, which made the monologues so extremely realistic, was the factor which rendered the legend accessible to poets who had nothing in common with either Faustus or Marlowe but unstilled desires and aspirations unfulfilled; that is to say accessible to every poet, and indeed to every human being, who has ever lived. This was to make the legend universal in a way which the fate of a mere black magician could never have achieved.

Immortalized in Marlowe's monologues, Faustus was also trans-figured by his passion for beauty, which shed a radiance over his tormented features when he saw it incarnate in Helen. 'Spiess' had done what in him lay to make this apparition alluring; but he was completely out of his depth when it came to transcendent beauty; and P.F., that intoxicated dreamer of glory and power, was hardly in better case:

This Lady appeared before thē in a most sumptuous gowne of purple Veluet, richly imbrodered, her hayre hanged downe loose as fayre as the beaten Gold, & of such length that it reached downe to her hammes, with amorous cole-black eyes, a sweete and pleasant round face, her lips red as a Cherry, her cheekes of rose all colour, her mouth small, her neck as white as the Swanne, tall and slender of personage, and in summe, there was not one imperfect part in her: shee looked round about her with a rouling Haukes eye, a smiling & wanton countenance. . . .[1]

Unlike 'Spiess' and unlike P.F., Marlowe worshipped beauty, which for him, and for the Renaissance as a whole, was enshrined in classical legend and myth and personified by Helen. It is there-fore almost as if fate, or the legend itself, had willed that he should live just long enough to raise the story of Helen and Faust on to a summit of beauty. In the Faustbooks she was merely a devil in disguise who put the crowning touch to Faustus's 'swinish and epicurean life'; in the drama love of beauty played an organic part in banishing thoughts of remorse and despair.

> Scarce can I name salvation, faith, or heaven,
> But fearful echoes thunders in mine ears,

<hr>

[1] Palmer and More, op. cit. p. 211.

'Faustus, thou art damned!' Then swords, and knives,
Poisons, guns, halters, and envenom'd steel
Are laid before me to despatch myself;
And long ere this I should have done the deed,
Had not sweet pleasure conquer'd deep despair.
Have not I made blind Homer sing to me
Of Alexander's love and Oenon's death?
And hath not he, that built the wall of Thebes,
With ravishing sound of his melodious harp,
Made music with my Mephistophilis?
Why should I die, then, or basely despair?
I am resolv'd; Faustus shall not repent.[1]—

It was to a mind receptive of beauty in all its manifestations that
the vision of Helen came towards the end of Faustus's allotted
span of life. Her first appearance was immediately followed by the
racking scene with the old man, the vain attempt to repent, the
wrath of Mephistopheles, the recantation, the second pact, the
outburst of hatred against 'that base and aged man'; and then, the
frantic appeal for satisfaction of one of the two ruling passions of
his life:

> One thing, good servant, let me crave of thee,
> To glut the longing of my heart's desire,—
> That I may have unto my paramour
> That heavenly Helen which I saw of late,
> Whose sweet embraces may extinguish clean
> Those thoughts that do dissuade me from my vow,
> And keep my oath I made to Lucifer.[2]

One of the noblest passions of the human mind, the love of beauty,
manifests itself here in its destructive form and is seen to be as
dangerous as the love of knowledge and the love of truth. In the
Faustbook these latter derived from arrogance and became inex-
tricably entangled with the lust for possessions and power. In the
drama they are wedded with the desire for beauty and are doubly
and trebly fateful. This was Marlowe's personal contribution, and
it gave a tragic significance to Helen which she had not had before.

Passing through the fiery furnace of Elizabethan poetic and
dramatic genius, the Faust-legend emerged with the dross very
largely purified from the countenance of the hero. Waist-high he

[1] Marlowe, *Tragical History*, p. 90.   [2] Ibid. p. 163.

stood, half disentangled from the grossness and crudeness of his earlier state, grappling with Mephisto, his tragic and sinister foe; and in his eyes an expression compounded of nobility and baseness, of disillusionment, rapture and such despair as no observer of any age or creed could regard unmoved. But from the waist downwards, forming as it were the base of this haunting monument, the elements untouched by the fire of genius had undergone a dramatic change. Galvanized into a semblance of life, they gambolled clumsily below and emitted coarse guffaws, heartlessly deriding and parodying the tragedy enacting above their heads. The dual vision of the Elizabethans had played over and transfigured the dark, uncouth, tormented German magician; but had pitilessly illuminated the nature of the wound with which the legend was born.

(c) *Farcical Fausts*

The popularity of the Faust-legend in England is vouched for, not only by the translation of P.F. and the dramatization by Marlowe, but in other ways too. As early as 1588–9 there was entered at the Stationers' Register *A Ballad of the life and deathe of Doctor Faustus, the great Cunngerer*, of which nothing further is known; and in 1594 there appeared the *Second Report of Dr. Faustus*, a sequel to the Faustbook, dealing with the adventures of Wagner. This is quite independent of the German Wagnerbook of 1593, and indeed totally different from it both in content and in tone. It is a very curious production, well worth study, but nevertheless far inferior to the English Faustbook; nor did it ever take the place in the popular esteem of P.F.'s translation, of which Thoms said in 1858:

> It is impossible, in the limits of this Introduction, to attempt to give a List of the various Editions of this Romance, which have been issued from Marlowe's time to the present day, in order to satisfy the popular curiosity respecting this Prince of Conjurors.[1]

As for Marlowe's *Faustus*, there is documentary evidence for twenty-three performances between the years 1594 and 1597, in which year Thomas Dickers was paid £1 for 'adicyones' to it. Samuel Rowley and William Birde received the fairly substantial

[1] W. J. Thoms, *A Collection of Early English Prose Romances*, London, 1858, Vol. III, p. 159.

sum of £4 in 1604 for further additions; and as this is the year in
which the first quarto was published, it will be realized that there
are solid grounds for supposing that the text as it now stands is
not the unaided work of Marlowe; moreover the fourth edition,
the 1616 quarto, differs in many respects from the first and contains some 550 additional lines, including the Saxon Bruno episode.
Finally in 1663 an alteration of some importance was made. This
was the ninth and appears to have been the last edition until the
nineteenth century. *Faustus* was therefore in great demand until
the Restoration. Moreover, frequent allusions to it and lines taken
from it in the works of other dramatists, among them Shakespeare
in *The Taming of the Shrew* and *The Merry Wives of Windsor*,
witness to the vividness of the effect Marlowe's tragedy made on
his contemporaries and on succeeding generations. At first the
effect was roughly what Marlowe aimed at and what one would
naturally expect:

> O, now you hitt it, 'twas indeed a spirit,
> To whom, for certaine tearme of yeares t'inherit
> His ease and pleasure with abundant wealth,
> He has made sale of his soules dearest health,
> And in a deed engrost, signd with his blood
> Sould soul & body with all hope of good
> In heavenly ioyes to come, vnto the devill.
> O horrid act, O execrable evill!
> Another *Faustus*, haplesse hopelesse man,
> What wilt thou doe, when as that little sand
> Of thy soone emptied houreglasse is spent?[1]

The widespread belief in pacts made with the devil and the
fascinated horror with which such actions were regarded were the
root cause for the hold of Faustus upon the public mind. It was
the content and not the form, the matter and not the manner, of
Marlowe's tragedy which conquered for the hero that fame mixed
with infamy that ensured the perpetuation of his name. But where
the vital belief was absent, a very different tone would be heard:

Another will fore tell you of Lightning and Thunder that shall happen
such a day, when there are no such Inflammations seene, except men go
to the *Fortune* in *Gelding-Lane*, to see the Tragedie of Doctor *Faustus*.

[1] R. C. Gent, *The Times Whistle*, 1614–1616; ed. Cowper in E.E.T.S.,
London, 1871, p. 53.

There indeed a man may behold shagge-hayr'd Deuills runne roaring ouer the stage with Squibs in their mouthes, while Drummers make Thunder in the Tyring house, and the twelue-penny Hirelings make artificial Lightning in their heauens.[1]

It is something of a shock to realize that this caustic description does not go beyond what is advocated in Marlowe's text, and indeed omits some of the spectacular machinery. So much, and of so grossly sensational a nature in his source, had been omitted by Marlowe that one had hardly noticed what had been added or left. It does not bulk large in the rubric, to be sure; but there was a sufficiency of thunder and lightning and devils and squibs to justify Melton's criticism. There was also the dragon in the conjuring-scene, a piece of stage-property mentioned by Henslowe in 1598 ('j dragon in fostes'); there was the throne of heaven descending and ascending, hell discovered and disappearing, quite apart from all the opportunities for strong effects offered by the good and bad angels, Alexander slaying Darius, the appearance of Helen between two cupids and the Seven Deadly Sins. For Marlowe was not the first and not the last to discover that when cosmic elements enter drama, they drag spectacular devices behind them, as the mystery and miracle-plays had shown. As a stage-play, therefore, *The Tragical History of Doctor Faustus* was not only highly susceptible to spectacular vulgarization, it might also on that account help to lower and corrupt the general standard of theatrical productions and public taste.

Meanwhile gradually but surely familiarity with the German magician's name was beginning to breed contempt, the sort of contempt which lumped him together with others of his kind under the general rubric of cheat and scoundrel:

O, art thou there, Saint Dunstan? thou hast undone me, thou cursed Friar Bacon, thou hellish Merlin. But I'll be revenged upon thee! 'Tis not your Mephistopheles, nor any other spirits of ruby or carbuncle, that you can raise, nor your good father-in-law Doctor *Faustus*, that conjures so many of us into your wives' circle, that with all their magic shall secure you from my rage.[2]

And even when Faustus's powers were accepted, he had become

[1] J. Melton, *Astrologaster, or, The Figure-Caster*, London, 1620, p. 31.
[2] T. Randolph, *Aristippus or the joviall philosopher*, 1630, in *Poetical and Dramatic Works*, ed. Hazlitt, London, 1875, Vol. I, p. 11.

a mere household-word for magician, a generic term, his indivi-
duality had disappeared:

Hee that can plucke this peece of my jawes, spight of my teeth, and
I keepe my mouth fast shut, Ile say, hee is more than a Cheater, and a
Doctor *Faustus* or *Mephostophilus* at least.[1]

But more often than not, scepticism was heard; as when Never-
Good in Randolph's *Plutothalmia* threatens his companions to
borrow a familiar spirit from 'this Faustus, the Mephistopheles of
his age, the wonder and the sole Asmodeus of his times' in order
to carry out his nefarious schemes. He goes off, leaving them
strangely unmoved:

Goggle. We fear not Dr. Faustus: his landlord Lucifer
   Says that his lease with him is out of date;
   Nor will he let him longer tenant be
   To the Twelve Houses of astrology.
Caryon. Let Dr. *Faustus* do his worst.[2]

It was but a step from this attitude to one of merry jesting and
jibing:

  The room was now a Conjurors Circle, and
  The pipes and pots for mystick figures stand;
  To one another they magicians were
  And their discourses charms to keep them here.
  Marry, their Host must be the Devill, for he
  Was truely glad of their impietie,
  And most officious in his malice lends 'em
  A boy-like *Mephostophiles* to attend 'em . . .
  By this time they had made more Ale away
  Than would have serv'd *Faustus* to's load of hay.[3]

  Or to plague thee for thy sin,
  Should draw a Circle, and begin
  To Conjure, for I am, look to't,
  An *Oxford* Scholer, and can doe't.

---

[1] J. D., *The knave in Graine*, London, 1640, Act v.
[2] T. Randolph, *Plutothalmia*, 1651, ed. cit. Vol. II, pp. 458f.
[3] E. Prestwick, *Alematch*, in *Divers Selected Poems*, 1651; quoted by
O. Francke in his edition of Mountfort's *Faustus*, Heilbronn, 1886, pp.
xxviif.

> Then with three sets of *Mops* and *Mowes*,
> Seaven of odd words and Motley showes,
> A thousand tricks, that may be taken
> From *Faustus, Lambe*, or *Frier-Bacon*. . . .[1]

Yet the play itself remained popular, though probably some of the heart went out of it during the Puritan period. Nevertheless it struggled through somehow:

The publication of the corrupt 1663 edition, 'as it is now acted', proves that, though mutilated, it was seen on the Restoration boards. On 26 May 1662 the audience had included Pepys, who notes in his *Diary*, 'by water to my brother's, and thence to take my wife to the Redd Bull, where we saw Dr. Faustus, but so wretchedly & poorly done that we were sick of it'.[2]

And sickened indeed one is by the scene at the court of the Turkish Emperor in Babylon replacing the episodes at the Papal Court in Rome. Not that the change of scene in itself is anything to grieve over; on the contrary the horse-play in the Vatican was tedious and tasteless enough; and it might seem a sign of grace to substitute the pranks played on the sultan in the Faustbook and leave the pope alone. But the new scene is so vapid, the humour so heavy and the atmosphere so stale that one begins to think wistfully of Rowley and Birde and of the gulf which separates them from their Stuart colleagues. All the more so, because the rank fustian of the language, printed as verse, is quite beneath criticism:

> *Faust.* Why, but tell me *Mephostophilis*, dar'st thou
> Attempt to venter on a man in his circle?
> *Meph.* Because thou art ours & sold to Lucifer, and I
> Have promis'd to serve thee faithfully, I'le not
> Conceal the secrets of our state from thee, thou darling
> Of great *Lucifer*: Know all those rights and
> Spells which mortals use to make us rise,
> Appear visible, answer to their demands,
> Fullfill their wills, and execute their malice on
> Their enemies, are very fables, forg'd at first
> In hell, and thrust on credulous mortals
> To deceive 'm.

---

[1] S^r J[ohn] M[ennis] and Ja[mes] S[mith], *Musarum Delicae or the Muses Recreation*, London, 1655, p. 54.

[2] Marlowe, *Tragical History*, ed. cit. pp. 49 f.

Nor is there such a power in signes & words, to
Make us to obey; that rule the elements, & in a
Moment, if we had but leave, would turn the
World to a confus'd nothing, 'tis true we seem
To come constrain'd, and by the power of their
Charmes: but are more willing to be imploy'd to
Hurt & kill mankind, than they are willing to engage
Vs in their service, and wheresoe'r we find one bent to our
Familiarity, we fly then willingly to catch him.

Faust. Thanks good *Mephostophilis* for this discovering
Of your misery. [? mystery][1]

Misery, indeed. Remembering Marlowe's mighty line:

We fly, in hope to get his glorious soul,

it seems that we have entered into an age in which poetry, mystery, beauty, blank verse and tragedy itself have been exorcized from the world.

It was only in a world so sadly bereft that William Mountfort's *Life and Death of Doctor Faustus, Made into a Farce* could ever have been produced and have found sufficient favour to be revived. It was acted 'several times' between the years 1684 and 1688 and then put on again in 1697, five years after the brilliant young actor-author had been stabbed to death, thus meeting the same fate which a century before had befallen the poet he desecrated. It was adorned with 'The Humours of *Harlequin* and *Scaramouche*', those madly popular Italian buffoons, which accounts for its vogue; but even so it is difficult to understand how a man of taste and feeling, as Mountfort's contemporaries describe him, could have perpetrated this enormity, or how an audience, if it remembered Marlowe, could have enjoyed it. The audience at that date must have forgotten Marlowe; and Mountfort, who certainly knew him, must have suffered from that blind spot for poetry which was evident in the 1663 quarto. For had he merely turned the whole situation into a farce, it would have been much more tolerable. Black magic is an ugly thing, and it could have done no harm to spend a hilarious evening laughing at Scaramouche and Harlequin in the semblance of wizard and dupe. And if the name of Faustus

---

[1] Marlowe, *Tragical History*, ed. cit. p. 205. This reads like a para phrase of the parallel passage in King James's *Daemonologie*, pp. 16f. in the 1924 reprint.

on the play-bills was there for a draw, this is one of the penalties one pays for fame. But to use as a background or as a skeleton-scheme the tragic scenes and even the tragic verse of Marlowe, deflowered and defaced but still recognizable, this was to be guilty of a deadlier deed. Scattered here and there through a roaring farce, they serve as a spice to the comic dish, a sacrilege that bears startling witness to the depraved taste of the age which knew not Marlowe and bowdlerized Shakespeare. To give two instances only: Scaramouche interrupts the conjuration-scene and ruins it with his foolery; then after Faustus's final monologue, shortened, garbled and printed in a way that murders the rhythm:

> *Enter old Man and Scholar.*
>
> *Old M.* Come, Friend; let's visit Faustus: For such a dreadful
> Night was never seen.
> > *Scene discovers Faustus's Limbs*
>
> *Schol.* O help us, Heav'n; for here are Faustus's Limbs
> All torn asunder by the Hand of Hell.
>
> *Old M.* May this a fair Example be to all,
> To avoid such Ways which brought poor Faustus's fall.
> And whatsoever Pleasure does invite,
> Sell not your Souls to purchase vain Delight. *Exeunt.*
>
> *Scene changes to Hell.*
>
> *Faustus's Limbs come together. A dance, and Song.*[1]

These examples show that the sub-title 'Made into a Farce' is a precise description of what Mountfort did to Marlowe; he really turned the tragedy into a farce; it was nothing so simple and legitimate as a parody. Retaining several of the comic scenes, he also kept many of the tragic ones, dislocated and truncated but still there, and still serious in intent. These noble and ravaged features he then distorted with a leer, reminding one of nothing so much as of that incomprehensible vandalism which delights in decorating the marble face of the Venus of Milo with a military moustache. As for Harlequin and Scaramouche, who replace Wagner and the Clown, and Robin and Ralph, they are on the whole rather livelier and gayer than their predecessors. Rather too coarse at times, and occasionally pointless, they have at least one

[1] W. Mountfort, *The Life and Death of Doctor Faustus, Made into a Farce*, London, 1697; ed. Francke, Heilbronn, 1886, p. 33.

scene which must have brought the house down. Preparing to partake of a magic banquet, they are thwarted of the meal, because that dolt Harlequin keeps on uttering proverbs which include the name of God. On the first occasion the table flies up out of reach: apologizing humbly, the two are then hoisted up after it, when Harlequin repeats his offence, and down flies the table leaving the wizards in mid-air. Finally, when an enormous pasty is opened, a stag's head appears, and birds fly out. One can almost hear the gales of laughter from the groundlings; and indeed one is ready to join in it and forget Marlowe for the space of an hour. But Mountfort will not allow one to forget; the maimed fragments see to that; the severed limbs of Marlowe's *Faustus* are executing this devil's dance. In view of the episode of the horse-courser, infallibly present here, this is a piece of poetic justice one would far rather waive. What is actually happening before one's eyes in this extraordinary playlet is the historically interesting fact that the comic sub-plot was achieving a degree of emancipation from the tragic theme which rendered the latter unnecessary and incongruous, an awkward residuum, an ungainly giant sprawling inertly across a neat little stage; the Lilliputian actors were busy dismembering it and carrying it off piecemeal to the shouts of delighted and derisive laughter; putting tragedy in its place.

Echoes of the effect can be heard in Rowland's unpublished play, *The Imposter or tis the Humer of the age, a Farce,* 1723, in which the plot was built round the figure of the stage Faustus, impersonated by the impostor Jack Daw, in order to pluck such predestined victims as Sir Credulous Shallow and his wife. It is full of sharp criticisms of the mangling of Marlowe's *Faustus* and of the parlous state of public taste in London altogether, and contains the following allusions to what seems to be Mountfort's play:

I have heard what universal success old *Faustus* have been received with in London. I [will] try, how the country folks will receive him too. For here's an old black cloak which . . . will make me look as like, if not more resemble the reall Doktor *Faustus*, then my friend Harlekeen did . . . and why should not the country folks be as great asses as these of the town. . . . I take upon me the name of Doctor *Faustus*, he being the most famous and yet the very silliest of all Congerors. . . . Lord, what manly exploits have been acted in the praise of this real and noble doctor here, o it would make ones hair stand an [sic] end to see the monsterous dragon come flying between the apple-trees with such fury as if it could blast the trees to such a degree, that one would not think to have had a bit of fruit in three or four years . . . that fellow, that fears to tell his name at the showhouse, where the Tag rag and bob tail flocked to see the Divill and Doctor *Faustus* for fifty nights together and made a perfect beargarden of the play-house. . . . Poh, but that silly fellow that You talked of is a silly whelp; if ours here is not wiser, I would not give a farthing for him nor his performance neither. . . . God I thought, this puppy had been an empty skulled fellow, such as that *Faustous* at London. . . . Ay, but we find him quite otherwise. . . . If it had been such a one, we need not have feared him. . . . No for all he was terrible in picking peoples pockets.[1]

A year later, in 1724, the loyal subjects of George I were gratified by the performance of a pantomime called *Harlequin Doctor Faustus*, composed by the dancing-master John Thurmond and produced at Drury Lane. It is a most eerie performance from the point of view of the legend, since it marks its complete dissolution. It is true that the magician signs the contract at the beginning of the ballet and is torn to pieces by devils on the stage after the following judgment by Time and Death:

> *Time.* Mortal, thy dreadful hour is come,
> Thy Days are past, thy Glass is run.
> *Death.* Tremble while Death strikes the Blow,
> Let thy black Soul propose to go
> To everlasting Flames below.[2]

But otherwise it is hardly recognizable, in spite of the fact that several old friends, now in fancy-dress, pirouette and whirl, swirl, turn somersaults, curtsey and kiss their hands across the footlights: stags' horns, wisps of hay, magic money turned to dross, peasants fooled with wizard wine, Faustus's leg pledged as a pawn. Hereupon a host of motley nether limbs comes dancing in, and the

[1] Mountfort, *The Life and Death of Doctor Faustus*, ed. cit. pp. xxxi f. Although the dragon is not mentioned in the rubric of Mountfort's farce, it was probably there, as it had obviously become a stock feature. But these allusions are very likely of a generic character, criticising Mountfort's version as well as other productions of *Faustus*. The MS. is in the Bodleian Library (MSS. Rawl. Poet. 49; fol. 130–178 according to Francke).

[2] A. Diebler, 'Faust und Wagnerpantomimen in England', *Anglia*, Halle, 1884, Vol. VII, p. 350. Except for these verses, the whole is in dumb show.

magician's choice falls upon a shapely member of female *provenance* with which to cut his capers. Would this ever have happened, if his limbs had not come together again in Mountfort's farce? Such is the flotsam and jetsam of the original body of anecdotes strewn through the hectic adventures of Harlequin, Scaramouche, Punch and Pierrot, in which transformations, acrobatics, and illusionisms of all kinds gave proof of the virtuosity of Thurmond's pupils and of the perfection of the stage-machinery. That, however, was yet another illusion; for during a pantomimic entertainment of *Doctor Faustus* at Lincoln's Inn Fields one of the machines broke, killing two of the occupants and maiming a third, so that in the future only dummy figures were permissible.

The second 'grotesque entertainment', as Thurmond disarmingly termed it, followed in 1727, either at Drury Lane or Covent Garden. It was called *The Miser, or Wagner and Abericock*, and was furnished with the following argument:

Doctor Faustus, some Time before his Death, in his Will, made his Faithful Servant Wagner his Sole Heir; and left the Spirit Abericock, by whose Assistance, Wagner (in his Character of Harlequin) Produces the following Magical Incidents.[1]

This information is contained in the English Faustbook, where the familiar spirit is called Akercocke (German *Auerhahn*, or mountain-cock). It therefore postulates that amount of acquaintance with P.F., but there is no other sign of knowledge either of the Faustbook or the *Second Report*; the name of Wagner was all that mattered.

Whilst *Harlequin Doctor Faustus* was delighting the audiences of Drury Lane, *Harlequin Shepherd* by the same script-writer was convulsing the crowds at Covent Garden; and the two together proved too much for Hogarth. In *A just view of the British Stage* the ghost of Ben Jonson is watching the rehearsal of a new farce representing *Dr. Faustus, Harlequin Shepherd* and *Scaramouch*; the face of the Muse of Tragedy is plastered over with a bill bearing the legend *Harlequin Doctor Faustus*, and the features of the Muse of Comedy are similarly defaced by *Harlequin Shepherd*. In his *Small Masquerade Ticket* (1724) the Academy of Arts looms neglected in the background; the works of Shakespeare, Ben Jonson, Dryden, Congreve and others are being carried off on

---

[1] *Anglia*, Vol. VII, p. 351.

Small Masquerade Ticket

A just view of the British Stage

barrows for waste-paper; whilst in the foreground a great crowd is streaming towards a masquerade, and an even larger one is jostling at the entrance of an enormous building where Harlequin is standing with a placard in his hands: '*Dr. Faustus is here*'.

Pope was equally emphatic:

> And [Cibber] look'd and saw a sable Sorc'rer rise,
> Swift to whose hand a winged volume flies:
> All sudden, Gorgoṇṣ hiss, and Dragons glare,
> And ten-horn'd fiends and Giants rush to war.
> Hell rises, Heaven descends, and dance on Earth:
> Gods, imps, and monsters, music, rage, and mirth,
> A fire, a jig, a battle, and a ball,
> Till one wide conflagration swallows all. . . .
> To aid our cause, if Heav'n thou canst not bend,
> Hell thou shalt move; for Faustus is our friend.

a sable Sorc'rer] Dr. Faustus, the subject of a set of Farces, which lasted in vogue two or three seasons, in which both Play-houses strove to outdo each other for some years . . . frequented by persons of the first quality in England, to the twentieth and thirtieth time.
Faustus, Pluto, etc.] Names of miserable Farces, which it was the custom to act at the end of the best Tragedies, to spoil the digestion of the audience.[1]

Well might Milton's nephew, Edward Phillips, have exclaimed some fifty years earlier of Marlowe:

. . . of all that he hath written to the Stage his Dr. *Faustus* hath made the greatest noise with its Devils and such like Tragical sport.[2]

For the sport *was* tragical; and, if Thurmond's pantomimes were pure farce, Mountfort's entertainment was not. From the very beginning the comic element had been there, and if the Elizabethan dramatists had stressed, and perhaps rather overstressed it, they were following a sound instinct, though not an aesthetic one. Sorcerers, magicians and necromancers belong to the mysterious taboo class; awe-inspiring, indeed terrifying because of the taboo, and risible because of their pretensions if one begins to doubt. One is often in two minds about them; and if one has the courage to laugh at them, their frightening power goes. To simple minds at

[1] Cf. *The Dunciad*, III, ll. 233 ff. and 303 f. with the notes (1729).
[2] E. Phillips, *Theatrum Poetarum*, London, 1675, Vol. II, p. 25.

least it is perfectly possible to fear and deride almost in one breath, as the medieval attitude towards the devil shows. Moreover, the trickery and charlatanism which seem inseparable from magic, even when the sorcerer is convinced of his own powers, made the Faust-legend and others like it peculiarly effective vehicles for that mixed emotion which craves for sensation and terror and yet wants to laugh such fears to scorn. To judge by the German texts, the English Faust puppet-plays also satisfied that irrational human desire. But in any case there he was in the early eighteenth century on the standing repertory of Robert Powell the showman, rubbing shoulders with Friar Bacon, Dick Whittington, the Babes in the Wood, Robin Hood, Mother Shipton and Mother Goose; what was worse, he and all the others with some even more eminent personages had to play second fiddle to Punch:

> Observe, the Audience is in Pain
> While *Punch* is hid behind the Scene,
> But when they hear his rusty Voice,
> With what Impatience they rejoice.
> And then they value not two Straws
> How *Solomon* decides the Cause;
> Which the true Mother,—which *Pretender*,
> Nor listen to the Witch of *Endor*;
> Shou'd *Faustus* with the Devil behind him,
> Enter the Stage, they never mind him:
> If *Punch*, to spur their fancy, shews
> In at the door his monstrous Nose.[1]

Perhaps Swift was exaggerating after the manner of satirists: and though Punch finally ousted Faust altogether from the English puppet-booths, the latter left him the legacy of the pact:

> 'Tis said, that he a compact sign'd
> With one they call 'Old Nich'las';
> But if I knew them, I've no mind
> To go into partic'lars. . . .
>
> At last, the Devil came to claim
> His own; but Punch what *he* meant

---

[1] J. Swift, *Dialogue between Mad Mullinix and Timothy*; in *The Poems of Jonathan Swift*, ed. Williams, Oxford, 1937, Vol. III, p. 776. Written in 1728.

Punch

Demanded, and denied the same;
He knew no such agreement!
'You don't! (the Devil cried:) 'tis well;
I'll quickly let you know it':
And so to furious work they fell,
As hard as they could go it.
The Devil with his pitch-fork fought,
While Punch had but a stick, Sir,
But kill'd the Devil, as he ought.
Huzza! there's no Old Nick, Sir.[1]

One need probably seek no further for the reason of the greater popularity of Punch; it was to all intents and purposes the same reason that was within an ace of obliterating Faust by Casper in Germany; the unconscious reason perhaps behind all the farcical

[1] *Punch's Pranks* (1791–1793); quoted in [J. P. Collier], *Punch and Judy*, 2nd ed., London, 1828, pp. 60 f.

Fausts in England, the desire to laugh magic out of court. And in this connection it is especially interesting to find Friar Bacon banished to the underworld of puppet-land with Doctor Faustus. They had appeared almost simultaneously on the Elizabethan stage, whether in deliberate rivalry or not, though it looks very like it: the Englishman a humane, pleasing and on the whole edifying figure; the German towering tragically above him. The one repenting and saving himself in the nick of time; the other rushing headlong down to perdition. Yet Bacon's grand gesture of repentance no more saved him from ultimate degradation than the sublime despair of Faustus when his hour had struck. Whether as a terrible warning or as a good example, or as fascinating conjurors, or as mere figures of fun, they were wanted by the mob. How was it that Prospero escaped? Was it because he had no commerce with the devil, or because his magic was made of the stuff of dreams? All things considered, one comes to the conclusion that the popular dramas and puppet-plays about Faustus were such a roaring success because the devil was in them; for however loud and long the laughter provoked on the stage and in the booths might be, the people as a whole were still under the ban of the conception of life which had given birth to the legend, and which a ballad published in 1675 had mournfully reiterated:

> All Christian men give ear a while to me,
> How I am plung'd in pain but cannot die,
> I liv'd a life the like did none before,
> Forsaking Christ, and I am damn'd therefore. . . .
> Woe to the Day of my Nativity,
> Woe to the time that once did foster me,
> And woe unto the hand that sealed the Bill
> Woe to myself the cause of all my ill. . . .
> You Conjurors and damned Witches all,
> Example take by my unhappy fall:
> Give not your souls & bodies unto Hell,
> See that the smallest hair you do not sell.[1]

It is therefore not as inconsistent as it sounds to contend that both Swift and James Ralph, whilst taking a diametrically opposite tone about the audience of the puppet-plays, gauged public opinion accurately and complement each other:

[1] Marlowe, *Tragical History*, ed. cit. pp. 208 ff. The ballad was entitled: *The Judgment of God Shewed Upon one John Faustus, Doctor in Divinity.*

The Plans of their little Pieces do not barely aim at Morality but enforce even Religion: And, it is impossible to view their Representations of Bateman's Ghost, Doctor Faustus' Death, or Mother Shipton's Tragical End, but that the bravest Body alive must be terribly afraid of going to the D—l.[1]

More than that, Ralph asserted that Thurmond's pantomime had a similar effect; and although he was writing with his tongue in his cheek, he may have hit upon the truth:

I cannot pass over in Silence, the Force that the Face of Religion has in *Stage-Entertainments*, urg'd from the most remarkable Instance the World can produce, than which we cannot bring a more powerful Argument to clench the Nail of an Assertion: which is the surprizing Run of Success that attended the Farcical, Musical Dance of *Doctor Faustus*, at both Houses: which must be owing to that Religious, Moral, Poetick Justice, so finely interwoven thro' the whole Piece; particularly, in the wicked Conjurer's dismal End, by infernal *Fiends* at one House, and a terrible *Dragon* at the other. These lively Ideas of Hell deservedly drew the Town after them. The Criticks may assign what Cause they please for what they term an Infatuation: but I insist upon it, I have only touch'd the true one.[2]

'The Lively Ideas of Hell' may really have had something to do with the extraordinary vogue of Thurmond's *Doctor Faustus*; and the relief of laughing at one's fears may have been present. Hell after all was just beneath the feet of the greater part of the audience, and the play itself had a sufficiently sinister stage history. Had not the theatre cracked and terrified those present during a performance mentioned in Middleton's *Blacke Booke* of 1604? Worse still:

. . . *the visible apparition of the Devill on the Stage at the Belsavage Playhouse, in* Queen *Elizabeths dayes, (to the great amazement both of the Actors and Spectators) whiles they were prophanely playing the History of* Faustus (the truth of which I have heard from many now alive, who well remember it,) *there being some distracted with that fearefull sight.*[3]

And in similar vein is the story of the performance of the play at Exeter which was brought to a sudden close because the actors in the incantation scene realized that 'there was one devell too many among them'.[4]

[1] [James Ralph], *The Taste of the Town*, London, 1731, p. 229.
[2] Ibid. op. cit. pp. 55 f.
[3] W. Prynne, *Histrio-Mastix*, London, 1633, Vol. 1, fol. 556.
[4] Marlowe, *Tragical History*, ed. cit. p. 49.

The same kind of thing was also said to have occurred at Shrews-bury according to the *Welsh Book* of 1703; and even as late as 1724 might have occurred again. For the dark age of superstition in which the Faust-legend arose was by no means over. Behind the hectic gaiety of sub-plots, farces and pantomimes lurked a grisly mass-obsession yielding very slowly to mockery and mirth.

CHAPTER III

HYBRID FAUSTS

(a) Vanished Fausts

Marlowe's *Faustus*, carried back to Germany by the English Players who began to visit the Continent in the last decades of the sixteenth century, underwent many vicissitudes in the country of its origin; but among these adventures it seems safe to exclude a theoretical encounter with a purely hypothetical original German Faust drama, which some patriotic scholars assume to have pre-dated and even influenced Marlowe. Their reasons, based on a laborious and at times hyper-subtle textual examination of the nineteenth-century German and Czech puppet-play texts, are not particularly cogent, and although the theory cannot be disproved, it merely darkens counsel in an already sufficiently obscure and complicated situation. For the popular stage *Fausts* who enjoyed such a vogue in Germany during the seventeenth and eighteenth centuries finally vanished from the boards leaving not a text behind; and the effort to reconstruct them, let alone a shadowy German ghost-original, from the puppet-plays only shows how little scholarship is apt to allow for the incalculable vagaries of the human mind. Guessing backwards, although in this case it has resulted in the accumulation of much valuable material and has shed some light on the whole problem, is to grope in the vague, and what is more it puts the puppet-plays themselves in a wrong perspective, the philological rather than the aesthetic. For these reasons, whilst conscious of the debt owed to such scholars as Creizenach, Krause, Bruiner and Bittner for their facts rather than for their fancies, I have decided to confine myself to surveying the data which can be gathered from entries in diaries, announcements and descriptions of the lost Faustian dramas scattered with tantalizing sparseness here and there through the literature of the period, and to theorize as little as may be.

The first performance of the Marlovian drama which has been traced was given by Greene's troupe in Graz on 10 February 1608, although there may have been an earlier one at the Frankfurt autumn mess in 1592 sponsored by Robert Browne. The play was originally produced in English, but the clowning was done in German, and before very long German versions supplanted the English texts, German companies sprang up to replace the English, and indigenous traditions insinuated themselves into the loose and yielding structure. Vulnerable as this drama proved itself to be in England to the intrusion of spectacle and farce, it must have been ten times more so in Germany, where the sublimity of the language in the tragic parts could exercise no restraining effect. But whatever its defects may have been, it maintained itself for nearly two centuries on the boards. We hear of it in Dresden in 1626; in Prague in 1651; in Hanover in 1661; in Lüneburg in 1666; in Danzig in 1668; in Munich in 1679; in Bremen in 1688 or 1690; in Basel in 1696; in Hamburg in 1738; in Frankfurt on the Main in 1742 and again in 1767; finally in Hamburg in 1770; whilst an already semi-literary and independent version appeared in the Tirol about 1790. These dates at least establish the longevity of the Faustian drama; whilst its frequency and popularity are vouched for by the supercilious allusions to it which Neumann made in 1683 and A. Keller in the notes to his edition of Grimmelshausen's *Simplicissimus* in 1684. Moreover a complaint was made to the clerical authorities of Berlin in 1703 in connection with the comedies Sebastian de Scio was then showing in the city guildhall; and it embodied a protest against the formal conjuration of the devils in *Faust* and the blasphemous rejection of God made by the hero. A gay little epigram published by a certain Corvinus in 1710 also witnesses to the notoriety of the play:

> You ask me, how it comes to be
> That the fair sex we never see
> (When *Faust* is given) at the play,
> Whereas at other times they go?
> My word, you must be very slow
> If you cant guess what makes them stay away!
> They fear through Faustus' magic arts to take
> A lesson (as he did) how horns to make.[1]

One is all the more grateful for this blithe reference to the trick

---

[1] W. Creizenach, *Versuch einer Geschichte des Volksschauspiels vom Doctor Faust*, Halle, 1878, p. 86.

with the horns, because factual details about the Faust drama are few and far between, and can indeed only be gathered by piecing together what is known about the representations in Danzig (1668), Bremen (*c.* 1690), Hamburg (1738), Frankfurt (1742 and 1767) and in the Tirol (*c.* 1790), and analysing Heine's account of two performances he witnessed in the early nineteenth century. In this way a dissolving and shifting panorama presents itself to the gaze.

George Schröder, a councillor, gave a brief account of the Danzig production in his diary; announcements have been preserved of the performances in Bremen by the Saxon High German Comedians, in Hamburg by the famous Neuber troupe, in Frankfurt, where *Faust* was produced in 1742 by Wallerotti and in 1767 by Joseph Felix von Kurz; whilst the Tirol play was described from a manuscript copy by Zingerle in his *Schildereien aus Tirol*, Innsbruck, 1877; and Heine recounted from memory in 1847 what he had witnessed a quarter of a century earlier. All these accounts have many features in common; but the first four resemble each other more closely than the last four, allowing for the fact that Schröder makes no mention of the comic element in his summary. Both in Danzig and in Hamburg certainly, and probably in Bremen and Frankfurt (1) too, the proceedings opened with a pandemonium or a prologue in hell. In Danzig Schröder reported that Pluto emerged from the nether regions and summoned various fiends in order to instruct them how best to deceive human beings, evidently with special reference to Faust, whom the 'clever devil' thereupon proceeded to lure into his toils. In this first group only Frankfurt (1) mentions the name of Mephistopheles. In Hamburg the following scene was listed first among the special features on the play-bill:

A great courtyard in the palace of Pluto on the rivers Lethe and Acheron in Hades. Charon comes sailing in his boat on the river and with him on a fiery dragon appears Pluto, accompanied by his whole hellish retinue and spirits.[1]

When therefore we find that in Bremen and Frankfurt (1) Pluto comes riding through the air on a dragon, we are probably right in postulating a pandemonium here too, although this 'particular attraction' may have occurred in the conjuration-scene. This inno-

---

[1] H. W. Geissler, *Gestaltungen des Faust*, Munich, 1927, Vol. I, p. 222.

vation, probably hailing from the earlier mystery and miracle plays, was both dramatically and scenically effective; the idea, moreover, is latent in the Urfaustbook and Marlowe's drama, and in the very assumptions of the legend itself. To stage a conspiracy of the hosts of hell against humanity and in particular against Faust was to give dramatic representation to the cosmic nature of the conflict. Inevitably this recalls the greatest pandemonium in all literature, the one described by Milton in *Paradise Lost* (1667).[1] Poles apart in execution and on entirely different spiritual levels in the epic and on the stage, nevertheless the underlying conception was the same, and corresponded to the mythological outlook of the age. This is one of the main reasons why the Faustian drama maintained itself for so long. The opening scene doubtless overshadowed the Marlovian monologue, of which no mention is made in any of the plays of the first group, though it can be deduced from the scene billed in Hamburg: *Dr. Faust's Study and Library*. Nor were the good and bad angels advertised as present, although in Hamburg 'an attractive celestial spirit' sang an affecting warning poem to soft music. Oddly enough, too, the spectacular effects which must surely have accompanied the conjuration-scene were passed over in silence by Schröder and do not figure among the special features advertised in the various announcements. Bremen concentrated instead on a sensational banqueting-scene, in which (*à la* Mountfort and probably taken from a Wagner comedy) the centre-piece disgorged human beings, dogs, cats and other animals, who came bursting through the pastry and flew off through the air. But if the conjuration-scene was scamped as far as terrifying manifestations were concerned, in Danzig it was enriched by a scene from the folkbooks, which, originally taking place at a banquet, was brought in very aptly here:

... D. Faustus, not content with ordinary knowledge, acquires magical books and conjures the devils to serve him, whereby he enquires into their speed and wishes to choose the fastest. It is not enough for him that they should be as quick as stags, clouds and the wind; he wants one as fast as the thoughts of man. And after the clever devil has declared himself to be such, Faust demands that he should serve him for twenty-four years, on which condition he would surrender himself to the devil.[2]

[1] Bodmer translated *Paradise Lost* into prose and published it in 1732.
[2] Creizenach, op. cit. pp. 5 f.

This incident harks back to the Erfurt Chronicle and to the 1589 and 1590 editions of the Spiess Faustbook. It was also used in the preliminary matter to a magical Faustian manual entitled *The Black Raven*, where again it was placed in the conjuration-scene; but whether the Faust drama or the handbook was first in the field in this respect cannot be determined, as the latter is impossible to date. In the folkbooks the gradation of speed began with an arrow, went on with the wind and finished with the thoughts of man. In *The Black Raven* the wind comes first, a bird in the air second and the thoughts of man third. In Danzig there were at least four devils, and there may have been more; for it was a scene which lent itself to endless variations and elaborations, as will be seen later.

In Danzig, the clever devil, having first obtained Pluto's permission, entered into a contract with Faust, who signed the document with his blood; in Hamburg a raven came out of the air and fetched Faust's signature. Sometimes evidently a mere string was used, and the contract fluttered away, to judge by Voltaire's account given in a letter to Carl Wilhelm Ferdinand of Brunswick:

Je ne connais votre fameux docteur Faustus que par la comédie dont il est le héros et qu'on joue dans toutes vos provinces de l'empire. Votre docteur Faustus y est dans un commerce suivi avec le diable. Il lui écrit des lettres qui cheminent par l'air au moyen d'une ficelle: il en reçoit des responses. On voit des miracles à chaque acte et le diable emporte Faustus à la fin de la pièce.[1]

It is fascinating to think of Voltaire (of all people) attending a popular dramatic representation of *Faust*; contracts and letters will have been all one to him, matter for sardonic chuckles. But this part of the performance at least was taken seriously by the vast majority of the audience, or so one assumes on reading the descriptions of Faust's end, which was scarifying, to put it mildly. In Danzig (which kept the vain warnings of the old man, here described as a hermit) Faust counts the hours until the clock strikes twelve; then the devils enter, tear him to pieces and drag him off to hell, where he is represented undergoing further torments and in letters of fire are seen the words: *Accusatus est*,

[1] Voltaire, *Oeuvres*, ed. Beuchot, Paris, 1834, Vol. XLIII, p. 501. Written in 1767.

judicatus est, condemnatus est.[1] In Bremen a fire-breathing raven announced his death and he was carried off by the spirits to hell, which was pictured with 'beautiful fireworks'; in Hamburg he was fetched away during a display of fireworks and then shown in Hades with the Furies dancing round him; in Frankfurt (1) he was torn to pieces by the Furies to the accompaniment of a ballet of spirits. Thus the piece came to its sensational end: and even the most critical must have felt that they had received good value for their money.

But there were other attractions too: fair Helen appeared in person both in Danzig and in Hamburg, where she disturbed the good doctor considerably by singing an aria in which she prophesied his destruction. Even more exciting was the part she played in Frankfurt (1), if (which seems tolerably certain) she was the woman 'publicly changed into a Fury'. This gave an opportunity for one of those transformation-scenes which had entered German drama from Italy through Vienna, where the famous Stranitzky did so much to domesticate the foreign spectacular and farcical elements, and whence they penetrated throughout Germany leaving many obvious traces in the Faust dramas too. Moreover these latter also pandered to the rage for machines, which were especially mentioned in the advertisement to the Frankfurt (1) production. As far as the famous feats of necromancy were concerned, these, like the trial by speed, allowed much scope for elaboration and development. In Danzig Faust contented himself with summoning up Charlemagne and Helen for his own delectation. In Bremen and Hamburg no conjuration of the spirits of the dead was featured on the play-bills; but in Frankfurt (1) Faust presented the following scenes to the Duke of Parma: the torments of Tantalus, the vulture of Tityos, the stone of Sisyphus and the death of Pompey. These displays, all drawn from classical mythology and history, show the same tendency towards the gruesome evident in the accounts of Faust's end, a natural, indeed inevitable, exploitation of those elements in the folkbook and Marlowe's drama which lent themselves to such treatment. As regards the

[1] This *motiv* probably derived from the Jesuit drama *Cenodoxus* by Jacob Bidermann, which scored a great hit when it was first produced in 1602. It was translated into German in 1625 and published in Latin in 1666. The words were previously used in the Bruno-legend and are to be found in manuscripts of the 13th and 14th centuries. They were echoed and answered by Goethe at the end of *Faust I*.

comic scenes, Schröder made no mention of any clowning, but there will certainly have been some; Hamburg retained the evidently very popular incident of the knight whom Faust decorated with a pair of stag's horns, and also the affair of the peasant whose horse turned into a bundle of hay and who was cozened into believing that he had pulled off the doctor's leg. Otherwise the traditional tricks seem to have been omitted in order to give more space to the sub-plot introduced into the Marlovian drama, in which the clown imitates and thereby parodies his master. In Bremen, still bearing the seventeenth-century name and nature of Pickelhäring, he tried to gather money and was tormented by all kinds of magic birds in the air; in Hamburg, now called Hans Wurst (an appellation Stranitzky had brought back into favour whilst lightening the rather lumpish original with the leaven of Italian wit), he was given a larger part to play:

Hans Wurst comes by chance upon his master Dr. Faust's magic circle. He has to stand still and cannot move from the spot until he has taken off his shoes. The shoes together dance merrily. . . . Hans Wurst wants to have a lot of money and, to please him, Mephistopheles permits him to cause a shower of gold. . . . Dr. Faust takes leave of his servant Christopher Wagner. Hans Wurst also clears out. . . .[1]

In Frankfurt (1) Hans Wurst was billed as a servant tormented by many kinds of spirits, and the scene in which he entered Faust's magic circle and was tormented by the spirits was mentioned among the 'noteworthy scenes'. In Bremen the proceedings closed with a masquerade of six persons, a Spaniard, two jugglers, a schoolmaster, a farmer and a farmer's wife, executing 'an especially humorous' dance; and in Frankfurt (1) there was a ballet and a 'merry comedy' at the end of the play, in order probably to relieve the tension created by the tragic fate of Faust.

Surveying this first group of Faust dramas as a whole, one gains the impression that they were gradually moving further and further away from Marlowe. In Danzig the scheme was still recognizable; but the introductory pandemonium and the speed-trial were radical innovations; and the final scenes in hell depicted in three of these plays were also original additions. The old jokes were evidently wearing thin, for new ones were replacing them; and although the notion of parodying the main action derived from

---

[1] Geissler, op. cit. p. 223.

England, there was much divergence in the actual incidents, and one seems to glimpse through the meagre allusions a lighter and more lively gaiety than the horse-play of Robin and Ralph, due to Italian influence. Nevertheless, however great the change and the distance between Marlowe's *Faustus* and the hybrid German stage versions, it was a logical and organic change, and there is nothing startling or puzzling about it.

The same can certainly not be said about the second group. The Kurz performance at Frankfurt in 1767 justifies the boast made in the announcement that it was to be presented in a way the like of which would have hardly been put on elsewhere. For, although items 1 to 9 of the individual attractions cover familiar ground, items 10 to 12 swerve off into alien regions as far as the Faust-legend is concerned. This is all the more unexpected as the first part of the announcement seems to show that the tradition was stronger than the earlier accounts revealed. The monologue, the conjuration, accompaniment by thunder and lightning in a dark wood at night and suscitating various hellish monsters, spirits and furies, among them Mephistopheles; Faust's contract with hell fetched through the air by a raven; his journey through the air with Mephistopheles; his necromantic feats at the court of the Duke of Parma (to whom he shows Judith beheading Holofernes, Delilah robbing Samson of his hair, and the Philistines over-coming Samson, the martyrdom of Tityos whose entrails are being devoured by ravens, the slaying of Goliath by David and the destruction of Jerusalem); finally the conjuring of a pair of horns on to the head of one of the courtiers—one rather opens one's eyes when reading these items, for so many Marlovian elements still remain; and though incidents from sacred history have replaced the appearance of Alexander the Great and his consort in the folk-book and on the English stage, and have also elbowed the later classical displays to one side, still it all belongs to the pattern which tradition had fixed. There were variations within it, to be sure; and the clown, now called Crispin, had at least three major scenes; but otherwise (having seemingly shed the prologue in hell and the trial by speed) the play went according to Marlowe's plan. But here the resemblance ends. Instead of the scenes with the old man and Helen, the action takes a different turn. A cemetery or grave-yard with many epitaphs and inscriptions is discovered, where Faust is engaged in excavating the bones of his dead father in order to misuse them in his magic. His father's spirit urges him to penitence, and he is converted, only to be seduced again by Mephistopheles through various illusions, during which the cemetery is transformed into a beautiful pleasure-garden. Too late Faust recognizes this for a deception; the garden is now changed into an open hell and the despairing Faust, after a plaint in verse, is carried off by the furies amidst thunder and lightning. Or, as an eye-witness put it:

After Faust has exhausted all other means to escape from the claws of the devil or to acquire undisputed mastery over him, the *Kabbala* of his despair suggests a last horrible resource: to tear the heart out of the body of his father, recently dead from grief. He plunges into this horrible deed, he comes to the graveyard, he opens the grave, and he is just about to accomplish the outrageous deed, when the corpse rears itself up, curses the unnatural son, and Faust falls unconscious to the ground.[1]

Although the features of Marlowe's old man are just discernible behind the warning ghost of Faust's father or the menacing mien of the corpse, there is nothing in the Faust-legend to account for this grisly graveyard scene, which is the first sign of the intrusion of witchcraft proper into the Faustian dramatic organism. It is also the first sign of something else: the deliberate borrowing from a German literary source, none other, or so it seems to me, than Gryphius's strange witch-drama called *Cardenio and Celinde*, written in 1657. In this play, the unhappy Celinde resorts to the same measure in order to win back the heart of Cardenio. Hearkening to the advice of the witch Tyche, who maintains that the only method is to concoct a love-potion from the blood of the heart of her former lover Marcellus whom Cardenio had recently stabbed to death, Celinde at first exclaims in horror at the notion, only to learn from•Tyche that such practices are a matter of almost daily occurrence:

> 'Tis misery's iron hand which so torments our lives,
> That souls were forced to mount and scan the starry skies,
> Were forced to summon aid from elemental spirits;
> Nay more, the dread abyss has yielded up its secrets.
> Blessings and curses fell have opened wide the gate
> Of deepest hell itself. Strange words, compelling fate,

[1] Creizenach, op. cit. pp. 170f.

77

Have loosed a mighty race who do what they are bidden.
The spirits in the air discover what is hidden,
And dead men from their graves the doom will prophesy
Which destiny has writ, and which we thus descry.
Nothing remains at length unconquered by that art
Which claims a dreadful price. No entrails, no fat part
Of calves was deemed enough; no stag on moorland wide,
Started by baying hounds; no steer in flawless pride,
No full-grown steed, no beasts this life depart
When spirits deign to men their mysteries to impart.
Thirsty for human blood, all other bait they scorn.
The victim must be pure. Some crave a child new-born,
Or else the mother's life. Sires at the cross-roads slaughter
(To pity blind and deaf) a chaste and virgin daughter.
Let me not mention those who, having slain their foe,
Seize the truncated head from which the blood does flow,
Wrapped in its native skin, with entrails for a handle,
And swing it censer-wise; or tender babes mishandle,
By flaying them alive; then on the skin indite
Letters which force the spirits or gain them by delight.
These also deign to speak and truly prophesy
Through heads of little boys, dissevered and awry.
From bodies manifold full many limbs we wrench
To sacrifice withal; we poke in charnel-stench
For pregnant women's hands, from stiffened corpses tearing
The mouldering winding-sheets. A reckless band and daring,
We go to any lengths where gain may be presumed:
A crumbling skeleton, a carrion half-consumed,
Bodies devoured by ravens; nor are we faint at heart
When thumb or hair at midnight from pilloried corpse we part.
Until at length by industry, courage and dauntless skill,
That is achieved which so allures the eager mortal will:
To bind and fetter nature with this new-found might . . .
For you are not the only one we've succoured in this plight;
The court, the township too, nay, the whole land's alive
With souls who prosper only by these arts and thrive.[1]

This passage has been quoted less for its value as a social document throwing a ghastly light on the beliefs (if not the practices)
everywhere current at the time, than as an illustration of the
violence threatening the Faust-legend from contamination with
witchcraft. Black magic and witchcraft tend to converge, though

---

[1] A. Gryphius, *Cardenio und Celinde*, Act II, Scene 2.

not so inevitably as white magic tends to become black. To force them together, as was done by Kurz in Frankfurt, is to cause a foul and turbid stream to flow into the black waters of a fathomless spiritual maelstrom. Yet Gryphius's drama is so powerful that one can well imagine how greatly a producer seeking for strong situations would be tempted by it. Celinde, over-persuaded by Tyche, comes with an accomplice to the vault at midnight, and confronts the corpse of Marcellus:

> Then, when I saw the corpse I trembled with amaze.
> Where was the forehead's sheen; where was the pupil's gaze?
> Where was Marcellus' self? Alas, for coffins cold
> Show but a carrion corpse covered with bluish mould . . .
> Distraught, in desperate straits, I lifted up my hands
> To perforate his breast; and as the linen bands
> Which covered him I rent (Oh, horrible the deed!)
> From that deep sleep of death his pent-up soul was freed.
> He stirred and raised himself upright upon his bier
> And spake (whilst Cleon fled away in panic fear):
>> Inhuman one, what leads thee here to me?
>> Is't not enough that I for love of thee
>> These wounds within my breast did not gainsay,
>> Through which my soul and blood have ebbed away?
>> Dost thou the silent death-vault dare to ope
>> And take my heart? Cannot a dead man hope
>> To lie in peace, and rest within the grave? . . .
> Thus spake he, rising up from out the dust of earth;
> I sank upon his tomb. . . .[1]

The similarity to the scene in the Kurz Faust drama is obvious; and indeed the borrowing was clumsily and carelessly done; for, though the heart of a dead lover might well be used in a love-potion, the heart of a dead father seems a singularly unlikely means of subduing a devil to one's will. Further proof (if proof were needed) that Kurz was plagiarizing Gryphius is offered by the transformation of the graveyard into a pleasure-garden and then into an 'open hell'. In *Cardenio and Celinde* the hero, pursuing (as he believes) his lost beloved Olympia, is brought to a beautiful garden, which is suddenly transformed into a horrible wilderness and the supposed Olympia into a skeleton aiming an arrow at Cardenio's heart and exclaiming:

[1] Gryphius, op. cit. Act v, Scene 2.

Behold this thy reward; my steel, the fruit of sin.[1]

Apart from the charnel-house atmosphere introduced into the Faust drama by contamination with witchcraft, the sentimental aura of family affection makes itself felt in the references to Faust's father, dying of grief (presumably induced by the wicked courses of his son), and warning or cursing him after death. This is a reminder that on the legitimate stage the domestic tragedy had already scored a notable success with Lessing's *Miss Sara Sampson* in 1755 and that the era of the middle-class hero had dawned.

The curious mixture of seventeenth-century baroque tragedy and eighteenth-century sentimental family drama invading the Faustian dramatic complex is more vividly illustrated by the long and detailed description of the Tirol play given by Zingerle with numerous quotations from a late eighteenth-century manuscript. It was in rhymed alexandrines, that exotic, feverish, eloquent metre, which Gryphius handled with such mastery and which, even in the unequal and often halting passages Zingerle transcribed, still bears a faint imprint of the strange genius who moulded the medium to his tragic themes and highflown purposes:

> Ye Furies, now come forth from out the jaws of hell,
> And tear me limb from limb, ye pitch-black hounds of hell!
> Ye mountains fall on me, let granite crush and grind,
> Whilst sorrow, terror, fear cease not to pierce my mind.
> May lightning, thunder, hail and fire from the clouds dart!
> Swallow me up, oh earth, beneath me split apart!
> Come, pallid skeleton, come call me to the bier;
> And cursèd goddess, thou, take my life's thread and shear!
> Let fire devour me quite, let storm-winds me down-hurling,
> Plunge me to darkest depths of waters wildly whirling!
> Whatever may have life, hunt me with might and main,
> Bring daggers, poison, ropes for ever burning pain![2]

Stray and vagrant echoes from Marlowe can be heard in this speech, the Bad Angel bidding Faustus gaze at hell:

> Into that vast perpetual torture-house.
> There are the Furies tossing damned souls
> On burning forks. . . .

and Faustus himself exclaiming:

---

[1] Gryphius, op. cit. Act IV, Scene 5. [2] Creizenach, op. cit. p. 32.

> Mountains and hills, come, come, and fall on me,
> And hide me from the heavy wrath of God!
> No, no!
> Then will I headlong run into the earth:
> Earth, gape! O, no, it will not harbour me!
> You stars that reigned at my nativity,
> Whose influence hath allotted death and hell,
> Now draw up Faustus, like a foggy mist,
> Into the entrails of yon lab'ring cloud
> That, when you vomit forth into the air,
> My limbs may issue from your smoky mouths,
> So that my soul may but ascend to heaven![1]

When hearing the Tirol Faust call for daggers, poison and ropes (whereupon Mephisto brings him poison, which he drinks), one remembers the 'Swords, and knives, Poison, guns, halters, and envenom'd steel' laid before Marlowe's hero to dispatch himself; and the dagger given him by Mephisto during the scene with the old man. But there is also a close verbal parallel to be found in Gryphius's tragedy *Papinianus*, where a highly eloquent tirade is woven round the three words 'daggers, poison, ropes' by Laetus, to whom the Emperor Antoninus has sent these three alternative methods of self-destruction. In a word it would almost seem that in the German stage *Fausts* of the seventeenth and eighteenth centuries the voice crying out in agony was the voice of Gryphius, though the words were sometimes the words of Marlowe.

This mingles oddly indeed with the shadow of Sir William Sampson (father of Lessing's unhappy Miss Sara Sampson, and ancestor of a long line of soft-hearted if sometimes rough-tongued parents) which looms over the action of the Tirol play, and which probably also made its presence felt in the Kurz production long before the grisly end. In the Tirol version Orkanus and Victoria, Faust's aged and pathetic parents, whose dire poverty is one of the reasons for the hero's pact with hell, appear almost as regularly as the good and bad angels on the one hand and the irrepressible Hans Wurst on the other. Helen is replaced by the wanton Meretrix, about whom there is nothing discoverably supernatural; Goliath, Judith and Lazarus are summoned up before the Duke of Parma, who exclaims that the art must be devilish; and much time is given to the wrestling with remorse and despair which

---

[1] Marlowe, *Tragical History*, pp. 170, 172.

Faust undergoes, whilst the good angel, Raphael, constantly urges him to repent and to hope. After one of these admonitions, the hero is nearly won over, and Mephisto hastens to offer to perform whatever Faust may desire in order to win him back. The request made is as startling to modern readers as it was to Mephisto: to paint the crucifix faithfully line by line, not omitting the super-scription. This *motiv*, which haled from the Catholic south, is to be found in several of the Czech puppet-plays and seems to have entered the Faust-legend before 1608, the date of a picture repre-senting a man kneeling in prayer before a crucifix, his guardian angel on his right and on his left Mephisto leading forth Helen in a devil's guise. An inscription dated 1746 under a picture of a crucifix with Mary and John in attendance attributes the painting to the devil under the orders of Faust. Moreover a Faust ballad, first published in 1818 in *Des Knaben Wunderhorn* from a Cologne fly-sheet, has the same eerie incident. Mephisto (in the Tirol play and elsewhere too) at first refused to obey and offered to return the pact and let Faust go rather than attempt this terrible task; and that strange little scene in Goethe's *Urfaust* flashes again before one's eyes:

A cross on the road-side, to the right on a hillock an old castle, in the distance a peasant's hut.

> *Faust.* What's up, Mephisto, whence this haste?
> Why pass the cross with eyes down lowered quite?
>
> *Meph.* I know it's prejudice, mere blind distaste,
> But yet, enough, I cannot stand that sight.[1]

In the Tirol play, Meretrix entered in the nick of time and Mephisto made off to seek advice from Lucifer and his consorts. Pluto, who was present at what was evidently a full-dress pande-monium, reproached Mephisto for his pusillanimity and ordered him to produce the picture of the crucifix by illusory means. This was done in the third act, and the evil spirit, his *morale* stiffened by Pluto, adopted a very menacing tone and informed Faust that he would have to pay for his presumption in commanding the picture by being carried off to hell that selfsame day.

---

[1] Cf. Goethe's *Urfaust und Faust, ein Fragment,* ed. Willoughby, Oxford, 1943, p. 84. This scene was placed immediately after *Auerbach's Cellar,* and later cut out.

To Faust, brooding despairingly over this news, Hans Wurst now enters and offers to fight Mephisto whilst his master hides, and a comic interlude ensues in which Hans Wurst plays the part of craven swashbuckler and braggart, a stock figure in comedy, which Gryphius had treated with great verve in his *Horribili-cribrifax*. During the wordy altercation, the clown notices that the crucifix has disappeared, and he slinks off to tell his master. This scene is followed by one in which Faust puts those fearful questions to Mephisto about hell and the torments of the damned which both the Urfaustbook and Marlowe placed immediately after the signing of the pact. Psychologically this cross-questioning is well placed at the beginning; dramatically it is more effective at the end, leading as it does to the hero's efforts to repent, foiled once again by Mephisto, who mocks him, and Meretrix, who completes the diabolical cure. Deserted at the last moment by Hans Wurst, who leaves Faust's service for God's, the unhappy magician after a final speech, part of which I have given above, drinks the poison, and the curtain falls with Meretrix bewailing the lot of her lover, whilst Mephisto and three other devils wait with satanic glee to seize the soul of the pact-maker.

Zingerle only had a fragmentary text, which began with the pact-scene; but the opening monologue and the conjuration may have figured, and there may have been a prologue in hell too; Mephisto's consultation with Lucifer and his consorts during the play makes this supposition likely. On the other hand, it is also possible that the traditional early scenes of the drama were omitted altogether; for another literary or semi-literary influence is discernible in the Tirol play besides the unconscious debt to Marlowe and the use of seventeenth-century tragic metre. The reconditioning by domestic tragedy, though ultimately due to Lessing, probably came into the Tirol play *via* Paul Weidmann, whose Faust drama, produced in 1775, gave an inordinate part to Faust's pathetic old parents and began the action long after the signing of the pact. However that may be, it seems abundantly clear from Zingerle's account that the play produced in the Tirol, whilst not altogether disregardful of tradition, was beginning to strike out from it in various directions, notably in that of family sentiment in which during the Storm and Stress the father became a dominant figure, and the mother played a supporting and sometimes a reprehensible part. On the other hand, the grisly sensationalism of the Kurz production was replaced by the highly poetical notion elaborated in the crucifix scenes. The origin, certainly Catholic, may have been popular. It is a strange, sinister and disturbing thought to imagine the devil producing by whatever means a picture of Christ on the cross; and it looks as if it had sprung from some deep layer of the subconscious popular mind.

But it is very dangerous to dogmatize about the popular mind, which appears at one moment to be many fathoms nearer to the secret processes of nature and of the supernatural than the sophisticated can ever come, and at the next to be so unutterably banal and childish as to be incapable of spiritual vision. The latter side is revealed in a Faustian ballet-scenario of an operatic kind, which Scheible dates about 1730 and which was therefore more or less contemporaneous with Thurmond's pantomimes in London. It was produced in Vienna on a Saturday, 9 June, in the Kärntner Tor Theatre, and advertised as follows:

D. FAUST: arranged from German comedies, English pantomimes and Italian music. In an action never in this manner presented here before, and particularly noteworthy because of the manifold machines and unsurpassed decorations.[1]

Like all the other popular German Fausts after Marlowe and before Lessing, this was a hybrid affair, including German, English and Italian elements, the presence of Columbine in the ballet vouching for the fact that the influence of Italy was not confined to the music. On the bare skeleton framework of an agreement between Faust and Mephisto, the former's incidental remorse and final end, a whole host of alien farcical and sensational *motivs* were introduced, with a *pièce de résistance* in the second act which even outshone Mountfort's banqueting-scene. It is possible that the incident of the virtuous young servant-girl whom Faust vainly attempted to seduce in Pfitzer's version of Widman's Faustbook inspired the notion of his successful overtures to a miller's bride at the wedding-festivities, with whom the magician triumphantly danced off at the end of Act I leaving the bridegroom plunged in suicidal despair. But the fact that the heroine of this incident was a miller's bride was dictated by other considerations. The second act represents a mill, and Faust and his willing captive are seen through an upper window engaged in singing love-songs and in

[1] Scheible, op. cit. Vol. v, p. 1020.

making love. The wretched groom climbs up the outer stairs after them, Faust dashes up to the attic, thence to the roof and then down by the sails of the windmill. The miller follows but is caught by the wheel and turned helplessly round and round whilst the lovers execute a mocking ballet and then dance off. The wheel (set in motion by Faust's magic arts) now stands still and down crawls the miller, dizzy and desperate but still determined on pursuit. He is hindered in this endeavour by sacks of flour dancing out of the mill and getting in his way. He slits them open in order to empty out the flour and finds himself surrounded by hosts of devils and monsters concealed in the sacks; thereupon he swoons away. Something similar must have featured in London at about the same time; for underneath one of the copies of *The Small Masquerade Ticket* (1724) were engraved the lines:

> Long has the Stage productive been
> Of offsprings it could brag on.
> But never till this age was seen
> A Windmill and a Dragon.
>
> O Congreve, lay thy pen aside,
> Shakespeare, thy works disown,
> Since monsters grim, and nought beside,
> Can please this senseless Town.[1]

The claim that the Viennese entertainment had borrowed from English pantomimes was therefore true; no windmill figures in the text of *Harlequin Doctor Faustus* discovered by Diebler; but it looks as if it had been present, since the *Small Masquerade Ticket* made a special feature of that pantomime. Both in Vienna and in London the real protagonist of the Faustian ballets and pantomimes was the stage-machinery; the magic and not the magician was the attraction, as had been the case in the anecdotal portion of the Urfaustbook; and this had now achieved choreographical status.

Comparing the Viennese ballet with the Tirol play and the Kurz production, one discerns two distinct trends in the direction in which the legend was going: the one group groping rather feebly upwards, putting out feelers and twining tendrils round the paling which still fenced the legend off from literature in Germany; the

---

[1] J. Heath, *The Works of William Hogarth*, London, 1822, p. 4.

other slithering gradually downwards into anonymous depths. Heine gave a tantalizing glimpse of Faust among the barnstormers in 1822 or thereabouts a quarter of a century after he had witnessed the performances in question; and there seems no reason to doubt his veracity, though his vivid imagination may have played some part in reconstructing from memory the scenes he had looked at and the speeches he had heard. In a little acting-booth on the so-called Hamburg Hill between Hamburg and Altona, he saw a company of strolling players acting a *Faust* whose author had evidently concentrated almost entirely on the love-interest, or perhaps it would be more accurate to say the love-life adumbrated in the Urfaustbook under the general rubric of the hero's 'swinish and epicurean' existence. Heine was particularly struck by the appearance of the devils in the conjuration-scene, heavily veiled and muffled in grey shrouds. When asked by the magician whether they were male or female they answered that they had no sex and no individual form, but that they always appeared to be identical with whatever conception their interlocutor had of them. After the contract stipulating for knowledge and the enjoyment of all things, Faust questioned the spirits about heaven and hell, and came to the thoroughly Heinesque conclusion that heaven sounded too cold and hell too hot, and that the climate of the terrestrial globe was preferable to either. Through the agency of a magic ring he was transformed into a handsome and graceful youth superbly clad, and by the same means all the most beautiful women in the world were at his disposal. Years of dissipation and debauch not unnaturally resulted, ending in a passionate love-affair with the most famous courtesan of Venice, a Signora Lucretia. Treacherously deserting his paramour, Faust then embarked for Athens, where the duke's daughter fell in love with him and proposed marriage. Faust was ready and willing, but he was reckoning without Lucretia, who had learnt the secret of the magic ring from the devil and was hot on his tracks. Arriving in Athens on the wedding-day disguised as a pilgrim, she snatched the ring from his finger just as he was giving his hand in wedlock to the blushing bride, and a terrible transformation immediately took place. Faust's youth fell off from him and he appeared as he really was: a wrinkled old man without a tooth in his head and with only a few sparse grey hairs on his withered cranium. Even the splendid clothes fell like autumn leaves from his bent and shrivelled body, leaving filthy rags behind. The disenchanted enchanter is quite unaware of what has happened, and cannot understand the disgust with which all the courtiers recoil from him, nor why his bride should exclaim: 'Remove that old beggar from my sight!' Then Lucretia confronts him with a mirror; he sees his real countenance and allows himself to be kicked out of doors like a mangy dog.

Heine made no mention of Mephisto in this version, which included the kind of transformation Rider Haggard made so memorable in *She*. The theme itself is as old as the hills, and was used by Julius von Voss in his melodrama, *Faust*, in 1823, although in a different fashion; Heine combined both versions in his dance-poem; and transformations had also occurred, it will be remembered, in the Kurz production and in Frankfurt (1), all of them scenes or cases of disenchantment, of which the barnstormers' variation was a simple and an extremely effective one.

The other performance seen by Heine in the early twenties took place in a village in the Hanover district during a horse-market. A little booth was erected on an open meadow, and the play was acted in full daylight. The circumstances notwithstanding, Heine found the conjuration-scene impressive. He was much struck by the fact that the part of Mephistopheles was taken by the spirit Astaroth, and gave some reasons to account for this departure from tradition. But he did not mention (although he probably knew) the most likely source to have supplied the unexpected name. This was that same Faustian Black Book, *The Black Raven*, which included in its preliminary matter the questioning of the devils conjured as to their relative degree of speed. These proceedings were inaugurated in the manual by Astaroth, who forced Faust to sign a pact with him, and then sent three devils to him, one by one, so that he might choose an attendant. None of these spirits was called Mephistopheles, so that the script-writer of the Hanoverian performance, if he were familiar with *The Black Raven*, might for that reason prefer the high-sounding appellation of Astaroth. And there is other evidence that he was acquainted with contemporary Black Books; for Astaroth, when summoned up by Faust, appeared at first in the shape of various animals. This was traditional in magical texts. In order to terrify the exorcist, the evil spirit called upon was apt to manifest in some hideous bestial form, whereupon the necromancer would order him to retire and reappear in *pulchra forma humana*:

87

> I charge thee to return, and change thy shape;
> Thou art too ugly to attend on me:
> Go, and return an old Franciscan friar;
> That holy shape becomes a devil best.[1]

This straightforward notion was fused in the Hanoverian drama with the idea of a crescendo underlying the choice of the fastest devil available, a scene which had enlivened the popular stage at least as early as 1668, when it occurred in Danzig, and which was also present in *The Black Raven*. A crescendo of fearsome animals was introduced here, possibly because a menagerie or circus was attached to the troupe. A swine, an ox, a monkey, a roaring lion and a gigantic snake made their successive appearances; and on each occasion the intrepid, not to say foolhardy, conjuror complained that the form assumed was not yet horrible and dreadful enough. Finally Astaroth donned the guise of a fine and handsome young man in a scarlet cloak. Faust expressed his astonishment at this far from frightening masquerade, and the evil spirit answered:

There is nothing more horrible and dreadful than man; all other beasts grunt and roar and bleat and hiss in him. He is as filthy as a swine, as brutal as an ox, as ridiculous as an ape, as wrathful as a lion, as venomous as a snake; he is a synthesis of the whole bestial kingdom.[2]

This pessimistic and 'philosophical' comment was probably Heine's; but the crescendo of frightfulness instead of speed shows the contamination of one tradition by another: the compulsion put upon the spirits to change their shapes from bestial to human; and the trial of the devils by speed. In both cases they are put through their paces; and Marlowe's caustic comment: 'That holy shape becomes a devil best', may even have been ultimately responsible for some similar remark in Hanover, which Heine then elaborated.

After the pact was concluded, Astaroth offered to procure for Faust various famous beauties as paramours. The magician rejected Judith, as he did not fancy an executioner, and Cleopatra, whose extravagance had ruined Antony and who drank pearls; the notion of speaking Greek with Helen appealed to him, however, and after having stipulated that he should become handsome and well

[1] Marlowe, *Tragical History*, p. 70.
[2] H. Heine, *Sämtliche Werke*, ed. Elster, Leipzig and Vienna [1890], Vol. VI, p. 504.

dressed in order to outrival Paris, he and his spirit retired and re-emerged outside the booth mounted on two tall steeds:

They throw their mantles off, and we now see Faust as well as Astaroth in elegant English riding-costumes performing the most amazing riding-feats, whilst the assembled horse-breeders stood in a circle and gaped at them with their red Hanoverian faces and slapped their yellow leather breeches so that a clapping was produced such as I have never heard at any other dramatic performance. And indeed Astaroth rode charmingly, being a slender, pretty girl with the big black eyes of hell. And Faust too was a comely lad in his elegant riding-kit and he rode better than any other German doctor whom I have ever seen on horseback. He galloped with Astaroth round and round outside the booth where the city of Troy was now seen and on its battlements stood Helen.[1]

Heine went no further in this description of a play which seems to have been in the nature of a circus side-show; and for us, therefore, Faust and his attendant spirit go galloping round and round the ring until at last they vanish. They vanish, as all their dramatic compeers vanished from the German stage, leaving an open field for infinite speculation and vain regrets; regrets, however, which were by no means shared by the more educated eighteenth-century worthies:

But, God be praised, the well-known wretched tragedies about him are now at an end, as people have at last put aside such childish things and have become attached to more rational conceptions. Faust now owes it principally to Rembrandt that he is remembered at all.[2]

Thus spoke an irate art-critic in 1771, a year after the 1770 performance in Hamburg, which seems to have marked the end of the appearance of the Faust dramas on the regular German stage; and there were of course any amount of reasons to account for such an attitude. Fascinating though it is to trace the spoor of the Marlovian drama through time and space in Germany; nostalgic though the emotions are with which one looks back to the Faustian circus-show in the little market-town near Hanover, to the mill turning so merrily in Vienna, to the crucifix raised in

---

[1] Heine, op. cit. Vol. VI, p. 505.

[2] Scheible, op. cit. Vol. II, p. 257; quoting from a catalogue of portraits, mostly of doctors, made by J. C. W. Moehsen in 1771.

the Tirol; still it all tells a story of progressive degradation, made yet more striking by latter-day contamination with witchcraft and literature. Spectacular, sensational, gruesome, farcical and sentimental agents of decay had been at work, like so many vermin infesting the decomposing carcase of Marlowe's mighty play. But the shade of the Elizabethan dramatist can comfort itself by affirming with Baudelaire the conquest of art over death and over life:

> Alors, ô ma beauté, dites à la vermine
> Qui vous mangera de baisers,
> Que j'ai gardé la forme et l'essence divine
> De mes amours décomposés!

(b) Miniature Fausts

Nothing either in the natural or the spiritual world is ever completely lost, annihilated or destroyed. Dozens and dozens of lusty little Fausts were already wriggling out from the mouldering remains of *The Tragical History of Doctor Faustus* before it collapsed entirely as an organic whole. When and where the first of these manikins made his bow in a puppet-booth cannot be determined; but it seems reasonable to assume that there were earlier productions than the one mentioned by Schutze[1] as having taken place in 1698; for puppet-plays were well-known features of German life from the Middle Ages onwards. In the nature of things they left no printed proofs behind them; and it was not until Goethe's *Faust* endowed them with an extrinsic value in the eyes of literary historians that the search for puppet-play texts began in earnest. Publication of the various 'discoveries' did not lag far behind their acquisition and has gone on almost until the present day, the late nineteenth century having brought a goodly number of Czech texts to light. The first German puppet *Faust* to appear in print was that of the showman Geisselbrecht, twenty-four copies of which were printed by von Below in 1832. Part of the very famous version played by Schütz-Dreher for many years in Berlin at the end of the eighteenth and the beginning of the nineteenth century was given by von der Hagen in *Germania* in 1841; and the play was also described by Franz Horn, Emil Sommer, Leitner and

---

[1] J. F. Schütze, *Hamburgische Theater-Geschichte*, Hamburg, 1794, p. 97.

Das
Puppenspiel
vom
Doctor Faust.

Leutbecher during the twenties, thirties and forties. Simrock used these various accounts as well as his own memories and Geisselbrecht's text for his quasi-poetical reconstruction in 1846. In the following year Scheible brought the complete Schütz-Dreher material, together with Geisselbrecht's play and puppet-plays from Ulm, Augsburg, Strasbourg and Cologne, in the fifth volume of *Das Kloster*. W. Hamm produced a Leipzig variant in 1850; Oskar Schade collated two Weimar texts and printed them in 1856; Carl Engel, who had been responsible for a spurious amalgam of the Faust and Wagner puppet-plays in 1862, edited an Oldenburg text in 1865; Lübke collated three Berlin versions in 1886; and Petsch weighed in with a very corrupt Franconian variant which he had seen in Würzburg in 1901.

This list is by no means exhaustive, for I am confining myself to the plays whose texts have been accessible to me. They were the very reverse to the original editors, as almost all the showmen strenuously denied the existence of a manuscript when approached on the subject. Indeed Schütz (the surviving partner of the Schütz-Dreher firm) persisted in his denials until the very end, and von der Hagen had to do the best he could from notes made during performances given in 1807. Hamm for his part was forced to resort to bribery. An underling was suborned by his clerk to 'borrow' the manuscript of the Faust drama from the showman Bonneschky without the knowledge of his principal. Hamm had possession of the precious but filthy volume bound in crumbling boards for the space of one day and two nights, and made good use of this opportunity. As for Lübke, he undertook a veritable paper-chase throughout Berlin and underwent all manner of trials and tribulations in order to get a sight of three texts:

The first showman with whom I became acquainted through the street directory was a brother of the once famous Linde. My first visit was in vain. I had great and unexpected difficulty in locating his lodgings; and when at last I discovered the poverty-stricken room in a rear building, I found the man ill in bed, extremely suspicious and at the moment not even in possession of the manuscript, as his grown-up children were performing in the town. I had to be content with the permission to return and the promise that I should then be shown the manuscript. Oddly enough, in spite of all their suspicion, this particular family never made the slightest attempt to conceal the existence of the manuscript. It is the only case of its kind which I remember. All the other puppet-showmen I visited, at least half a dozen, declared at first, feigning great surprise, that they had never possessed such a thing. All but one however were easily persuaded to change their tune when I told them that this was an old trick. They then either described the manuscript more or less frankly, or even allowed me to see it.

Thus a certain Wolfram, whom I visited immediately after Linde, placed two manuscripts at my disposal without further conditions, as soon as I had persuaded him that I did not belong to his craft. Both of them were lying mournful and neglected, on a heap of rags and bones, for he is also a rag-and-bone man. . . . Unhappily Wolfram did not keep his promise to procure me other manuscripts.

Returning to Linde after this success, I found the children at home, and here too rather more confidence was shown in me. I was allowed to see the manuscript but not to take it away. It goes without saying however that my attention could only be very divided in that fearfully overheated room, which did duty as sitting-room, bed-room, sick-room and kitchen. I therefore made every effort to obtain permission to take the manuscript home; and after much pleading and negotiating I was allowed to do so. . . .

My third visit was completely unsuccessful, and all my subsequent exertions there bore no fruit but tired legs and vexation. The showman whom I have to thank for that is called Handt. He too admitted (or pretended?) that he had an old manuscript . . . and he spoke of old theatre-bills which he would let me have, and so on; but he never gave me a sight of either, although I begged for them in a way which would have melted the heart of a stone. . . .

Soon after this I discovered the name of Schlüssel in another directory, and this old showman made the best impression of all. It is true that he too did not spare me the customary denial of any manuscripts; but when I had sufficiently convinced him of my status in the matter, he turned the whole place upside down to find the manuscript, which was finally discovered at the very bottom of a pile of puppets and properties. He placed it at my disposal for an indefinite period, and finally sold it to me. . . . The discovery of this old manuscript was my last success. The investigations which I undertook on the advice of the above-mentioned Handt failed completely; and I was even once suspected of hunting for a pair of old boxing-gloves [*Fausthandschuhe*] instead of a Faust manuscript, so little did the person to whom I was sent know about the matter. One puppet showman, Kallista, really had no manuscript, for it had been stolen.[1]

[1] H. Lübke, 'Die Berliner Fassung des Puppenspiels vom Doctor Faust', *Zeitschrift für deutsches Altertum und deutsche Literatur*, Berlin, 1887, Vol. xxxi, N.F. ix, pp. 105 ff.

The suspicions of the showmen were therefore not altogether unfounded; they were jealously guarding their copyrights from rivals, and since each of the versions had individual attractions, this seems natural enough; moreover, they all probably believed that they and they alone were in possession of the 'genuine' text and that the incalculable element of luck attached to the grimy copy which had been handed down from father to son. By the time Lübke was on their trail, however, the day of the masters of the art of puppetry, of a Geisselbrecht, a Dreher, a Schütz, a Bonneschky, was over; the showmen, like the texts, had suffered deterioration at the hand of time. In their heyday they had ministered, and ministered royally, to popular and simple tastes, whilst the more sophisticated surveyed their performances with a supercilious and jaundiced eye:

Faust among his books and magical apparatus spoke incoherent stuff and nonsense. A pot-bellied angel came flying in to warn him against the devil. . . . One of Mephisto's cheeks was painted black. I don't know whether this is traditional or a special invention. . . . The action was shamefully mutilated. . . . The principal person of the puppet-play, Hanswurst, was bad, not a spark of wit, and what little remained of traditional jokes curtailed almost beyond recognition.[1]

This carping critic, significantly enough writing for the *Morgenblatt für gebildete Stände* about a performance of the showman Lorgée in Frankfurt during the month of April 1824, was a mere onlooker; those who, like Hamm, had a personal interest in the Faustian puppet-plays took a kindlier view, which did not preclude occasional sharp criticisms of details:

A rather narrow, gloomy and smokily illuminated hall had accommodated a relatively enormous crowd of onlookers, who were staring at the curtain in tense expectation. It was brick-red, painted in boldly draped folds, ornamented with rather fantastic emblems of dramatic art and seemed undoubtedly to be concealing something unusual behind its mysterious veil. It must be confessed that the majority of the audience belonged to the rising generation and that nursemaids represented the higher grades of the middle-classes. But there was also a sprinkling of *haute volée*. We saw several gifted ladies of our acquaintance, who waved to us with smiles and shrugs; the literary profession was adequately represented, and curiosity had impelled some artists to attend. After a

[1] Creizenach, op. cit. pp. 17 f.

far from classically executed overture—as far as I remember it was the one to Spohr's *Faust*—the curtain rose, and the black-clad doctor, jaded with learning, stood upon the stage. What ought one to say, and what can one say about the acting and the eloquence of these three-foot wooden personages, about the gaily coloured magnificent decorations and the expenditure of gun-powder and fireworks? It should all be seen and experienced, not written about and read. In a word, the impression was on the grand scale. Not only the youthful element in the audience, but we grown-up children too were enchanted and clapped until our hands were sore. . . .

The infernal spirits make an indescribably comic effect when they appear. Wretcheder creatures have never yet been cobbled together from black calico and tow than these puppets without hips or joints. Their disappearance is brought about gloriously. For they hang on threads and jerk upwards into the air with the boldest swinging motion, whereas they ought by rights to be wandering to the underworld. Only Alexo, the slow Alexo, jolts up gradually and by degrees and excites rapturous applause from the gazing 'populace' as he (or she?) hangs floundering calmly in the air. . . .

In the representation [of David, Goliath, etc.] the figures invoked appeared as brightly lit transparencies on the right side of the stage in an apparatus which looks suspiciously like an upright flour chest with a lid. The art of painting and·lighting generally contributes just as little to the heightening of the illusion as the 'soft adagio' of the music.[1]

This state of innocence was not to last; already when Hamm was writing, the eyes of the highbrows were watching and the era of art-and-craft puppetry was at hand. Kleist's wonderfully imaginative essay on the marionette-theatre was published in 1810, illuminating the subconscious reason for the eternal fascination of puppet-shows. It thereupon became conscious, as Rilke's essay on dolls and his marionette-elegy were later to show, quite apart from the repercussions on the puppet-stage itself, which by the end of the nineteenth century had become a thing of great beauty, charm and eeriness, miles removed from its primitive origins, in a different world from the performance Hamm witnessed in Leipzig:

The Salzburg Marionette Theatre was founded by Anton Aicher who, from 1884–1912, was professor at the School of Arts and Crafts at Salzburg. . . . The company included 350 puppets with 400 settings. . . . The performances at Salzburg are distinguished by their skilful

[1] [W. Hamm], *Das Puppenspiel vom Doctor Faust*, Leipzig, 1850, pp. xviif., 72, 76.

manipulation and the high artistic quality of their presentation. The figures are finely designed and carved with a delicate appreciation of period and mood, and are invested with an old-world charm and refinement rarely equalled. . . .

George Deininger is an author and a man of taste who is well versed in the technique of puppetry; and all these gifts he brings to bear on his productions. For instance, his Dr. Faust is much more than a new edition of a classic play. He has introduced various devils, such as the demons of drunkenness, lust, gluttony, and riches; he has changed Hanswurst from a figure of farce to a humorous character endowed with a quick wit and peasant cunning; his Mephisto is the destroyer of reason. Deininger's productions are noteworthy for the artistry and fantasy of their conception and realisation.[1]

Given the choice, one would nevertheless rather witness the performance described by Hamm than the artistically dolled-up versions of Aicher and Deininger. And this is not merely the perversity attendant on a sophisticated mind. Coming to the parting of the ways, one realizes with a pang that conscious art of this nature does violence to the unconscious poetry informing native traditions.

This intrusion is already noticeable in the texts that have survived. Even Ulm, considerably the simplest and most artless, shows signs of having been tampered with, although (very similar to the Danzig performance) it is recognizably modelled on the Marlovian scheme. Geisselbrecht, considered by those who knew both to be far inferior to Schütz-Dreher, is lively, light and tuneful in the comic portions, which go with a swing; but is (with one exception) not at the height of the tragic moments. The reconditioning of this text seems to have been chiefly concerned with getting the humour across to laughter-loving audiences. The language of Leipzig and of the fearfully long-winded Weimar text is the very reverse of popular and shows few signs of age. The Augsburg play had picked the brains of Lessing, Müller and Klinger; and whoever was responsible for the Strasbourg text sported the plumes of Lessing, Klinger, Müller and Goethe. As for Cologne, a most paltry pot-boiler, it swerved away from tradition entirely, although some *motivs* from the Faustbook of the Christlich Meynender prove, if proof were necessary, how feeble

[1] C. W. Beaumont, *Puppets and the Puppet Stage*, L ndon, 1938, pp. 82, 104.

the inspiration deriving from that source was. Otherwise most of these plays exhibit borrowed poetical plumes and storm-stressed sentiments, whilst adhering faithfully (with the exception of Ulm) to a pattern which the author of the Schütz-Dreher text probably laid down.

To the audience (for the most part child-like) which gathered round the booths in the towns, villages and hamlets of Germany during the eighteenth and early nineteenth centuries, the entertainment offered must have seemed of a high order, for there was never a dull moment and any number of thrills. All the best titbits of a well-known legend were there and, what is more, they were most dramatically unfolded, with a breathless speed which left the slower-moving stage-drama far behind. The very stiffness of the puppet's movements suggested the unseen presence of an inexorable, indeed an automatic, fate. And a fourth dimension, eeriness, eddied on to the miniature stage where the destiny of an immortal human soul lodged in a tiny wooden body was being decided. The very neatness, completeness, briskness and slickness of the action made it all the more frightening; and it was terrifying enough in all conscience for those in the audience who believed in the devil and the possibility of invoking him in order to sign a pact with the powers of evil. In that case such adjurations as *Conjuro vos per omnes Deos, qui vos Kakadaemones sitis, ut statim appareatis!*[1] must have sent cold shivers coursing down the spine of literate and illiterate alike. A band of gypsies who delighted the villagers of Suabia in the eighteen-thirties with a puppet-play version of their own probably made the simple summons *Devil, I call thee!* sound sinister enough for the juvenile listeners; but nearly all the other texts aimed higher, summoning the fiends by the great seal of Solomon, or by the mystic numbers three, nine and eleven, or by such mysterious names as Bibet Rapaton Pessanos Kaldonai;[2] or by outlandish formulae such as *Siste, siste, Phlegethontia Styx! Hejus! hejus!*,[3] or by corrupt and incomprehensible mumbo-jumbo: *Orum infessorum interminato!*[4] So strong was the belief in

[1] Scheible, op. cit. Vol. v, p. 793; Ulm.

[2] Ibid. Vol. v, p. 864; Strasbourg.

[3] O. Schade, 'Das Puppenspiel Doctor Faust', *Weimarisches Jahrbuch*, Hanover, 1856, Vol. v, p. 278; Weimar.

[4] R. Petsch, 'Das fränkische Puppenspiel von Doktor Faust', *Zeitschrift des Vereins für Volkskunde*, Berlin, Vol. xv, p. 254; Berlin.

the potency of conjurations like this that expectation will have been roused to fever-pitch, and one can imagine the Berlin public gasping for breath when the hero bade the still invisible spirits: *Audite vox Fausti, Furiä, vox Tartarie, parete.*[1] As such conjuring was even then going on all over Germany in the ceaseless search for buried treasure, this scene had an element of realism in it which it lacks to-day; whereas the prologue in hell, retained in Ulm, Berlin and Strasbourg, probably needed the spectacular effects of the legitimate drama to make its full effect. The other puppet-plays did not use it.

But only the author of the Cologne text was strong-minded or ignorant enough to exclude the stock examination in speed which followed immediately after the conjuration and which gave scope for so much imagination and good clean fun. To the arrows, the winds, the birds, the clouds, the stags and the thoughts of man which had already been laid under contribution, the puppet-plays added cannon-balls and plagues, rushing streams and ships at sea, mountain-cocks, darting fish, flashing mirrors, autumn leaves falling, storms, thunder and lightning, the arrows of slander and gossiping women. Only the number of manikins available limited these various flights of fancy, all leading up to Mephisto's brag that he was as fast as the thoughts of man; although in a Czech version this was altered to the impressive speed of flying from Persia to Bohemia in one minute. In several plays a good laugh was raised by introducing the series with a slow-coach spirit who was as fast as a snail or (as Weimar had it) as an old woman. Leipzig went one better by producing the snail-like Alexo just before Mephisto. And then Lessing stepped in and ruined the scene. He was too clever by half with his philosophical witticisms on the speed of arrows, plagues, winds, the light, the thoughts of man, the vengeance of the avenger and the sobering reflection that the transition from good to evil holds the record for speed. Strasbourg copied this faithfully; Augsburg watered it down to the transition between the first and second step in vice. Something had gone for ever from the game. Already in Weimar there seems to have been a contamination between this scene and the appearance of the Seven Deadly Sins in the Marlovian play; for a series of this kind goes on developing until the theme exhausts itself by elaborations and complications; but it was the hand of Lessing which dealt the

[1] Lübke, loc. cit. p. 131.

death-blow. Krummschal, Vitzliputzli, Auerhahn, Asmodeus, Haribax, Xerxes, Megera, Audium et Gugulorum, Pick, Polümor, Wauwau, Alexo, Mexico, Astaroth, Pomon, Chill, Oron, Leviathan and Dilla: those active little devils made of black calico and tow would never really stir an audience to fear and laughter again. Out and alas for the heavy hand of our humourless intellectuals!

Chosen for his velocity, Mephisto manifested in human form, having first appeared as a fury or as a monster in some of the plays; and in Weimar by command first as a lion and then as a bear, much as he was to manifest in Hanover.[1] He took on various pleasing forms, appearing in the guise of a dashing cavalier, of a huntsman in blue, of a postillion, of a handsome and well-dressed youth, but never habited like a monk as in the days of the Urfaust-book. A very solemn pact-scene then ensued. What did the puppet Faust demand, playing before a simple, semi-literate audience in the market squares and on fair-days in little German towns, before he became fashionable and ceased to be popular, that is to say before Lessing started the intellectual and aesthetic deluge? It is difficult to answer that question, the published texts having been overlaid with later and more sophisticated accretions. Nevertheless, like the opening monologue (on the whole flat, philistine and uninspired) the desires of the nigromantic midgets were proportionate to their size. The melancholy and sombre sinner in the first part of the Urfaustbook was chiefly intent on truthful answers to those dark questions which for ever haunt human kind and which had driven him distracted. Marlowe added visions of unutterable glory and power. Ulm only bargained for twenty-four years of diabolic service before his surrender to the powers of hell. Other versions are more explicit, and material benefits bulk very large in nearly all. Augsburg and Strasbourg insisted that they should have a lavish supply of food and drink during the period of Mephisto's service; Geisselbrecht concentrated on money, desiring that all the buried treasure in the world should be his and in addition an inexhaustible purse whose coins should be valid everywhere. Weimar stipulated in this connection that the money he was buying with his soul should not vanish away in human hands. Fairy gold had a bad enough name among

---

[1] The Weimar Faust allows Mephisto to choose between male and female form, and although the former is chosen, this also reminds one of Hanover.

99

the people, infernal gold a worse one; and this particular stipulation
is to be met with again and again in the Black Books attributed to
Faust as well as in other manuals. In fact, no one drawing up a
list of the boons asked for in the puppet-plays can fail to be struck
with the marked similarity between the texts of ritual magic and
of the marionette theatre in this respect. They were both drawing
on a common stock of popular beliefs, it is true; but the showmen
may also have had some knowledge of the magical hand-books.
Wealth, beauty, pleasure, glory, fame, health and happiness, and
even (though less frequently) knowledge, learning and the truthful
answer to all questions figured on the catalogue of *desiderata* made
by the insatiable little wooden magicians; and most of them
demanded as well to be carried with lightning speed wherever they
wished to go, without danger to themselves, said Augsburg and
Weimar, whilst the Franconian Faust expressed the same notion
more poetically:

Can you build me bridges over the wild, red sea and streets in the
air?[1]

The gipsy Faust, first cousin to Don Juan, was of a more romantic turn of mind than his Gorgio namesakes, and clamoured for
one thing only, the love of a beautiful princess; whilst Cologne
comprehensively stated that he wished to be the foremost magician
in the world and to have everything he wanted. They were all of
them ready to pledge body and soul for these benefits, although
Leipzig at least had some mental reservations; nevertheless most
of them boggled slightly at Mephisto's counter-conditions. These
generally began with a prohibition against washing themselves,
and cutting or combing their hair and paring their nails. The bad
little puppets, about to embark on a splendid career, naturally
objected to that; but they gave in with a good grace when Mephisto
assured them that their outward appearance would be as clean,
smart and handsome as the most fastidious could desire; he would
see to that. This popular superstition about the glamour produced
by devilish arts was widely held at the time and was also reflected
in the sad transformation undergone by the Hamburg Faust when
Lucretia pulled off his magic ring. Never to darken the doors of
a church again, and yet to seem God-fearing men; to shun lecture-
rooms like the plague, what time Mephisto garbed in their robes

[1] Petsch, loc. cit. p. 254.

would keep up their reputation for learning (Goethe remembered this); never to lend money or to bestow alms—on the whole these conditions were not unduly onerous. But in nearly every instance there was a tussle on the subject of marriage, a hoary Faustian theme; and Mephisto had to use all his wicked wit and wiles to disgust his victims with that holy state, especially in the case of Strasbourg, who had taken a leaf out of Klinger's book and was already a *paterfamilias*. But there are better fish in the open sea than in the shallows of matrimony, and the devil won the day. The contract was signed with the signatories' blood, and only Berlin had the common-sense to read it through and insert a saving clause:

I the undersigned attest herewith that for twenty-four years I will use the power of the hellish prince Pluto and keep the following agreements,

1. This contract is valid as from the present date and terminates at midnight twenty-four years hence.
2. During this time I will neither wash nor comb myself nor cut any nails on my hands or feet.
3. During this time I will neither utter any prayers nor enter a church.
4. And I also promise never to marry.
5. I further declare that I am signing this contract in full possession of all my faculties.

For his part Pluto binds himself:

1. To serve me by land and by water,
2. To procure me all possible happiness and pleasure,
3. To make me appear always clean, decent and honoured, and never to allow me to lack money.

Finally I declare that I will give myself to Pluto body and soul after twenty-four years. But should he be unable or unwilling to keep the clauses detailed above, I herewith give notice that I shall take back my word and demand the return of the contract at any moment. This I sign with my blood.

Anno 1525.   Johannes Faust.[1]

I think that undoubtedly the saving clause derived from a study of the Faustian Black Books, where instructions are sometimes to be found how to word a binding bilateral pact in a way which

[1] Lübke, loc. cit. pp. 137f.

allows a loop-hole for the signatory to wriggle through. But it did not help the wretched Berlin, who, like almost all the other puppet Fausts, having pleaded for forty-eight years and been granted twenty-four, was fetched off at the end of twelve, because he had used the services of Mephisto by night as well as by day. This sudden curtailment was particularly hard on Leipzig, who had counted on the last twelve years of the contract in order to gain enough power through knowledge to escape the devil's clutches. The same situation arose with the gipsies' Faust. He had been warned that he would belong to the devil after his third murder, and was claimed after the second, because forsooth the pact with Mephisto counted as number one. Truly he who would sup with the devil needs a long spoon. But, in spite of a good angel intoning or even singing solemn warnings, and in spite of sinister laughter from the evil spirit on the left, one and all put their names to the contract, signing it in their own blood, miraculously and painlessly drawn by Mephisto. Though startled by the letters H.F. (*Homo Fuge*) which thereupon appeared in red letters on the palms of their hands, they were easily reassured by the various ingenious explanations produced by the fiend, one of the most frequent being that the message meant: 'Fly into the arms of thy Mephistopheles!' A raven black as night then fluttered in to fetch away the blood-stained pact (which possibly accounts for the title *Black Raven* on one of the Faustian magical manuals); and this apparition terrified Geisselbrecht's Faust to such an extent that Mephisto had to suggest a journey to the court of the Duke of Parma in order to distract his mind.

Cologne did not go there; Geisselbrecht and Strasbourg were not seen there; the gipsy Faust rushed off to Mantua and his beloved princess, where he behaved as an ardent lover; but otherwise the ensuing episode, whether laid in Parma, in Prague, in Florence or in Portugal, during which the puppet heroes became puppet-showmen, represented the apex of their careers. They had sold their souls to the devil in order to produce Alexander the Great and Padamera (his paramour, complete with the wart originally bestowed upon her by 'Spiess'),[1] Samson and Delilah, David and Goliath, King Solomon, Judith and Holofernes, the whole Assyrian camp, Lucretia, the Queen of Sheba, Aetna, a storm at sea, and the Duke of Parma's supposed friends in their

[1] In Ulm. For the wart see my *Myth of the Magus*, p. 141.

true shape (an unpopular proceeding); finally in Bohemia Alexander again, with beautiful Helen (Krasna Helenoria), both of them with horses' hoofs. Strutting about and hoping to impress their princely patrons, they managed to alienate either them or the courtiers, especially those Fausts who made advances to the ducal or royal consort. But, whatever the reason for their disgrace, they all had to leave the scene of their triumph in double quick time with Mephisto's aid, having gained nothing but hatred, ill-repute and downright danger from their showmanship.

When next met with, back in their home towns, they are discovered in the clutches of remorse and fear. The poetic energy of 'Spiess' which had so greatly moved Marlowe still invests the prayers for mercy, the desperate, unavailing remorse, the anguished questions, the vain efforts to repent which transform the least life-like of these manikins for the space of a few short telling scenes into tragic heroes in their own right. They are heirs to a tradition which held them in its grip, and to a certain extent they had even improved upon tradition. For, by a dramatic regrouping of Marlowe's scenes (probably first undertaken on the legitimate stage) the questioning and remorse come all together at the end; the old man has disappeared; but Mephisto's answers to their frantic questions are such that his victims wildly throw themselves upon the mercy of God and come within an ace of salvation. The Czech version gave the crucifix scenes here. In Augsburg a very imaginative use was made of this *motiv*. The scene is laid in a wood with a crucifix behind a tree, which divides and discovers Christ bleeding on the cross when Faust breaks into prayer, but closes and hides the crucifix when Mephisto enters. 'What would you do in my place, Mephistopheles, to obtain the grace of God?' the tragic puppets ask the fiend, almost in the selfsame words their namesake had used so many years ago. And the Augsburg devil answers:

Ah Faustus, if there were a ladder stretching from earth to heaven, made of swords instead of rungs so that I should be cut into a thousand pieces with every step I took, yet would I still strive to reach the summit, so that I might behold the face of God but once more, after which I would willingly be damned again to all eternity.[1]

This heart-shaking answer, one of the great moments in Faustian literature, bears a strange resemblance to the passage in the

[1] Scheible, op. cit. Vol. v, p. 842.

English Faustbook where Mephisto describes the ladder in hell reaching up to heaven which the damned vainly attempt to ascend in order to seek the blessing of God.[1] The tragic vision is more piercing here, and comes at a tenser moment; the efforts to heighten it by substituting razor-blades for swords and lengthening the speech, made by Strasbourg and Weimar, only detract from the greatness of this inspired utterance.

The mythological marionettes—for during these scenes their mythological character is very much in evidence—fall to prayer when Mephisto roundly refuses to answer any more questions, and he makes off in fear and trembling. Left alone, they petition for mercy, and mercy seems to hover round them; for neither riches, fame, pleasure, nor glory, dangled anxiously before them by their evil genius who returns to find them escaping from his clutches, have any allure for them now. As a last resort Mephisto produces Helen of Troy, and a tragic landslide ensues. For not only does Helen gain an extremely easy victory; but this scene is one of pure bathos after the spiritual tensity preceding it; the idea is poetical enough but the execution is pitiable and labours under the further disadvantage of the inevitable comparison with Marlowe. Leipzig alone (and I strongly suspect Hamm of complicity in this) made shift to be at the height of the situation, and produced a few lines in prose which sound like a faint echo from the great speech in Goethe's *Faust, Part II.* All the other manikins took one look at Helen and surrendered, only to discover either immediately and on the spot or swiftly behind the scenes that she was a Fury in disguise and that they were now irretrievably damned.

Although this is not the end of the play, the end cannot be recounted without confessing to a major omission comparable to the proverbial absurdity of reproducing *Hamlet* without the Prince of Denmark. For Faust became more and more inseparable in the popular mind from his farcical double Hans Wurst, Pickelhäring, Crispin, Casper, or by whatever name he went. And it must remain a moot point whether the crowd collected outside the showman's booth really came to see Faust, or whether the same restlessness did not prevail during the opening scenes which Swift had noted in England among the audience waiting for the appearance of Punch. Certain it is that, whereas in Ulm the clown played a very minor part, it had increased to such an extent in the Leipzig text

[1] See above, p. 34.

as to run into thirty-four pages, whilst Faust had only twenty-seven. Moreover if some or all of the other puppets were rather clumsy and stiff, he (at least in the Leipzig and Geisselbrecht productions) was the best articulated of all: he could move his head, roll his eyes, walk on his heels, tap-dance and gyrate, clear his throat and even spit to the delight of all beholders. The chief actor, or the showman himself (when there was more than one mechanician behind the scenes), always took this part and allowed himself any amount of licence as regards gagging. Strasbourg had one scene to be played extempore; and Augsburg merely gave some general directions for all Hans Wurst's appearances, to be played *à la gusto*. This truly popular figure was held so high in general esteem because he represented, even though he caricatured, the 'little man', and was a fanciful projection of the grinning and chuckling individuals who watched him disporting himself on the stage. He gave them what they wanted, and gave it them in their own dialect too, hot and strong, coarse, loud and piercing. He may have been full of Latin wit, nimble repartee and general *joie-de-vivre* when he first arrived from Italy, and flashes of these characteristics remained with him throughout; but it must also be owned that he was sometimes rather a boor—worse still, occasionally a bore, and that the fooling was apt to degenerate into horse-play. Nevertheless his importance can hardly be exaggerated; for he was there to parody Faust and the situations Faust encountered from beginning to end and always to get the better of the devils. So that the two actions, serious and comic, went on side by side, until they were finally merged together in a most remarkable *finale*.

To my mind Casper is most engaging in Geisselbrecht's play, where all his songs are given; but he plays much the same part in all the versions except Ulm and Cologne. Rushing on to the stage in the highest spirits, he takes Faust's house for an inn at first, and when Wagner undeceives him agrees to become the magician's servant, for he hasn't a penny to bless himself with, his knapsack is empty and so is his insatiable stomach. From the very outset he gives proof of an artless (but successful) low cunning which stands him in good stead when he blunders into Faust's magic circle, stumbles on the word which summons the fiends, and then has much ado to get rid of them. This juxtaposition of Casper and the devils is truly and gloriously comic. It is a comic situation, a comic idea and involves comedy of character too. Moreover there is the underlying comedy of contrast between the powerful arch-necro-mancer and his ignorant and illiterate servant who, in the direst straits, discovers, or remembers, or is even obligingly informed by the fiends that if *Perlico* (or *Berlicke*) conjures them up, *Parlico* (or *Berlocke—per li, per là*) dismisses them. He thereupon has them flying on and off at will and finally with such lightning speed that one begins to feel quite sorry for them; and yet there is also some-thing sinister in their reiterated and emphatic demands for his soul, especially perhaps in Geisselbrecht, where the monotonous refrain: 'Bind yourself over, bind yourself over, bind yourself over' sounds like a tolling bell. Needless to say, Casper knows a trick or two worth that and gets out of the circle and out of the *impasse* (after a good rough and tumble) by declaring that he hasn't a soul, or that it's only of wood, or that he doesn't know how to sign his name, or that he'll give it them later, or by getting round them somehow and getting away.

Far be it from me to follow him painstakingly through scene after scene, all in some sort parodying Faust's, but few of them at the height of the one I have just sketched. They need the dark framework in which they occur for their full effect. For though Faust could do very well indeed without Casper, a parasite if ever there were one, Casper couldn't do without Faust. He almost smothers his host in this play; one can hardly see Faust for Casper; but without the organism he is battening on he could not exist at all. Turning from aesthetic considerations to philosophical ones, however, it is possible to regard Casper in a more favourable light: as a dose of rather bitter medicine offered to a world sick at that time of a fearful disease, the belief in demonology and witchcraft. If 'Spiess' delivered in season a dreadful word of warning, Casper struck a shrewd blow at the accredited power of Satan. Amidst gales of raucous laughter the people relearnt the lesson Luther had taught them to forget: that the devil can be outwitted and made to look a fool, even by such an ignoramus as Casper, whose instinctive shrewdness and horse-sense save him from the fate of his master. And here the hoary and flattering notion that the simple are wiser than the learned and that 'a little child shall lead you' also paid dividends. For on the puppet-stage the greater wisdom of Casper was the interesting addition to the implicit mockery of magic which the Marlovian drama had introduced. To parody the main action by means of a comic sub-plot was not new (*pace* Creizenach and other German scholars), but to set up a counter-ideal in the person of an illiterate and far from holy clown certainly was. The annihilating power of laughter, unleashed in *The Tragical History of Doctor Faustus*, achieved the status of enlightenment on the puppet-stage, enlightenment as dispensed by and for the people, and with a very cruel side to it.

Perhaps all enlightenment has this cruel side: something insensitive, blunt, unimaginative, cocksure and scornful being its less admirable aspect. The puppet-play writers betrayed these qualities in the final scenes strangely wedded with their opposites. It was a flash of genius which in some unknown author's mind at some unknown date (but evidently before 1767)[1] promoted Casper to the office of nightwatchman as Faust's end drew near. This gave the clown an organic function in the last scene, and linked Marlowe's wonderful notion of the striking of the clock with that of a watchman telling the hours. Never perhaps in the whole history of the drama have tragedy and comedy been welded together so closely as this or by a more genuinely poetical idea; but the execution leaves much to be desired. The scheme is as follows. During Faust's last night on earth the clown enters and sings a ribald song at each striking of the clock which brings the hero's end one hour nearer; he also haggles with the desperate man about his unpaid wages and sees through the stratagem by which Faust hopes to effect his rescue: a change of garments with Casper in lieu of the money owed him. He is completely unmoved throughout by his erstwhile master's tragic situation and avoids a like fate. Meanwhile those solemn words which had figured as transparencies in the Danzig production were intoned by a voice off the stage in sometimes rather garbled Latin:

> Fauste, praepara te!
> Fauste, accusatus es!
> Fauste, judicatus es!
> Fauste, in aeternum damnatus es!

Faust's own despairing speeches answer these inexorable declarations.

In the Augsburg version, which is altogether the most imaginative, Faust, having implored Wagner to burn his books on magic,

---

[1] In the Kurz performance in 1767 Crispen was billed as 'a foolish nightwatchman'; but no scene was sketched.

is left alone on the stage; the clock strikes nine and Hans Wurst enters, sings a lewd little ditty and retires; the voice is heard uttering the first warning and Faust breaks out into impassioned verse (alexandrines). Ten o'clock strikes and the sequence repeats itself, recurring in the same order for the hours of eleven and twelve. It goes like clock-work with uncanny precision which must have been extremely effective to watch. And the impression is heightened because in this version Faust and Hans Wurst do not address each other, seem unaware of each other, and appear to belong (as indeed they do) to totally different worlds, the world of black nightmare and the wide-awake world of reality, brought rather violently together by the final utterance given to the joker:

Huzzah, the devil has fetched him away with drums and pipes![1]

Except for this one jangling note the sinister and macabre atmosphere of the last scene in the drama is heightened by the presence and the bawdy songs of the unconscious fool; but in the other versions his wordy intrusions jar terribly; his triumph over the magician is cheap and nasty and his victorious escape from the devil after his master has been taken off is an outrage on the emotions. Perhaps only an age inured to the trials and burnings, the tortures and executions of witches and warlocks which were still taking place when the first Faust puppets met their lamentable fate could have enjoyed this savage but salutary ridicule. For though the puppet-play texts were published when the age of enlightenment was already a thing of the past, the shows themselves were being given before the dawn of that age which gradually filtered down and affected the libretti. Pacts with the devil were 'common knowledge' when the Faustian marionettes made their first bow on the miniature stage, and indeed long afterwards; the search for buried treasure with the help of 'Faust's' books of black magic was still continuing when Goethe was an old man. Superstition dies hard and belief in the powers of evil is in itself an evil thing. So that Casper Triumphans ought to be commended rather than condemned for throwing doubt on the subject. If by this means the fear of evil forces could be diminished, no aesthetic considerations should elbow him off the stage. Nor does he always come off scot-free; the devils belabour him now and then, but he escapes them in the end; and the stock joke that they retire in

[1] Scheible, op. cit. Vol. v, p. 852.

terror on hearing that their prospective victim is a nightwatchman, or a native of Augsburg, or Strasbourg or Weimar, may actually have reassured some of the simpler souls among the audience, as is said to have been the case with Paddy, who, seeing a corpulent Faust stuck fast in the trap-door to the infernal regions, exclaimed with heartfelt relief: 'Thank God, hell's full!'

Incredulous smiles may meet this anecdote; but it can be paralleled by the strange story of the showman Geisselbrecht, a native of Berlin, already grey-haired in the first decade of the nineteenth century, who toured all Germany with his puppets, visiting the messes, markets and fairs. In his text Casper is at his lightest, gayest and most debonair and was carved and jointed with particular care. All to no avail. A great many passages were underlined in the manuscript, and Scheible printed them in spaced type. They include Faust's conjuration formulae, part of a chapter read out by Casper from a magic book on the subject of the rejuvenation of old women, Wagner's plea towards the end that Faust should remember his Creator and the Day of Judgment, Faust's own remorseful efforts to repent, his fearful outcry at the end that the devil is coming for his soul and a sudden irresistible desire for the bottomless pit:

Come forth, ye devils, come forth, ye furies, take away my life, I am already lost. . . .

> Let the thunder at once destroy me,
> Open wide
> Ye gates of hell,
> *I would come to you.*

(The devils come and fetch him away with them)

THE END

(ALL THE PASSAGES I HAVE UNDERLINED ARE THOSE WHICH HAVE DECIDED ME NEVER TO PLAY FAUST AGAIN)[1]

In spite of Casper, the daimonic power in the legend has seized upon the old puppet-player:

The oftener he played the piece and the older he became, the more questionable for the salvation of his soul appeared the blasphemies, impieties and conjurations which it contained. At last he became so nervous during the representations that he cut out the most effective bits which he had underlined as blasphemous in his manuscript. . . .

[1] Scheible, op. cit. Vol. v, p. 782.

But the devil nevertheless pursued him like a roaring lion, and the old showman at last wrote despairingly at the end of his manuscript that he would never play Faust again.[1]

Geisselbrecht's version had no explicit renouncement of God and the Christian faith in the pact, as some of the others had. But it looks as if he knew something about witchcraft. Casper's mother had been burned at the stake as a witch (this was underlined), and Mephisto declared that he would lead Faust and Helen first to the Blocksberg and thence to hell. It was all evidently a living reality to Geisselbrecht; and perhaps nothing that has ever been written in story, drama or poetry about Faust's fearful end rings quite so tragically true as the final confession:

'*I would come to you.*'

---

[1] [Hamm], op. cit. p. xvi.

PART II. BRAVE NEW FAUSTS

Chapter IV.   ESCAPING FAUSTS

       (*a*) An enlightened Faust, 1759–1784

       (*b*) A lucky Faust, 1775

       (*c*) Womanizing Fausts, 1772–1778

   V.   STORM-TOSSED FAUSTS

       (*a*) A titanic Faust, 1776–1778

       (*b*) A Faust forlorn, 1777

       (*c*) Faust in fragments, 1790

       (*d*) A sombre Faust, 1791

   VI.   FORGOTTEN FAUSTS

       (*a*) Faust in Grub Street, 1792–1801

       (*b*) A quasi-Goethean Faust, 1804

   VII.   POETICAL FAUSTS

       (*a*) A romantic Faust, 1804

       (*b*) An imperishable Faust, 1808

ESCAPING FAUSTS

(a) An enlightened Faust, 1759–1784

A twofold painful shock must be faced on turning from the German puppet-plays to Lessing's Faust scene and Faust schemes. In the first place the change-over from the popular to the portentous in the speed-scene is a most disenchanting process. It is true that the showmen themselves felt no scruples or misgivings on the subject of plundering from literature; but it was so artlessly and clumsily done that it actually heightens the effect of extreme simplicity of mind which is the overriding impression made by the German Fausts before they attracted the attention of the *littérateurs*. And that is why (with the exception of Widman and his suite) they are so refreshing and at times so powerfully moving. There is a spontaneity, a directness, a reality in the total experience they offer which not all the glaring faults of detail can obliterate; and this provokes an emotional recoil from Lessing's elaboration of the trial by speed in the seventeenth *Literaturbrief* in 1759. This truly dramatic event in the history of the Faust-legend shows literature condescending to folk-poetry and folk-poetry laughing at literature, not a very happy omen for the threatened 'ennobling' of Faust.

Hovering on the verge of a sweeping statement about the absurdity of the attempt, one remembers just in time that Marlowe had triumphantly performed a similar task, and that the German stage Fausts whom Lessing wished to reinstate were direct descendants of the immortal Elizabethan; why then should one instinctively resist this well-meant effort to reclaim their rightful inheritance? The answer to this question is not merely the obvious one, that Lessing was not Marlowe; it involves the whole complex and baffling relationship between primitive poetry and literature. The history of the myth of the magus shows that the Faust-legend of the sixteenth century was a battered and blackened hulk from the wreckage of a great magical tradition. Marlowe launched it on

to the ocean of poetry with 'the proud full sail of his great verse';
but it foundered again almost immediately, and this time, it would
seem, irretrievably. The flotsam and jetsam of the second shipwreck sank slowly downwards, and when Lessing's salvage operations began, everything to do with Faust had suffered a sea-change,
encrusted with popular notions, petrified in a popular form,
glistening and glittering with popular wit, exhaling a briny, salty,
bracing tang, and sometimes emitting a murmur like a sea-shell
held to the ear. How could a rationalist such as Lessing make
anything of that?

Moreover literature and folk-poetry as a whole had drifted so
far apart in the eighteenth century that they were out of sight and
sound of each other. It needed such explorers and discoverers as
Percy and Herder to bring news of a whole lost continent to the
modern world and to produce specimens of the flora and fauna
which sometimes turned out to be spurious; for it required extraordinary perception in Herder's day to tell the true from the false;
it still needs the utmost in poetical gifts to exploit the beauties of
folk-poetry in the service of art. A Goethe, a Heine and the
inspired generation of the romantic poets in Germany; a Keats, a
Synge and a Yeats over here; isolated instances everywhere, but
no one remotely resembling Lessing. And yet, is this equation of
folk-poetry and the Faustian puppet-plays a satisfactory one? The
first came bubbling up from the soil or even the subsoil of life
in naïve, refreshing song: poignant, mysterious, humorous and
matter-of-fact turn by bewildering turn; the other, a by-blow of
literature, rather out at elbows, went gambolling in the market-
squares, where it came to a sad bad end. At first sight they seem
to have nothing in common. But both were impregnated with
popular habits of mind; and both for that reason are in the highest
degree intractable to sophisticated reconditioning.

It was sophisticated reconditioning which Lessing undertook in
the seventeenth *Literaturbrief*, and the result proved that he was
fundamentally out of tune with the spirit of his model, a popular
stage version according to his own account. The particular scene
which he chose in order to illustrate the native quality of the Faust
drama and its Shakespearean aura (he actually knew nothing of
Marlowe) was in fact one of the most genuinely popular elements
in the Faust-legend and had been reintroduced from the folkbooks,
where it went like this:

After several weeks he comes again from Prague to Erfurt with splendid gifts which had been given to him there, and invites the same company to be his guests at St. Michael's. They come and stand there in the rooms but there is no sign of any preparation. But he knocks with a knife on the table. Soon someone enters and says: 'Sir, what do you wish?' Faust asks, 'How quick are you?' The other answers: 'As an arrow.' 'Oh no,' says Dr. Faust, 'you shall not serve me. Go back to where you came from.' Then he knocks again, and when another servant enters and asks the same question, he says: 'How quick are you?' 'As the wind', says he. 'Well, that's something', says Dr. Faust, but sends him out again too. But when he knocked a third time another entered, and when he was asked the same question, he said he was as quick as the thoughts of man. 'Right,' said Dr. Faust, 'you'll do.'[1]

Already in Danzig (1668) this scene was part of the conjuration-scene, and the ambiguous servants of the folkbook were unambiguous devils. In the Ulm text after the invocation accompanied by thunder, all the devils appear:

Faust. Holla, that storm is over! What kind of a devil are you?

Krummschal. My name is Krummschal, and I am bound to appear at your command.

Faust. How quick are you?

Krummschal. As quick as the bird in the air.

Faust. Away, hell-bound, you're no good to me! And what is your name?

Vizibuzli. I am a flying spirit and I am called Vizibuzli, the love-devil.

Faust. And how quick are you?

Vizibuzli. As an arrow from the bow.

Faust. Be off, you're no use to me!—But tell me, what kind of a spirit are you?

Mephistopheles. I am a spirit of the air, and I am called Mephistopheles, the speedy.

Faust. Then tell me, how fast are you?

Mephistopheles. As fast as the thoughts of man.

Faust. That's fast indeed. You'll do.[2]

---

[1] Palmer and More, op. cit. p. 114. Word for word the same in the Spiess Faustbook of 1589. This is taken from the *Erfurt Chronicle*.

[2] Scheible, op. cit. Vol. v, p. 794. The 'love-devil' may be an echo from Marlowe.

As I said before, there were many variations, permutations and elaborations of this scene, all tending to bring out suspense and humour combined, and all directed to the final victorious announcement: 'As fast as the thoughts of man.' Now let us listen to Lessing:

Faust and seven spirits.

Faust. You? Are you the quickest spirits of hell?

All the spirits. We are.

Faust. Are you all seven equally quick?

All the spirits. No.

Faust. And which of you is the quickest?

All the spirits. I am!

Faust. What a miracle! Only six liars among seven devils. I must get to know you better.

The first spirit. So you will! In the future!

Faust. In the future? What do you mean? Do devils preach repentance too?

The first spirit. Yes indeed, to the obdurate. But don't detain us.

Faust. What's your name? And how quick are you?

The first spirit. It would be easier to give a proof than an answer.

Faust. Very well then. Look here. What am I doing?

The first spirit. You are moving your finger quickly through a candle-flame—

Faust. And I haven't burnt myself. Go you then and proceed seven times equally fast through the flames of hell without burning yourself.—You fall silent? You remain where you are? So devils boast too, do they? Ah yes; there is no sin so paltry that you would surrender it.—Second spirit, what is your name?

The second spirit. Chil; in your longwinded language that means the arrows of the plague.

Faust. And how fast are you?

The second spirit. Do you suppose that I bear my name in vain?—I am as fast as the arrows of the plague.

Faust. Then be off and serve a doctor. You are far too slow for me.— What's your name, third spirit?

The third spirit. I am called Dilla; for I am carried by the wings of the wind.

Faust. And you, the fourth?

The fourth spirit. My name is Jutta, for I travel on the rays of light.

Faust. Oh you miserable creatures, whose speed can be expressed in finite terms—

The fifth spirit. Don't honour them with your anger. They are only Satan's messengers in the material world. We are his emissaries in the spiritual world. You will find that we are much quicker.

Faust. And how quick are you?

The fifth spirit. I am as fast as the thoughts of man.

Faust. That is something!—But the thoughts of man are by no means always fast. They hesitate when truth and virtue summon them. How slothful they are then!—You can be fast when you want to be fast; but who can guarantee that you will always be fast? No, I can trust you as little as I should have trusted myself. Ah me!—(*To the sixth spirit*) Tell me, how quick are you?

The sixth spirit. As quick as the revenge of the Avenger.

Faust. Of the Avenger? What Avenger?

The sixth spirit. Of the mighty, of the terrible, who said that vengeance was His, because He took pleasure in revenge.

Faust. Devil, I see that you are blaspheming, for you tremble. As quick, you say, as the vengeance of the—I nearly named Him! No, He shall not be named between us! And His vengeance is fast?—And I am still alive? And I am still sinning?

The sixth spirit. Vengeance enough, that He still allows you to sin!

Faust. Oh, that a devil should have to teach me that!—And yet not till today! No, His vengeance is not fast, and if you are no quicker than his revenge, then be off with you.—(*To the seventh spirit*)— What is your speed?

The seventh spirit. Insatiable mortal, if I am not quick enough for you—

Faust. Well, say how quick you are.

The seventh spirit. No more and no less than the transition from good to evil—

Faust. Ha! You are the devil for me! As quick as the transition from good to evil!—Yes, that is fast indeed; there is nothing quicker than that!—Away with you, you snails from Orcus! Away!—Than the transition from good to evil! I know from experience how quick that is! I know it from experience![1]

[1] This scene is given in German in Palmer and More, op. cit. pp. 275 ff., where it may be most convenient for English readers to consult it.

Meaning to go one better than the folk-scene, Lessing decidedly went one worse; for if thoughts are sometimes laggards the transition from good to evil is also a very variable quantity, is rarely lightning-quick and may take months and even years. But quite apart from this heavy-footed anticlimax, the scene sags beneath the weight of laboured irony, hefty sermonizing and hair-splitting theological subtleties. The native freshness and quick-wittedness of the original; the unexpected introduction from another category of speed, whereas Lessing laboriously prepared the ground; all the fun has gone; in fact it is almost like seeing a deliberate and weighty caterpillar emerging from a butterfly. Lessing proved incapable of retaining the popular mother-wit and lightness of the original, and he was also not imaginative enough to endow his version of the scene with mystery and fear. One's heart warms to the contemporary critic who complained that Lessing's devils were as witty as any *bel esprit*, as serious-minded as a naturalized Englishman, as honest and as open as a German and as pious as the most sanctimonious bigot.

Now why should Lessing, as shrewd a thinker, as acute a critic and as great an intellect as could be met with in a day's march, have blundered into the Faust-legend like this, since its fundamental assumptions were completely outside his sphere of interests and actually antagonistic to them? The man who laughed miracles to scorn in *Nathan the Wise*, for whom religions had no value apart from their ethical content, and whose deism was essentially rationalistic and optimistic was emphatically not the man to believe even for half a moment in pacts with the devil or in a torture-chamber called hell, let alone in eternal damnation. Moreover not only did he share with the nobler minds of his age a high-minded faith in the essential incorruptibility and indefinite perfectibility of man; he was also (like his ancestor Socrates) fundamentally convinced that human error and the unhappiness it entails can be cured by knowledge and wisdom. Yet from the very beginning the Faust-legend had taught the opposite doctrine: that the desire for knowledge and more light was in itself a dangerous and sinful desire. Lessing, it must be granted, stated in a famous passage that pure truth was for God alone; but in the same passage he made it quite clear that the unremitting search for truth was the noblest activity of man. If, therefore, he wished to do more than merely bait Gottsched by boosting German as against French wares; if he really wished to elevate Faust to the status of a national hero; and if he designed to have a hand in this himself, he would be forced to alter as radically as possible the assumptions of the legend.

It will be clear presently that this was the aim he had in view, and there were probably three reasons why such apparently intractable material exercised such a fascination over his enlightened mind. In the first place the deep philosophical undertow was there, and his was a philosophical spirit; in the second place the legend represented a challenge: a work of liberation to be accomplished; and in the third place his critical faculty was involved. Perhaps this was his supreme gift, so much in excess of his imaginative and almost non-existent poetical qualities that it continually impelled him to create. Had the German stage not been in the deadly condition in which he found it, he might never have contributed a single play to its repertory. But the absolute divorce between life and the theatre displayed by the pompous pseudo-classical tragedies with their swollen and hollow alexandrines goaded him into producing examples in prose of tragedy in real life, taking place in and conditioned by the contemporary social structure (*Miss Sara Sampson* and *Emilia Galotti*); whilst the stilted, artificial or grossly farcical comedies which were then in vogue were responsible for *Minna von Barnhelm*, a piece of constructive criticism taking the shape of a model to be copied. Native talent, native characters, native tradition—Lessing aimed at furthering all this; and being Lessing, he was clear-sighted enough to see the possibilities latent in the Faust drama which he had witnessed in 1754 given by the Schuch troupe in Berlin. This was something as different from French tragedy as well might be; and Gottsched, who had located Faust among the rabble rout and prophesied his imminent extinction, must be made to eat his words. In this way it came about that Lessing directed the attention of the literary world to a piece of folk-lore embedded in an organism which had lived such a full and varied life since the days of the Urfaustbook in 1587.

Yet, even had Lessing not lent a helping hand, the Faust-legend (perhaps not unmindful of the days of Marlowe) would probably have accomplished the come-back into literature which it seemed rather warily to be staging. It was reaching up into those regions by clinging on to Gryphius; and the now rather shaky ladder of poetical alexandrines was used by Johann Friedrich Löwe in his semi-satirical poem *The Witches' Sabbath*, 1756, in which Faust was invoked in the first canto and later shown hobnobbing with Beelzebub on the Blocksberg, singing a drinking-song and protesting against the false rumours current about him, notably that he had been torn to pieces by fiends. This rather tedious product of enlightenment at .least shows that the current was settling towards an aesthetic revival and even an ethical salvation of Faust; but the publicity given to him in the seventeenth *Literaturbrief* was decisive for the rising literary generation. The magic name had been uttered by Lessing; and the magic name had power.

It had power over Lessing too. As early as 1755 he confided to Moses Mendelssohn that he was working at a *Faust*. All that is left of it is the so-called Berlin Scenario, published posthumously in 1784, and statements made by friends. The scenario sketched a pandemonium to be held in a ruined cathedral; this traditional feature taken in conjunction with the speed-scene makes it appear likely that at one time (in the 1750s) Lessing was chiefly intent on a literary version of the popular drama. It would also obviously have been a 'philosophical' version. In the pandemonium-prologue Beelzebub is discovered taking counsel with his subordinates, and they are reporting their nefarious activities to him: a town delivered up to the flames, a whole fleet wrecked by a storm. Much more to the point, however, is the seduction of a saint through the agency of strong drink leading first to adultery and later to murder. Faust's name is then mentioned with the rider that it would be more difficult to lead him astray. The devil who had undermined the virtue of the saint undertakes to deliver Faust up to hell in twenty-four hours, being evidently a stickler for the unity of time. And is not Faust even now burning the midnight oil and searching in the depths for truth? And is not too great a desire for knowledge a fault from which all vices may spring, if one gives way to it too much? (And had not Lessing himself in an early play called *The Young Scholar* signalized, if not the danger, then the folly of too much learning?)

The first act shows Faust in the attitude described by his would-be seducer, and full of doubts on the subject of scholastic wisdom. He decides to attempt contact with the shade (or entelechy) of Aristotle, and the devil rises up in the guise of the Greek philosopher. The short dialogue Lessing sketched has something embryonically awe-inspiring about it; and considering Lessing's reverence for Aristotle, this is exactly what one would expect. On the disappearance of the devil in this shape, another demon is summoned, with whose entry upon the scene the fragment breaks off.

If this were all that we knew of Lessing's *Faust*, his place in the history of the legend would be confined to the rather saddening publicity he gave it in the seventeenth *Literaturbrief*, and the spectacle of the first stage in its literary metamorphosis. But it is by no means all. Either one or two almost completed Faust dramas written by Lessing have disappeared if all the accounts are true, lost with other Faustian material in a wooden box which somehow went astray in a coach plying between Dresden and Leipzig. They have never turned up; but several of Lessing's acquaintances and friends came forward after his death and testified to his schemes and their partial or actual completion. Engel in particular elaborated the prologue and put it into dialogue-form. Piecing together the various sometimes conflicting statements, one certainly gains the impression that Lessing fully realized the magnitude of his undertaking; and it is at least probable that, dissatisfied with both solutions of the almost insoluble problem, he destroyed what he had written and invented the story of the lost case of papers. He certainly seems to have made few efforts to trace it. He is reported to have said, at a time when *Fausts* were being announced all over Germany and when everybody who was anybody in the literary world was gossiping about Goethe's, that the devil would fetch his *Faust*, but that he would fetch Goethe's. A hearsay witticism of this sort is not evidence; nevertheless it can be interpreted as a reference to the ultimate fate of his hero. If so, then he later changed his mind, and we must now brace ourselves to meet the consequences.

Of the two versions reported, one was said to be a domestic tragedy without supernatural elements, depending solely on the machinations of a villain. It was to be so cleverly contrived, however, that the onlookers would exclaim at every new development: 'That is Satan's work!' When the curtain fell on the last act they would be disabused of this notion. This sounds like a rough draft of the benevolent lecture later given by Nathan to Recha about angels and miracles, a rationalistic effort to explode tenacious superstitions. The audience, having been led up the garden path, might have been in no very receptive state to experience tragic emotions; nevertheless Lessing clearly wished to keep the tragic content at the expense of the supernatural element. The second version set out to do the opposite: to pay lip-service at least to the traditional assumptions and to reverse the tragic conclusion of the situation. Rational optimists cannot but allow that tragedies may be brought about in life by the wickedness or folly of mankind; but that there should be divine sanction for eternal tragedy after death is a completely inconceivable and indeed a blasphemous notion. Both Blankenburg and Engel stated categorically that Lessing's Faust was to be saved. Hovering over the pandemonium in which his damnation had been the main item on the infernal agenda, an invisible angel announced in clarion tones when it was over: 'Ye shall not conquer!' This celestial being then plunged the hero into a profound slumber and created a phantom in his stead. The deluded devils set about corrupting this *eidolon*, only to see it disappear in the hour of their illusory triumph, and to hear the angelic voice broadcast the good tidings that hell had not been victorious over humanity and that God had not endowed man with the noblest of all instincts (the desire for truth) in order to encompass his eternal ruin. The real Faust then awakes from the dream in which he had seen the fearful fate of his double enacted, and renders thanks to the Almighty for the timely warning. He is now stronger in virtue and truth than ever.

In a conversation with Maler Müller in 1777 about the latter's *Situation in Faust's Life*, Lessing actually suggested that the hero of that scene (who had just reaffirmed his pact with Mephisto) should be led back to salvation and repentance on the model of the parable of the prodigal son. He also praised Müller for his 'ironical' handling of such a pregnant but dangerously quaint theme, and continued:

Anyone who today should attempt to represent such a subject as probable in order to awaken serious belief and conviction in the thing itself, as Dante did in *The Divine Comedy* and Klopstock in *The Messiah*, would be courting failure.[1]

Although Klopstock did not die until 1803 and his *Messiah* had only been completed in 1773, it was already on its way to the libraries which house books never read; and there is much truth

---

[1] R. Petsch, *Lessings Faustdichtung*, Heidelberg, 1911, p. 45.

in Lessing's contention that the age of enlightenment was not propitious to a straightforward treatment of the Faust-legend. The question that thereupon arises is whether or not the Faust-legend would lend itself readily to an 'ironical' rendering.

To judge solely by the report of Lessing's schemes, his solution of the difficulty was also courting disaster. The 'irony' is represented both by the phantom and by the dream, which is rather overdoing it. Had the whole thing been a nightmare, it would at least have had its own unity, and might have been very effective if well developed. But the prologue in hell is outside the dream-sphere, the angel too is real, and the phantom belongs (fittingly enough) to both realms. The use of the phantom Faust inevitably recalls Euripides' *Helen*, which in its turn brings the same author's *Trojan Women* back to the mind: the one a romantic comedy, the other a sublime and heart-searching tragedy. Great drama cannot be written about a phantom; and the 'quaint' assumptions underlying the Faust-legend are not susceptible of such a manipulation. The effort to equate tragic mythology with a humane ethic by dematerializing Faust would have resulted in nonsense, had not Lessing very fortunately lost that mythical box.

And yet Faustian scholars of the present day have actually claimed for Lessing a 'loftier conception' and a 'higher plane' than Marlowe's. Perhaps it was symptomatic of the early twentieth century that those eighteenth-century *clichés* (complete with the 'ennobling of the character' of Faust) seemed to be coming home to roost again. Marlowe's hero was spiritually destroyed, it is true, whereas Lessing's merely had a bad dream; a dream, by the way, from which the eighteenth century as a whole was struggling to awake: the nightmare dream of demonology and witchcraft. This is the historical perspective from which Lessing's Faust plans should be viewed in order to do them justice. His conception was not 'loftier' than Marlowe's; his proposed drama was not on a 'higher plane'; it was on a different plane, the rational plane, the morally optimistic plane, the enlightened plane. The sombre glory of Marlowe's *Tragical History* comes from another, a deeper and a darker world, the world in which Faust was born, and the world to which he belonged. Could he be transplanted into Lessing's and become that anomalous creature I have called an enlightened Faust? Only by denying the basic assumptions of his being and therefore by denying himself. But unless he did this, could he continue to exist in an age which was resolutely putting behind it the belief in such childish things as the devil and hell? If the danger were no longer real, why attempt to represent it?

All these questions must have been seething in Lessing's mind as he hesitated between a 'domesticated' and a 'traditional' Faust, and finally allowed both to disappear unobtrusively in that convenient wooden box. Yet all things are possible to poets; and from the earliest times they can be found reversing mythological assumptions to suit their own conceptions of life. Aeschylus showed mercy usurping the throne of nemesis in the *Oresteia*, and probably also in *Prometheus Unbound*, which was exactly what Lessing was attempting in his dream-drama. Yet there is a vital difference. Orestes' crime would be a crime in any society and would always be regarded with horror, although some religious systems might sanction it in certain circumstances. Moreover it is a crime capable of being committed in any society, whatever its beliefs. But Faust's crime could only be performed (or made credible to the extent of arousing pity and fear) under a religious sytem which believed in the reality of the devil and hell and infernal pacts. Take that belief away, and the hero becomes an allegorical, or at best a symbolical, abstraction.

Marlowe's hero arouses tragic emotions, and so to a lesser degree does the hero of 'Spiess', because his creator expressed through his mouth with the utmost intensity what was then universally held to be true. Euripides did the same in the *Bacchae*. Swept into the orbit of those dramas, no one questions the validity of their assumptions whilst the experience lasts. But 'ironical' treatments of such subjects insist on questions being put. A rational attitude towards Faust might (and evidently did in Lessing's drama) result in his ethical salvation, but spelt his poetical doom.

(b) A lucky Faust, 1775

It seems highly unlikely that *Johann Faust, an allegorical drama* by Paul Weidmann (1746–1810), which appeared anonymously in 1775, owed the idea of the hero's salvation to Lessing; for it is by no means proved that Lessing himself contemplated such a solution before that date, and it is almost certain that none of his friends had any inkling of it until later. If Blankenburg and Engel, to whom we owe our knowledge of Lessing's final intentions, were in the know before 1775, they certainly respected his confidence, and did not reveal the secret until after his death, Blankenburg in 1784, Engel in 1786. Yet there may have been a leakage somewhere, although it is not necessary to postulate one; for not only was the current of thought setting in that direction at the time, but Weidmann showed himself so remarkably original in other respects too that his 'happy ending' may well have been his own unaided invention. Be that as it may, the peak years of Storm and Stress productions, including the year in which Goethe went to Weimar with the completed *Urfaust* in his baggage, were the same years in which an anonymous Austrian playwright rescued Faust publicly in Prague and Munich (1775), in Nördlingen and Ulm (1776). This was certainly an historical occasion for the black magician of legendary fame.

Weidmann's drama represents such a complete break with tradition that only a very impervious or a very ignorant writer could have ventured on the task. Whence Weidmann's inspiration came, it is impossible to say; but he was quite clear that, though Melanchthon and other contemporary authors believed the story to be true, he thought otherwise, and hence the allegorical treatment:

I found something so dark and shattering in the subject, which does not accord well with my imagination, that I could not deny myself the pleasure of describing this tragic human situation and of communicating my ideas on the subject to the public. It is true that Melanchthon and other contemporary historians try to pass it off as a true story; but even if it is only a chimera, it is the sublime privilege of poetry to transcend the limits of what is probable.[1]

Carl Engel (never the most reliable of Faustian scholars) electrified the late nineteenth century by his discovery of this forgotten play, and his declaration that it was none other than Lessing's lost drama. This was soon disproved and the real author brought to light; but the startling coincidence of the similarity between the optimistic assumptions, though it cannot justify, explains the mistake. Moreover Weidmann's drama is almost like a fusion of Lessing's two schemes: the domestic tragedy and the allegorical comedy; for both elements contend uneasily together throughout the action, each ruining whatever feeble chance the other might

[1] P. Weidmann, *Johann Faust*, in K. G. Wendriner, *Die Faustdichtung vor, neben und nach Goethe*, Berlin, 1913, Vol. III, p. 32.

have of arousing any interest. The author began the action on Faust's last day on earth, possibly in the interests of the unity of time. By so doing he sacrificed the opening monologue, the invocation and the pact-scene, although this may have been an unconscious sacrifice, since there is nothing to show that Weidmann had ever read a Faustbook or witnessed a puppet-play. Presuming that he had done so, his determination to adopt a line of his own illustrates the double-edged nature of originality, especially when brought to bear on traditional themes. Weidmann's drama opens with Faust's aged, penurious and virtuous parents who are seeking their son in an opulent palace and being falsely informed by Wagner that he does not live there. Theodore and Elizabeth thereupon retire; but we have not seen the last of them; nor should we wish to do so; for it is possible that, with the exception of the galvanized corpse in Frankfurt, it is their first appearance on any Faustian stage. It seems highly probable at least that the Tirol drama of the late eighteenth century copied Orkanus and Viktoria from Theodore and Elizabeth. But whether this is so or not (and the dating of the Tirol play is conjectural), the parents in Weidmann's drama represent part of an advance-guard of domesticity into the legend, a special instance of the conquest of the boards by the middle-classes, bringing the family-group on to the stage, a composite hero, gaining, it was thought, in breadth what had been relinquished in eminence. Weidmann's *Faust* is therefore another landmark in the revolution inaugurated by Lessing in *Miss Sara Sampson* in 1755.

The Faustbooks, although they sometimes emphasized the virtue and blamelessness of the hero's upbringing, were not interested in family life; and Marlowe was at least equally indifferent to pathetic, plaintive and poverty-stricken parents; but such personages were now greatly in demand in the fashionable domestic drama, and they wormed their maudlin way into the Faust-legend owing to the good offices of Weidmann. They brought in their train two other figures whom Lessing had introduced into *Miss Sara Sampson*, a woman of doubtful virtue and an innocent but dramatically important child. The woman was called Helena in Weidmann's drama and was the mistress of Faust; Edward was the offspring of their unhallowed union. So opaque is the mind of Weidmann that it is not possible to determine whether or not he knew anything of the traditional Helena of the Faust-legend. The Tirol play called a similar heroine Meretrix; in neither is there any vestige of the supernatural nor the slightest reference to a Greek prototype. Actually Helena's original was Lessing's Marwood, an eighteenth-century Medea, a revengeful and menacing woman scorned. Her power over her lover Mellefont, vacillating and contemptible rather than wicked, is vested in the child Arabella, whom she threatens to kill if Mellefont should desert her for virtue and Sara. In exactly the same manner Helena threatens to stab Edward should Faust leave her in the lurch and rejoin his pious and pleading parents. Much more flabby than Marwood, however, she soon becomes enamoured of virtue for its own sake and is ready to embark with Faust on that humble cottage life which would ensure the salvation of her lover. Mephistopheles by seizing Edward as a hostage counters this treachery on her part, and forces her, in order to save the infant, to stab Theodore to death. The mute little hostage clearly owes his existence to Arabella, who indeed was ultimately responsible for a whole nursery of babies and children squeaking, babbling and prattling in the dramas of the Storm and Stress. He has no discoverable connection with the strange little being called Justus Faustus in the Urfaustbook who could foretell the future and disappeared when his father died. Except for the fact that the villain of the piece is a spirit called Mephistopheles, the action so far described is far more like *Miss Sara Sampson* than any version of the Faust-legend which had hitherto appeared; and this may help to account for Engel's amusing blunder. It makes one duly grateful that Lessing's domesticated Faust never saw the light of day.

But Weidmann's action also takes place on a higher plane, the plane he called allegorical; and this is represented by the conflict between Faust's bad angel Mephisto, and his good angel Ithuriel, both in human guise playing the part of friends of the hero. Not only do these two supernatural beings argue and reason with Faust; not only do they ally themselves with his nearest and dearest (Mephisto with Helena and Edward, Ithuriel with Theodore and Elizabeth) in the tug-of-war for his soul; they are also represented contending verbally with each other in two 'cosmic' scenes; and this dramatic development of the situation inherent in the notion of Marlowe's good and bad angels should be put down to Weidmann's credit.

It was a bold notion, from which others were to profit more

than he did; but even so the two scenes in which the cosmic adversaries confront each other are the only tolerable scenes in the drama; and moreover they prepare the reader (and were very necessary to prepare the audiences of 1775) for the final triumph of good over evil and of mercy over justice. Not that Faust himself ever seems to merit anything so excessive as eternal damnation. He occasionally refers to the unthinkable deeds he has committed, and his parents take a very dark view of the luxury by which he is surrounded; he is seen trying to stifle his remorse at a banquet and again by witnessing an erotic mythological ballet; he never can resist the pleadings of Helena, whom he loves devotedly; but he is equally ready to be moved by the admonitions of his parents and the counsels of Ithuriel; he has evidently signed a pact with Mephisto, but no one could regret it more deeply than he; he has used his magical powers to bestow boons on his friends; and although these turn out to be curses by making them rich, beautiful, clever, powerful and so on, he meant no harm; whilst his attempts to ruin an enemy have actually resulted in the spiritual beatitude of the intended victim. Weak as water, unstable as sand, and completely ineffectual, he is such a very poor specimen that neither eternal blessedness nor eternal misery seems to meet his case. He rants at times, and so does Helena, for he was not born in 1775 for nothing; but even so he remains one of the dimmest and dreariest of the countless figures who have borne the name of Faust.

It is therefore not surprising to discover that the *agon* between Ithuriel and Mephisto is on a slightly higher level than any of the scenes in which Faust himself takes a part. This is not entirely due to Weidmann; for Ithuriel was borrowed either from Milton or from Klopstock, and possibly from both. In *Paradise Lost* Ithuriel and Zephon were despatched by Gabriel to discover and thwart the evil machinations of Satan in the Garden of Eden:

> Him there they found
> Squat like a toad, close to the ear of Eve,
> Assaying by his devilish art to reach
> The organs of her fancy, and with them forge
> Illusions as he list, phantasms and dreams. . . .
> Him thus intent Ithuriel with his spear
> Touched lightly. . . .
> Up he starts,

Discovered and surprised . . .
So started up, in his own shape, the Fiend.[1]

Put Mephisto for Satan and Faust for Eve, and this is roughly the situation between the two adversaries when they meet in the second act, although the ensuing dialogue falls far indeed below the level to which Milton rose; nevertheless, especially in the third act, some of the splendour glimmers faintly through Ithuriel's prophecy of final victory. Klopstock transformed Ithuriel into the guardian angel of Judas Iscariot, vainly attempting to avert the tragic treachery, and detailed to be Simon Peter's second guardian after Judas' death. The resemblance of situation is not so close here, for in *The Messiah* Ithuriel's influence is anything but successful and his lot far from enviable; but he knew a moment of great triumph when listening to the virtuous sentiments of Nicodemus:

> Thus spake he, nor recked he aught of the presence of Satan,
> Who might list if he would. But Satan beheld him
> Absorbed in his rapture and foresaw th' inevitable triumph
> Of the seraphs sublimer than he.[2]

In Weidmann's drama Ithuriel's triumph does not come about until Helena has first stabbed Theodore and then herself; until Faust has drunk the poison (preferring that to the other alternatives offered by Mephisto: sword, pistol and rope);[3] and until Elizabeth is also ready to give up the ghost. All the human actors, now at death's door, are praying piteously for mercy, and Faust loudest of all, when Mephisto and his furies appear and begin to prowl round the group transfixed at that moment into corpses. But the triumph of the evil spirit is short-lived; Ithuriel and a host of angels enter, splendidly clad in shining armour, to the accompaniment of thunder and lightning; Mephisto and the furies tremble, the thunder is stilled and Ithuriel announces:

The Almighty whose throne is in the heavens, who with one word can create thousands of worlds from nothingness, who makes the suns to shine and the thunder to roll, Himself has judged the sinners. The scale of justice has found them too light, but infinite mercy has caused their crimes to kick the beam! Tremble, ye wicked, and adore his just

---

[1] *Paradise Lost*, bk. IV.

[2] F. G. Klopstock, *Der Messias*, Canto IV.

[3] For the same *motiv* in the Tirol play, cf. pp. 80 ff. above.

judgments!—He gathers the repentant into his fatherly bosom and hurls you, ye accursed tempters, into eternal hell. (*The thunder roars. Mephistopheles and his companions are felled to the earth.*)

N.B. *During this scene all the stage lighting must be on the side occupied by Ithuriel; the completest darkness must reign on Mephistopheles' side.*[1]

Well produced, that scene might be effective enough, if only anything in the drama had seemed to warrant it; but the incongruous mixture of *Miss Sara Sampson*, *Paradise Lost* and *The Messiah* is too indigestible to be leavened by this transcendental yeast; nor do the satirico-didactic figures of Thunderclap (a lame officer), Nose-to-the-Ground (a pedant-poet), Silvergrub (a usurer), Full-of-Care (a courtier), Beautymad (a coquette), and others of that sort do anything to enliven the tedium of the dramatic proceedings. Unless the very blunt satire they embody be taken for humour, there is no comic relief in Weidmann's *Faust*, and only one joke, made by Wagner when Nose-to-the-Ground asks to be made invisible so that he may spy on his bride. Wagner tells him to return in a week's time; for at the moment he has several regiments of soldiers on his hands who all wish to be made invisible at the frontier. Those scenes in which Wagner is solicited to dispense various magical specifics are meant to amuse; and they possibly represent the seed from which Goethe's similar scene in *Faust, Part II* sprang. They occur in Act I; the more serious pendant in Act II displays the follies and vices of those whom Faust's magic arts have rendered clever and powerful, beautiful and rich. This may have been an off-shoot of the Seven Deadly Sins in Marlowe's drama; and the words written by a shadowy hand in golden letters after the ballet: 'Faust! Evening is falling' may have been inspired by those transparencies which exhibited similar warnings in Latin in the traditional plays.

In spite of these reminiscences, an abyss yawns between Weidmann's *Faust* and the popular stage versions as preserved in the puppet-play texts. The latter are undoubtedly much more dramatic and moving; they are basically poetical, an adjective which could never be applied to Weidmann; and, however embryonically, they exhibit a real spiritual tragedy. Weidmann, on the contrary, purveys moral uplift by means of the allegorical element in a domestic drama of the most conventional and philistine nature

---

[1] Weidmann, *Johann Faust*, ed. cit. Vol. III, p. 118.

imaginable. Yet, if aesthetically he is almost beneath contempt, historically it would be hard to overrate his importance in the development of the Faust-legend in literature. The spirit of the age laboured in Lessing to express itself in an eighteenth-century Faust. It achieved its aim in Weidmann, producing a domesticated hero and a happy ending in one fell swoop; accomplishing in a single drama what Lessing had striven to achieve in two, and openly announcing that the supernatural element must henceforth be regarded as allegorical. A bolder series of innovations could hardly be imagined, nor one executed with such complete *sangfroid* at the psychological moment. Lessing might struggle for the better part of his life to solve an insoluble problem and die without succeeding; Weidmann ruthlessly hacked the Gordian knot in two and presented to his contemporaries the ragged and unsightly ends. It remained to be seen what they could make of them.

(c) *Womanizing Fausts*, 1772–1778

I have also a very nice drawing of Krause's, in which Goethe is sitting reading *Faust* out loud, the Duke of Weimar and all the others round him.[1]

This is a picture to be borne in mind when surveying the Faustian plans, fragments and completed works between Lessing's publication of the speed-scene in 1759 and the appearance of Goethe's *Faust I* in 1808. All kinds of elements, old and new, were flung into the Faustian melting-pot during this period by eager and anxious alchemists who were only partially in the know about Lessing's plans until 1784, and not fully enlightened about Goethe's even when he published the *Fragment* in 1790. Both were felt as a challenge; speculation and inside information acted as a ferment; and since Goethe had communicated the main outlines of the Gretchen tragedy to a wide circle of literary friends, and Weidmann had publicized the redemption of Faust, these two revolutionary notions were factors to be reckoned with by the poets and dramatists of the Storm and Stress period who tackled the legend. Goethe is supposed to have taken the idea of Gretchen from the virtuous servant girl whom Faust vainly attempted to seduce in Pfitzer's version of Widman's Faustbook, an episode

[1] Letter from Merck to Lenz, 8 March 1776; given by M. N. Rosanow in *Jakob M. R. Lenz*, Leipzig, 1909, p. 542.

included in the condensed account by the Christlich Meynender; and it is possible that this anonymous young heroine played a minor part in the infiltration of the domestic element into the Faustian organism. The tendency to associate Faust with a real woman instead of the legendary Helena is apparent in Weidmann's play; and the theme of seduction often coupled with infanticide had been gaining popularity ever since the days of *Miss Sara Sampson*. It was now at the height of its prestige: Lenz in *The Private Tutor*, 1774, and *The Soldiers*, 1776; Klinger in *The Suffering Woman*, 1775; and Wagner in *The Infanticide*, 1776, all contributed their versions of a social tragedy which held an incalculable appeal for that age. Moreover the general tendency since *Emilia Galotti* in 1772 was to represent the woman involved as of lower social standing than her betrayer, helpless before the glamour of nobility; and this made of a titanically-conceived Faust a fit and proper person to play the part of seducer. One hardly knows whether to say that the Gretchen *motiv* entered the Faust-legend in the 1770s or that the Faust *motiv* entered domestic tragedy. They gravitated together naturally; and if they had not fused in Goethe's mind, they would have fused (indeed they were already fusing) elsewhere. It is not therefore in the combination of two heterogeneous elements in the *Urfaust* that Goethe's originality is most manifest, it is in the manner of their fusion, the level at which he combined them.

Lessing levered them up on to the plane of enlightened literature, where he proved finally incapable of dealing with Faust. Weidmann, combining the Faust theme with the *Miss Sara Sampson* theme, reduced both to utter absurdity in the forlorn attempt to mate allegory and realism. But Goethe saw that the sixteenth-century sorcerer and the maid betrayed were both inhabitants of the world of folk-tales and poetry and could meet in those regions naturally. His opening monologue, beginning in Hans Sachsian doggerel, set the key in which the *Urfaust* was composed; and however much it rose above the level of that naïve rhythm, the poem kept on returning to it. Soaring upward, swooping down, air-borne and earth-bound, it was there as the basic harmony of the whole. Moreover Goethe had steeped himself in the study of medieval alchemy and mysticism and was acquainted with the works of Faust's great contemporary Paracelsus. This ministered to his own inborn feeling for mystery, nature and the oneness of all life, welling up from submerged mental depths where the legend itself had its being. Lessing's enlightened Faust had summoned up the shade of Aristotle, Goethe's hero called to the Earth Spirit, and it came in a terrible guise ('in a repulsive form'), as was rumoured to be the custom with the elemental spirits as well as with the fiends. This operation, if not exactly white magic, since no angel was invoked, was not black magic either. It belonged to that mixed type which practitioners believed to be innocent, but which was considered by others to be excessively dangerous, and generally ended in delivering up the exorcists into the power of the fiends.[1] Hence the apparition's rejection of Faust and its prophetic allusion to Mephisto before it vanished, a brief and glorious incarnation of the dreams of Paracelsus, Bruno and Swedenborg, shedding the aura of real magic over the opening scene of the drama: dazzling and disillusioning in one breath. The following conversation with Wagner shows that this engaging and aspiring pedant was modelled rather on his namesake in the puppet-plays, where he enacted a sober and virtuous part, than on the graceless young scamp of the folkbooks, who followed in his master's footsteps and inherited his magical texts. But the notion of looking up to and imitating Faust as a disciple is the same. It will be remembered that Mephisto promised the puppet nigromancers to perform their academic functions for them. He is now discovered fulfilling that promise by giving the most pernicious counsel to a young freshman, gibing at the faculties of logic, metaphysics and medicine, advocating sensuality, satirizing all the manifestations of University life mercilessly and more than satisfied with the probable results. This gave Goethe scope to make merry over the University of Leipzig and at the same time to expand those criticisms of the academic disciplines which (since Marlowe's day) had been a constant feature of the first monologue, but which he had passed over rapidly in the wonderful opening speech. In the same fashion *Auerbach's Cellar* combined the folkbook tales about Faust's magic pranks, many of them performed for the benefit of University students, with vivid memories of wine, woman and song which he himself had enjoyed in the seat of learning.

The four-line scene 'On the High Road' is also both traditional and subjective. Mephisto's fear of the cross or the crucifix and his forcible juxtaposition with it are to be found variously represented

[1] Cf. the story of Thomas Parkes in my *Ritual Magic*, pp. 281 ff.

in art and poetry, on the stage and in the puppet-plays. They figured, too, in the Faustian Black Book *Magia naturalis et innaturalis*, where the terrible demon Aciel was forced to kneel before the crucifix and swear by it that he would keep his word.[1] Mephisto's repugnance to the sight, as they passed it on the high-road, was in line with Goethe's own attitude, privately and publicly expressed.

All these loosely-connected episodes at the opening of the dramatic poem stem from tradition and yet have such an individual stamp that no reader can fail to see in the hero a projection of Goethe's youthful personality. It was an identification which struck down to the very roots of his dualism; he was Faust and Mephisto too: the satire on Leipzig and the recoil from the cross both witness to that. If the arch-enemy of mankind has lost considerably in stature when compared with Marlowe's mighty fiend, and is undeniably less impressive than the terrible familiar of the Urfaustbook, this is because, as he himself confessed later, he was only a fraction of the whole: slighter and lighter than his creator, pure intellect and therefore devoid of temperament, completely cynical, a master of irony and persiflage; but never, even at his most diabolic, going beyond those potentialities for baseness which lurk in humanity itself.

His icy coldness permeates the Gretchen tragedy and conditions it. Unfolded after the fashion of ballad-poetry, moving forward by leaps and bounds, with much left unuttered and much said by song, poignant, lovely, simple and sad, it found a place for the sinister forces which haunt folk-poetry, condensing them in the person of Mephisto, that satanic third in the human conflict. This miraculous fusion of black magic and pure love (Mephisto and Gretchen) is the high watermark of Goethe's youthful genius and probably of his whole poetical life; it sprang forth, as if by magic, from the ballads of the past. The dynamic energy of the poem is directed to detaching Gretchen from everything and everybody around her capable of saving the situation. Her father, her most important natural protector, is dead before the action begins; her mother (who dies before the crisis, owing to the action of the sleeping-draught) is too severe and too rigid to win the girl's complete confidence. She is therefore thrown into the arms of Frau Marthe, as Juliet was thrown into the arms of her nurse;

---

[1] Cf. my *Ritual Magic*, p. 177.

and both these well-meaning counsellors help to precipitate the tragedy, because they are fundamentally wanton light o' loves. Mephisto immediately nosed out Frau Marthe as the ideal go-between and exploited her possibilities to the full in that inimitable scene which echoes back again to Hans Sachs. Furthermore the distance between Faust and Gretchen, social, intellectual and spiritual, brought out whenever they meet, and vividly exposed in the religious discussion, is another isolating factor. After the seduction the growing solitude of the apprehensive girl among her own kind and the censoriousness of her one-time playmates is brought home by the spiteful gossip of Lieschen about Bärbelchen at the well. Another leap forward in time shows Gretchen, frightened and desperate, appealing to the Mater Dolorosa for help. The anguished cry is answered in the cathedral by the evil spirit whispering in her ear that her sins are too great to be pardoned, that she has brought about her mother's death, and is bearing in her body the stigma of a guilty and shameful love. He speaks to the fearful accompaniment of the hymn about the Day of Doom and Judgment, expressing the collective belief of the crowd all round her and also of her own. It is the very voice of the wrath of God, proclaiming an isolation so absolute and terrible that darkness blots out everything and she swoons away. Outcast from divine mercy and about to be delivered into ruthless human hands, she has nothing to hope for from the one remaining member of her own family, her young soldier-brother Valentine, whose narrow personal sense of honour is up in arms against her; and Faust's wild outburst against his own dangerous and destructive nature and the despairing prophecy of how his ruinous passion will inevitably destroy her show that his unavailing self-tormenting remorse will hasten rather than avert the looming catastrophe.

It has taken place irretrievably when Faust and Mephisto are met with after another downward plunge of the action. Half out of her mind with panic, Gretchen has committed infanticide and is now incarcerated and awaiting execution. Faust, overwhelmed by the fate that has overtaken her whilst he had callously left her to her own devices, hurls titanic invectives at the head of the unruffled Mephisto, during which it becomes clear that the latter had been sent to him by the Earth Spirit and was the unholy result of his evocations. It is further in line with magical tradition as enshrined in the Black Books that Faust threatens Mephisto with the most fearful curse, to last for thousands of years, unless he obeys him on the instant and saves Gretchen. Mephisto then promises to do what he can, and they make off together, passing the criminal gallows on their magic steeds, and glimpsing shadowy figures making dedicatory gestures before the place of execution as they storm past. They are witches according to Mephisto, and this weird tableau reminds one of *Macbeth*; it is on the same eerie plane as the episode 'On the High Road'.

The final scene in prison, although written in prose like the two preceding ones, seems to be saying what Gretchen says in her agony of mind: 'They are singing songs about me: . . . but it is a fairy-tale that ends like that, they are not singing it about me.' For the universal aspect, the primitive folk-poetry aspect, is concentrated in a way that positively rivets the attention. Not only does Gretchen, half-demented with grief, sing a gruesome ballad of guilt, cruelty and infanticide (as Ophelia before her had sung about illicit love); but the whole lay-out of the scene recalls those tragic songs in which snatches of heart-breaking dialogue are heard amidst the fearful preparations for death as the victim mounts the scaffold. And as the grey dawn creeps upon this desolating scene, her wedding-day with death, the pattern of the whole becomes clear. It is based on the *aubades* or *albas* of the *Minnesinger*, in which two lovers who must separate at dawn to avoid discovery and danger are warned by a watchman that the hour is at hand and refuse to believe it. Alternatively one of the lovers warns the other, as in *Romeo and Juliet*, where the nurse plays the part of watchman, whereas Mephisto plays it here. In both tragedies the two lovers are on the eve of an eternal separation, the one urges speed and flight, the other is unpersuadable, although Juliet gives in to the parting at last. Shakespeare's rendering and Goethe's have only the model in common; a comparison between them brings out the German poet's far greater closeness to folk-poetry, for he treats it with the brevity and simplicity which it had assumed when, abandoning the art of the court, it penetrated to more primitive levels. Shakespeare's scene is much more highly wrought and more nearly resembles the original model.

This summit of Faustian poetry was practically complete in 1775, whereas the traditional story of Faust had hardly been begun by Goethe before he broke it off in its fragmentary and inconclusive state. Those who heard it read out loud will doubtless have been impressed; but the Gretchen tragedy must have had a far greater effect. It certainly had an immediate and unforeseen reaction, Wagner's *Infanticide* in 1776, in which the sleeping-draught, the swoon in church, the parallel case, and the distraught crooning of folk-songs by the heroine were clearly bare-faced plagiarisms from the *Urfaust*. Not only that, but Mephisto's cynical sneer: 'She is not the first' was echoed by the seducer. 'You are not the first,' he exclaimed when faced with his victim's dire distress after the accomplished fact. Goethe had every right to be annoyed and to be less expansive about his poetical plans ever afterwards; but, despite the petty thefts and the similarity of the theme, the two works are so totally and utterly different that neither suffers from a comparison with the other. Not only is there no other Faustian element in Wagner's play than a Mephistophelian false friend of the far from titanic hero; but the crass and at times masterly realism, crossed with didactic and melodramatic elements in Wagner's unequal but powerful drama (which opens in a disreputable house and ends with the infanticide committed on the stage), puts it on another plane where it can exist in its own rights. Its relationship with the Gretchen tragedy is superficial; but it illustrates the vigour and vitality of the secondary theme which Goethe grafted on to the legendary parent-stem.

Gretchen herself represented a triumph for girlhood in the modernization of the myth, in which women were now demanding their rights as creatures of flesh and blood rather than as glamorous phantoms. Weidmann's Helen was a sign of that. Another straw flickering maliciously in the wind was the engaging story by Count Hamilton, *L'Enchanteur Faust*, written about 1700 but not published until 1777 in his *Œuvres Diverses*. It was immediately translated into German by Mylius, Schink doing the occasional verse, and appeared in 1778. The speed with which it was brought to Germany is symptomatic of Faust's rapid rise in literary esteem in the land of his birth. Hamilton's wicked and witty trifle presents the magician at the court of Queen Elizabeth, who, with Sidney and Essex dancing attendance, watches like a lynx whilst the exorcist summons up at her command four famous beauties of the past: Helen of Troy, Marianne, Cleopatra and Fair Rosamund. The point of the tale is the light-hearted fun at Elizabeth's expense. Inordinately and unjustifiably vain, she makes derogatory comments on the personal appearance and habiliments of the first three as they appear one after the other. Sidney and Essex uneasily agree, stifle their own admiration and dispense that flattery to the royal virgin which was her object in commanding the display. Fair Rosamund had a much warmer reception, because it had been craftily announced beforehand that she bore a striking resemblance to the Queen, although far inferior to her in beauty. After she had disappeared, nothing would satisfy Elizabeth but that she should be summoned again. In vain did Faust warn them all that this was a difficult and dangerous thing to do, and apt to anger the spirits; the Queen insisted. The magician undertook extreme and exhausting efforts to conjure Fair Rosamund back, and at length she stepped down into the gallery through an open window:

> The Doctor was bathed in sweat, and whilst he was mopping his brow, the Queen, who thought her incomparably more amiable than on her first appearance, forgot her usual prudence in a transport of affection, and quitted the circle with open arms, exclaiming: 'Oh, my dear Rosamund!' Hardly had she pronounced the words before a violent clap of thunder shook the whole palace, a thick black vapour filled the gallery, and several little baby flashes of lightning snaked round their ears, to right and to left of the petrified party. The obscurity having gradually dissipated, the magician was seen stretched on his back, legs and arms in the air, his bonnet to one side of him, his wand to the other and his magical Koran between his legs. No one in this adventure got off scot-free.[1]

Undoubtedly this high-spirited story was at the back of Goethe's mind when he came to represent the raising of Helen and Paris in *Faust II*. But more interesting just now is the intrusion of the 'eternal feminine' in the shape of Queen Elizabeth into the traditional conjuration-scene. In the Faustbooks Helen had been summoned up at the request of University students, Alexander the Great and others at the command of the Emperor Charles V. In the puppet-plays conjurations of the spirits of the dead were undertaken to delight a Duke of Parma, or a King of Hungary, or some other potentate; nevertheless the consort of the ruler began to make herself felt in these scenes; the magician made advances to her, and she responded or not as the case might be. In Hamilton's story the command-performance is for a queen; the male

---

[1] Cf. A. Tille. *Die Faustsplitter in der Literatur des sechzehnten und achtzehnten Jahrhunderts*, Berlin, 1900; cf. p. 343 for the original version; pp. 753f. for the German translation.

element has shrunk to the status of courtier. The coming deluge of womanhood into what had been a peculiarly masculine legend could hardly have been more gaily foreseen.

If the 'eternal feminine' came off rather badly in this story, her next appearance was in the guise of a domesticated angel of salvation. This was in Schink's little operetta, *Doctor Faust, a Comic Duo-drama*, 1778. Expanded in 1782 under the title *The New Faust* it found its way on to the Augsburg puppet-stage, where it was called *Johann Faust or Hoaxing the Doctor*. It was well housed in the booths, as Schink, who modestly deprecated any expectation of 'a *Faust* such as Lessing, Goethe and Müller are writing', might possibly have agreed. From this unassuming beginning onwards to his magnum Faustian opus, Schink was always on the side of his 'lord and master' Lessing, and therefore on the side of the angels. He never faltered in his determination that his Faust should be saved, and saved moreover by the love of a pure woman, an expedient which Lessing had certainly not contemplated. In the operetta a fascinating young widow (called Dorinde in the introduction but thereafter Rosalinde), who had fallen in love with Faust, determined to cure him of his nigromantic leanings. She therefore disguised herself in male attire as a student to incite him further and to bring matters to a head by means of a book of conjurations which she presented to him. She next dressed up as a devil, in which shape she tempted him to sell his soul for knowledge and then mocked at him for his folly; finally she appeared before him as Helen of Troy and put him to the following test. If he could withstand her, his contract would be returned to him and his soul would be saved. He was therefore in the same dilemma as his tragic namesakes on the stage and in the puppet-plays; and like them he chose eternal damnation for the sake of Helen. But *amor vincit omnia*. Rosalinde discovered herself and her philanthropic plot, and wedding-bells were set a-ringing. It is hopeless nonsense, but agreeable nonsense. Schink had a slight but pleasing lyrical gift, very much to the fore in the recurrent snatches of song. More than that, some of Faust's speeches sound well; and the short conjuring-scene is not altogether unimpressive:

Chorus
Who called us, who called from the void and the whirling,
Who called us aloft from abysses dark-swirling,
Who called us from flames that are roaring below?

Faust

What voices are these? Is it wings that I hear?
They are coming, the spirits, they come and fell fear
Doth seize me as down sinks the night.
Where are you? For darkness covers my sight.
Let the night be gone, and the day be near!
Spirits of evil, appear, appear!

Chorus

We're coming, we're coming in dim moonlight,
We are here. What wouldst thou? We know thy might,
We fear thee; we rise from the abyss to thee.[1]

There is something curiously Goethean in the conception and at times in the language of this musical playlet. It reminds one again and again of the minor poet in Goethe who cohabited so peaceably with the transcendent genius, and was for ever flinging off trifles like this, which have charm and lightness, if not much else, to recommend them. When reading this half-serious, half-gay, half-mocking, half-warning operetta, one feels that Goethe would have enjoyed it; though it was probably inspired by Lessing's Faustian schemes and his youthful comedy, *The Young Scholar*, in which much heavier fun is poked at excessive learning and pedantry. But it is strange indeed to think that, if Lessing was the first to envisage a happy ending to Faust's situation, Schink was the first to conceive the notion of a woman as the agent of redemption. It is represented playfully in an operetta written by a man with a very mediocre mind, a mind almost as mediocre as Weidmann's; and yet the result not only anticipated the solution offered in *Part II*, but also bears a haunting resemblance in the texture of the style to Goethe's lighter works.

[1] Scheible, *Das Kloster*, Vol. v, p. 899.

CHAPTER V

STORM-TOSSED FAUSTS

(a) A titanic Faust, 1776–1778

> We've put behind us
> All that did bind us;
> As the wind free,
> God-like are we![1]

It would seem to be a fortunate conjunction of circumstances which brought the Faust-myth, that wandering star of legend, across the literary firmament in Germany at the very moment when a galaxy of talent was observable on the poetical horizon. Under the sign of the Storm and Stress, surely, Faust would conquer for himself a permanent position in the literary heavens; for there were elements in that explosive movement peculiarly and almost explicitly Faustian. England had played her signal part in achieving immortality for the legend, and now two other countries, although much less directly, helped to condition its German rebirth. No one will ever appreciate the Storm and Stress, so unduly derided, so little understood, who does not realize that it was impregnated from the beginning with Slavonic elements; that Hamann, the Wizard of the North, came from the Baltic provinces, and so did Lenz, who died in the streets of Moscow; whilst Klinger also gravitated to that country where he spent the greater part of his life. It was from Hamann that the great seminal ideas proceeded which made the movement what it was; Hamann from whom Herder, the East Prussian, derived his enthusiasms; and it was Herder who revolutionized and fertilized the mind of the youthful Goethe. Hamann's proclamation of the daimonic nature of genius and its untutored, inspired knowledge and power fired one inflammable mind after the next; and his belief that poetry is the mother-tongue of the human race changed the face of contemporary aesthetic opinion. Hardly less important was the manner

[1] M. N. Rosanow, *Lenz, der Dichter der Sturm- und Drangperiode*, Leipzig, 1911, p. 145; written by Lenz.

of his delivery. Oracular, obscure, enthusiastic, rhapsodical, it created a new style and set up a new ideal. Greatness rather than perfection was now felt to be the goal, an incommensurable greatness and limitless spiritual horizons. These dimensions and the dynamic impetus towards extremes are essentially Slavonic. The voice of the Wizard of the North was answered by the Wizard of the South, the Swiss pastor Lavater, whose deeply religious but indiscriminate fervour, whose reverence for greatness, which he saw wherever he looked, had something of the sensational sublimity of Swiss scenery, and added that note of extravagance, that lack of proportion and humour which is the Germanic equivalent of Slavonic immensities. From these two seething sources of inspiration the movement took its being; and all the rest—the worship of great men, the enthusiasm for folk-poetry, for the Bible, for Homer, Shakespeare, the English sentimentalists and Rousseau—followed as a matter of course.

It was a heady ferment, producing something like a literary explosion which scattered seeming works of genius broadcast over Germany; Goethe, Gerstenberg, Maler Müller, Klinger, Leisewitz, Lenz, Wagner and finally Schiller each flung at least one red-hot product of poetic or dramatic inspiration into the common pool, and most of them contributed more. Then the spurts of energy became feebler and soon all was over and the *débris* was swept away. With the exception of Goethe and Schiller, the virtue had gone out of them and they died young, whether actually, or poetically, or mentally as in the saddest case of all, that of the unhappy Lenz. The latter bore the stigmata of genius as well as of insanity; but the others, gifted and enthusiastic, became violently creative under the spell woven by Hamann, Lavater and Herder, and then relapsed into more normal existence.

The signs were singularly propitious for the rebirth of Faust. Utterly antagonistic to the rationalism of enlightenment, the Storm and Stress writers betrayed no disposition to shirk the supernatural assumptions of the legend; and in particular they were drawn to rather than repelled by the dark demonological aspect and the inferno raging in minds distraught. Moreover their preference was for heroes of titanic stature whose magnanimous spirits were darkened by some tragic stain. Greatness was by no means synonymous with goodness in their eyes; it was in a different category of values. This fruitful aesthetic concept had been forgotten during the period of enlightenment; it now determined the attitude to heroism. As the young writers were emotionally rather callow their efforts to depict titanism often degenerated into rant, but their will-to-greatness saved them from downright puerility; and the nature of the ideal with which they were all grappling is illustrated by Goethe's preoccupation with Ahasuerus, Prometheus, Socrates, Julius Caesar and Mohammed, before compromising with *Götz von Berlichingen* and finally turning to Faust. Gerstenberg portrayed moral greatness in his Ugolino, allied with the granite pride, the ruthless ambition and the uncontrollable wrath which had brought him to the pass where his heroic endurance increased his stature. Guelfo in Klinger's *Twins*, great-souled but hag-ridden by satanic pride, ends as the murderer of his brother; Guido in Leisewitz's drama *Julius von Tarent* and Müller's Cain are hounded by envy and jealousy along the same path; whilst the original nobility of Müller's Golo ends in fearful moral degradation brought about by thwarted and ungovernable passion. Nearly all the heroes tend to be supermen, and incline to be hero-villains: Gerstenberg's Ugolino and Goethe's Götz are at one end of the scale; Guelfo, Guido, Golo and Karl Moor at the other. Generally speaking, original magnanimity is the mainspring of their actions; they are daimon-driven, according to Hamann's conception of genius. However questionable and even dangerous aesthetically this ideal was, it was obviously more likely to produce a convincing Faust than Lessing's notion of a high-souled dreamer, let alone Weidmann's solution of an amorous weakling.

Maler Müller (1749–1825), as his title implies, was a painter-poet; he achieved distinction in neither field, ending his days as an unsuccessful artist in Rome; but his beginnings were instinct with promise. To compare the Faust fragments he published in 1776 and 1778 with his later schemes is to become vividly aware of the deterioration he and others underwent once the inspiration emanating from Hamann had died down. Yet he went on labouring at his *Faust* until the end of his life, and certainly produced in the early years the most characteristically storm-tossed of them all:

Lessing and Goethe are both working at a *Faust*. I did not know that, at least not at the time when I felt impelled to write this thing down. Faust was always one of the favourite heroes of my childhood, because I took him at once to be a great man, who knew his own strength and was irked by the rein with which fortune and fate checked him. . . . To soar upwards to the very height of one's powers, to become completely what one feels that one could become—that is surely innate in all of us. . . . Who would not venture to the topmost rung of the ladder of fame and honour? . . . If self-interest and self-love are the mainsprings which propel the world, what wonder that a strong man should assert his rights and seek out another being to content him, even if this hardihood should drive him beyond the confines of the natural world. There are moments in life, who has not felt that and felt it a thousand times, when the heart overreaches itself and when even the best and noblest man alive passionately desires to outdistance and outstrip himself, in defiance of justice and law.[1]

This is the very voice of the Storm and Stress speaking through Müller, and speaking much more explosively and vehemently than is apparent in translation. As one would expect from a writer of this calibre, his Faustian drama opens with a pandemonium in a ruined Gothic church; and as one would also expect from one's general knowledge of the man and the movement, it is not a striking success. The wilful lack of aesthetic restraint, the belief that power was synonymous with violence, the besetting sin of the whole group, the uncouth style varying between strident fustian and hysterical guffaws' make the whole excessively tedious. The criticism of contemporary society, with special reference to the nullity of poets and artists, is too topical to be interesting; the ugliness and the noise are overdone. But the scene improves markedly towards the end. The underlying idea that the world is barren of great men, the reason for the diabolical conference, begins to assume dramatic importance when Lucifer announces that he is proposing to abandon humanity altogether and to tempt them no more, since there are no souls to be found who are worthy of the tragic fate of damnation and hell:

Berlicki, Vizlipuzli. Hold, oh King!

Mephistopheles. Hold!

Lucifer. And why? If you are speaking in praise of humanity, my rod shall smite your neck, and I will trample all those under foot who dare to disagree with me even in their thoughts.

[1] F. Müller, *Fausts Leben Dramatisiert*, in *Sturm und Drang*, ed. Freye, Berlin, n.d. Vol. IV, p. 225.

Mephistopheles. I have been going up and down and round about the earth and have found, as you say, flabbiness and feebleness in abundance, a middling amount of strength and firmness and little that is glorious or great.

Lucifer. Nothing, absolutely nothing! Who is great? Come, tell me: Where is greatness to be found in the world? If I could discover one single great man, one solitary specimen of strength and firmness, of whom one could say: 'He is ripe and ready';—do you dare to tell me that you can show me a man like that?

Mephistopheles. Here's my hand on it.[1]

This Job-like conversation (going widdershins) serves to introduce the name of Faust as the one great man who is to justify humanity in the eyes of Lucifer. Calling his seven minions, Mephisto proclaims that Faust shall that very night summon them up from the depth of hell. A wild outburst of jubilant malice in spirited doggerel from these fiends, who have already prepared the way by engineering Faust's financial ruin, brings the prologue to a stirring close. Radically shortened and toned down, it would make an effective introduction to the action.

This opens with a dialogue in near-Yiddish between two frenzied Jews who have learnt of the flight of an absconding debtor and, gabbling and gesticulating, lay their plans for squeezing the ducats from Faust, who had stood surety for the debt. The shade of Shylock dwarfs his German progeny, who nevertheless in their realistic squalor vividly represent the intolerable pressure which the sordid side of existence exercises upon soaring minds such as Faust's, who is musing restlessly in his study:

Why only five senses with such boundless feelings? Why so constricted the power to perform? . . . I feel how the god flaming in my blood falters and yields to my mortal sinews and frame. . . . Adored divinity, thou mirror of my soul, what message is thine? Skill and intellect, honour and fame, knowledge, achievement, power and wealth; everything wherewith to be the godhead of this world, in very truth the god! A voracious lion roars in my breast, for I am the first and foremost of mankind.[2]

A titanic spirit such as this could never be brought to brook abject

---

[1] Müller, *Fausts Leben Dramatisiert*, ed. cit. Vol. IV, p. 235.

[2] Ibid. pp. 239f. Faust is represented as reading this passage from a book of which he must have certainly been the author.

poverty nor confinement in a debtor's prison; and so lofty a mind would suffer cruelly from the knowledge that the money he had forfeited belonged morally at least to his struggling family dependants. This distressing aspect of the situation is revealed in a conversation between Wagner and a student called Eckius; whereas the malice and hatred of pretentious mediocrity for aspiring minds is concentrated in the person of Magister Knellius, who hopes to ruin Faust irretrievably. He has reckoned without the student population however, which is Faust's to a man, a turbulent, riotous, unmanageable element, equally enthusiastic in love and in hate. By placing his action in a University setting, Müller achieved realism whilst also showing himself mindful of tradition. The academic *milieu* in which the legend arose had played a very atrophied part in the puppet-plays and Weidmann had ignored it completely. Goethe was reintroducing it in the *Urfaust*; but Müller went considerably further by bringing the background of the Faustbooks into the foreground of his action. In 'Spiess' the hero was represented as a University man who was much in the company of the students. His carousals with them, the boon-fellowship and skylarking he indulged in, his production of Helen of Troy for their delectation; his last banquet with these 'dear friends' and his piteous confession and farewell to them, their horror, compassion and grief—all this represents the human side of the life of the black magician. Müller brought it strongly to the fore in his dramatization of the opening scenes, and used it with some skill for the sake of the contrast it offered between the brooding and tormented hero and his care-free, indeed devil-may-care, associates:

Kölbel. You've missed the most glorious fun. There are two Strasbourg girls here, whom I used to be very intimate with, and there's a regular old beaver of an uncle with them playing Argus. It was an awful bore at first; you couldn't say a word to either that he didn't hear; and as for getting one of them alone, what a hope! . . . At last Herz came to the rescue, the old rascal, put on his landlady's clothes (you know that fat dressmaker), made up his face just like a woman's, and I introduced him to uncle and nieces as an old acquaintance of mine and called him a school-master's wife. And by Jove you should have seen how well he played the part; that man's a born actor. . . . I looked for you at once to share the fun, for they're two jolly nice girls, so come along and join us. Aren't you listening? I say, Faust! He doesn't hear me. He's staring round like a sleep-walker; what's the matter with him? And what is he muttering between his teeth? Faust!

Faust. It would be shameful not to venture;—perilous to undertake it, and yet shameful to abstain! Whence this concentration of my thoughts on one point to which they keep returning, a point where all fortune's gifts lie spread out at my feet? My soul resists and suspects some dangerous presence near which would fain snare me, the instinct of the dove when the marten is at the cote. I feel a beating and a hovering all round me urging me onward without surcease. Let it be what it may, follow I must.[1]

The combination of Charley's Aunt and the powers of evil runs throughout the action, a grotesque and gruesome contrast between light-hearted ragging and a fearful spiritual danger. It emphasizes the isolation of Faust from those who are nearest to him, as he goes forward into regions where they cannot penetrate and where even the most devoted cannot follow. But before surrendering outright to the sinister temptation, he tries to retrieve his fortunes in a gambling-den, a step duly reported to Knellius by his spies, and which nearly ends in arrest. Trapped and surrounded, he hears voices and sees visions of wealth, power, honour, pleasure and glory; for the evil spirit is at hand, and urges Faust to summon him to his aid. Faust does this, although not by a formal invocation, but much in the same fashion as Goethe's hero calls up the Earth Spirit, by expressing a fervent desire for his appearance. A scarlet-clad stranger enters, and after a short conversation in which Faust comes to the conclusion that he was fated to become the Columbus of hell, and that his very hesitations and misgivings were all part of the plan, he allows the stranger to rescue him from his plight. The police are now thundering at the door, all the other gamblers have fled; there is a great uproar, a very effective urgent dialogue in doggerel in which a chorus of devils joins; and, as the door bursts open and the crowd rushes in, Faust disappears with the stranger through the air. He has put himself into the power of the fiends by accepting their assistance.

This fateful capitulation in a moment of stress was unnecessary. The students were hot on the heels of the police and determined to rescue him. They make up for their disappointment at finding

---

[1] Müller, *Fausts Leben Dramatisiert*, ed. cit. Vol. IV, pp. 249f.

him gone by savaging Knellius and they rally round Faust with wild enthusiasm when he appears among them in the market-place. Conspicuous amongst them is Herz, whose relationship with Faust is modelled on that between Falstaff and Prince Hal, Herz being a fat, jolly and lovable rogue who is bewildered and hurt by the change in his former boon-companion; for the latter is withdrawing from his intimacy and is no longer willing to join in noisy and undignified pleasures. Deaf to the voice of comradeship, he is shaken by the pleadings of his old father, who has heard rumours of the pass to which his son has come and appears in Ingolstadt to warn and save him. There is tragic power in the scene between them, in which diabolic voices mingle, unheard by the father but audible to the son, insisting that he should keep his word and meet them that same midnight. For the paternal intervention is too late: the irretrievable step has been taken. The father retires to rest and pray; his lost son creeps out to the cross-roads; whilst Kölbel brings a charming serenade to Gretchen from Strasbourg and a night-watchman is heard telling the hours.

The conjuration-scene is based on the traditional trial by speed as reconditioned by Lessing. It is not unimpressive and the sinister doggerel chanted by the fiends at intervals seems in truth to come from the nether regions. The first devil, Curballo, claims the speed of light, and Faust answers that he is both too slow and too fast for him. Sight and hearing are quicker than light; moreover:

Does not man often wish to clip the wings of time? How often in life is one fain to call out in its sweet moments: *da capo*![1]

This almost anticipates Goethe's Faust in the pact-scene. The second devil, also very speedy, is sin. The third, called Mogol, offers gold and all the buried treasure in the earth and the sea. Cacall, the fourth, is lechery; and Faust rejects him because he feels too old for this. The fifth, Pferdtoll the destroyer, is told to wait till the last trump. The sixth promises to fulfil all Faust's wishes with lightning speed, and once more a wrangle about the nature of speed sets in. The seventh offers Faust a fresh world, an entirely new creation where the sun of the magician will rise and set; but before this dazzling gift can be examined, the seven exclaim that their master is near and sink down out of sight. Faust falls into an entranced slumber, and Mephisto appears and holds

[1] Müller, *Fausts Leben Dramatisiert*, ed. cit. Vol. IV, p. 29.

a tragic soliloquy over the victim who is to surrender his soul, and whom he must destroy despite the love he experiences for Faust as a part of that world of light from which he is an exile in the dark depths of hell.

Had Müller possessed the vital virtue of aesthetic restraint as manifest in selection and concentration, this first act of *Faust's Life Dramatized* would have been a notable contribution to Faustian literature. The titanism of the hero and his fearful isolation amidst the riotous life surging round him; the hero-worship he inspires in the students who feel his greatness but do not fathom him; the harrowing scene with his father; the sinister atmosphere distilled by the fiends who approach him; the tragic devil who is to destroy him: all this endows the subject with grandeur and power. But if the conception is extraordinarily interesting, the execution almost kills it. Müller's volubility and verbosity, the inordinate length of the scenes and the speeches, long-winded and unnecessary episodes and a very imperfect style make this act a labour to read and quite impossible to produce. This is all the more regrettable because the realism of the setting has contributed in a remarkable way to enhance the supernatural action. The ordinary everyday life depicted, far from injuring the theme, acts like a floodlight illuminating the hidden recesses of a dark and desperate soul.

The second act, published two years before the first under the title *A Situation in Faust's Life*, is more dramatic but much less powerful. It also opens with a pandemonium, in which Mephisto reports that the first twelve years of his service with Faust will be up at midnight; and that, according to the contract, he must remind his master that half the term is run and that Faust may, if he so desires, break the agreement. This combines two traditional themes. In the Urfaustbook the hero was forced to ratify the first pact by signing a second after his attempts to repent owing to the persuasion of the good old man. Müller seized upon the notion of a second chance given and rejected in that episode and linked it up with the scene in the puppet-plays which showed Faust at the climax of his fame as a practising magician, performing before some monarch, duke or prince. He is here represented at the court of Spain, madly in love with the Queen of Aragonia and about to pledge her after having produced a marvellous magical display. Invisible to all but the magician, Mephisto intervenes and offers him the contract to destroy if he will:

... but in that selfsame moment that you touch it with the tip of your little finger, you will be again what you were before, a down-trodden, wretched, starving beggar ... and I will then as a humorous reward for twelve years service bring you so low, so sickeningly low, that the servants of this palace will spurn you with their heels like a mangy cur, and your proud, beloved Queen will toss alms with averted head on to your ragged cloak. Come on, take the contract!

Faust (steps back). A million torments and miseries upon your head, you treacherous, poisonous liar!

Mephisto. Take it, I say. Ha, ha!

Faust. I refuse to take it.

Mephisto (pressing forward). Twice damned unless you take it. What do you choose?

Faust. Woe is me! Unhappy the man who has any truck with devils![1]

The choice between good and evil, with the scales heavily weighted against good, comes to all those who have usurped power and must either relinquish it or accept the ethical consequences. Schiller represented such a situation in *Wallenstein* and in *Demetrius*, and in both cases the choice was a tragic foregone conclusion. It was humanly speaking impossible for either to go back into the obscurity from which they had so gloriously emerged. Faust could not contemplate the surrender of everything his bargain with the powers of evil had gained for him. The picture of what he would become if he broke the contract was too degradingly dismal, and seems either to have been suggested by the transformation undergone by his namesake in the play Heine saw later near Hanover when Lucretia pulled off the magic ring, or else to have inspired that sensational scene.

The remaining three parts of Müller's *Faust* (with two acts in every part) have never been published, but seem to have been more or less complete when he died. After the appearance of Goethe's *Faust I* in 1808, Müller transposed seven of the eight acts into very poor verse, if the whole resembles the part of Act I printed in the *Frankfurter Conversationsblatt* in 1850. There seems little reason to regret the non-publication of what Seuffert called Müller's Roman *Faust*, to judge by this specimen and other details,

[1] Müller, *Situation aus Fausts Leben*, ed. cit. Vol. IV, pp. 305 f.

some of which are to be found in Müller's letters. At some point in the work he introduced a long episode taken from the Magellone folkbook which sounds more like a baroque novel than a Faustian drama; but at least he adhered to tradition by representing voyages to the North Pole and the centre of the earth as a variant of the terrestrial and supernatural journeys in the Urfaustbook. It was undoubtedly owing to Goethe's Gretchen that a young girl called Lenchen was smuggled into the versified Act I, Faust declaring himself to be violently in love with her in the opening monologue. One can make what one likes of the fact that Lenchen is an abbreviation of Helena, but there is no other point of contact between them. On the contrary, plagiarized from Goethe, Lenchen was conditioned by the fact that Müller had become a Roman Catholic. He therefore placed the seduction in a convent to emphasize the heinousness of the offence. Deserted by her lover and brought to despair when her condition becomes known, she dies on giving birth to a son, for whom, in ignorance of his identity, Faust later conceives an unnatural passion. This pleasing notion may well have been inspired by Schink's *Johann Faust* published in 1804; but the idea of Lenchen and Faust's father interceding for him in heaven with the Virgin Mary was entirely Müller's own, though Schink by making a woman the agent of salvation had already paid a signal tribute to the fair sex. The Virgin Mary is not inexorable; she allows Lenchen and Faust's father to appeal to the souls suffering in purgatory to aid them; and they attempt to bring Faust to repentance and remorse, so that the heavenly powers may come to his assistance:

This succeeds several times far enough to induce, although only for short periods, conflicts between the children of light and those of darkness; but the latter, by the might with which they are able to arouse Faust's passions and thus to govern him, soon bring about his backsliding and emerge victorious. Meanwhile he himself, falling ever lower from sin to sin, finally disgracing human nature, sinks into the deepest pit of abomination, despairing of God's mercy, that sin for which, according to the Bible, there can be no forgiveness, in which I then allow him to go under, not without the approval of poetic justice. . . . It is true that I would not have allowed this annihilation (which goes against my own feelings) to have overtaken a protagonist whose being shows undoubted traces of nobility of soul . . . were it not for the effect of the whole and the moral necessity; and also because from the outset

I had the means in readiness to justify the lost soul to the sympathies of my readers and bring him back, a free man, into the present again, as you will see for yourself in the last act which I hope that you will approve. . . .[1]

If this means anything (and it is most confusingly written) Müller was going to save in the eighth act a soul damned in the seventh; and since he went on immediately to quote Lessing's opinion that this Faust should finally be saved, one can only marvel at the extraordinary *dénouement* brought about in almost equal parts by the rationalism of enlightenment and Catholic mysticism. Neither of these elements was present in the Storm and Stress fragments which were clearly directed towards a tragic ending, or the hero would hardly have been permitted to choose damnation for the second time. Müller's early Faust scenes, rooted in tradition, were an independent and interesting contribution to the developing literary structure. His Roman *Faust* owed the idea of salvation directly to Lessing; Lenchen was borrowed from Goethe; the supernal conflicts derived from Weidmann; Faust's son was probably taken from Schink and so was the notion of redemption through a loving woman. If all this finally witnessed to failure of inspiration and to intellectual deterioration, not to say confusion, it should not be forgotten that the storm-tossed Faust of the seventies was saved in the early eighteen-twenties by the intercession with the Blessed Mother of God of a woman he had loved and ruined.[2]

(b) A Faust forlorn, 1777

In affliction, timeless, toneless,
And in unimagined loneness,
Nothing left to fear or brave,
Erebus' waters round me lave.
Oh bitter waters, had you loved me,
Into your bosom downward sinking,
I might have died, oblivion drinking,
But out, alas, you hated me!
You recked not of the balm you gave me

---

[1] A. Tille, *Die Faustsplitter in der Literatur des sechzehnten bis achtzehnten Jahrhunderts*, pp. 704f. Letter to Therese Huber from Rome, 14 September 1820.

[2] Although the letter addressed to Therese Huber is dated 1820, Müller had probably conceived the notion of intercession earlier.

Because your flaming flood did lave me,
Nor how it cooled my agony
When, torn away from all around me,
I felt that something did surround me,
And thought that something still loved me.
Befooled, befooled, alas untrue!
You cruel waves, you hate me too.
Could I but one sole creature find,
Neither compassion nor love to give,
But to suffer me near it, that I may live,
I, the most wretched of mankind![1]

The pregnant Faustian fragment which Jakob Michael Reinhold Lenz (1751–1792) published in the *Deutsches Museum* in 1777 has that flickering fascination which plays over nearly all his works; and since his latent insanity first declared itself for what it was in the same year, the three dozen lines in which he sketched Faust's state of mind in hell have a peculiar poignancy. They are typical too of his general method, which was impressionistic, outlining characters and situations by subtle touches and brief flashes which etch themselves on the mind. Careless often, tasteless sometimes and wilfully bizarre, he was a past-master in delineating progressive moral degradation, and had he attempted a full-length *Faust* he would probably have concentrated on that aspect of the situation. But he was nothing if not original, this extraordinarily gifted young man, whose poems were taken for Goethe's by their contemporaries, who fell in love with Frederike in Goethe's wake and was such a thorn in the flesh of Weimar. Far from imitating the Gretchen tragedy, he was planning a farce on the subject of Faust, although he got no further than the opening lines in which Bacchus is represented as going down to hell to fetch a soul up to earth again. He finds Faust bewailing the unthinkable loneliness of his life after death. On the appearance of Bacchus, the magician prays for final and utter annihilation; but the god tells him that he has been redeemed from his fate because his heart was great, and that he is now to come back to earth.

Lenz therefore actually represented what Müller finally planned: the salvation of a soul already suffering torments in hell; and this was a preliminary scene to a farce to be modelled on Aristophanes'

<hr />

[1] J. M. R. Lenz, *Die Höllenrichter*, in Wendriner, *Die Faustdichtung vor, neben und nach Goethe*, Vol. III, p. 147.

Frogs. Lenz had the gift of wit in no small degree, and the farce would in all probability have been lively enough; but the fragment he achieved is steeped in that almost Russian melancholy which Chehov once described as 'the limitless sorrow of the steppe'. The utter loneliness, desolation and despair of Faust are wonderfully rendered. And the verdict of Bacchus, 'Thy heart was great', outweighs all the rhetoric about the titanism of Faust which the Storm and Stress produced. Moreover Lenz's conception of hell as eternal loneliness was a wonderful solution of the dilemma for future poets who might wish a tragic ending for Faust and yet could not swallow hell fire. The solution was Greek, a vision of that underworld so greatly dreaded, cold, grey, shadowy, formless, to which Lenz added from his own bitter experience lovelessness and loneliness of the soul. In this strange fragment the doom which waits on those who are different from their fellow-men was expressed in words of human sorrow and grief which penetrate deep into the tragic fate of magicians. This was to present the legend in a new light, the light of unutterable and hopeless sadness which no one else has ever attempted either before or since.

(c) *Faust in fragments*, 1790

Except in Weidmann's paltry drama and Schink's airy operetta, Faust's attempts to enter German literature had hitherto been arrested in mid-career. Singing and orating on the Brocken; awakening thankfully from a terrible nightmare in Lessing's mind; conjuring up fair phantoms at Elizabeth's court; surrounded by tumult and shouting in Ingolstadt; rejecting a second chance of salvation when at the zenith of his power and glory in Spain; wandering wretchedly in the underworld; these tantalizing and fragmentary glimpses were all that the eighteenth century had so far succeeded in giving of Faust. Since none of the poets of the Storm and Stress contemplated a simple and straightforward version of the legend, their failure to satisfy their own standards is the reverse of surprising. From Lessing onwards the impulse to deepen Faust's character and to throw it into high relief against the dark background of diabolism had been decisive; and (as with Lessing) this impaled the writers on a dangerous dilemma: preposterous to damn a person potentially so noble; yet how to save him without having recourse to Weidmann's unconvincing

Ithuriel, to Lessing's undramatic dream or to Schink's merry widow, Rosalinde? Müller worried at this problem until the day of his death, and wrestled with his Faust drama for fifty years without completing it; Goethe took even longer over his. For though the Gretchen tragedy was finished in 1775, the drama of Faust had been barely begun, and was far from easy to continue. It had come in spurts and flashes in his youth; a soaring monologue, inspired by pantheistic longings and intimations which had led to the invocation of the spirit of creative nature in a mighty scene; the merry mocking at pedantry in the person of Wagner: the satire on University life through the mouth of Mephisto; the drinking, singing and brawling in *Auerbach's Cellar*; the devil shying like a jibbing horse before the Christian cross. Then the Gretchen tragedy, pressing to be written, had banished all other scenes; and after that Weimar had intruded and brought about an emotional revulsion from the early works and *Faust* amongst them.

In the year 1788, wishing to include this drama in an edition of his collected works, Goethe began the long, intermittent but never wholly abandoned struggle to complete it which continued for the rest of his life. His groans reverberate in the *Italian Journey*, and one can almost see him poring over his yellowing manuscript and wondering how on earth to fill in the 'great gap' between the opening scenes and the Gretchen tragedy as he sat in the Borghese gardens and tried to pick up the broken threads. Reading it dispassionately after such a long interval, he became aware of a discrepancy between the Faust of the opening monologue and the hero of the Gretchen tragedy; the first being a deeply disillusioned scholar with a tragically soaring mind, the second being a passionate young titan violently in love. There was also the gap to bridge between the vision of the Earth Spirit and the appearance of the totally different Mephisto. The two Fausts were of a different age, the two spirits were different in kind. Would the scholar of the opening monologue, for instance, ever really have lent himself to all that foolery in *Auerbach's Cellar*? Probably not; but there was a simple remedy for that. Let him be kept in the background, obviously bored, and let Mephisto perform the jugglery with the magic wine; moreover by versifying the scene some of its coarseness and crudity could be smoothed away. It might be more dignified too, and tone better with the general level to be aimed at, if some of the indecencies in the dialogue between the student and

Mephisto were also dropped. Their place could be taken by including law and theology among the faculties satirized, which meant reconditioning much of the scene, to its undoubted advantage. So far so good; none of this presented insuperable difficulties. It was a different story when it came to the introduction of Mephisto, who still had to be invoked. The calling up of the Earth Spirit barred the way to a second conjuration-scene. Goethe could neither scale those heights again, nor would it be in line with Mephisto's nature to do so; and yet if possible an anti-climax must be avoided. He decided to wait and see, and meanwhile began to reflect upon the pact-scene, on Faust's state of mind when signing it and the benefits he hoped to derive from it:

> And all of life for all mankind created
> Shall be within mine inmost being tested:
> The highest, lowest forms my soul shall borrow,
> Shall heap upon itself their bliss and sorrow,
> And thus, my own sole self to all their selves expanded,
> I too, at last, shall with them all be stranded![1]

That was the kind of language the Faust of the monologue would use and the kind of desires he might harbour on the emotional rather than on the spiritual plane, thus bringing him nearer to Gretchen. Mephisto naturally made short work of these aspirations; but was ready and willing when the student was announced to interview him for Faust, and characterized the latter when he went off in a manner that brings back the desperate aspirations of the opening scene. But still it was not enough. The magician was clearly too old to be the impassioned lover of Gretchen. Goethe now faced the difficulty squarely, and let Faust declare that his long beard and set ways and scholarly habits debarred him from finding solace in the world and enjoying that intensification of life which Mephisto could procure him. Desperate ills need desperate cures. The two Fausts were still so far apart in years that only magic could fuse them. Magic therefore should do it; and rightly so, since the play was about magic; and magicians have since time immemorial been rumoured to know the priceless secret of rejuvenation by means of the elixir of life or philosophers' stone. Though not traditional about Faust, it was in harmony with his legend and no violence would be done to it by these means. But

---

[1] Goethe, *Faust I*, ll. 1770 ff. tr. Bayard Taylor, London [1949], p. 71.

what possessed Goethe, the sometime student of Paracelsus, to drag in witchcraft where it had no right to be? If so far all the alterations had been made with a view to dignifying and ennobling the poem, why degrade it by contamination with a baser and more squalid element than tradition warranted, let alone demanded? The answer to these questions is a sobering one. Goethe had grown up and grown away from that vital emotional belief in the powers and nature of magic which had compelled the Earth Spirit to appear, and had dictated the sinister little scene before the cross, now ruthlessly cut out. Quite as rationalistic and as optimistic as Lessing, Goethe now considered the assumptions of the legend silly and absurd. By debasing magic to the level of witchcraft in the *Witches' Kitchen* he cocked a snook at it and passed on.

He had certainly found a skilful way out of his immediate difficulty, and, as far as Faust was concerned, he handled the scene with consummate skill. Keeping to the conception of the brooding speculator of the opening monologue, he showed his hero to be disillusioned in advance on the question of the efficacy of anything so grotesque as witchcraft, bored and *blasé* by what he sees, and in much the same superior frame of mind as in the reconditioned *Auerbach's Cellar*. Accessible only to higher lures, he is nevertheless caught and held by the appearance in a magic mirror of the most beautiful woman in the world, and swallows the potion which, as Mephisto plainly hints, is an aphrodisiac too. The bridge between the two Fausts had been built. Passing over it Faust Senior became Faust Junior by a species of magical transformation which was, technically speaking, a triumph of engineering. The problem was solved, and the satire on witchcraft and all its hocus-pocus had been cleverly associated with magic proper as represented by the elixir of life. It would be uncritical to demand of an author who felt like this that he should have attempted to portray the poetry of witchcraft like Shakespeare, Middleton or Ben Jonson. But one may nevertheless suggest that to mock at the powers of evil in this light-hearted way is out of place in a drama intending to portray the conflict of a human soul with the might of hell. Perhaps Goethe would retort that by means of the magic mirror Faust was caught after all and leave the critic silenced if not absolutely convinced.

The gradual expansion of the *Urfaust* into *Faust Part I* through the intermediate stage of the *Faust-Fragment* resembles nothing so much as the blowing of a shimmering iridescent soap-bubble, still adhering to the pipe in the *Fragment*, but showing more play of colour than before. *Woodland Cavern* was part of the expansion. Placed immediately after the scene at the well, it served to illuminate the state of mind of Gretchen's lover and to show Mephisto in his true nature as *advocatus diaboli*. It also drew the two parts of the dramatic poem more closely together by defining the relationship between the Earth Spirit and Mephisto more precisely than in the hint given during the quarrel between the hero and his evil spirit about the fate of Gretchen in the *Urfaust*. In a powerful and moving address to the sublime spirit of nature, Faust renders thanks for the wonderful gift he had bestowed upon him by allowing him to penetrate deeply into the very heart of the natural world and to feel himself animated with its spirit. In fact all that he had asked for in the early scene had been granted. But such superhuman, supernormal or supramundane gifts are never obtained without a price being exacted. If the lives of the magicians throughout the ages teach nothing else, they certainly teach that. And the price in this instance was the companionship of the cynical Mephisto who blighted the gift of communion with nature. The Earth Spirit had dispatched him to play that part, and Faust, though he loathes his familiar, is well aware that he can no longer dispense with him. Mephisto, entering after this apostrophe, proves to the hilt both that he takes a devilish delight in belittling and destroying Faust's nature-worship, and that as an evil counsellor in the affair with Gretchen he is firmly in the saddle and wilily directing operations. The functional connection between the Earth Spirit and Mephisto is manifest in *Woodland Cavern*, but the spiritual and temperamental incompatibility remains. It is hard to accept the sneering, fleering devil as an emissary of the mighty spirit of creative nature. Welded together in this scene, they exhibit a disturbing join.

This was as far as Goethe went in 1788–1790. With the scheme still in the melting-pot, he even felt it advisable not to print the end of the Gretchen tragedy, but to break it off after the swoon in the cathedral; so that the *Fragment* represents a half-way house up the steep Faustian hill looming above him. The problem of the two Fausts in the original version had been solved by magic; that is to say it had not solved itself naturally. The problem of how to introduce Mephisto still awaited solution, and as a vassal of the

Earth Spirit he was not a striking success. Without the pact and stopping before the end, Goethe's *Fragment* must have sorely puzzled his contemporaries. Had he or had he not joined the ranks of the salvationists? Impossible for the general public to guess. The Earth Spirit, the *Witches' Kitchen* and Gretchen must have aroused great interest as well as enthusiasm; but speculation too will have been rife. It was 'all a wonder and a wild surmise', and hardly capable of imitation or influence in its baffling uncompleted state. But at least Goethe's claim to be writing a *Faust* had been made publicly and strikingly valid.

(d) A sombre Faust, 1791

Although the storm-tossed fragments produced by Müller and Goethe between 1775 and 1790 were destined to flutter into serenity at last, a consummation foretold by Lenz in the opening lines to his farce, their tone was tragic, and defiant titanism informed the utterances of the heroes. The full-length novel *Faust's Life, Death and Damnation*, published in 1791 by Friedrich Maximilian von Klinger (1752–1831), represents the answer of the Storm and Stress to the optimistic rationalism of Lessing. The author had in fact renounced his allegiance to that tumultuous movement long before his *Faust* came out; but the conception if not the execution belonged to the earlier period. It might have been differently presented in the seventies, when Klinger's tragedy *Storm and Stress* baptized the whole unruly school; and the recurrent use of dialogue throughout the book suggests that the form might have been dramatic. The quality too would surely have betrayed the hand of the author of *The Twins*, that breathless, violent, oddly impressive study of envy, hatred, love and jealousy run mad which concentrated and released into literature the dangerous passions seething in many hearts. But fifteen years is a long time, especially when there is a mind to develop as distinct from a temperament to manifest; and the intellectual nature of Klinger's *Faust* distinguishes it from Müller's no less sharply than from his own early works. Nevertheless the titanism of the hero, the satanic mercilessness of the fiend and the cruelty of the final damnation bear the imprint of that intense and tragically minded movement which shook Germany out of its literary complacency towards the latter end of the eighteenth century.

Klinger, who had been an intimate friend of Goethe's at that time, must have been familiar with his Faustian schemes, but cannot be said to have been influenced by them to any marked degree; for his whole conception of the problem is totally different as he emphatically pointed out in the preface to the anonymous first edition:

The author has neither used nor desired to use anything of all that has hitherto been written about Faust in prose or in verse. The present work is his own, let it be good or bad. So much at least every reader will easily see for himself from the method of presentation, the characterisation and the purpose.[1]

In a long letter to Goethe in 1814, Klinger analysed at some length the impulse behind the novel, the desire to probe into the evils generated in the world by political, social and psychological forces. It is in truth an unflinching revelation of such evils, and the mind of the reader is forced into a strait-jacket whilst the hero pursues his investigations, the conclusions of which can best be given in the words of Job:

The earth is given into the hand of the wicked: he covereth the faces of the judges thereof.[2]

This sombre discovery is complicated by Klinger's preoccupation with the law of cause and effect or fate and the guilt involved in any arbitrary interference with its natural workings. As this is exactly what magicians aim to do and claim to do, the fundamental question of the ethics of magic is raised on the philosophical as well as on the religious level. These are the two leading ideas behind the book: the causes and the nature of evil and the workings of fate. Klinger disclaimed any borrowings from Faustian literature; but he was conversant with the popular tradition, and made use of some of the magic pranks in the Faustbooks. He was also well read in demonology and witchcraft. Many of the tales told and the incidents represented are impregnated with such elements and they do not seem out of place in the fifteenth-century framework of the novel, which in this aspect somewhat resembles Grimmelshausen's *Simplicissimus*. Neither author could exclude

---

[1] F. M. von Klinger, *Fausts Leben, Taten und Höllenfahrt* in *Stürmer und Dränger*, ed. Sauer, Stuttgart, 1890, Vol. I, p. 142.

[2] Job ix, 24.

the dark superstitions of the times they were depicting from the broad canvas on which they worked. It was not, however, because demonology and witchcraft were more prevalent in the fifteenth than in the sixteenth century (for they were not) that Klinger chose to identify the black magician who called himself Faust with Fust, the reputed co-inventor of printing who died about 1466, a hundred years before Faust. According to his own statement he was adopting an identification already popularly current; and Heine also declared that Faust and Fust were confused by popular tradition. The Strasbourg puppet-play certainly rolled the two into one, and in other ways too resembles Klinger's novel. He may therefore have used that text, although it seems more likely that Strasbourg borrowed from him. Otherwise I have not found the identification in popular sources, and it was certainly the first time that it was made in literature. Klinger used it for two reasons. In the first place the fifteenth century offered him particularly rewarding material for his pageantry of evil (though to make full use of it he silently added another thirty years or so to Fust's life); and in the second place it enabled him to make a striking point about printing.

The book opens by introducing Faust as a married man with children. Domesticity had now gone a step further with its attendant complications of mouths to feed; and the unhappy printer is hoping to stave off family starvation by selling the Latin Bible he has printed with his own hands. Finding no eagerness to buy it in his home town Mainz, where the population was entirely occupied by a monastic scandal (shades of Grandier and Gauffridi), he offered it to the Frankfurt Senate, which seemed equally unenthusiastic. Filled with despair and shaken with rage, Faust thereupon undertook a diabolical conjuration. He did so in an evil hour for himself. A feast was toward in the nether regions, for there was much joy at his invention of printing, the root of untold future evils, leading among other things to religious wars and fearful carnage, a result also to be confidently expected from the forthcoming discovery of the New World. A toast was brought to Faust as the purveyor of poison to the children of the earth, and when his conjuration echoed down into hell, Leviathan was immediately dispatched to attend him:

The devil flung back his cloak and stood in a sublime, stately, bold and mighty form before the circle. . . . His countenance was that of a fallen angel, once illuminated by the godhead and now covered by a sombre veil. . . .

Devil. Faust, I am a spirit created of flaming light and I saw the colossal worlds come forth from nothingness; you are made from dust and are but of yesterday; am I to flatter you?

Faust. And yet you must serve me if I so desire.

Devil. I shall reap a reward for that and the applause of hell. Neither man nor devil does anything for nought.

Faust. What reward do you expect?

Devil. To make of you a thing like myself, if you have the strength for it. . . .

Faust. Shake off that form, I wish to see you as a spirit.

Devil. You speak folly—look at me if you choose—I shall be, but you will not see me. I shall speak and you will not understand.

After these words the devil Leviathan dissolved into a bright flame and disappeared.

Faust. Speak, and reveal all riddles.

There was a murmuring round the brow and ears of Faust like the soft west wind whispering over a flowery meadow and gently caressing the tender flowers. Then the murmur changed to a mounting, persistent, roaring blast, like the rolling of thunder, the breaking of waves on the surf and the howling and growling in rocky clefts. Faust sank down in his magic circle and only recovered slowly. . . .

Devil. . . . You wished to hear the speech of the spirits: you heard it and sank down overcome by the sound.[1]

There is a certain similarity between this scene and the rejection of Goethe's Faust by the Earth Spirit; and Goethe's Faust sounded later as if he were quoting Leviathan when he said that the devil was an egoist and unlikely to do anything for nothing. But Klinger's Faust was intent not so much on union with the spirit of nature as on answers to his spiritual and ethical questions:

I wish to learn the destiny of mankind and the cause of the moral evil in the world. I want to know why the just man suffers and the wicked man flourishes. I want to know why we must purchase one moment's

---

[1] Klinger, *Fausts Leben*, ed. cit. Vol. I, pp. 164 ff.

pleasure with years of pain and suffering. You shall reveal to me the root cause of all things, the hidden mainspring of the physical and moral phenomena in the world. You must make me comprehend Him who has ordered all things, even should the flaming lightning splitting yonder black cloud singe my head and hurl me down without life in this circle of damnation.[1]

The compact is in the form of a wager. Faust declares that he will make Leviathan believe in the virtue of humanity, in which case the pact is to be returned; and he also forces the devil to agree to perform good deeds. The similarity here with Goethe's *Prologue in Heaven* (written in 1797) is marked; for God was to make the same kind of wager with Mephisto and to maintain that he furthers good in spite of himself; but whereas Goethe's premises were optimistic, Klinger's were pessimistic in the highest degree.

The remaining four books of the novel develop this despondent point of view, by representing the successive disillusionments of the hero on the subject of his fellow-men, a theme lending itself admirably to that violent criticism of society to which the Storm and Stress writers were prone and which Müller had concentrated in the expectorations of the pandemonium-scenes. Klinger did likewise and even more fiercely; but he also emphasized it relentlessly throughout the whole course of the novel. Thus the burgher-master of Frankfurt is ready and willing to sell his wife's honour (and she is willing too) for a patent of nobility; a pious hermit is induced to attempt murder for gold; Faust's own family, in particular his wife, begin to slide downhill rapidly when affluence comes their way through him. Justice is found to be corrupt; the Church and the State cruelly oppress the poor; a self-styled deliverer, Robertus, is seeking his own ends; a prince apparently amiable and wise is in reality the reverse, and his court rotten with intrigues and rank with hypocrisy. Faust, who tries to right the wrongs he finds flourishing everywhere, gradually attains to the state of mind of Karl Moor in *The Robbers*, a revengeful state of mind in which he sets out to act the part of nemesis on the evil-doers, though the devil warns him to desist:

Devil. Faust, you are forestalling the vengeance of the Avenger!
Faust. His vengeance is asleep, and the just man suffers; I wish to see *him* annihilated who wears the mask of virtue. . . .

[1] Klinger, *Fausts Leben*, ed. cit. Vol. I, pp. 167f.

Devil. . . . The results be on your own head. . . . Faust, I obey, but consider that the office of judge has not been given to you.[1]

As one would naturally expect, the innocent suffer with the guilty in Faust's reckless efforts to punish the crimes of his fellow-men; and the number and nature of the vices and sins he unveils begin to arouse very dark thoughts in his mind:

He still sought to find the cause [of evil] in mankind itself; but his restless, doubting spirit, his imagination always ready to fly from the near to the far, his embittered and passionately compassionate heart were already beginning to feel darkly that the Creator of humanity was, if not the originator, then the accomplice of all those things which outraged Faust's sense of right; for He tolerated them.[2]

Yet in spite of Faust's fearful and genuine moral indignation; in spite of his frantic attempts to help the oppressed and the virtuous, he was far from leading a blameless life himself, and in particular enacted the part of Don Juan with the women who crossed his path. Foremost amongst these was an innocent victim called Angelica, whom he seduced by means of devilish arts and who finally suffered the fate of Gretchen. The influence of Goethe seems obvious here; but the episode is only one of many and not given much prominence; for the novel is planned on a very large scale in which individual fates merely contribute their quota to the overwhelming impression of the whole: corruption and evil everywhere, corrupting the hero's mind. One apparently disinterested act of benevolence, not dictated by any desire to punish or reward, was performed by Leviathan at Faust's command before they left Germany to visit Europe. This was the rescue of a drowning man, whom the devil unavailingly warned Faust to leave to his fate unless he were prepared to pull him out of the water himself. Faust refused to bestir himself and Leviathan did as he was bid.

The traditional journey round the world, which had been a feature of the Urfaustbook, was most skilfully handled by Klinger in the interests of his main theme. Faust and Leviathan visited France under Louis XI (1461–83), England under Richard III (1483–5), Italy and Spain, where Torquemada was in the ascendant

---

[1] Klinger, *Fausts Leben*, ed. cit. Vol. I, p. 219.
[2] Ibid. p. 204.

(1420–98), and finally came to the Papal Court, where Alexander VI (1492–1503) was disporting himself. With the help of Voltaire's *Essai sur les mœurs* and other sources, Klinger presented such a fearful picture of evil in high places and gave such a dreadful description of innumerable grim, grisly and ghastly crimes that one sickens as one reads. In Rome especially, it is almost like meeting Widman over again, a much better educated and better informed Widman, gifted with a more lurid imagination and a far more telling style, but with the same intolerable determination to blacken and blast the reputation of the Holy See.

Having watched the Borgias drain the cup of vice to its unsavoury dregs, Faust decided to return to Germany. On the way back he had a visionary dream in which he saw himself excluded from a great temple humanity was building in despite of the assault of foes; and the atmosphere lifts for a moment during the description of the dream. Only to descend inexorably when Germany is reached. Family misery and family guilt meet the returning hero. His eldest son is found hanging from the gallows, brought to this fearful end by the drowning man whom Leviathan had been ordered to save, and who might have refrained from ruining the lad had Faust rescued him personally and earned his gratitude for the deed. Powerless to restore his son to life or to render any effective aid to his desperate family, Faust has further to submit to a diatribe from Leviathan, who mercilessly recapitulates all the deeds he has been responsible for and proves how all of them, good and bad, have had far more disastrous consequences than would have resulted had Faust not interfered. He is now, and the world with him, reaping the whirlwind of his impious interventions with fate. Conspicuous amongst his failures was the rescue of Robertus from prison and the saving of his life. That far from disinterested political agitator who had spoken so eloquently about the tyranny of the nobles, had precipitated a fearful catastrophe by inciting the peasants to revolt and acting as their leader. The consequences of this was unthinkable carnage in which the peasants themselves suffered most of all. This fearful retributive speech has a crushing grandeur unparalleled elsewhere in Faustian literature. Modelled on the outburst of Mephisto towards the end of the Urfaustbook, it adds a historical perspective to the Lutheran indictment of the sinner and a vastness to the power he has abused which make it terrible in the extreme. Unlike the hero of the

Urfaustbook, Klinger's Faust shows titanic rebellion and defiant greatness in his retort:

Torment me if you will, but you cannot resolve the doubts and questions of mankind. . . . Never did they penetrate more insidiously into my heart than in this hour when I survey my past and future life. What is human life but a web of pain, vice, torment, hypocrisy, contradictions and squint-eyed virtue? What is freedom, choice, will, and the famous power to distinguish between good and evil, if passions outroar weak reason, like the tumultuous sea drowning the voice of the pilot whose ship is being driven against the rocks? And what is the cause, what is the reason of evil? He willed it so. . . . I hate the world, humanity and myself more bitterly than before. Why was I given the longing for happiness, since I was born to suffer? Why the yearning for light, since I was born for darkness? Why the thirst for freedom, since I was born a slave? Why the desire to fly, since I was made a worm? . . . Of what kind is the government of heaven if a worm like me, through the means of an outcast like you, can, with heaven's permission, botch its own work? Is this justice? Was it necessary that Faust should have been born and developed in such a way and think and feel in such a fashion that thousands came to misery through him? Undo the magic which fetters me in this circle, and I will not flee from you. I would not if I could. For the pains of hell cannot be greater than what I am suffering now.[1]

Having cut down the body of his son and dug his grave, Faust hurls a last defiance at Leviathan, is annihilated, carried off to hell, welcomed with acclamation as the inventor of printing, curses God and meets his everlasting fate:

Drag him into the worst corner of hell [says Satan], and let him languish there in sombre solitude, sunk in the contemplation of his deeds and of this moment that can never be expiated. Let no other shade come near him! Go and hover alone and for ever lost in that land where no hope, no consolation and no sleep dwell. The doubts which tortured you in your life shall eternally gnaw at your soul, and never shall one of the riddles be resolved for whose solution you came here.[2]

The fearful cumulative effect of this powerful and painful novel is not easy to shake off. The follies, vices and crimes of humanity as seen by Faust, and the fearful and revolting practices so inexor-

[1] Klinger, *Fausts Leben*, ed. cit. Vol. I, pp. 296 f.
[2] Ibid. Vol. I, p. 302; the description of Faust's situation in hell is similar to that given by Lenz.

ably described, would be quite intolerable were it not for the bracing breath of moral indignation which mitigates the total impression. Moreover in his final denunciation of Faust, Leviathan does something to readjust the balance:

You pushed your way into courts and palaces, where humanity is mocked, misused and trampled underfoot, the while the means of subsistence robbed from the poor are shamefully wasted. The rulers of the world, the tyrants and their executioners, wanton women, priests who use your religion as an instrument of oppression:—all these you have seen; but not those who groan under the heavy yoke, who patiently bear the burden of existence and console themselves with hopes of a happier future. Proudly you passed by the hovels of the poor and humble, who do not even know the names of your sophisticated vices, who earn their bread with the sweat of their brow, share it faithfully with wife and child and are happy in their last hours to have finished their labours at last. . . . Without your priests and philosophers, Faust, the gates of hell would soon be closed. Can you pretend to know mankind, when you sought men only in the haunts of vice and of your own base desires?[1]

It may seem incongruous to hear the devil preaching the gospel of Rousseau in all good faith; but throughout he has shown himself a stern moralist; and whether by Leviathan or another, this speech is at least a make-weight against the indictment of humanity apparent in the book. Like Schiller's *Robbers* and to a lesser extent Goethe's *Götz*, Klinger's *Faust* is both revolutionary and anti-revolutionary: revolutionary in its attitude towards the great and the structure of society as a whole; anti-revolutionary, since it scourges as with scorpions Faust's attempts to right the wrongs by violence and also his arrogance in setting himself up as a judge. Yet, low as Faust sinks, he never loses the issue from sight; wrestling obdurately with the question of moral evil, he draws his tragic, despairing and finally blasphemous conclusions and goes to his eternal reward.

This impressive and sobering version of the legend is one of those exceptional works of literature in which poetry plays no part and has no place. Even in the allegorical dream-vision, beauty eludes the author; and so does humour, which Jean Paul (who well knew its nature) once defined as the conquest of the suffering induced by the world. Klinger was still suffering bitterly in his

[1] Klinger, *Fausts Leben*, ed. cit. Vol. I, p. 289.

mind when he wrote his *Faust*; but a certain sardonic quality sometimes relieves the tension, as in the well-imagined scene at the Borgias, where, in connection with the sale of indulgences, the party is composing a list of new and fashionable sins to replace the old:

Faust. Absolution for all those who practise magic and make a pact with the devil. How high do you tax that crime?

Pope. My son, you won't enrich the Papal Stool by that. The devil is blind to his own advantage; he does not come when called.

Faust. Holy Father, don't tempt him and name a sum.

Pope. Well, for the sake of its rarity, let us say a hundred golden guilders.

Faust. Here they are, just in case I succeed; prepare an absolution for me and sing the chorus.

Chorus. Absolution for him who makes a pact with the devil.[1]

The irony in this scene is brought forcibly home when Faust meets Alexander VI in hell, despite the promised indulgence.

Klinger genuinely believed that his conception of Faust was entirely original; but the germ of his grandiose notion of Faust's tragic guilt, his aspiration to become the nemesis of humanity, lies in that paltry scene in Weidmann's drama in which the friends whom the hero had tried to benefit showed that he had thereby irretrievably corrupted them. It is more than likely that Klinger had read or seen the play and that this seemingly unpromising seed fell on fertile soil. Inspiration often derives from very unlikely sources; and it is sometimes observable that the intrinsic significance of the source and the magnitude of its effect are in inverse proportion. Weidmann certainly affected the general trend the Faust-legend was taking towards salvation and 'domesticity'; he may also have been responsible for Klinger's striking conception of the hero's tragic guilt.

[1] Klinger, *Fausts Leben*, ed. cit. Vol. I, p. 271.

CHAPTER VI

FORGOTTEN FAUSTS

(a) Faust in Grub Street, 1791–1801

With the publication of Goethe's *Fragment* and Klinger's novel, the Faust theme definitely caught on and began to circulate in Grub Street.[1] The first sign of this was the publication in 1791 of *Scenes from Faust's Life*, whose anonymous author, Aloys Wilhelm Schreiber (1763–1841), was a professor of aesthetics who had already written some travel books. It speaks volumes for the taste of the time that a second edition of the *Scenes* came out with the author's name in 1794 under the altered title of: *Pictures in Softer Colouring from the Life of the Black Magician Faust*. It also speaks volumes for the *naïveté* of the author that he dedicated the work to Goethe in these touching lines:

> Oh, be not wrath that I with thee
> Should dare to tempt the self-same goal!
> No wreath upon my brow thou yet canst see;
> But one small leaf of thine contents my soul.[2]

Posterity will be apt to see the minute laurel-leaf Schreiber laid claim to nestling in these verses, and to deny any other token of fame to the modest author. And yet modest is probably not the right word; pretentious seems nearer the mark when the loosely connected scenes, strung together on a narrative thread, come to be examined. According to the preface they were written to prove that man is not fitted for intercourse with higher beings and will not venture with impunity outside the circle of humanity. Faust is introduced, full of vague dissatisfaction and having already

---

[1] Nepomuk Komareck, *Faust von Mainz*, 1794, shows the influence of Klinger in the use of the name Faust for Fust the printer. This play is a domestic drama dealing with the love affairs of Faust's daughter Christine. It contains no supernatural elements.

[2] [A. W. Schreiber], *Szenen aus Fausts Leben*, Offenbach, 1792, dedication.

seduced a young girl called Therese. She has given birth to his illegitimate son and confides in Wagner that she is totally averse from entering a convent in order to expiate her sin:

Thoughts of hell and eternity always hover round me in church where God appears to me only as the stern judge. . . . The stone saints in the convent make me shudder, and when I kissed a stone Madonna the other day, it struck cold to my soul.[1]

This wan echo of Gretchen's experiences in the cathedral is the only Goethean element to be found in the subsequent account of the hero's peregrinations in search of light and truth. After taking farewell of his old father he sets out to see the world, visiting monasteries, inns and peasants' huts. He is seen in stage-coaches, walking on the high-road, wandering by the sea-shore, attending the debates of learned societies and everywhere dissatisfied or disgusted with what he finds. Nor can he accept the doctrine of limitation and usefulness preached to him by the initiate of some esoteric order; although this episode may help to account for the totally unexpected fact that he is next met with on the Ganges, having come to the East to consult the Holy Men of India on how best to step outside the circle of humanity in order to find what he seeks. A voice instructs him in the four tests he must undergo if he wishes to become a higher being. These consist in withstanding the temptations of the senses, of wealth, of pity and of family affection. Faust resists them all, even refraining from the impulse to save an infant from a venomous snake, and refusing to be touched by the disembodied voices of his father, Therese and Wagner urging him to return home. He thus attains to superhuman indifference and becomes a member of the order (Brahmanical or Buddhistic?). His guardian angel, a youth called Helim, now appears to him and reveals the interesting fact that after their death all human beings become guardian angels (good or bad as the case may be) to members of their race. Faust further learns from Helim that the future is incapable of being influenced, and that a girl they had saved from being seduced will nevertheless become a bad woman, for that is her destiny. This depressing piece of news increases Faust's discomfort at finding that his emotions are now in truth dead, and that he can feel neither sorrow nor joy. Back in Germany, his heart remains unmoved by the reunion with

[1] Schreiber, op. cit. p. 11.

his old father and by his first sight of his son. He agrees languidly to marry Therese; but neither this nor his father's death has the power to touch him. He is finally redeemed from the flesh by a thunderbolt, after Helim has assured him that he is to become the guardian angel of his son after death and thus mount up to godhead. This is one of the most original and one of the silliest of the many silly *Fausts* on record. Neither as a study of the Faustian temperament nor as an exposition of Brahmanical or Buddhistic doctrine has it the slightest value. Nor can one quite see where the supposed warning against intercourse with higher beings comes in; for in the company of Helim (that antithesis of Mephisto) Faust treads, however flabbily, the path leading to sainthood. The only interest attaching to the feeble nonsense of Schreiber's *Scenes* is that it shows the obstacles in the way of those desirous of redeeming Faust at whatever cost.

The determination to damn him out of hand was on the contrary the simple aim of Count Friedrich Julius Heinrich von Soden (1754–1831), whose *Doctor Faust* appeared in 1797. Unlike Schreiber, Soden's faults cannot be attributed to straining after originality. On the contrary, this engaging playwright, who was among other things a patron of E. T. A. Hoffmann, owed Faustian debts all round the compass. His so-called *People's Drama* was vigorously cobbled together from shreds and patches torn from tradition and literature with a fine impartiality. But the whole has a personal colouring: ardent patriotism, socialistic tendencies, and the dream of a great and united fatherland. Otherwise the simplest way of describing his drama is by listing the borrowed plumes with which he adorned it, beginning with Lessing's speed-scene treated with characteristic verve:

(*Seven Spirits appear*)

Doctor Faust. Welcome, brothers! Your course is now mine! Who will follow me?

All. I!

Doctor Faust. You are willing, and I'm grateful for that. But are you strong as well? (*To the first Spirit*) Are you bold?

First Spirit. As bold as a courtier.

Doctor Faust. Away with him! Vermin like that is only bold with women and the weak. (*To the second Spirit*) And you?

Second Spirit. As bold as the eagle of Hermann, the German.

Doctor Faust. You are my man. (*To the seventh Spirit*) And you?

Seventh Spirit. As bold as the struggle of a free man for the fatherland!

Doctor Faust. Good enough. . . . But are you quick and speedy too?

First Spirit. As the flaming lightning.

Doctor Faust. Faugh! Lazybones!

Second Spirit. As the wrath of the Avenger!

Doctor Faust. That crawls compared with the flight of my thoughts.

Third Spirit. As the transition from good to evil.*

Doctor Faust. You are in error. One cannot fly with sore feet. Every
step is marked by the blood of the wanderer.

Seventh Spirit. As fast as the transition from the first step to the
second!

Doctor Faust. Ha! You've hit it. You're the spirit for me. Come forth!

* *This is what Lessing lets his Spirit answer in the well-known scene in
his Faust, the only scene still extant. Does my idea deserve to stand beside
his?—Let those who know human nature decide.*[1]

The later summoning up of Socrates, Cato and Solon was probably
also due to the fact that Lessing's Faust had called up Aristotle.
But much more important is the bodily transference of Ithuriel
from Weidmann and the scenic 'cosmic' conflict between this angel
of light (a charming genius in a floating white garment and with
a starry crown) and Mephisto, clad in black with flying hair and a
veil over his face. Weidmann and Klinger combined contributed
the idea that all Faust's attempts to benefit mankind and make
human beings happy render them either corrupt or else more
wretched than before; and the identification of Faust with Fust
was clearly owing to Klinger too. Müller was behind the introduction of scenes from University life in the first act, and supplied
the motive for the pact: bankruptcy and imprisonment. Soden
added a human double to Mephisto in Brenner, corrupt, vicious
and urging Faust along the road to ruin. To Weidmann originally
and to the Storm and Stress as a whole Soden was indebted for
the introduction of Faust's family, an aged father, a loving mother,
and (shades of Gretchen) his bride Liese, a sweet and simple

[1] J. Soden, *Doktor Faust*, in Wendriner, op. cit. Vol. III, pp. 198–200.
The Augsburg puppet-play has this version.

peasant-girl. Her illegitimate offspring called Gürgel is tactfully introduced to the notice of his father when the latter suggests that he should reform, marry Liese and share his parents' hut with her:

Faust's Father. But you see, the hut is small.

Doctor Faust. Oh, it's big enough for two happy couples.

Faust's Father. Yes, it would be big enough for that; but you have already sent us an unbidden guest.

Doctor Faust. I, my father?

Faust's Father. Gürgel! Come along and show yourself.

Gürgel (embracing Faust's knees). Father!

Doctor Faust (lifting him up and embracing him). Heaven and earth! What joy is this? Son! My son?—Liese! Father! Mother!

Faust's Mother. It wrings my heart!

Doctor Faust. Ah, senseless that I am, the world is abhorrent to me! I never knew the joys of fatherhood! Oh, it is well with me now. Now I am happy and at peace. (*He embraces them all, one after the other.*)[1]

The fiery writing on the wall: 'Faust, your time is up!' was probably inspired by Weidmann's 'Faust, evening is nigh!'; although it may have been suggested by the menacing Latin mottoes which figured in transparencies on the popular stage. Certainly the appearance of Helen of Troy at the traditional moment to dispel Faust's remorse was modelled on the puppet-plays; and her subsequent transformation into a fury, not represented but described, was in the popular tradition too. Soden also owed an important debt to Schiller, for Faust speaks the language of Karl Moor in Act I and switches over to the accents of the Marquis Posa in Act IV. In the same way *Götz von Berlichingen* as well as Klinger were laid under contribution in Act V. Faust, attempting to break away from his evil courses after the shock of Helen's transformation, retires to his home, where, as we have seen, he was contemplating a virtuous life with his parents, Liese and the grotesquely named Gürgel. But his hatred of tyranny and love of the people make it impossible for him to refuse his aid when the mob comes surging in on the idyllic family tableau urging him to become their leader. Like Götz before him he leads the Peasants' Revolt, only to arouse their

---

[1] Soden, *Doktor Faust,* ed. cit. Vol. III, pp. 282f.

murderous fury when he tries to persuade them that some form of government is necessary. In order to escape from this deadly peril he summons Mephisto to his assistance (much as Müller's Faust had done in the gambling den), thereby irretrievably forfeiting his soul, and is haled off ranting to everlasting perdition whilst the clock strikes twelve.

There is no adequate reason why Soden's hero should end in hell; on the contrary his own essential nobility, let alone the presence of the powerful Ithuriel, make nonsense of the conclusion. Having created a sympathetic and finally selfless Faust to adorn his theatrical clap-trap, Soden was hoist with the same petard which gave Lessing such an infinity of trouble. But the high-handed if democratic count saw nothing to hinder him from bringing his drama to a stirring close and letting logic look after itself. Although one can no more deny his mediocrity than Weidmann's and Schreiber's, he had more spirit than they; and his patchwork of patent plagiarisms is the very reverse of dull.

And indeed can one fairly talk of plagiarism when dealing with a traditional theme of this nature? A question by no means easy to answer, though it is raised in a peculiarly acute form by an anonymous book entitled *Faust, the Great Man, or his Wanderings through the World and into Hell* which appeared in 1798 and was reissued in 1835. The author openly stated in the preface to this work that he had used all the oral and written material available, and a trial by speed *à la* Lessing was therefore inevitably one of the episodes. Incredibly enough he thereafter compiled the book by interleaving Klinger and Schreiber: whole passages were copied bodily from the novel, although sometimes condensed, and diversified at intervals by Schreiber's Brahmanical scenes. The ending is pure Klinger; and the juxtaposition of this with Faust's gradual attainment to sainthood in India is indescribably comic. It might be taken as a symbol for the struggle over the soul of Faust which had been going on in German literature for a quarter of a century at least, a most confused struggle in which some very odd combatants were engaged; and few odder than Karl Friedrich Benkowitz (1764–1807), who produced his *Jubilation of Hell or Faust the Younger, a Drama of the end of the Eighteenth Century* anonymously in 1801. This obscure official, an uninspired hanger-on of the Storm and Stress movement, died by falling out of a window, probably the most remarkable thing he ever did. His Faustian drama certainly did not inaugurate the nineteenth century in a promising manner. Yet it was reprinted under the author's name in 1808, the year which saw the appearance of the first part of Goethe's *Faust*. Unlike Soden and the bookmaker who mated Klinger with Schreiber, Benkowitz went his own way, and complacently stated in his preface that to the best of his knowledge all the other Faustian works of literature derived more or less closely from tradition, from which he was boldly departing. His Faust is a married man with a wife and two grown-up children, a boy and a girl. He has also acquired a mistress, the daughter of his deadly enemy, a fact of which he is in happy but improbable ignorance at the beginning of the action. Seductions, intrigues, fearful complications and villainous plots fill the first two acts, the supernatural element being supplied by a pandemonium-scene in Act II, Scene 1, closely modelled on Klinger's. In Act III Faust, entangled in a hideous snarl of domestic and extra-marital coils, resorts to magic in his despair and conjures up the devil Gog to cut the Gordian knot for him. He makes what he believes to be a wily and reasonable contract with the fiend, by which he is to suffer torments in hell for as many years as Gog serves him on earth. Needless to say he has damned himself irrevocably to all eternity by signing the impious pact, and is received with great rejoicings in the nether regions when he dies.

This lamentable effort at a Faustian domestic tragedy proved again, if indeed further proof were needed, that the two conceptions of life, the metaphysical and the mundane, are so incompatible that only great poetry can unite them; and the traces of Klinger in Benkowitz's drama also suggest that the former's powerful statement was militating strongly against the optimism advocated by Lessing. As far as Goethe's and Müller's public utterances went, the issue of the conflict for Faust's soul still hung in the balance with the scales weighted against salvation in Müller's *Situation*. Weidmann, Lenz and Schreiber were on one side; Klinger, Soden, the anonymous bookmaker and Benkowitz on the other; and the only outstanding work was Klinger's. This was felt to be the case at the time, as is shown by Tieck's *Anti-Faust, or the Story of a Stupid Devil*. With so many and such fantastic *Fausts* bobbing up all over Germany, it was not surprising that the humour of the situation should have appealed to that lively young satirist and ironist. In a gay little farce (begun in 1801 and never completed) which was published posthumously as a fragment in 1855, Tieck, according to the fashion favoured at the time, laid the scene in the Underworld, and the first act plays in hell. The now threadbare complaints about the flatness, paltriness and pettiness of all the phenomena of the day with special reference to literature gave the witty romantic writer scope to make merry over some of his literary butts and over the mania for producing *Fausts*. Satan, beside himself with anger on discovering that the devil Auerhahn has set up a lending-library in the nether regions, is still further incensed to find that all the little imps of mischief are borrowing books from it:

Satan (*flying out at them*). I've never seen such a thing in my life! What? Do you mean to say that you're actually reading? What have you got in your hands, young feller-me-lad?

A little devil (*showing him the title-page*). *Faust's Life* by Klinger, from which I hope to learn how to become a promising devil.

Another. And I am reading *The Eastern Faust* in the mornings.

A third. Everything we read is about our old friend Faust, who is sitting inside there and burning like blazes. There are at least fifty books about him in the lending-library. . . .

Satan. And do you imagine that you'll learn to be devils by that?

All the little devils. Yes!

Satan. Now look, Mephistopheles! We're bringing them up to our sorrow and shame!

Mephistopheles (*takes a book away from one of them and boxes his ears*). You silly idiot, how can you have the face to read that book?

Auerhahn. What are you beating him for? I hope it's not indecent or obscene? If it is and if it's done him any harm, we must undo the mischief with a rattling refutation.

Mephistopheles. You fool! It's *Faust*, the real *Faust*, in which I figure myself; something rabble like you can't understand.

Satan. Away with the book! There's nothing worse than when lousy little fellows like these read a poem about a real devil! They then try to copy him and the result is contemptible.

Dümmling. It's a good book, Mephistopheles, for those who can understand it. There's a lot in it. It's a pity that it's remained a fragment.[1]

---

[1] L. Tieck, *Nachgelassene Schriften*, ed. Köpke, Leipzig, 1855, pp. 150–2. *The Eastern Faust* was also by Klinger, but the hero was Ben Hafis. There is a pun here: *Morgenländer-Morgenstunden*. The 'real Faust' is of course Goethe's *Fragment*. Only the prologue and the first act of this farce were written. It was to have had five acts.

(b) A quasi-Goethean Faust, 1804

Klinger's novel and Goethe's *Fragment* were the only two of the 'fifty' Faustian products Tieck bothered to name. Yet he knew another, and had probably read it, or at least looked through it:

> The other day, a man filled with curiosity
> Asked me if by chance I absolutely
> (Which seemed to him unreasonable)
> Preferred Goethe's *Fragment* on Faust
> To Schink's poetical version.
> Incredulously he shook
> His thoughtful head
> When I assured him
> That I knew not the second,
> Nor felt any desire
> To attempt to enjoy it.[1]

Chasmisso for his part confessed in 1806 to having read Schink's *Faust* from cover to cover; and Weimar clearly had a sardonic eye on the author, for, on the publication of some scenes by Schink entitled *Doctor Faust's Pact with Hell* in the *Berliner Archiv der Zeit und ihres Geschmacks* in 1796, the following epigram appeared in Schiller's *Musenalmanach* for 1797:

> Unhappily Faust has often in Germany leagued himself with the devil,
> But so prosaically as here ne'er concluded the terrible pact.[2]

In the preface to his operetta in 1782 Schink had modestly declared that others might feel bold enough to tackle a subject which Lessing had handled, but that he did not. In the dedicatory poem to his completed work he announced triumphantly that his longing had constrained Lessing's shade; and if unremitting labour for more than twenty years on the Faust problem (1778–1804) counts for anything, then he deserved to succeed. He had published the prologue to his dramatic poem in 1795, the scenes just referred to in 1796, a musical lyric on Faust in 1800, and finally came forward in 1804 with the completed product: *Johann Faust. A Dramatic Fantasy based on a Legend of the Sixteenth Century.*

[1] L. Tieck, *Gedichte*, Dresden, 1823, Vol. III, p. 178. Written between 1804 and 1808.

[2] *Schillers Sämtliche Werke*, Säkularausgabe, Stuttgart, 1904–5, Vol. II, p. 119.

This exasperating production makes manifest the mysterious way in which the spirit of the age was moving in order to achieve its *Faust*. Weidmann was one proof that it was not particular in the choice of agents, and Schink is another; for at this juncture it almost appeared to be indifferent or uncertain whether to speak through the mouth of Goethe or through the mouth of Schink. In the pandemonium-prologue it is (to put it mildly) disconcerting to hear our old friend Ithuriel announcing the good tidings of Lessing with a Goethean message tacked on in would-be Klopstockian language:

> To his human heart I with human sounds
> Will speak, and as virtue is never more victorious
> Than through the soft eloquence of noble women,
> A virtuous female, the companion of his youth,
> Shall gently approach and save him!
> For Thou didst adorn womanhood
> With beauty and grace;
> Gave her a tender heart and a spirit mild,
> That she might tame man, rebellious and uncontrolled,
> And be his *visible* angel![1]

Here therefore, says one critic in incredulous tones, it would seem as if, for the first time in Faustian literature, we were meeting the idea of Faust's salvation through the love of a pure woman. But, adds the same critic reassuringly, so deep a conception as this was certainly far from Schink's mind.[2] It was as certainly present in this prologue as it had been in the operatic scenes published in 1778; and Schink, whether one likes it or not, must be given the credit for originating a notion which was to receive its final unction in the second part of Goethe's *Faust* more than thirty years later, when the 'penitent once called Gretchen' performed much the same function for Faust as Schink's Rosalinde and Mathilde had performed on earth and Müller's Lenchen had attempted in paradise.

Except for Ithuriel's heavy-handed prophecy, the pandemonium, written in spirited and at times eloquent verse, is much more readable than Müller's or Klinger's, being neither overweighted

---

[1] J. F. Schink, *Johann Faust*, Berlin, 1804, Vol. I, pp. 22 f.

[2] R. Warkentin, *Nachklänge der Sturm- und Drangperiode in Faustdichtungen*, Munich, 1896, pp. 80 f.

with satirical matter nor rendered unpalatable by repulsive descriptions of the torments of the damned. The reports of the various devils on their destructive commissions go with a swing; and though Schink was merely elaborating and versifying Engel's account of Lessing's scene here (as he frankly acknowledged), he added an episode of a seduction begun in church which is a vivid rendering of the advances made to Emilia Galotti by the Prince of Guastalla. This is only one among many signs of his allegiance to the spirit of Lessing as conceived by him; his affinity with the mind of Goethe is a much more puzzling matter. If he anticipated the part to be played by 'the eternal feminine' in Faust's apotheosis at the end of Goethe's poem, there is another striking coincidence in the second scene of the prologue, laid in Faust's study in Wittenberg. The hero, strongly drawn to magic, discovers a book of incantations on his table, utters invocations and is rewarded by some manifestations. His faithful Famulus Eckard interrupts the *séance* and tries to persuade Faust of the truth of Christianity. When he goes, Mephisto materializes in the guise of Paracelsus claiming foreknowledge of his own imminent demise as a proof that magic arts can unveil the future. Left alone, Faust in great gloom and doubt is temporarily cured of his despair by a girlish voice singing about the joys of heaven to the accompaniment of a lute:

> *Faust.* Thou heavenly one, and hast thou heard my prayer
> And seen my hand stretched forth to thee in longing?
> Come ye from heaven, oh sweetest tones, to me,
> That I may know who dwells above the skies?
> Oh yet sound on, ye envoys from on high,
> With rapturous ears your message I receive.[1]

Not only does the situation resemble the crisis at the end of the second monologue in Goethe's *Faust I* when the angelic chorus breaks in upon the attempted suicide, but there is also a haunting verbal similarity:

> *Faust.* Your messages I hear, but faith does still elude me . . .
> Oh yet sound on, ye heavenly songs so mild,
> My tears spring forth, and earth wins back her child.[2]

[1] Schink, op. cit. Vol. I, p. 46.
[2] Goethe, *Faust I*, ll. 765, 783f.

Schink could have known nothing of this passage until it was published in 1808; Goethe may have read Schink; but neither could have owed the following line to the other, since Goethe had written his in the dedicatory poem in 1797 and kept it by him until 1808:

> *Faust.* Ye waked in me of fairer days the memory.[1]

> *Faust.* Of happy days ye bring the pictured memory.[2]

Less effective in translation, these strange echoes are bewildering in the original, although one is not disposed to listen to them long; for it was no wonderfully impersonal manifestation from another world which gave Schink's hero pause, it was the voice of his deserted bride Mathilde, to whom Ithuriel, appearing in a dream, had entrusted the salvation of her former lover's soul:

> Tis thou shalt save him. Love, the angel which
> Shall overcome hell's dark and lying spirit.[3]

But it is to be no easy victory; for hardly has her song (off-stage) induced a softened and more hopeful mood in Faust, before Eckard rushes in to announce the approach of an infuriated mob of creditors and of equally incensed priests who are determined to arrest Faust for debt and also for his nigromantic practices. A letter announcing the death of Paracelsus determines Faust to have recourse to magic in good earnest, since the former's claim to foresee the future has been made good, or so the deluded hero believes; whereas, as the reader knows, it was that arch-deceiver Mephisto who made the 'prophecy'. Faust retires in a reckless mood, and Mathilde now enters disguised as a boy to hold a council of war with Eckard. He decides to disguise himself in the habit of a clown, and together they hope to save Faust from spiritual and moral ruin. The prologue is now over and the conflict engaged. In the first act Mephisto has it all his own way. Grotesquely disguised as the great-great-great-grandchild of the Witch of Endor (inevitably one thinks of Mephisto as Phorkyas in the second part of Goethe's *Faust*) he stages a Blocksberg farce or Witches' Sabbath for Faust's benefit, during which he conjures

---

[1] Schink, op. cit. Vol. I, p. 48.
[2] Goethe, op. cit. l. 9.
[3] Schink, op. cit. Vol. I, p. 59.

up gnomes, nixies, salamanders and elves, the whole diversified and enlivened by choruses of spirits. Although totally different from Goethe's *Witches' Sabbath*, this anticipates the notion of introducing such a scene into the drama; moreover Goethe's Faust was later to exorcise Mephisto by incantations addressed to salamanders, nixies, sylphs and kobolds. And the following incantation has a ghost-like affinity with the spell-binding, hypnotic, sliding and gliding rhythm with which the spirits were to sing Goethe's Faust to sleep after the invocation-scene:

Softly from hither
Flow, melt and slither
Vaporous and airy,
Breath-taking fairly,
Lightest of flimmer,
Rosy-red shimmer
Rises from gorges,
Flashes from far.
Sparks like a star,
Leaping they come,
Forcing the foaming
Mass that is roaming
Bubbling anon.
Hissing and swirling,
Magic unfurling,
Towering it plashes,
Then over it splashes
Right round the rim of the old
    mossy well.[1]

Lo! in a shower
Grapes that o'ercluster
Gush into must, or
Flow into rivers
Of foaming and flashing
Wine, that is dashing
Gems, as it boundeth
Down the high places,
And spreading, surroundeth
With crystalline spaces,
In happy embraces,
Blossoming forelands,
Emerald shore-lands!
And the winged races
Drink and fly onward.[2]

Much more important, however, than these vagrant verbal and rhythmical coincidences is the nature of the pact made subsequently between Schink's Faust and Mephisto in the Spesser Wood. From the Urfaustbook onwards the agreement between the hero and his familiar spirit had been a binding bilateral pact. Mephisto bound himself to serve and obey Faust absolutely for a specified number of years, and Faust swore to renounce God and the Christian faith and to surrender his soul to the fiend when the years ran out. Implicit in this contract was the clause that Mephisto must keep his part of the bargain in order to gain the reward. The English translator inserted it:

[1] Schink, op. cit. Vol. I, pp. 68f.
[2] Goethe, *Faust I*, ll. 1472ff.; tr. Bayard Taylor, op. cit. p. 65.

Further I couenant and grant them ['the hellish prince of Orient and his messenger *Mephostophiles'*] by these presents, that at the end of 24 yeares next ensuing the date of this present Letter, they being expired, and I in the meane time, during the said yeares to be serued of them at my wil, they accomplishing my desires to the full in al points as we are agreed, that then I giue them full power to doe with mee at their pleasure. . . .[1]

Marlowe kept this caveat:

. . . and furthermore grant unto them . . . four and twenty years being expired, and these articles above written being inviolate, full power to fetch . . . the said John Faustus, body and soul. . . .[2]

The Berlin puppet-play put it more positively, as we have seen;[3] but whether implicit, explicit or emphasized, the saving-clause was never put into operation; the nearest approach being in those versions of the legend in which Mephisto offered to return the contract rather than obey Faust's command to paint a faithful picture of the crucifixion. But that the deed might be rendered null and void by divine grace was tacitly acknowledged in the Urfaustbook when Mephisto forced Faust to sign a second pact after the pleadings of the good old man had nearly brought about a state of genuine repentance. This, however, was rather in the nature of a dramatic heightening of the spiritual conflict as the end drew near than due to any desire to throw doubt on the binding nature of the pact. To the rejection of God, Widman added an oath of celibacy, aimed at the Roman Catholic Church, and most of the puppet-plays kept this condition, inserting further prohibitions as the fancy took them and as popular tradition dictated.

So far all was plain sailing, and naturally so, since the hero of the action represented or described was headed inexorably for perdition. On the other hand, if he were to be saved a different kind of pact seemed desirable. So far this issue had been balked. There is no pact to be found in Lessing's Faustian fragments; Weidmann began his drama long after the agreement had been made and barely mentioned the subject. Goethe had left the relevant scenes unwritten both in the *Urfaust* and in the *Fragment*. Müller also omitted the signing of the pact, and all that we know

[1] Palmer and More, op. cit. p. 143.
[2] Marlowe, *Tragical History*, p. 85.
[3] See above, p. 101.

about it is the clause that it had to be confirmed by Faust after half the stipulated time had run. It was thus confirmed, and was therefore in line with the second deed in the Urfaustbook and in Marlowe's drama. Comprehensibly enough, Schreiber and Lenz had nothing to say about contracts. All those, in fact, either committed to the salvation of Faust or still undecided on the subject, or doubtful at least how to bring it about, had evaded the knotty problem of the pact. Those who adhered to the traditional ending were less perplexed. It needed the fearful pessimism of Klinger, however, to insert the stipulation that the pact should be returned if the devil could be forced to acknowledge the virtue of humanity, and to show how that contingency was the forlornest of all forlorn hopes. Soden for his part, although he gave no text, clearly had the traditional Faustian agreement in mind, which his hero swears to and signs; and Benkowitz emphasized the irretrievable nature of the deed by the hopeless attempt of the eighteenth-century magician to curtail the period of his torments in hell.

The binding bilateral pact was the only model which Faustian literature had to offer to the salvationists. Faustian ritual texts, however, and other well-known Black Books were considerably more helpful in this respect. There was, to start with, the unilateral agreement, which constrained the spirits to the utmost in obedience and service and explicitly preserved the exorcist from any injury either to his body or soul. 'Agrippa' described the process to be adopted in order to bring about this desirable result in the *Fourth Book of Occult Philosophy*; a German version of the *Grand Grimoire* gave the text of such a pact, and so did the Faustian *Magia Naturalis et Innaturalis* and the *Black Raven*, as well as directions how to obtain it. The spirits invoked were forced to append their seal or sign; the magician did not put his name to the bond, and was committed to nothing. But, however satisfactory such a state of affairs might be to the practising magician, and however deeply imbued with that ritual optimism which no experience can shake, it went too far in the direction of complete control and ascendancy as well as absolute immunity from danger to be of any use to a dramatist. Determined though such a writer might be to save Faust eventually, the peril must be real and the conflict too. A bilateral pact was therefore essential, and there were two types of this agreement to be found in the texts of ceremonial magic which offered a loop-hole for the exorcist. There was the conditional pact, and the ambiguous pact. There is a conditional pact in the famous *Grand Grimoire*, by the terms of which the spirit (called Lucifuge) is bound over to the service of the exorcist, who for his part must keep the secret of their commerce inviolable, be charitable to the poor and give to Lucifuge a gold or silver coin on the first day of every month. If he fails to keep these conditions, he will forfeit his soul and belong eternally to Lucifuge. These conditions are relatively easy to fulfil; nevertheless the danger is there, and the word secrecy underlines it. The version of the ambiguous pact in the *Grand Grimoire* depends for its point on the wording. For although Lucifuge expressly demanded the body and soul of the exorcist after twenty years, the document reads thus:

> I promise the grand Lucifuge to reward him in twenty years' time for all treasures he may give me.[1]

Lucifuge in his reply shows that he is well aware of the contemplated chicanery. 'Faust's' *Magia Naturalis et Innaturalis* did better still. Far from renouncing God and the Christian faith, as the legendary Faust had been forced to do, the exorcist is earnestly advised to frequent Mass during the preliminary proceedings so that he may be in good odour when and if he wishes to renounce the pact; and this advice is followed by instructions as to the rite to be performed in order to break the agreement. There was therefore ample precedent in the Black Books for conditional and ambiguous pacts which were not as binding on the exorcist as they seemed to be. Moreover the ritual texts and notably those attributed to Faust (reacting against the direful assumptions of the legend) always adopted a highly pious tone, invoking the blessing and aid of God when dealing with the fiends. Here again they went too far for a Faustian dramatist. A compromise had to be found between the inexorable pessimism of the legend rooted in the apostasy of the hero and the childish optimism of the ritual texts, based on genuine if very primitive religious beliefs. Schink attempted such a compromise. His Faust, having bargained for supernatural knowledge, magical flights, the bloom of youth and the love of women, now has to face the conditions imposed:

> *Meph.* Renounce the faith in an eternal God,
> Creator of the Universe, and preserver,

---

[1] Cf. my *Ritual Magic*, pp. 80 ff., 206 ff., 303 ff.

> Transcendent Lord Omnipotent of all.
> Confess there is no God but thine own will,
> And thine unaided strength is Providence.

Faust. (*After a pause for thought*)
> If God's in me, why should I need another?
> If I'm the maker of my fate, why then
> Demand a Providence? I will renounce
> The old God then in favour of the new.[1]

Arrogant, overweening, impious, this is nevertheless no formal allegiance to Satan, such as was made in the legend; it is rather the choice of an immanent as against a transcendent God; nor is there any explicit rejection of Christ. It shows a dangerous but not an incurable state of mind, also evident in the responses made to the further conditions: to forswear marriage and legal paternity:

Meph. Nor son's nor daughter's voice shall sound for thee;
> Against the call of nature close thy heart.

Faust. If thou canst ever bring me to that pass,
> And rob me of humanity, I'll swear.

Meph.   Then promise too
> After twelve years to give thyself to hell.

Faust. That might sound fearful, but it frights not me.
> I know myself and know mine own free will,
> And that defies thee and thy devilish arts. . . .
> And if I swear to thee, I brave thee too,
> Thee and the whole host of thy hateful hell.
> Yea, I'll be thine, if thou upon my soul
> But *one* decisive crime canst ever roll,
> But keep thy word, as I my word shall keep.[2]

On reading this, the mind leaps forward to Goethe's *Prologue in Heaven*; for Schink's condition anticipates God's wager with Mephisto and Schink's Faust obviously believes that he will never commit that glaringly ambiguous 'decisive crime'; and who in any case is to be the judge of that? He is now in the same position as the protagonist of the gipsy puppet-play, whose soul could only be claimed after he had committed three deadly sins. He virtuously determined to stop at the second, only to discover that the pact with Mephisto counted as the first. Klingemann also made use of

---

[1] Schink, op. cit. Vol. I, p. 122.   [2] Ibid. pp. 123 f.

this device. By means of a similar diabolic sophistry Pope Sylvester II (Gerbert) and Faust's Polish double Twardowski were carried off from places named after the cities (Jerusalem and Rome) where the pact was to fall due. Uncertainty of time, place and condition always redounded to the devil's advantage in Faustian legend and to the advantage of the magician in ritual texts. Schink followed their example.

From now onwards his drama creaks slowly forward through monstrously swollen episodes which cannot conceal the extreme simplicity of the mechanism. The stock or permanent figures are Faust and Mephisto, Eckard disguised as the jesting Casper Fröhlich and Mathilde habited as a youth. Though perpetually on the verge of recognizing their identity, Faust never quite does so until the fourth act. It is hard to see why he has to be kept in ignorance, at least as far as Eckard is concerned; but Mathilde, whom he once loved and is to love again, did well perhaps to hide her maiden blushes under an assumed masculinity. Faust calls her his Agathodaimon, and bursts out thus after she has been lecturing him for his own good:

> Oh, that I could but from mine own self hide!
> Am I still Faust? I know myself no more.
> A boy I stand deserving of the rod.
> Oh wretched Faust, fling far the sceptre's power![1]

> What do I here? Why is my heart so sore?
> Oh wretched Faust, I know myself no more.[2]

This echo from Goethe's Faust in Gretchen's chamber shows the debt to have been Schink's, even if unconsciously. It does little to reconcile one to the part Mathilde is called upon to play throughout the drama in close collaboration with Eckard. Whenever Mephisto is on the point of achieving his object and plunging Faust into crime, Mathilde sings a song, or (more rarely) Eckard stages an interruption, and Faust is dragged back in the nick of time from eternal perdition. In the second act, for instance, he falls violently in love with a beautiful girl called Isabella whom he sees praying to the Virgin in church. This harks back once more to *Emilia Galotti* and the cognate scene in Schink's prologue; but it

[1] Schink, op. cit. Vol. II, p. 30.
[2] Goethe, *Faust I*, ll. 2719 f.

is still more obviously a pendant to the scenes in the Gretchen tragedy before the Mater Dolorosa and in the cathedral. For Isabella is imploring the Virgin Mary to sanction the love she feels for her ardent young wooer Theodore. The answer to this petition is in the affirmative as Isabella rapturously informs her lover:

> I *may* love thee, for by a miracle
> The Blessed One has sanctified our vows:
> She smiled on me, as saints do smile in heaven.[1]

Not only is this a thoroughly Schinkian recasting of the tragic scenes in the *Urfaust*, it also puts one uneasily in mind of the re-orientation Goethe was to give to the heart-broken prayer to the Mater Dolorosa when he came to the last scene in the second part of *Faust*. Almost more than anything else this unwelcome coincidence seems to prove a fantastic affinity between two minds which were nevertheless poles and poles apart. This makes the reappearance of Frau Marthe in the semblance of Isabella's nurse Susanna a mere unimportant reminiscence. She and Mephisto are hand in glove, and everything seems set-fair for a seduction when Mathilde steps in to foil the plot. Faust's heart is so much softened by the representations of his Agathodaimon that, far from ruining Isabella, he now magnanimously makes it possible for her to marry Theodore instead of the old man for whom her father had destined her. In the third act, after Eckard, disguised as Casper Fröhlich, had taken a leaf out of the puppet-play texts by summoning and dismissing devils with lightning speed, the University was brought strongly into the foreground. Faust was made honorary doctor of the four faculties of theology, law, medicine and philosophy, and held a lecture to the assembled senate expounding Fichte's system, strongly ironized by Schink. Goethe did much the same thing with the young Baccalaraeus as exponent in *Faust II*. The rest of Schink's third act was taken up by a riotous and rowdy version of *Auerbach's Cellar*, partly based on Goethe's, but also enriched by many traditional tricks and feats from the Faust-books, ending in the famous exit of Faust and Mephisto on a barrel. In the fourth act farce gives way to pathos. Faust's aged and virtuous parents (Gotthard and Anna) appear at a masked ball disguised as a hermit and pilgrim respectively and urge their son to return to the path of virtue. Eckard and Mathilde add their

[1] Schink, op. cit. Vol. I, pp. 177 f.

prayers to those of the parents, everyone unmasks, all identities are discovered, and a moving scene of mutual recognition and sentiment ensues. Mephisto is within an ace of losing his victim, when he saves the situation by a magic mirror, in which the bewilderingly beautiful countenance of Schirin ('sweet and lovable') puts all other thoughts in Faust's mind to flight. He immediately makes tracks for Italy, where he hopes to find Schirin, accompanied by the triumphant Mephisto and a lad of sixteen called Faustin:

> Now this youth was, hell's fiend revealed it not,
> The son of Faust, begot in volupty
> In former years, when in the strength of youth,
> All flown with wine and fiery kisses bold.
> The hapless girl he then abandoned quite
> And she paid with her life for the child's birth.
> The orphan son unto her sister's care
> In far Vienna then was given up.[1]

This is a peculiarly Schinkian 'improvement' on Goethe. The heroine herself, the devoted Mathilde, although engaged to and deserted by Faust in the past, had never been seduced by him, and was therefore unsullied and unstained and a suitable instrument for Ithuriel. A son of Faust being needed at this juncture, the function of illicit motherhood was given to a dead girl. Müller combined Mathilde and Gretchen in his Lenchen, thus making the best of both worlds, for he followed Schink in using the son of Faust as an agent of temptation. Mephisto's aim was to corrupt Faustin through his father, and in this way to ruin them both. But, what with the ever-watchful Eckard and the ever-songful Mathilde, he never really had a chance. Mutual recognition again thwarts the fiend; and although by the terms of the pact Faust may not love his son Faustin, the hope that he will corrupt him can no longer be entertained. Eckard has meanwhile also interrupted a promising love-affair between Faust and a statue animated by the magician, in reality a fiend; and Mephisto is now forced to play his last card, the irresistible Schirin.

This vision is discovered to be a magic likeness of Raphaele, the lovely young wife of the old Count of Montaldo, at whose court the whole party is now gathered and where Faust is to hold a magic

---

[1] Schink, op. cit. Vol. II, p. 233.

display. Here again the traditional scene was used by Schink and by no means unsuccessfully. For Faust transformed Raphaele into the semblance of the Venus of Paphos, the audience-hall became a classical grove and all the attendants were similarly transformed. This marvellous performance led up to a passionate love-scene between Raphaele and Faust, in which, however, their better natures won the day; renunciations were made and an affecting farewell was taken. It was such an emotional good-bye, however, that the old Count, engineered on to the scene by Mephisto, not unnaturally mistook it for something else. He made to stab his wife, but Eckard and Mathilde prevented him and convinced him of the purity and faithfulness of Raphaele. Mephisto, maddened by this, swears that she is guilty, and (clad as a Dominican monk) is about to stab her to death in the name of Holy Church, when a heavenly music is suddenly heard, a supernatural light fills the scene, Mephisto trembles, the dagger slides from his grasp, his monk's robe disintegrates into dust, and he himself, dissolved into a nebulous phantom, hovers wavering on the ground. Ithuriel now comes shining down from a silver cloud and makes a long and forgiving speech to all and sundry. Not to be outdone, Faust also speaks some improving words, and Ithuriel then turns to Mephisto:

> Fly, fallen angel, and bring in your company
> Bettering remorse down to the seat of rebellion!
> Let her companion you back to truth, the life of the Spirits!
> Then may you rise from the night, sons of the morning, like us!
> Then will hell cease to be the dwelling of sad compassion,
> No longer a realm of night. Peace and light too and truth
> Shall reign in the kingdom of souls.

(*Mephistopheles disappears. Ithuriel vanishes in a haze of light. The heavenly melodies continue. Faust's son enters with his grandparents. They throw themselves into his arms. Universal expression of joy and sympathy.*)[1]

The belief that the hosts of hell might attain to salvation finally had been held by Origen and by the author of the *Clementine Recognitions*; although later rejected as heretical, it had been adopted by a few of the magical rituals. Some of the fiends in the *Lemegeton* or *Little Key of Solomon* cherished this hope, which was held out as a bribe to the cohorts of Infernus when taking their oath of allegiance to the exorcist in 'Faust's' *Magia Naturalis*

[1] Schink, op. cit. Vol. II, pp. 329 f.

et Innaturalis, and it was explicitly mentioned by the arch-fiend Aciel in that compilation when swearing to keep his word.[1] It is expressed by Schink in Klopstockian language which recalls the pardon granted to the remorseful devil Abbadonna in *The Messiah*. Goethe also at one time contemplated a similar forgiveness for Mephisto; for, whether through their knowledge of magical rituals or not, Goethe and Schink had many points of contact. Schink anticipated Goethe in representing Faust's salvation brought about by the supernal powers working through a young girl loved and betrayed in his youth. The 'angelic' music breaking in upon Faust's despair; the *Witches' Sabbath*, Mephisto disguised as a 'Norn'; the elemental spirits, the ambiguous conditional pact; the satire on Fichte's philosophy, the Greek transformation-scene: all these disparate elements reappeared either in the first or in the second part of Goethe's *Faust*. On the other hand the Gretchen tragedy inspired the episode of Isabella and Theodore as well as the sad story of Faustin's mother; and the debt to *Auerbach's Cellar* and to the magic mirror in Goethe's *Witches' Kitchen* is plain to see. As for the rhythmical and verbal similarities, it must be acknowledged that Schink had it in him to write a Goethean line or two now and again. Yet he has never been regarded as a forerunner and is almost completely forgotten to-day. This is because his 'Fantasy' is on the whole mere stuff and nonsense, inordinately long and for the most part execrably written. But analysis lays bare the same mental attitude as Goethe's to the problem of Faust and its eventual solution. One seems to see the spirit of the age hovering uncertainly over the minds of both, labouring now in one medium and now in the other as it propelled the legend forward, and tossing Schink carelessly aside after twenty-six years of arduous collaboration.

[1] Cf. my *Ritual Magic*, pp. 69, 173 f, and 177.

CHAPTER VII

POETICAL FAUSTS

(a) A romantic Faust, 1804

Had it not been for the publication of Goethe's *Faust-Fragment* in 1790, an early nineteenth-century critic would have argued ill for the future development of the legend in German literature. After a very unpromising beginning in Weidmann's drama, it had struggled gamely upwards during the Storm and Stress period and achieved completion at last in Klinger's novel. This was followed by a vertiginous downward descent which bade fair to land it among anonymous bookmakers or deliver it bound hand and foot to the tender mercies of a Soden or a Schink. And so far, with the signal exception of Goethe, the only poet who had been drawn to the legend was the strange, unhappy Lenz.

And would even Goethe prove to be the Saint Christopher needed to carry the misleadingly light little Faust of the puppet-plays across the narrow stream dividing popular from literary poetry? The stream developed into a rushing river when Lessing made the attempt, and he gave it up. With every subsequent effort to lift him, the manikin put on weight. In 1804, before Goethe was even half-way across, the river was so wide and the burden so heavy that it looked as if nothing short of a miracle could accomplish the feat. In view of the general awareness of the formidable nature of the task, which the experiences of the Storm and Stress writers and Goethe's *Fragment* had greatly increased, Chamisso (1781–1838) modestly called his dramatic poem *An Attempt*. It appeared in the *Musenalmanach* for 1804, and he later defined it as an almost boyish metaphysical effort, a disarming piece of humility which does less than justice to his presentation of the problem. Chamisso was a real poet, whose *Castle Boncourt* is perhaps one of the most melting statements of longing and loss ever made even by a German romantic poet. Moreover in *Peter Schlemihl* he was later to give a highly personal, queer and wistful rendering of the Faustian situation in one of its aspects. The hero sells his shadow to a sinister stranger for the purse of Fortunatus, and then realizes that he is a lost man without it, tragically different from his fellow-men. His action was guilty and disastrous, and the benefits accruing to him from it are tainted at the source. In a very fine scene, he nevertheless refuses to trade his soul to the devil in order to get his shadow back, and casts the inexhaustible purse from him, lest it should act as a link between him and the fiend dogging his footsteps. This is a romantic version of the Faust-legend, and it seemed to promise that the new movement would contribute yet more to the weaving of the Faustian web. For *Peter Schlemihl* ranks high amongst the spate of kindred stories poured out in fascinating profusion from romantic pens. The poets who wielded them had reverted one and all to the belief in another world surrounding ours, alluring but also sinister and fraught with perils for mortal men. Such writers, it would appear, were even more fitted to produce acceptable Fausts than the titanically-minded Storm and Stress; for the legend belonged to the same stratum as those about Undine, Melusine, and Fortunatus, not to mention a score of others either invented or re-created by the romantic poets in their subtle, imaginative or eerie way.

This possibility was not realized; but Chamisso's *Faust* is romantic in a special sense, indeed almost in a specialized sense; for this short dramatic sketch has deep philosophical implications, and the fairy-tale world of German romanticism was based on contemporary philosophy and notably on Kant. His contention that it is absolutely impossible for human beings to know the reality behind the apparent world, since the senses are delusory, went back to Plato and electrified his own generation. Kleist was one of those to whom the tragic 'discovery' was almost fatal. Others found it extremely inspiring and bent their energies to the representation of the illusory nature of what is generally taken to be real, or tried to penetrate beyond the barrier between the world we know and the reality which it masks. Chamisso took a different line in his *Faust*, combining the Kantian idea of the impossibility of knowing reality with the religious notion of the guilt involved in making the attempt. This harks back to Genesis and was strongly emphasized in the Urfaustbook. Schiller had given it expression too in *The Veiled Statue of Saïs*. To condemn the thirst for knowledge as sinful was a retrogressive step, completely in harmony with the general trend backwards to medievalism and beyond of the German romantic movement; and Chamisso harmonized this attitude with the most modern philosophical thought in a manner tragically profound. The action is concentrated into a few pages covering a period of an hour at most, during which Faust learns the terrible lesson which Kant had inexorably proclaimed:

Faust.   Eternal riddles, grim and dreadful vipers,
    Forever self-begetting, self-consumed,
    You waste my heart by winding and uncoiling
    In circles intertwined and ever new.
    I cannot banish you, I cannot crush you,
    My labouring soul no respite from you knows.
    Ah, woe to him who must accept your challenge!
    The thinker's brow with deep-etched lines is furrowed,
    And doubt is all the prize he'll wrest from you.

    No! That fell snake-bite doubt shall now no longer
    Gnaw slowly on at my grief-sickened heart,
    No longer still the burning wound envenom,
    I *will* be whole in the full light of truth.
    Distant the goal as stars, yet I'll assault it,
    Since vainly striving I can ne'er attain. . . .
    Oh you, in dread and darkling veils enveloped,
    Spirits surrounding me, obey my will,
    The firm and rock-like will that summons you.

Evil Spirit (a voice on the left).
    The firm and rock-like will obeyed shall be,
    Thou son of earth who boldly spurnest it,
    Resembling us; speak, what is thy desire? . . .

Faust.   Tis knowledge I desire, wisdom and truth.

Evil Spirit. Thy lofty words transcend the thoughts of mortals,
    Yet, didst thou call me up in sober earnest,
    Then swear to me the price for this: thy soul,
    And I'll unlock for thee truth's priceless treasures,
    And what a man may know, it shall be thine.

Good Spirit (a voice on the right).
    Faust! Faust!
    To blessed amidst mortals
    The Father permitted
    To taste of all fruits
    That grew in the garden;
    To blessed among mortals
    The Father forbade but
    The one single fruit. . . .

Faust. No spirit good art thou, liar, avaunt!
      I turn away from thee, I follow *him*.
      Tis knowledge I desire, wisdom and truth.

Evil Spirit. Tis well, oh Faust; but swear to me the price,
      And I'll unlock for thee truth's priceless treasures,
      And what a man may know, it shall be thine.
      Now break the staff thyself over thy soul. . . .

Faust. The staff is broken!

Good Spirit.   Broken!

Evil Spirit.   Broken!

       (*Long pause.*)

Faust. And now?

Evil Spirit. I mock at thee, thou gimcrack bauble thou,
      And mock the greedy wishes of thy heart,
      I mock at thee, rash fool whom I despise,
      And render thee the price which I agreed: . . .
      Like unto speech, like to the sound of words
      Which are the go-betweens and signs of thoughts,
      So are thy sense-impressions and thy thoughts
      But language only, empty, idle signs
      Of that reality thou'lt ne'er unveil.
      Thou thinkest only with the help of words,
      Seest nature only with the senses' aid,
      Canst grasp her only with the laws of mind.
      Hadst thou a hundred, nay a thousand eyes,
      Thou still wouldst see but shadows thrown by thee,
      And never penetrate beyond that veil.[1]

Only death can rend the veil; and death means for Faust the price he has paid for that bitter knowledge, an eternity in hell. But his desire for the truth is a heroic desire, and he puts an end to his existence on the spot in order to discover the ultimate reality he has vainly sought on earth.

This arresting dramatic sketch, written in very fine verse into which the melodies of Goethe's *Parcae's Song* from *Iphigenia* enter when the good spirit bewails Faust's choice, is a poetical commentary on the first monologue, that stock feature of Faustian drama since the days of Marlowe. It penetrates the subject with an incurably tragic philosophy, and is complete in itself, narrowing

 [1] *Chamisso's Werke*, ed. Tardel, Leipzig and Vienna [1907], Vol. 1, pp. 433 ff.

the issue down to the one fundamental point, on which (or so it seems to me) Chamisso said the last sorrowful word, representing a dilemma from which, humanly speaking, there is no possible escape.

(b) An imperishable Faust, 1808

And now at last Goethe brought himself to publish the first part of his dramatic poem in full, uttering first of all that long, lovely sigh in the dedicatory poem which expelled from his anxious heart the doubts and hopes, the joys and sorrows, the regrets and fears which assailed him and indeed shook him when in 1797 he finally decided to complete what he had begun in his now almost legendary youth. His emotions were so mixed and mingled, so much shot through with grief, that they must be exorcized by poetical expression before he could apply himself to the alluring but perplexing and painful task. It had been rather like an intellectual conundrum when he had picked up the threads for the *Fragment*; but now a strong emotion had the upper hand and dictated the poem (one of the most moving of his personal confessions) as well as the tragic lament over his vanished youth which the poet gave vent to in the curtain-raiser. In this spirited discussion about plays, the public and the theatre, Goethe was groping like a blind man among his contemporaries and the demands they were likely to make on a work so long awaited, so much talked of, so famous already. Was it fitted for the stage? he seemed to be asking. Would it ever satisfy the general public, let alone a theatrical manager? Could any actor ever make anything of Faust? But these symbolical questions expressed a deeper doubt, a profound sense of isolation from that once so ardent and enthusiastic public, spell-bound under the appeal of works from which he was now estranged and whose tone he neither could nor would recapture.

For middle age was upon him, and one of the signs that this was so is the ironical element in the *Prologue in Heaven*. Mephisto, who had the diabolic monopoly of irony in the *Urfaust*, was now treated with patronizing irony by Goethe and by God. This detached, benevolent and elderly attitude differentiates Goethe's opening scene from the hectic pandemoniums of Müller and Klinger and the heavy solemnity of the reassuring conclusion to

Schink's. Otherwise the basic idea, the choice of a great man whose virtue is to be put to the test, is the same in all, and derived from the Book of Job. But Goethe kept closer to the common model and brought his prologue into line with the tone of the opening monologue by bringing God on to the stage very much in the style of Hans Sachs in *The Dissimilar Children of Eve*. A kind of wager between the Lord and Mephisto as to the possibility of destroying the soul of Faust was an earnest of the hero's eventual salvation, although many of Goethe's readers did not live to see the accomplished fact. But the omnipotent and omniscient ruler of the universe was in no doubt as to the result, and was explicitly using Mephisto as a goad to activity. The devil was therefore a mere tool in the hands of the Lord, who according to medieval tradition (based on Job) often permitted diabolic temptation in order to search or purify the hearts of His servants. It is true that such trials sometimes came to a tragic end; but here we have it on the highest authority that no permanent harm will result from the intercourse between Faust and the evil spirit. This diminishes the stature of Mephisto, who, after an informal and friendly chat with the Almighty, goes about his task with the divine patronage and approval. Goethe thus deliberately renounced the Marlovian and Miltonic conception of satanic greatness which Müller and Klinger in their different ways had striven to achieve. Mephisto, as he later confessed himself, was now but part of that power which, always willing evil, always furthers good. Irony could hardly go deeper than this; and one can imagine the approving smiles it would have drawn from Lessing, who had so sagely and unavailingly preached irony to the uncomprehending Müller.

Endearing and engaging as the *Prologue in Heaven* is, a masterstroke of poetical diplomacy, it nevertheless placed the Earth Spirit in an anomalous position; for the *Woodland Cavern* scene in the *Fragment* was retained, and this ratified the claim put forward in the *Urfaust* (and also retained in *Part I*) that Mephisto was the servant of that mighty apparition. Faust may of course have been mistaken in believing this; but that supposition leaves the Earth Spirit hanging in the air, and deprives him, if not of greatness, then of significance, a sacrifice to the altered conception which one can only reluctantly accept. It is a symbol of the devaluation of magic to mere witchcraft made in the *Witches' Kitchen* and emphasized in the *Witches' Sabbath* now introduced into *Part I*. As we have seen, there were precedents, if not very reputable ones, for inoculating the Faustian organism with the virus of witchcraft. There was Löwe's poem of 1756, semi-satirical nonsense, showing Faust on the Blocksberg; there was the Kurz production of 1767, in which Faust was preparing to tear the heart out of his father's body; there was Schink's light and not unpleasing version of a Sabbath in which Mephisto summoned up at too great length tuneful elemental spirits. Goethe, who introduced his *Sabbath* with its attendant *Dream* immediately after the scene in the cathedral, ironized the whole proceedings, which began however with some magnificent natural descriptions.[1] Coming where it does, this fantasy transports the reader from one of the most heart-breaking moments in all poetry, and moreover heart-breakingly real, into a whimsical world of make-believe which is not meant to be taken seriously. Far from affording relief to the emotions, it is an outrage upon them, and would perhaps have seemed less deliberately heartless if Goethe could have brought himself to represent the Sabbath as evil instead of merely ridiculous. This was not within his power, as the *Paralipomena* show. He had meant to depict, even if only ironically, the obscene and blasphemous final worship of Satan in which the Sabbaths were supposed to terminate; but he swerved away from that impossible task and substituted the *Witches' Sabbath Dream*, a jingling and jangling puerile little entertainment in which some of the verses he had written about his literary and other butts (already satirized in the *Sabbath*) were economically used up. One can forgive Goethe the less easily for this because the paltry *Dream* comes hard on the heels of a moment on the Brocken when real danger to Gretchen and the stirrings of real evil in Faust's mind were darkly adumbrated:

> *Faust.* Mephisto, seest thou there,
> Alone and far, a girl most pale and fair?
> She gropes along and very slowly too,
> As if her feet were bound. Can it be true?
> I must confess, it seems to me
> That my dear Gretchen she might be.
>
> *Mephisto.* Let that alone, don't look, for mercy's sake,
> It is a magic spook, a likeless fake. . . .

[1] How little Goethe was disposed to take the matter seriously at this time can be seen in the poems *Die erste Walpurgisnacht*, 1799, written a year before his *Witches' Sabbath*. It gives a rational explanation for the superstition, very much on the lines of modern thought.

> *Faust.* Ah no, those are the eyes of one, whom dying
> No hand with loving pressure closed;
> That is the breast whereon I once was lying,
> The body sweet, beside which I reposed!
>
> *Mephisto.* Tis magic all, thou fool. . . .
>
> *Faust.* The woe, the rapture so ensnare me,
> That from her gaze I cannot tear me!
> Fain would I see around her fairest throat
> A single scarlet stringlet gleaming,
> No broader than a knife's back seeming!
>
> *Mephisto.* Quite right! The mark I also note.[1]

The last three lines of the passage are ambiguous; they read like a wish, although Mephisto's answer seems to suggest that it is not a wish but an aesthetic appreciation. In either case there is a fearful sadistic gloating in the lines, the only ones in the *Witches' Sabbath* which bring the shadow of real evil over the motley throng assembled on the Brocken. Otherwise this scene is quaint, grotesque, satirical, ironical, playful; anything but sinister. And perhaps Goethe did well to go no further with the vision of Gretchen; for originally the hint of the coming decapitation was to be given more broadly: the head was to fall off from the body. It is clear that he was not to be trusted on the Brocken at all. But, if it does nothing else, this scene at least gives the impression of the passage of time during which Gretchen's fate is running its tragic course. Fairley maintains that it is an evocation of the folk-myths among which Gretchen was born and bred, the dark subsoil from which the legend sprang, and that it is almost like a nightmare during her swoon. This would be a brilliant suggestion if the *Witches' Sabbath* were not so ironical; but when was the folk-consciousness ever that? And when did the folk-consciousness ever rise to satirical gibes at literary notabilities of the day? Besides, the whole is too light and playful to be a suitable nightmare for a girl in her terrible predicament. Goethe probably placed

---

[1] Goethe, *Faust I*, ll. 4183–206; translation based on Bayard Taylor, op. cit. p. 133. He translates: 'And, strange! around her fairest throat/A single scarlet band is gleaming'. Goethe says: 'Wie sonderbar muss diesen schönen Hals/Ein einzig rotes Schnürchen schmücken.' The literal translation of the last lines runs thus: 'How strangely that fair neck would be adorned by a single scarlet thread,' or 'How strangely well a single scarlet thread would adorn that fair neck.'

it where he did to bridge the gap in time between the scene in the cathedral and *Dull Day, Field*; but one can hardly resist the conclusion that he chose to represent a Sabbath in order to laugh the whole phenomenon of magic and witchcraft out of court. The *Dream* confirms this impression. Fairley interprets that as the thinning out of the nightmare until we come back with a start to consciousness and hear the angry voice of Faust loudly berating Mephisto. This is the best defence ever offered for that tedious intermezzo; one's reason accepts it grudgingly; one's instincts continue to rebel and to sorrow over this damage done to a masterpiece.

If Goethe dislocated the Gretchen tragedy at this crucial point, partly in order to discredit the power of evil, all the other alterations to it show that he was far indeed from wishing to sabotage the most beautiful of his works. There was very little he could do to improve it; but the slight alterations and amplifications which he made all tended to bring out the tragedy of Gretchen's situation more strongly. He altered the position of *Woodland Cavern*, placing it before the actual seduction, where it acquires a more poignant significance. He developed the situation latent in young Valentine's monologue about the loss of his sister's reputation into an attack on her lover, in which Faust with Mephisto's aid mortally wounds him and absconds. The dying lad then turns upon Gretchen and rends her before the assembled villagers, who have already answered her trembling question as she emerges from her house: 'Who lies there?' with the fearful indictment: 'Your mother's son.' The sleeping-draught has done its work: her brother curses her and dies; and only Frau Marthe raises her voice in protest and defence. Racing and toppling over each other, the Valentine scenes finally dash the terrified girl on to the menacing shore where looms the dark cathedral. And here again the place finally chosen for the utter repudiation by her own kind before the seeming repudiation by God heightens the intensity of the tragedy. Nothing now remained but to transpose into poetry the stark and vivid prose of the prison-scene, a transposition which brought out in even greater beauty than before the parting of the lovers at a dawn which precedes death, enacted again and again in the *aubades*. And the voice calling out that Gretchen is saved is the first voice proclaiming salvation in Faustian poetry to which one lends a willing and grateful ear.

The labour with the Gretchen tragedy was light labour, for it was a labour of love; the Faust drama itself presented a much more formidable problem. Two links in the chain drawing Faust and Mephisto together had been forged in the *Fragment*: the *Witches' Kitchen* and *Woodland Cavern*. In both of these, as well as in the reconditioned *Auerbach's Cellar*, Mephisto played a conspicuous part; but he had yet to be summoned up by the magician, and the contract between them had yet to be drawn up in form; and still the Earth Spirit threatened bathos to that undertaking. Space enough must be made between the two conjurations; and greater despair must be Faust's portion before he could be brought to accept in lieu of the spirit of creative nature the disparaging, sardonic and cynical familiar who was to companion him through life. The despair which the rejection by the Earth Spirit had induced in the magician was the obvious and organic point of departure for this. Hence that wonderful second monologue uttered by Faust after Wagner has been dismissed, sinking into an abyss of despair and then rising to an ecstasy of suicidal resolve, to that supreme moment when he pledges a new dawn and lifts the poisoned goblet to his lips. He was by no means the first of his tribe to choose and welcome death:

> Or come you, as your gentle face
> Does seem to promise, full of grace,
> To annihilate me utterly?
> Receive my thanks and linger not![1]

The measure of my misery is full, break the vessel which can no longer contain it. But I still have courage to fight with you for my life; for I refuse to die like a slave who sinks down passively under the might of his master. . . . It is my own heart which has conquered me and not you.[2]

> Into thy bosom, everlasting doom!
> Maybe to mere extinction, perhaps to knowledge,
> To certainty whate'er betide![3]

Lenz's Faust is moving, Klinger's heroic and Chamisso's is great; but only the musings of Socrates on the immortality of the soul before he drank the cup of hemlock can be compared with the

[1] Lenz, *Die Höllenrichter*, ed. cit. Vol. III, p. 148.
[2] Klinger, *Fausts Leben*, ed. cit. Vol. I, p. 298.
[3] Chamisso, op. cit. Vol. I, p. 443.

spiritual fortitude shown by Goethe's Faust as he prepares for death:

> Out on the open ocean speeds my dreaming;
> The crystal flood before my feet is gleaming,
> A new day beckons to a newer shore!
>
> A fiery chariot, borne on buoyant pinions,
> Sweeps near me now! And I can ready be
> To pierce the ether's high, unknown dominions,
> To reach new spheres of pure activity!
> This godlike rapture, this supreme existence,
> Do I, but now a worm, deserve to track?
> Yes, resolute to reach some brighter distance,
> On Earth's fair sun I turn my back!
> Yes, let me dare those gates to fling asunder,
> Which every man would fain go slinking by!
> Tis time, through deeds the proof of this to thunder:
> That with the height of gods Man's dignity may vie!
> Not from that gloomy gulf to shrink affrighted,
> Where Fancy doth herself to self-born pangs compel,—
> But to strike on toward that pass benighted,
> Around whose narrow jaws flame all the fires of hell,—
> To take this step with cheerful resolution,
> Even should Nothingness be the dread conclusion.[1]

At the great moment, when Faust is raising the cup to his lips, the Easter bells and the Easter chorus ring out from a near-by church, like voices from another world. This sudden irruption of Christian ideas about resurrection into pagan dreams of a further state is one of the most beautiful dissonances in all poetry, shattering Faust's mood and breaking his high resolve. The long and fearful strain of the night is over; memories of childhood, of lost happiness and vanished faith overwhelm him: a flood of tears unmans him and life reclaims him. Although the situation, and even some of the lines, bear a real resemblance to the parallel scene in Schink's drama, it is nevertheless not possible to compare the two seriously. The glorious despair of Goethe's Faust soars out of sight and sound of the mere gloom of Schink's; and poor Mathilde with her twanging lute cannot compete with the triumphant outburst of

---

[1] Goethe, *Faust I*, ll. 699 ff.; cf. Bayard Taylor, op. cit. p. 47. I have made some alterations. It is known that Goethe contemplated a drama on Socrates during the *Urfaust* period.

Easter joy. In fact no one but Schink's Faust would ever have taken her for a divine messenger. But if she was responsible for that wonderful invasion of the Christian into the pagan world, ringing in a different dispensation, then her literary existence has been justified by no less a poet than Goethe.

Though the spell of the night was broken by what seemed like a direct divine intervention and Faust had been won back to life, yet the fearful isolation of his spirit remained, and he essayed to break through the solitary confinement of his mind by mingling with others in a walk with Wagner outside the city gates on that same Easter Sunday. The highly refreshing atmosphere of that scene, with nature so fair, and lads and lassies so gay, and everything so full of movement and life, is a marvellous poetical comment on the hero's tragic difference from humanity as a whole; it condenses into a few snatches of song and exchanges of dialogue what Müller drew out so interminably in his student-scenes. Moreover the admiration and respect felt for Faust by those who remembered how he had helped his father to fight the plague are revealingly contrasted with Faust's own savage criticism and mockery of the means they had ignorantly and (according to him) disastrously employed. This is the same refusal to be comforted by any ordinary means which Müller's Faust also manifested; and both show too that the only solace their minds can receive is through and with nature:

How happy is he [says Müller's Faust to Herz] who can enjoy the splashing of little fishes in a pond or the humming of gaily coloured insects; how happy is he, how quiet and peaceful his soul. The golden evening beckons him upward; the swaying willows scatter sweet scent from their brown tree-tops; he lies down near a murmuring waterfall and falls asleep until the silence of the night awakes him. . . . Everything is balm to his soul: green fields with pasturing lambs, streams, hills and moors; all nature opens her stores to pleasure him with her manifold treasures. . . . He is the son of happiness, lying in ecstasy on the breast of nature.[1]

Soothed at first by the glorious natural panorama before him, Goethe's Faust is rapt away by longing as he contemplates the setting sun and he calls upon the spirits of the air to transport him to a new and happier existence elsewhere. Wagner utters a warn-

---

[1] Müller, *Fausts Leben Dramatisiert*, ed. cit. Vol. IV, pp. 277 f.

ing; but too late; this is Mephisto's cue and he appears at once in the shape of a black poodle, one of his traditional disguises. It was very generally believed that a desperate state of mind was sufficient to attract the devil into the vicinity of a prospective victim, as happened with Müller's Faust in the gambling-den. King James described the general way in which such encounters took place:

And finding them in an vtter despair . . . he prepares the way by feeding them craftely in their humour, and filling them further and further with despaire, while he finde the time proper to discouer himself vnto them. At which time, either vpon their walking solitarie in the fieldes, or else lying pansing in their bed . . . he either by a voyce, or in likenesse of a man inquires of them, what troubles them. . . .[1]

Goethe's Faust was walking in the fields, Müller's Faust heard voices; both were in utter despair, and both proceeded to a conjuration-scene shortly afterwards. It was rather forced upon Goethe's hero, who had accepted Wagner's assurance that there was nothing supernatural about the poodle, and took him home. The walk had refreshed and restored him: and in order not to let his happier mood escape, he set about translating the first chapter of the Gospel of St John into German. This rather incongruous 'Lutheran' occupation much displeased the poodle, who began to howl and growl. And naturally enough; for either all or part of this chapter was often inscribed in the protective ceremonial circle when summoning up fiends, and was an outstanding feature of those described in 'Faust's' *Magia Naturalis et Innaturalis*. There was a copy of this manual in the Grand Ducal Library at Weimar, and Goethe was acquainted with it in 1829. He may have known it earlier; he certainly had some idea by the time he wrote the conjuration-scene of the general lines laid down in the Black Books; whereas when calling up the Earth Spirit Faust had made use of the 'mysterious book' of Nostradamus. This famous collection of prophecies contains nothing to the purpose as regards evocations; but Nostradamus was reputed to practise magic, and there was no reason why a book of conjurations should not be ascribed to him by a poet. Goethe clearly had him in mind in his references in *Before the Gate* to the curing of the plague by alchemical remedies; for Nostradamus ascribed his almost mira-

---

[1] King James I, *Daemonologie*, p. 32.

culous successes in this field to his possession of the elixir of life. In conformity with Goethe's altered attitude to magic, however, Nostradamus, who had once been a name to conjure with, was now derided by implication in Faust's account of the deadly nature of the 'remedies' his father had concocted in the retorts. Familiarity with alchemical text-books is certainly calculated to breed contempt, and the same is true of invocation ceremonies on the whole. Goethe evidently thought so; for when the poodle (whom Faust was exorcizing without knowing it by repeating the text from St John: 'In the beginning was the word') began to assume a terrible bestial form, the magician exclaimed scornfully that for mere half-hellish spirits of that nature the *Key of Solomon* was good enough. Goethe obviously did not know this particular magical classic, or he could hardly have spoken of it like that; for it is much the most solemn and impressive of them all, and (though it describes the elemental spirits) it is concerned chiefly with a powerful series of conjurations addressed to the potentates of hell. Nor did the so-called *Claviculae Salomonis et Theosophia Pneumatica* for communicating with the Olympic spirits supply any grist to Goethe's mill. In fact he used the term generically, or he may have seen one or other of the many little handbooks of magic which used Solomon's name. There are several series of invocations for the elemental spirits in *Magia Naturalis et Innaturalis* as well as elsewhere, totally unacceptable however to a poet; and Goethe had naturally no difficulty in supplying his own brief and vigorous constraints. They proved ineffective, because the spirit in the erstwhile poodle was not an elemental being; and Faust thereupon proceeded to stronger measures: the cross used as a symbol and a wonderfully poetical formula for Christ. This again was in line with *Magia Naturalis et Innaturalis* and with most of the Faustian ritual texts; but not with the *Key of Solomon*, which was a pseudo-Kabbalistic and genuinely Jewish production. The evil spirit tried to escape and dissolve into mist; but the threat to scorch it with the threefold flame of the Trinity forced it to materialize and to step forth in human form. Highly condensed and poetically expressed, this conjuration-scene derives far more clearly from traditional rituals than from the descriptions given in the Faustbooks or the scenes enacted in the puppet-plays. For in the magical texts failure to manifest on the part of the spirits was followed by more powerful and threatening conjurations and often culminated in a threat of ritual burning which sometimes was actually implemented.

Goethe therefore, like Marlowe before him, showed some knowledge of the so-called Black Books, enough to make his conjuration-scene lively and realistic. It has none of the sombre atmosphere of Marlowe's nor the grandeur of the invocation of the Earth Spirit, because it was addressed to a much less formidable creature than Marlowe's satanic Mephisto, and to a spirit much inferior to the mighty being who had denied that Faust could comprehend him. Mephisto's appearance is an ironical anticlimax to the 'noise' the magician has been making in exorcizing him. Out he steps from behind the stove in a very *dégagé* manner, presenting his credentials urbanely as:

> A part of that same might
> Which wills the evil cause, and furthers right.[1]

Throughout this scene he emphasizes his harmlessness and ineffectiveness for evil and keeps the conversation on a light and ironical level. His refusal to enter into a contract on the spot was part of the legendary tradition dating back to the Urfaustbook. His uneasiness at being kept too long and his demands to be released are in the ritual tradition. Many of the texts contain injunctions not to force the spirits to remain beyond the statutory time, and the Lucifuge summoned in the *Grand Grimoire* complains that his repose has been disturbed and asks to be left in peace. The pentagram too is an orthodox protective device; the spell-binding verses which lull Faust to sleep on the other hand belong to the magic of poetry. In fact this whole scene is a mixture of poetry, humour and irony which harmonizes completely with the *Prologue in Heaven*, and to a lesser extent with the *Witches' Kitchen* and the *Witches' Sabbath*, where satire is more in evidence than humour, but where poetry also mediates between black magic and rationalistic scorn.

The next scene, the last one necessary to fill in the great gap originally yawning between the Earth Spirit and Mephisto, is on a different level from the conjuration-scene, depicting Faust in such hopeless and yet rebellious despair, such wild and desperate unhappiness, such misery of mind, and so utterly sceptical of relief, that for the first time in Faustian literature the signing of

---

[1] Goethe, *Faust I*, ll. 1335 f.

the contract is represented as an act of complete despair. Faust consents in order to prove to Mephisto and himself that he will never in this life know one moment's happiness. Should he ever do so, let that moment be his last, and let come what will afterwards. And yet, since this tormented and defiant being was to be saved, the contract must not be binding. Like Schink before him, Goethe resorted to a conditional and ambiguous agreement. But nothing so simple as a 'definite crime' would suit his purpose. His Faust, now in much deeper spiritual despair than when he was about to venture across the threshold of life in the suicide-monologue, declares that he hopes nothing and fears nothing from the next world and that Mephisto is welcome to his soul if and when he can satisfy its longings:

> *Faust.*　If e'er, appeased, I lay me down to rest,
> Let me be done for in that hour!
> Canst thou with flattery ever rule me
> And lull me to complacency,
> Or with base pleasure ever fool me.
> Let that day be the last for me!
> That wager's offered.
>
> *Mephisto.*　　　　　　　　　Done!
>
> *Faust.*　　　　　　　And once again!
> If e'er I hail the moment flying:
> 'Ah, stay awhile, thou art so fair!'
> Then bind me in thy bonds undying,
> My final ruin then declare!
> Then let the death-bell toll the token,
> Then art thou from thy service free!
> The clock may stop, the hand be broken,
> And time may then stand still for me![1]

The time when the contract was to fall due was a matter of much haggling on the puppet-stage, the period of service generally being reduced by half in the agreement, and then halved again by Mephisto, because he had worked by night as well as by day. Goethe seized on this uncertainty with respect to the moment when Faust's soul should become forfeit and tied it up with the condition on which he was willing to lose it, a condition which Faust (like Schink's hero) was morally certain would never be

---

[1] Goethe, *Faust I*, ll. 1692 ff.; cf. Bayard Taylor, op. cit. p. 70.

fulfilled. And again the uncertainty in the wager told in favour of Faust when taken in conjunction with the *Prologue in Heaven*. For (and could irony and ambiguity go deeper than this?) Mephisto himself will be obliged to bend his utmost efforts to sting Faust to activity and thus preserve him from lethargy. It is the function he has been sent to perform; it is the deepest instinct of his nature: goading, tormenting, egging him on; frustrating, irritating and maddening his victim, he will poison every pleasure he procures him and never give him peace.

In the Faust-legend and in Goethe's opening monologue transcendental knowledge was the overriding reason for the resort to magic which led to the signing of the pact. But at this stage of the drama Goethe's hero has abandoned all hope of penetrating into the mysteries of nature and life, and expressly demands the intensification of all human experience: activity, passion, rapture and pain. Through a series of wonderful modulations—the second monologue, the scene outside the city gate, the conjuration and the pact-scene—the ageing scholar in his Gothic study has been transformed into an ardent and palpitating human being whose quest is not knowledge but life. This makes the *Witches' Kitchen* actually unnecessary. The Faust who burst out after signing the pact that he wished to bear in his own breast all the woe and rapture of humanity and finally be shattered by it had no need of any magic potion to restore his youth. He was now ready to play his part in the Gretchen tragedy, the part of a demon-driven lover, vainly struggling against the destructive passion in his own breast and against the evil incarnate in Mephisto. Continually defeated by the one because he cannot control the other, as is made very clear in the argument about perjury, he attempts to make a stand in *Woodland Cavern*, looses his foothold, is carried away by despair and swoops downward, cursing himself in vain, to accomplish his destiny and Gretchen's doom. He has fallen lower still at the beginning of the Valentine scene; he is a murderer at its close, and plumbs the depth of degradation in the *Witches' Sabbath*. Nor is his violent determination to put the blame on Mephisto when he learns of Gretchen's fate a sign of moral regeneration, in fact quite the contrary. Shaken and indeed shattered by the scene in prison, he yet comes to heel when Mephisto snarls out: 'You, follow me!'

Goethe's *Faust I* is peerless in one sense, for it has no peer in Germany. But peerless does not mean perfect; and, quite apart from being incomplete, this wonderful dramatic poem is full of imperfections. It lacks homogeneity, for the upper stratum did not develop organically from the lower, as the middle stratum shows. Moreover, taken as whole, it is not a shapely work of art. The Gretchen tragedy has not been harmoniously fused with the Faust tragedy. The *Witches' Kitchen*, a useful enough expedient in the *Fragment*, is a mere tiresome excrescence in *Faust I*, and makes the third of a consecutive series of scenes in which the hero is either absent or deliberately kept in the background. *Woodland Cavern* on the other hand drew the two parts of the poem closer together: and they might have been knitted into a whole, were it not that Goethe attempted to do this by means of the *Witches' Sabbath*. Instead of readjusting the balance between Faust and Gretchen, this complex of scenes, ending in the *Dream*, pulled them further apart and made the Gretchen tragedy lopsided. Do what Goethe would, and he accomplished one poetical marvel after another from the second monologue down to the pact-scene, it was still Faust's drama at the beginning and Gretchen's tragedy at the end; and the discrepant attitudes towards magic disturbed the depths and ruffled the surface of the poem.

Goethe's *Faust I*, peerlessly beautiful, impressively imperfect, exhibits the effects of the two spiritual forces (human and divine love) which had split the legendary atom and produced a poetical chaos; the chaos blooms and blossoms in bewildering luxuriance in Goethe's *Faust I* on the ruins of an ancient myth.

PART III. INTERIM FAUSTS

Chapter VIII.   A Medley of Fausts
        (*a*) All sorts and conditions of Fausts,
           1809–1823
        (*b*) Would-be Goethean Fausts,
           1811–1833

    IX.   Helena and Faust
        (*a*) A histrionic Helen, 1815
        (*b*) An unearthly Helen, 1827
        (*c*) A vanquished Helen, 1829

    X.   Don Juan and Faust, 1829

    XI.   The Apotheosis of Faust, 1832

A MEDLEY OF FAUSTS

(a) All sorts and conditions of Fausts, 1809–1823

The predominant influence on the many and various Fausts written between 1759 and 1808 was undoubtedly Lessing, as the mouthpiece both of enlightened optimism and of middle-class realism. But from 1791 onwards Klinger's attitude gained many adherents, for he represented the tragic outcome of the situation in a manner consonant with the general point of view of the Storm and Stress, and so powerfully as to sway many minds. His introduction of revolutionary ideas in connection with the Peasants' Revolt, by enlarging the canvas and actualizing the theme, revitalized it in a more fruitful way than the domestic element was capable of doing, unless manipulated by the poetic genius of a Goethe. Soden made effective if superficial use of the political approach and the anonymous bookmaker cribbed it; Benkowitz repeated Klinger's effects when it came to the damnation of his hero, and Komareck snapped up the notion of identifying Faust with Fust. So did Niklas Vogt (1756–1836) in *The Dye-Works or Printing-Press in Mayence*, 1809, and went even further. This fairly eminent professor and romantic historian, who counted Metternich among his pupils, wrote his Faustian three-act drama after a nervous break-down, which (as was unkindly pointed out at the time) was evidently far from over. He presented Fust the printer, Faust the black magician and Mozart's Don Juan as one and the same person, and became so confused in the process of plagiarizing from Mozart that he switched over to the names of Don Juan and Leporello half-way through his drama. Mephisto is responsible for the invention of printing, an instrument of corruption as in Klinger's novel; and when the devils hear that this diabolic device is to be communicated to Faust, they chant in unison:

A B C D
E F G;
H I J K
L M N O P;

Let black printing be
Our war-magazine, he, he![1]

In spite of this gay little ditty, the play as a whole is a tissue of incoherent and almost insane nonsense, according to those who have seen it, which I have been unable to do.

Nor did Carl Christian Ludwig Schöne (1779–1852) profit much by his deliberate borrowings from Klinger in *Faust, A Romantic Tragedy*, 1809. His first and final acts began and ended in plagiarisms from the novel; the intermediate stages were devoted to a court intrigue which has a marked family resemblance to the parallel action in Klinger's work, representing corruption in high places, in this particular case at the court of the Emperor Frederick III. Finally Leviathan's great speech of indictment closed the whole. Unintelligent imitation and downright thefts, a forgery issued under the imprint of blank verse: that is a justified judgment of Schöne's first Faustian drama.

It disposes one to view with some indulgence the rather amusing little tale contributed by August Friedrich Ferdinand von Kotzebue (1761–1819), called *The Loquacious Pockets*, 1811. Kotzebue was a skilful if superficial playwright whose box-office successes resounded throughout Europe. He would certainly have brought the house down in Berlin, Vienna, London and Paris if he had dramatized the Faust-legend, and he would also have considerably enlivened this particular section of the history of Faust. Unhappily he contented himself with inventing a story, in which Faust, the famous magician, is called in by a young man anxious to marry but fearful of choosing wrong, who begs to be given the power of reading women's hearts. The wily sorcerer causes a little devil to slip into one female pocket after the next, whence the imp discloses his finds. These throw valuable sidelights on the characters of the various owners, and enable the hero to make a happy choice. Achim von Arnim (1781–1831) may well have read this tale; certain it is that he described a Faustian episode in his unfinished novel *The Guardians of the Crown*, 1817, also depicting the practising magician and also regardless of the soul at stake. Being a romantic poet enamoured of the past and of medievalism, he produced a vivid and realistic sketch of the person glimpsed in the stories told about the historical sorcerer and also

---

[1] Warkentin, op. cit. p. 62.

about the hero of the Urfaustbook. His Faust is a quack, and acts and talks like one; but there is some knowledge of medicine behind all his mumbo-jumbo, as was probably also the case with the real vagabond. A seemingly incurable invalid called Berthold, who has been practically bedridden for thirty years, is persuaded by a painter doing his portrait to consult Faust, and the latter cures him by means of a blood-transfusion, described with realism and spirit. The braggings and boastings of Faust are well documented by the humanists of the sixteenth century, and Arnim's Faust indulges in them recklessly. He is also shown to be a very awkward customer, since he demands as a reward for his services the lad Anton, the other party to the operation, whom he wishes to train as a herb-gatherer and body-snatcher. The request is refused, because Anton is the painter's apprentice, and Faust thereupon threatens the former with ten deadly illnesses, among them consumption and dropsy, before making off in a fury. Arnim then described how, while the town was celebrating the cure of Berthold, a terrible clamour was heard from the inn, where Faust, as drunk as a lord, was showing off; he became involved in a brawl, was thrown out on his ear and spent the rest of the night in a pig-sty.

Kotzebue and Arnim, each in his different way, were off the beaten track; Julius von Voss (1768–1832) returned to it in 1823 with a five-act Faustian tragedy, enlivened by music and dancing. This shows the same kind of all-round indebtedness as Soden's drama, but not so effectively handled. Klinger was responsible for the identification of Faust with Fust, whose partner and friend Guttenberg acts the same part as the faithful Eckard in Schink's drama. The devil Leviathan derived from Klinger too, as well as the figure of Robertus, the would-be liberator, ennobled here, but also responsible for the Peasants' Revolt. The invention of printing is once more shown to be the root of many evils and notably of religious wars; and the good deeds which Leviathan performs at the bidding of Faust provoke the same kind of nemesis as in Klinger's novel. The temptation-scene is a fantastic development and elaboration of Müller's; and Faust's father is dragged off to a debtor's prison because he had stood surety for his son. This repeats Müller's *motiv* of family penury precipitated by Faust and leading him to perform the desperate act of invoking the devil. Leviathan, appearing after a rather feeble summons, frees Faust's father, punishes his enemy, rewards his friend, promises money in abundance and mistresses galore; but speaks like Chamisso's evil spirit on the question of unveiling hidden knowledge:

> As far as earthly senses' measure goes,
> And forms of thought resemble life and death,
> The light of truth shall brightly shine upon thee![1]

Faust on the other hand takes a leaf out of the book of his Goethean predecessor when it comes to the pact:

> Thine am I—wilt thou make this pact with me?—
> When senses cease to urge and mind to strive.[2]

In spite of these shreds and patches torn from the poets, the most important debt after the one to Klinger was the one Voss owed to Schink. We find Faust's former sweetheart Seraphine donning male attire and following him round in this disguise, attempting to win him from his evil and Don Juanesque courses by singing songs. We also find a pious maiden Clara praying to her patron saint in a church in Florence, and thereby inspiring Faust with the same passion Schink's hero had conceived for Isabella in the wake of the Prince of Guastalla in *Emilia Galotti*. Held fast in the toils of Klinger, Voss attempted by transporting his hero to Italy and by introducing Machiavelli, the Borgias and the Medici into the action to give it breadth; but he failed lamentably. They arouse no interest; nor does the civil war raging in Germany, though Voss tried to instil some human drama into the conflict by representing how it embroiled the gentle and moderate Robertus with his wife Aurelia, a fanatic for freedom. The conflict between Clara, who has now taken the veil, and her brother Cinthio, whose views of convents are Lutheran, is equally ineffectual, even when both fall victims to the religious wars unchained during the fifth act. It is all excessively tedious, not excluding Voss's boldest flight of fancy, which occurs in the fourth act. In order to corrupt Faust irretrievably, Leviathan transports him to a magic island, a paradise of beauty, inhabited by the most ravishing odalisques. The inopportune arrival of Seraphine disenchants the island, however; it is then transformed into a horrible desert, and the odalisques into monsters who fling themselves into the crater of a suddenly erupt-

---

[1] J. von Voss, *Faust, Trauerspiel mit Gesang und Tanz*, in *Berliner Nachdrucke*, II, 2, Berlin, 1890, p. 17.
[2] Ibid.

ing volcano. Maddened by her meddling, Faust stabs Seraphine to death, only to recognize his former sweetheart when the deed is done. This is the death-blow to the 'senses' urge'. It only remains for Leviathan to check the striving of Faust's spirit, which is brought about by his realization of the fearful evils resulting from his attempts to free the human mind by the invention of printing, and the no less catastrophic effect upon humanity of his efforts at social liberation. He loses his wager and throws up the sponge. Seraphine appears on a shining cloud to confirm his damnation, whilst a chorus of evil spirits gleefully proclaim it:

> The hour has struck.
> Down with thee, down,
> For hell is now thy tomb.[1]

Although Vogt, Schöne and Voss bear witness to the persisting influence of Klinger and the continued attraction of the Faust theme, they are in all other respects entirely negligible. Yet Voss's magic island, perhaps inspired by Schink's Greek transformation-scene, was to catch the attention of no less a poet than Heine; and Vogt's confusion between Faust and Don Juan may have fallen on the fertile soil of Grabbe's brooding mind. Minor writers are of greater importance to poets than the poets can ever be to them.

(b) Would-be Goethean Fausts, 1811–1833

That last statement forms an introduction to the extraordinary sequence of works inspired by Goethe's *Faust I*, amongst which Grillparzer's contemplated schemes must be given a place of honour: the fragment and notes written in 1811 and the notes added in 1822. The short scene sketched in 1811 is a pale and wistful reflection of the state of mind depicted by Goethe in *Woodland Cavern*, enlivened by Mephisto's airy cynicisms. In the accompanying note Grillparzer confessed that he had intended to represent the awakening of a young's man's love in a continuation of Goethe's *Part I*; something, he said, which no one had yet attempted with the exception of Beaumarchais' delineation of Cherubin in *Le Mariage de Figaro*. Although far from exhausting the possibilities of the subject, he considered Cherubin a fascinating study, especially when interpreted by the 'soul-music' of

---

[1] Voss, op. cit. p. 85.

Mozart. It is strange that Romeo did not occur to Grillparzer's mind; but highly interesting that he was evidently contemplating a masculine counterpart to the Gretchen tragedy. His elaboration of the scheme written in 1822 sounds much more like a repetition than a pendant, however. Grillparzer's hero, after Gretchen's death, was to retire into a modest and contented existence, all passion spent. But not for long; he was to fall in love again with a young girl very like Gretchen, and she with him. Longing to enjoy this happiness in an innocent and natural way, he finds himself continually relapsing into his former ruthlessness, recklessness and depravity, egged on of course by Mephisto. One can imagine that Grillparzer would have done this extraordinarily well; for he had a real genius for creating young men and women who were a law unto themselves: cruel, predatory, unscrupulous and irresistible. Jason in the first part of *The Golden Fleece*, Zawisch and Kunigunde in *King Ottokar*, Otto von Meran in *The Faithful Servant*, Rustan in *A Dream-Life*, Rahel in *The Jewess of Toledo*—they are all instinct with a devouring individualism which recoils before no devastation their egotism may wreak. Nor was Grillparzer much less successful in his portrayal of innocent young lovers in the clutches of passion, such as Hero and Leander. So that if anyone could have created another Gretchen, it would have been Grillparzer; and if anyone could have represented a more youthful, irresistible, dangerous and daimonic lover than Faust in the Gretchen tragedy, it would have been the man who knew so intimately and described so accurately the terrifying integrity, pitilessness and single-mindedness of youth. Jaromir in *The Ancestress* and Don Cesar in *House Hapsburg* also show that the portrayal of love in its destructive and potentially criminal aspect was well within his powers; and it was probably the consciousness of his special gifts which suggested a repetition of the Gretchen tragedy. Unpromising though this sounds when put baldly, it is nevertheless possible that Grillparzer's genius might have seen him through; and that he would have added to his list of violent and fearfully attractive young men the Faust whom he envisaged playing a peace-destroying part in a second love-tragedy. Unlike most of his kith and kin in Grillparzer's works, however, he was to experience excruciating remorse and attempt to tear himself away from the girl. But she will not let him go, even though he confesses his identity to her and the whole story of his past. Rather than precipitate another catastrophe, he then summons Mephisto and commands him to fulfil the contract here and now:

> This was how I had imagined the last scene on the stage. Faust, with the girl still clinging to him, calls to the evil spirit, and when the latter appears they go off together into a rock which opens with thunder and lightning. The girl and her relatives are assembled, praying fervently for the unhappy man. Then the rock opens again and Faust comes out with Mephisto, his face deathly pale. Both are wrapped in black mantles and are wearing hats with black plumes. They are talking together, ignoring the bystanders completely. 'Where are the horses?'—'They are snorting and stamping at the gate.'—'Let us hasten.'—'We have far to go.' Meanwhile the others are praying: 'Lord, have mercy upon him.' Faust looks at them and asks Mephisto: 'Who's that?'—'It's Gretchen.' —'Really?—Let us hasten: we have a long way to go.' And they make off.—The parents rush to the girl and begin to question her. 'Let us be good,' she answers, 'and do what is right. That man is no longer one of us.'[1]

This sinister sketch shows that Grillparzer did not subscribe to the optimism expressed in the *Prologue in Heaven*, but reverted to the tragic tradition. The other would-be Goethean dramatists of the interim period between the first and the second parts of *Faust* were all ardent salvationists, foremost among them the egregious Schöne, who turned his coat completely once he had had time to assimilate *Faust I*. He did more than that; having waited for over ten years for Goethe to finish his masterpiece, Schöne took it upon himself to do so for him, sending him the manuscript with the following dedicatory epistle in 1821:

> To His Excellency Baron von Goethe, Privy Councillor and
> Minister of State
>
> Thy pupil, Master, timidly draws nigh thee,
> Shrinking before the radiance of thy sight,
> To offer thee this work, and yet I fear me;
> Halting my steps, my courage leaves me quite.
> Give me thy hand, and spurn me not, but hear me,
> Thou, crowned with laurel-leaves so green and bright;
> My whole endeavour, Master, was to please thee.
> Oh, that not blame but praise might sound to ease me! . . .
>
> No German but must venerate the story
> Which thou so beautifully hast told anew;

[1] Wendriner, op. cit. Vol. III, p. 326.

Oh wouldst thou deign to shed the crowning glory
On what, though incomplete, enchants the view!
Ah, that thy years were young instead of hoary,
And the grave's goal were still a distant view,
Ah then! But silent thou, thou wilt not end it,
Trembling I dared, and finished now I send it!

For man must dare his all to reach the highest,
What's glorious only cherish to his breast;
Thus with thy *Faust*—I've worn it ever nighest
My heart, of all life's pleasures far the best.
And once a light shone forth, I dare be biased
And say I saw thy plan; I've now confessed;
Trembling I wrote the end which still it needed;
'Tis done, and thou alone canst say if I've succeeded.[1]

It would be short-sighted to hope for much from a writer who was capable of a folly of this nature, sending a so-called continuation of Goethe's *Faust* to the author, lamenting his hoary years and his imminent demise, which was not to take place until eleven years later. But, however modest one's expectations, and however fresh in one's memory Schöne's plagiarisms from Klinger may be one is hardly prepared to find a mere bad copy of Gothe's *Part I*, dragged out like a piece of elastic and divided into thirty-nine scenes and an *Epilogue in Heaven*. Besides recapitulating the tragedy at every turn, and depicting a similar seduction and betrayal in the Faustina episode which plays in Venice, Schöne modelled at least eleven of his scenes so closely on Goethe's that there is no escaping the inevitable comparison. The play opens with a pendant to *Dull Day, Field* and is followed by *Woodland Cavern* (of which several specimens under other names occur later); there is an obvious imitation of *Auerbach's Cellar*, containing reminiscences from the *Witches' Kitchen*; there are scenes in a convent garden and garden-house following the lead given by Goethe's two couples who passed and repassed each other in Frau Marthe's garden, a pattern used again by Schöne at a masked ball in Venice; and there is an intermezzo called *A Winter Night's Dream* which is a slavish copy of the *Witches' Sabbath Dream*. Moreover Faustina keeps on singing songs and holding monologues which are watered-down replicas of Gretchen's, so that her suicide by poison is a happy

---

[1] C. C. L. Schöne, *Fortsetzung des Faust von Goethe. Der Tragödie zweiter Teil*, Berlin, 1823, pp. v ff.

release for all. This is followed by a scene in St Peter's in Rome, during which Faust undergoes the same kind of experience Gretchen had undergone before him, but with a good angel to counter the bad and to produce a cathartic effect upon Faust, though not upon the reader. The versification throughout is so imitative, so near and yet so far from Goethe, that one can hardly force oneself to read it; but there is one moment in the play which must raise a laugh even from the most unwilling. It occurs towards the beginning in *Woodland Cavern*; Faust, exalted and consoled by the purifying power of nature, exclaims lyrically:

> I feel myself enraptured, ardent;
> Oh, what a blessing, what delight!
> To heaven I now can lift my sight—
> Ah, stay awhi— no, no!

Mephisto (*appearing suddenly*). Go on, that's right!

Faust.   Ha, villain, thou? What horror's mine!
>   The pact? But no, I stopped in time.[1]

In the last scene by the gallows on which Gretchen's body is still hanging, Faust, overcome by remorse, demands to die and end his earthly existence, trusting in God's mercy. Mephisto has other views:

> *Mephisto.* Into my hands the pact delivers thee,
>   Despair, thou doubter, and give up the ghost![2]

He thereupon disappears with his victim into the flames, but only temporarily. In the *Epilogue in Heaven* we find him making his report on Faust to the Almighty, who is supported as in Goethe's *Prologue* by the trusty archangels; and the rogue is probably no more surprised than the reader when commanded to bring Faust back from the nether regions at once:

> Therefore fetch Faust up from the earth's abyss,
> That clarity, so longed for, may be his.[3]

Goethe's self-control when he received Schöne's *Faust* was remarkable. He thanked the author courteously if coolly, refused to comment on his work, but added with an irony which quite

---

[1] Schöne, op. cit. p. 16.   [2] Ibid. p. 370.

[3] Ibid. p. 378.

escaped the object of it that he had every reason to appreciate Schöne's efforts. He told Zelter that it passed his comprehension how a sensible man could imagine a mere repetition to be a continuation; and he pilloried him in the following lines which were published posthumously:

> The *Iliad's* but primer for the fool;
> How much a reader of this sort we dread;
> He reads the Bible as he did at school,
> Thus Schöne read my *Faust*, the dunderhead![1]

Little dreaming of this, Schöne went into ecstasies over what he chose to regard as Goethe's encomium on his 'continuation', declaring in hysterical verse, prefaced to the published play in 1823, that the Master had acknowledged his apprentice, and that he would not part with his 'indenture' for a fortune.

It seems almost incredible to-day that anyone should have had the nerve to write *Goethe's Part II* for him whilst he was still alive, even acting on Schöne's assumption that a man of seventy-two has one foot in the grave. But, though only J. D. Hoffmann was to go to the same lengths, there was a general itch at the time to do something about Goethe's *Faust*, since it seemed as if he had abandoned it altogether. Gustav Pfizer (1807–90) succumbed to that itch. This minor bard of the Suabian school of poetry was later to be one of Heine's favourite butts, and the series of *Faustian Scenes* published in the *Morgenblatt für gebildete Stände* in July 1831 are not very impressive and remained unfinished. There is a footnote at the beginning stating that the action sets in at the 'end of Goethe's tragedy': and accordingly we find Faust plunged in remorse on the subject of Gretchen, wrangling with Mephisto and interviewing that same student whom Mephisto had corrupted at the beginning of Goethe's drama. He makes a blustering entry here, declaring himself to be Faust's 'brother in diabolo'; but he is well snubbed by Faust and goes off with his tail between his legs. This is sufficiently like his re-entry in Goethe's *Part II* (already written) to arouse attention; but the second scene in a garden does more than that. In this scene the spirit of Gretchen plays a part. Appearing to Faust earlier, she had begged him to release her, and this he had done, swooning away afterwards in his great despair. She now summons a chorus of sylphs and elves

---

[1] Weimar edition, I, 5, p. 191.

to soothe his remorse and make him whole, and they sing a lullaby which ends thus:

> But hush now, for quietly he's sleeping,
> A slumber restoring and deep,
> Whilst his pale cheeks seem to be weeping
> That for long he's known no such sweet sleep.

Gretchen's Spirit. Oh kindly Might, allowing these small sprites
(Forever children) harmlessly to play,
And soothe an alien grief away,
As o'er a head accursed they hover light.[1]

The startling resemblance in thought to the opening scene in Goethe's *Faust II* (which was already in being) can only be attributed to the kind of spiritual kinship earlier discerned between Goethe and Schink; although here it is less disturbing, for Pfizer was a poet, and perpetrated none of those glaring follies of which Schink and Schöne were guilty. Nevertheless there is not much to be said for the development of his scenes, which had opened in a fairly promising way. Gretchen's spirit now urges Faust to break with Mephisto and to go to Rome, which he does, accompanied by the incurably pedantic Wagner. Rome has a purifying effect upon him; and though in the last scene Mephisto is seen summoning demons to help him recapture Faust, the erstwhile black magician is clearly booked for salvation.

Meanwhile a discernibly utilitarian aim was seeping into other minds, who wanted a vehicle for satire and saw the possibilities in *Faust*, since Goethe himself had included that element. Harro Paul Harring tried his hand in this vein. A political adventurer and wanderer, who dubbed himself 'The Frisian from Ibsenhof on the North Sea', Harring was a Carbonaro and an impassioned friend of Greece and Poland. Exiled at one time and another from Russia, Prussia, Austria and France, he lived for some years in London on the bounty of Mazzini and other patriots. Forgotten and embittered, he later removed to the Island of Jersey, where he committed suicide in 1878. He prefaced his *Faust in Modern Dress. A Shadow-Play with Light*, 1831, with the following lines:

> I wrote this once in Russia, though the land
> Poland is called. In dark and empty hours

[1] G. Pfizer, *Faustische Scenen*, Morgenblatt für gebildete Stände, Tübingen, 7 July 1831, p. 369.

To while away the days I wrote it down.
That country, torn three times, is now no more;
And a prophetic voice I cannot still
Keeps whispering that my motherland herself
May fall a victim to that same fell might.[1]

There is nothing of this sombre, brooding, tragic spirit in Harring's *Faust*, however, which is one of those topical satires posterity passes by, unless some man of genius under great emotional stress has been the author. Poor Harring only succeeded in being dull and dreary in his efforts to be devastating. Nor is Karl Rosenkranz (1805–79) much more enlivening. His *Spiritual Epilogue to the Tragedy of Faust*, 1831, followed rather more closely in the footsteps of Goethe than Harring, although without the dogged persistence of Schöne, and with less intent than Pfizer to continue the action of *Faust I*; for Rosenkranz was chiefly concerned with ridiculing various theological and philosophical schools, especially Catholicism. He must therefore have been considerably disconcerted when he read the final scene of Goethe's masterpiece, whose first part inspired the following dedicatory epistle:

To Goethe

The regal minster has been built by thee,
The mighty pillars well and firmly founded,
The aspiring dome in graceful curves is rounded,
From which the cross sheds grace for all to see.

And that thy people may in future be
Full of great deeds and highest hopes unbounded,
Thou gav'st this work to them, in faith well grounded
That now no more fear of life's cares shall be.

The strife of spirits clashes ever faster,
And one thing only cools the fervour wild:—
That lies are vanquished, and that truth is holy.

Sublime and mighty, well-beloved Master,
Oh be not wrath if, tim'rous as a child,
I add to thy great fane this chapel lowly.[2]

This at least shows a more modest attitude than Schöne's; and

[1] H. P. Harring, *Faust im Gewande der Zeit. Ein Schattenspiel mit Licht*, Leipzig, 1831, p. 7. The original is in rhyme.

[2] K. Rosenkranz, *Geistlich Nachspiel zur Tragödie Faust*, Leipzig, 1831, on the fly-leaf.

the author, a prolific philosophic writer, deprecated the comparison with that bumptious playwright; but there is a sufficient
admixture of Goethean reminiscences in the opening scenes to
lend colour to the reproach that he was a second Schöne which
was made at the time. The first scene, for instance, is a mere
rehash of the *Prologue in Heaven*, with the Almighty, supported by
the familiar archangelic caste, prophesying from his throne that
all shall be well with Faust, who is discovered immediately afterwards quarrelling with Mephisto about the fate of Gretchen and
the terminology of the pact. This is followed by a scene *Before the
Gate*, during which Faust recalls his earlier walk with Wagner,
contemplates a similar sunset, and bursts out into a rhapsody
composed by combining various Goethean odes and hymns with
the lyrical address to the setting sun which Faust uttered in *Part I*.
Thereafter literary and theological satire prevail over plagiarism.
Towards the end Mephisto attacks Goethe's *Faust* for insinuating
the belief that absolute truth can be known. To the horrified
question put by the assembled mystics, critics and similar gentry,
as to who has ever maintained such a heresy, he answers categorically:

Mephisto. Why, who but Faust, whom Goethe brought to life
And promised in the Prologue that he should have light?
That book's a scandal and merits burning,
From paths well-trod it takes a wrongful turning,
A revolutionary book indeed!
And this our age with lightning speed
Keeps bringing out new versions.
But the greatest of perversions
Is Faust himself.

All. What! Is he still alive?

Mephisto. Alas, he is; and he's escaped from hell
To plunge head-first into truth's abstract well.[1]

The assembled throng, who have met in a cemetery containing
Gretchen's grave, then determine to lie in wait for Faust and
bundle him off to a lunatic-asylum. They conceal themselves on
the entry of Faust, who holds an edifying monologue on Gretchen
and 'eternal truth', to which he is now a convert. He is assaulted
by the angry mob, deaf to his improving harangues, but forced to

---

[1] Rosenkranz, op. cit. p. 75.

yield before St Michael, who intervenes in highly evangelical vein, whilst a church chorus brings this tendentious entertainment to a welcome close.

One cannot help feeling that Schöne, Pfizer, Harring and Rosenkranz were asking for trouble in their various Faustian ventures, and fully deserved the nemesis about to overtake them with the posthumous publication of Goethe's *Part II* in 1832. But even Schöne did not attain the height of folly achieved by Jakob Daniel Hoffmann, whose *Faust. A Tragedy by Goethe. Continued by J. D. Hoffmann*, appeared in 1833. It was evidently completed and sent to press before 28 August 1832, which is the date affixed to the introductory poem;[1] and it may have been impossible to withdraw this 'continuation' at the eleventh hour; but surely some words of explanation could have been added to the introductory matter. As it is, there is nothing to show whether or not Hoffmann knew that *Part II* came out before his so-called Goethean tragedy, which contained this statement in the *Prologue*:

Amateur. I am interested to see how you have tackled it [the Faust theme]. Goethe's *Faust* seems so well rounded-off and complete.

Author. There I entirely agree with you! Goethe's *Faust* is complete, but *Faust* itself is not.

Amateur. What do you mean?

Author. Goethe and Goethe alone could represent Faust surrendering himself to the devil. But Faust has to struggle out of the devil's clutches again; the second part of the tragedy demands that, and so does the deep inner meaning of this glorious legend.[2]

Taken in conjunction with the word 'fertig' (which means 'done for' as well as 'finished'), twice used of Goethe's *Faust*, this would seem to mean that Hoffmann doubted Goethe's powers to depict the salvation of his hero, and one does not grudge him the shock in store. But it may not have cured his conceit; the almost megalomaniacal boost he gave his own wares in the Prologue ('a work of art that still must seek its peer')[3] shows that he was in the last stages of the fatal disease of self-satisfaction, and certainly

---

[1] Goethe was born on 28 August 1749, and died on 22 March 1832.

[2] *Faust. Eine Tragödie von Goethe. Fortgesetzt von J. D. Hoffmann,* Leipzig, 1833, pp. 7 f.

[3] Ibid, p. 10.

envisaged the departed sage of Weimar as a back-number super-
seded by himself:

> But let us not forget times now gone by,
> Nor that old man who recently has died,
> But taught our eyes to gaze far into space,
> And bid us too to look within ourselves.
> Uniting manly strength with gracious beauty,
> Small wonder that he led a life serene.
> Let us acknowledge gladly what we owe him,
> Nor seek to stanch the gently flowing tears,
> But let our spirits follow him aloft
> On freely moving wings to realms eternal.

(The background opens. The *Realm of Eternity* is disclosed, and the
Sun of Truth surrounded by its rainbow. All the poets of olden times
are assembled and salute it with song and stringed instruments. The
volume of the music swells, the assembly rise from their seats and retire
backwards. *Goethe* enters, a laurel-wreath round his brow. *Schiller*
comes forward to meet him, welcomes him warmly and leads him
towards the Sun of Truth. [This is a particularly happy touch.] *Goethe*
does obeisance and lays down his laurel-wreath. Then *Homer* steps
forward, hands him his own and his harp as well and conducts him to
the seat of honour prepared for him. Silence.)[1]

Handsome, but final: the Realm of Eternity and the Sun of Truth
for Goethe; the plaudits and the ovations for Hoffmann. And
indeed, just at first, one is inclined to applaud Faust's recapitula-
tion of the prison-scene in rather effective free verse; and to greet
as a good idea the description of Gretchen's execution overheard
by Faust and Mephisto in the village inn, where the onlookers
have foregathered after it is over. The pastor who is drinking with
his flock doubts her salvation because she went to her death still
loving Faust. Unfortunately this otherwise realistic and credible
scene ends with thunder, lightning and the collapse of the inn in
a universal conflagration, and the play never lifts up its head
again. Hoffmann steered an unaided course from then onwards,
except that, by laying some of his scenes at the court of the
Emperor Maximilian, he was in the puppet-play tradition. Words
seem totally inadequate to describe the Faustian nadir reached in
this drama, made all the more evident because of the pretentious-

---

[1] Hoffmann, op. cit. p. 13. If Hoffmann had read *Part II* he might
have had the sense to substitute Aeschylus for Homer.

ness of the *Prologue* and the asthmatic efforts to scale spiritual heights at the end. The body of the play is a flabby and fantastic love-tragedy, ending in the suicide of the heroine Clara, who drowns herself rather than face her returning lover Hugo, because Faust has won her heart. He and Mephisto are meanwhile seen contending for her person in the clouds, the evil spirit having also lost his heart to Faust's *inamorata*. Hugo stabs himself and an irrelevant little girl called Therese dies of the accumulated shocks. So much for the 'domestic tragedy'. Faust and Mephisto are next seen on Olympus, surrounded by the vanished and invisible gods; but Faust most ungallantly refuses to meet and mate with Helen's shade:

> *Faust.* I feel for Sparta's Queen no base desire,
> Nor do I wish to woo a paramour. . . .
>
> *Meph.* And yet the legend has proclaimed long since
> How charmingly you sinned with Helena.
>
> *Faust.* Legend speaks true, but reason goes astray
> When it attempts the meaning to disclose.
> I'll show this web of lies for what it is,
> Legend must conquer in its purity.[1]

We are left conjecturing what that purity may be, while Faust and Mephisto converse together in hexameters about the Trojan War on the citadel of Troy, deserting that historic ruin for the Holy City, where they fall in with the Wandering Jew. The pact now becomes null and void because Mephisto refuses to follow Faust to the Holy Sepulchre; but he and the Wandering Jew nevertheless put in an appearance there in good time to partake of a vision of Christ in the skies surrounded by hosts of angels strewing flowers upon His grave. All three sink reverently to their knees, the angels sing a hymn to the glory of God and the pageant passes on. Hell is now discovered, and its inmates are in despair, for they have lost not only Faust but Mephisto too. Meanwhile the author of this peculiar play is allowed by St Peter to enter the first heaven because he has brought about the salvation of Faust. He will therefore presumably meet Weidmann, Schink and Schöne in these regions, where there will be an opportunity for comparing the four different versions and wrangling over their respective merits. The final scene takes place in the third heaven, where

---

[1] Hoffmann, op. cit. p. 211.

God, Love and the author, now transformed into St Michael, hold parley with Faust, Ahasuerus and Mephisto, all three of whom are pardoned and saved. Comment seems superfluous.

It is symptomatic of the very low level obtaining in this Faustian medley that Platen's poem *Faust's Prayer*, written in 1820 and dealing with the desire for infinite knowledge, is so far inferior to Chamisso's dramatic sketch on the same subject. After a course of Vogt, Schöne, Kotzebue, Arnim, Voss, Grillparzer, Platen, Pfizer, Harring, Rosenkranz and Hoffmann, one inclines to the conclusion that the Faustian vein was worked out, since even poets like Arnim and Platen could do so little with it; and a tragic dramatist of the calibre of Grillparzer got no further than a scheme. It is more than possible that Goethe's *Faust I* inhibited the poetically gifted; its influence on the smaller fry was positively pernicious. Unless taken in a light-hearted stride, the would-be Goethean Fausts are distressing in the extreme.

CHAPTER IX

HELENA AND FAUST

(a) A histrionic Helen, 1815

The total disappearance of Helen from sight, except in Soden's drama and as a name in Weidmann's, is a noteworthy feature of Faustian literature since the days of Lessing. Granted that this glamorous wraith squared ill with the spirit of enlightenment, the same is true of Ithuriel, Schirin, the Earth Spirit, pandemoniums, scenes in heaven, magic islands and the Wandering Jew. It was not enlightenment, it was Gretchen (using her name symbolically) who put Helen to flight; for the mania for love-interest was at its most obsessive at the time, and Goethe's Gretchen increased that mania to fever-pitch. From the appearance of the *Faust-Fragment* onwards until 1815 it was a series of victories for 'Gretchen', so complete that, except in Soden's tragedy, the Greek ghost was exorcized and ceased to haunt the legend. In 1815, however, she reappeared charged with demoniacal energy and took a signal revenge on her human adversary. This was in the *Faust* of Ernst Friedrich Klingemann (1777–1831). A playwright and man of the theatre, Klingemann became director of the Brunswick Court Theatre in 1818, and produced Goethe's *Faust I* there in 1829 for the first time in all history, although in a stage version of his own. It was not because he underrated the beauties of Goethe's dramatic poem that he felt impelled to add to the number of other *Fausts*, but because (as he stated in his preface) it *was* a dramatic poem and had not been designed for the stage. He also deprecated the too-philosophical approach of Lessing and his followers:

If therefore I have ventured on a new version of this subject, it is because of the reasons given above, and also because I wanted to represent the old legend in a thoroughly dramatic way and further to embody in my drama that medieval, mysterious and gruesome element which has vanished away from the enlightened works of other Faustian poets.[1]

[1] E. A. F. Klingemann, *Faust*, in Geissler, *Gestaltungen des Faust*, Vol. III, p. 21.

One becomes rather attached to Klingemann as one battles through his five-act tragedy. He obviously enjoyed writing it so much; and, like Soden before him, he succeeded in being spirited and grotesque, eloquent and bombastic in almost equal degrees; never allowing a single dull moment to intrude, and fringing poetry at times in his spate of fervent and pseudo-Goethean verse. No wonder that his *Faust* achieved real popularity on the stage, being frequently acted in Germany and maintaining itself for a considerable time in a Russian translation on the repertories of St Petersburg and Moscow. It had Goethean elements in it, in the nature of superficial adornments, reminiscences and echoes rather than plain plagiarisms. An imitation of *Auerbach's Cellar*, in which Faust grimly listens to the legends current about him, will offend nobody's taste; but many will flinch when the magician, on his way to invoke the evil one, pauses by the chapel where his mother lies buried and hears the same requiem being sung as Goethe had used in *Part I*. Throwing himself heart and soul into the manufacture of what he conceived to be the appropriate atmosphere, Klingemann was liberal of sinister devices, such as an ambiguous Stranger (the devil in disguise), the fearful black dog in which the familiar spirit lurks, the dreadful Black Book which subdues him, and so many and such resounding thunderstorms, such lurid and menacing flashes of lightning as to deafen and blind whole populations. Tirades and rant abound, sentiment reeks and drips; but, whittled down to its essentials and shorn of its melodramatic trimmings, the essence of the drama is a triangular conflict between Faust's sweet and virtuous but wronged wife Käthe and the fiendish spirit masquerading as Helen of Troy for the undoing of his soul. His blind old father Diether bears the chief burden of the ponderous pathos, and staggers with it to his grave; Wagner, a useful go-between and stop-gap, is otherwise negligible; Faust between Käthe and Helen is the focus of the play. It exhibits an unequal contest and a foregone conclusion. Faust, already impatient, neglectful and even brutal with Käthe (whilst Diether moans and mutters menaces and impotently wrings his hands), has no further use for her once he has set eyes upon the magic picture of Helen which the devil has insinuated into his house. He must and will find and possess the original; and the sinister Stranger, under the guise of her protector and friend, leads the magician to her side. She is discovered slumbering under a bower of roses on a grassy bank:

> *Faust* (*gradually regaining the power of speech*).
> Am I myself? And can these eyes be mine
> Which (as the earth sucks the sun's flaming orb)
> Life's utmost charms absorb
> And greedily shine?
> And is this breast still mine, and this my heart?
> Or will the whole like magic drift apart?
> And will this strange life truly stand the test
> With its supernal powers at my behest?
> You live—Ah then I feel that I live too;
> I have arisen from the night of yore,
> My vital flame is fanned again by you.
> No need to struggle now to reach heaven's shore![1]

Is there the very faintest echo of this delirious outburst (which reads better in the original) in the impassioned speech uttered by Goethe's Faust in the first act of the second part (composed between 1827 and 1830)?

> Have I still eyes? Or is it in my soul,
> This source of beauty lavishly unsealed?
> My dreadful journey brought me to this goal.
> How empty was the world and unrevealed
> Before my priesthood. But now all that is past;
> 'Tis firmly founded, stable, loved at last.
> If ever my allegiance I withdraw,
> Then let me perish, let me be no more. . . .
>
> I owe to you the quickening of all power,
> And passion's inmost meaning; for your dower
> I give you love and worship, madness too.[2]

Klingemann's beautiful and fatal devil in disguise refuses to give herself to Faust until he murders his wife, whom, after a struggle, he duly poisons; only to learn from her dying words that she is with child by him and that he has unwittingly committed two crimes. This is a serious blow, since the pact is to fall due after the fourth (as in the gipsy puppet-play). Moreover as a result he kills his old father in self-defence, which makes a total of three, or so he thinks. But he is sadly mistaken; for (again as in the puppet-play) the pact with Infernus counts as crime No. 1. And none of

---

[1] Klingemann, op. cit. ed. cit., p. 77.   [2] Goethe, *Faust II*, ll. 6487 ff.

them profit him, since Helen is transformed into a skeleton. He is thereupon claimed by the Stranger, whom he defies with his last breath:

Faust (*with mounting strength*).
>   Thou'lt torture *me*? Ha, fiend three times accurst,
>   With all thy flames of hell attempt thy worst!
>   For I defy them, and defy thy might,
>   The fiercest pains I'll welcome with delight,
>   Nor haggle with them; desperate, wild and bold,
>   Thee, and thy wrath, and hell in scorn I'll hold;
>   To crown my wild existence I'll endeavour;
>   I will! I'm Faust! I'll mock at thee forever!

Stranger (*at the height of his rage*).
>   Down with thee, cursed wight!

(He drags him into the background by his hair. The scene changes to the accompaniment of violent thunder and lightning into a dreadful wilderness with a yawning chasm in the background into which the devil flings Faust. Fire rains down on all sides, so that the whole of the interior of the chasm seems to be in flames. A black veil descends over both when the devil is lying on the top of Faust.)

Faust (*exulting in wild defiance*).
>   Ha, down with us, down[1]
>   (Thunder, lightning, fire. They both sink down.)[1]

This is another of those instances which illuminate the difference between folk-poetry and literature, in this case the difference between the undeniably impressive ending of Geisselbrecht's puppet-play[2] and Klingemann's melodramatic finale, which arouses at most indulgent or ironical amusement. One begins to see too, in view of his undoubted feeling for the theatre, that, if the salvation of Faust was almost impossible to represent convincingly, his damnation was even less likely to go down well, and that the Faustian dramatists were in truth faced with a very delicate problem.

Weidmann, Soden and Klingemann, three undistinguished playwrights, transparently reflect the general ideas of the times in which they wrote. All three have in common the emphasis on

---

[1] Klingemann, *Faust*, ed. cit. pp. 120f.   [2] See above, pp. 109f.

family life; otherwise (although Soden borrowed from Weidmann) they represent the changes which were taking place between 1775 and 1815. In the peak year of the Storm and Stress Weidmann emphasized the cosmic nature of the issue involved by introducing the conflict between Ithuriel and Mephisto and giving it prominence. In the turbulent political years following on the French Revolution Soden transformed Faust into the foe of tyranny, scourging (as Klinger had done before him) the corruption of the spiritual and temporal rulers, and deprecating the excesses of the revolutionaries, which was the prevalent state of mind on the subject in Europe as a whole.

Klingemann for his part wrote under the setting star of romanticism. He was utterly indifferent to politics, freedom, tyranny, the people or any questions of state. Nor was he unduly concerned with the problem of evil, being a superficial and facile writer intent on theatrical effects. The crux of the situation as far as he was concerned was love-interest of the most glamorous, erotic and eerie nature imaginable. He embodied this ideal in the person of Helen, whereas Goethe had shown the reality, truth and beauty of love in Gretchen. Not being a genius, Klingemann failed utterly with his Käthe (a milk-and-water misery), but was fairly successful in a stagy and clap-trap way with the fateful and fiendish Helen. She was a bastard sister of the race of the Loreleis, those fatal, unearthly beauties luring men on to destruction and sin, a tinsel Venus in a pasteboard Venusberg. But, though Klingemann's Helen will not stand the test of poetry, she represents the organic development of the Faust-legend under romanticism. There was no romantic poet equal to the task of incorporating in a Faust drama those weird and lovely creatures to whom Brentano, Eichendorff and Heine gave poetic substance and whom Keats immortalized under the name of *la belle dame sans merci*. So that it devolved upon Klingemann to dramatize the dream which romanticism was dreaming. He came perilously near to caricaturing it irretrievably; and yet behind the garish mask and the basilisk eyes one has occasional glimpses of that vivid dream.

(b) An unearthly Helen, 1827

Although Klingemann's heroine derived from the Helen of the Faustbooks and the puppet-plays, he was no more interested in

Greece than in politics and revolutions; and the Stranger, whilst hinting at the mysterious pagan origin of his *protégée*, wasted no words over the glory that was Greece and the tragedy that was Troy. It was far otherwise with Goethe, whose impassioned Hellenism was one of the most fundamental things in his life, so fundamental that it was the chief obstacle blocking his path to the completion of his masterpiece. For if he continued beyond *Part I*, then he would have to introduce Faust to Helen; and as he told Schiller, his mind misgave him at a juxtaposition which threatened to distort her beauty. Indeed he felt this so strongly that he abandoned the Helena-act in 1801, after completing 265 lines, and did not take it up again seriously until 1825. The question naturally arises as to why, if he felt the incongruity of Helen in the Faust-legend so acutely, he yet felt that he could not omit it if he continued the poem. He had shown himself anything but a slave to tradition in *Faust I*; and a spate of contemporary *Fausts* showed at least, if they showed nothing else, that Helen was not essential to a further development of the action. But since Goethe's *Faust* was, amongst other things, the greatest, the deepest and the truest of all the 'fragments' of his confessional life-work, he could no more ignore Helen if he continued it than he could have banished the Earth Spirit from the Gothic study. Truth will out. Moreover the predicament seemed less cruel in 1825 than it had done in 1801; for Goethe had now resigned himself to the stark impossibility of a Renascence of Greek beauty in modern times; and this melancholy realization brought with it a mood and an emotion which suggested the perfect solution of what had earlier seemed an impossible task.

According to legend the Helen who became Faust's paramour was a devilish being, typifying the lusts of the flesh; Marlowe irradiated her with beauty; the puppet-plays transformed her into a Fury, whom Klingemann romantically beglamourized, and Goethe turned her into a heart-hauntingly lovely ghost. The first scene of his Helena-act, published in 1827 with the sub-title *Classical-romantic Phantasmagoria*, is one of the most fascinating ghost-stories in all literature; indeed only *The Sense of the Past* by Henry James can be compared with it for subtlety. The state of mind of Helen is the crux of the situation, a dream-like state of mind, into which doubts of her own reality intrude and bewilder her. Mephisto (in the guise of Phorkyas) knows that she is a shade and takes a fiendish delight in dropping broad hints to that effect; the chorus of attendant Trojan maidens are also aware that they have temporarily escaped from Hades and they try to keep the knowledge from their mistress; for if she remembers her past she will sink back to the shades and take them with her. Yet she herself appeals to Phorkyas to enlighten her, for she wants to know the truth:

> Can it be memory? Is illusion seizing me?
> Was I that woman? Am I still the same? And am I yet to be
> The dream and terror of city-wrecking men?[1]

Phorkyas, ready and willing to oblige, begins to recapitulate her past history, slyly insinuating her essential unreality, since she had been seen in Troy and Egypt at one and the same time; and she is distressfully uncertain herself as to which of the two she is: the virtuous wife who (according to some Greek legends) remained hidden in Egypt during the Trojan episode, or the fatal beauty whose face wrecked a thousand ships—whether she is the heroine of Euripides' *Helen* or the lovely siren of his *Trojan Women*. Not content with this, Mephisto goes a step further:

Phorkyas. And then they say that from the hollow Shades,
    Achilles too was joined in passion to thee,
    Who earlier loved thee despite all Fate's decrees.

Helen. Eidolon I, and Eidolon he, yes, we were wed;
    It was a dream, the words themselves proclaim the truth,
    I vanish hence, a dream now to myself.[2]

The chorus revives her; but the tragic irony of her situation remains: feeling and thinking as a real woman, she is but a shade, and one perhaps who has never had a real existence except in the minds of men, a strange, beautiful, mythological being.

Such as she is, she is involved here and now in a highly dramatic action. She has just disembarked with her maidens in Sparta before the palace of Menelaos after the downfall of Troy; for Goethe took up the tale where Euripides left it in the *Trojan Women* and her fate at the hands of her husband is still undecided. He has been silent and hostile throughout the voyage, and has sent her on ahead to prepare the sacrifice as a thanksgiving for victory. Mephisto-Phorkyas, in the role of aged female retainer,

---

[1] *Faust II*, ll. 8838f.   [2] Ibid. 8876ff.

breaks the news with barely concealed malice that Helen has been designated as the sacrifice by her lord, together with her damsels. He thus paves the way for the appearance of Faust as her deliverer; and when the chorus is sufficiently panic-stricken, she is brought to the point of accepting the assistance of the unknown hero as the only way out of the danger. There is of course no real danger; there is no Menelaos at hand to revenge himself on Helen, not even his shade, since that has not been summoned up from Hades. The whole situation has been invented by Mephisto, building on her confused and cloudy memories of the past. As soon as Helen agrees to trust herself to Faust, the scene before the palace is transformed into the interior court of a Gothic castle.

This first scene of the act, shot through and through with poetic irony, is written in close imitation of the style of Greek tragedy. It is stately, slow-moving, almost statuesque; it aims deliberately at producing a feeling of unreality, and would therefore leave one stone-cold, were it not that Helen's half-and-half awareness has emotional value, a sorrow which gradually extends to the reader, who mourns that she is no longer in the land of the living, and indeed perhaps has never lived. Goethe's grief for a vanished ideal penetrates the scene; it is one of his strangest and most beautiful confessions.

The meeting between Helen and Faust occurs in the second scene. Goethe had taken a quarter of a century to bring it about; and Faust himself had been similarly occupied from the middle of the first act onwards: seeking, glimpsing, yearning and striving. Inevitably the achievement sank into anti-climax. Too long delayed in Goethe's life, it was also (as would become apparent in 1832) too long delayed in the drama. But even presented as an independent dramatic fantasy in 1827, the meeting between these two legendary figures was not the great moment it might have been. Faust is preternaturally solemn and formal; and (just as Goethe had feared) Greek beauty lost its radiance in Nordic surroundings, all the more so perhaps because of the overwhelming Germanic enthusiasm which it aroused. This emotion was expressed by the watchman Lynceus, for Faust's awe-stricken reverence was inarticulate and could only be broken down to mating-point if Helen stooped to conquer. The playful little duologue in which she learns to speak in halting rhymes prior to the first embrace brings her gliding down to his level, thus proving, as the chorus lightheartedly points out, that she is not fastidious but knowledgeable about men. This comment on the public billing and cooing of the mythological mates shows that Goethe's heart was not in the trivial love-scene, opportunely interrupted by Mephisto announcing the imminent arrival of Menelaos. The noise of battle is now heard; armies are glimpsed on the march; speeches of a pseudo-historical nature are made; and a wonderful description of a modern Greek pastoral Arcadia brings the second scene of the act to a close. Quite as deliberately unreal as the first, it has none of that haunting quality of sorrow for an irreparable loss which impregnates the opening of the act.

By this time the action has deserted symbolism for allegory; and when Mephisto-Phorkyas announces that Faust and Helen have produced a son, one looks back with something like nostalgia to the queer little sprite of the Faustbooks, who had so tactfully disappeared. Hitherto overlooked in literature, which much preferred real infants provoking their mothers to infanticide or growing up to make things awkward for their sires, Justus Faustus, now called Euphorion, was to personify modern poetry, sprung from the union of the classical with the romantic spirit, not a very promising theme. Nor does Euphorion, when he first appears, seem to fit the part he was created to play. Why should perfect beauty wedded to the illimitable dreams of romanticism (or, to speak Schiller's language, the combination of naïve and sentimental poetry) result in this hectic young creature, skipping and hopping, dancing and singing, calling and climbing, whilst his parents wring their hands at his recklessness, and Faust (Faust of all people) implores him to be moderate? But, just as the episode threatens to become too fantastic, a martial note intrudes, something sterner and more adult comes into the piping young voice, something real into the allegorical situation, and there is great poignancy in the sudden Icarus-like fate of Euphorion, whose attempted flight ends in disaster. The shadow-show has vanished. Byron lies dead. The irruption of that extraordinarily compelling poet into the Helena-act, whilst the chorus sings a dirge over him, perhaps the most beautiful of all Goethe's elegies for the dead, is comparable in its effect to the sudden pealing of the Easter bells when Faust was about to commit suicide. A real day dawns over the twilit realm of allegory, and a moment of great and startling beauty has been achieved. In the fourth scene, after Helen has vanished in the wake of her son, and Faust has been upborne by her cloak and disappears from sight, the chorus disperse to fresh fields and pastures new. The leader, it is true, elects to follow her mistress down to Hades; but the others choose to become tree-nymphs or water-nymphs or dryads of the vine rather than go back to that grey and formless abode; and the act ends with a rollicking and rather satirical description of Bacchic revelry, probably because at the Dionysiac festivals a satyr-play followed on after three tragedies and brought the solemn proceedings to a light-hearted close.

(c) *A vanquished Helen*, 1829

One cannot help speculating on the effect which Goethe's very baffling Helena-act made on the rank and file of his literary parasites in 1827, isolated as it then was from its context. Pfizer, Harring and Rosenkranz resolutely ignored it. J. D. Hoffmann, if we are to judge by his remarks about Helen and Faust in his drama, was far from satisfied with it; and Karl von Holtei (1798–1880) was frankly puzzled by it when he studied it in order to include it in the *Faust*-readings he was holding in Weimar in 1828; so puzzled that he actually ventured to ask Goethe's help. The latter, who (very wisely) did not attend Holtei's recitations, seized an opportunity one day when they were in society together to give a courteous but rather laboured explanation for his absence:

'Your Excellency,' I said firmly, for I was determined to get some-thing positive out of him; 'tomorrow I am to read *Helena* as an integral part of *Faust*. Now I have taken great trouble with it, but I still don't understand it all. Couldnt you explain to me for instance what is meant when Faust, seated by Helena, divides certain lands among individual commanders-in-chief? Is it a definite indication. . . .'

He did not allow me to finish, but interrupted me very genially: 'Well, well, if only you young people werent such blockheads!' And left me standing there.[1]

Not very helpful, one must admit; but then, though Goethe was very friendly with Holtei and considered him a social asset in Weimar, he clearly thought poorly of him from the poetical point of view, and unhappily he was right. Holtei is far and away the

---

[1] K. von Holtei, *Vierzig Jahre*, 4th ed., Breslau, 1898, Vol. II, pp. 172 f. footnote.

most engaging of all the minor Faustian dramatists, and has the added if adventitious attraction of personal acquaintance with Goethe and the great man's distraught and unhappy son August. A versatile talent and a lively creature, poet, novelist and playwright, Holtei had a hopeless passion for the stage, and was a highly successful professional reciter, but too much of a vagabond and a play-boy to become emiment in any branch of art. His gift to posterity is his autobiography, which has the beguiling merit of making the past and all its forgotten celebrities, with their triumphs, glories and defeats, come to life again. Amongst them Holtei himself arouses one's sympathy and holds one's interest throughout, but particularly in everything associated with Faust. His first connection with the subject was as an actor, playing the part of Wagner in Klingemann's tragedy. In the year 1827 he visited Weimar for the first time and became acquainted with Goethe and the circle round him. Returning in January 1828 to give a course of recitations, including Goethe's *Faust*, and staying until April, he became intimate with Eckermann and August. He then conceived the daring notion of preparing a stage-version of *Faust I* to be acted at the Berlin Königstädter Theatre on the occasion of Goethe's birthday on 28 August of that same year. Warmly encouraged by August and Eckermann, he sketched a scenario on his return to Berlin, and sent it to August for his father's perusal in June. One can imagine his delight when the reply came that Goethe approved the scenario and gave his consent to the proposed performance. Unluckily the Königstädter Theatre had no licence to produce tragedies. Holtei tried to wriggle out of this difficulty by calling the work a melodrama and giving it a sensational title copied from the folkbooks; but the authorities were not deceived. He thereupon sent the completed manuscript to Weimar, and was terribly mortified to hear from August that Goethe did not approve of the version, but withdrew his promised support and co-operation. This was a fearful blow, and Holtei suspected some intrigue behind the Goethean *volte-face*; but it is equally possible that the completed manuscript was more scarifying than the scenario:

Unlike my successors in the field, not excepting Tieck and Goethe *himself*, I was not content with mere cuts, but had invented a really theatrical form, getting the whole action into a prologue and three acts, insinuating individual speeches and passages, which occurred in scenes totally unfit for the stage but which were psychologically significant, into other portions of the drama. In this way I combined in one great act, the second act, all the scenes between Gretchen and Faust, from the first word onwards to the sleeping-draught, which she gives her mother on the stage. Owing to a device of my own invention, this act demanded no single change of scene. There is nothing more disturbing than the eternal bell-ringing and scene-shifting during this part of the tragedy, as I have always felt whenever I saw *Faust* performed.[1]

This last criticism is true enough, but one rather shudders to think of Goethe reading a manuscript which had manhandled his poem so drastically. What gave some colour to Holtei's suspicions of something going on behind the scenes was the acceptance of Klingemann's version shortly after. Holtei thereupon burnt his own in pain and anger. Produced in Brunswick on 29 March 1829, Klingemann's version was acted in Weimar on 28 August as part of the celebrations for Goethe's eightieth birthday. Holtei was present at this performance and was naturally extremely critical of it:

As far as the performance of *Faust* was concerned, this was given in *eight* acts and in a very odd arrangement. A great deal which I had omitted in my despised version not only because I thought I *could*, but because I thought I *ought*, had been left in and made, as I had foreseen, no impression on the stage, or the wrong impression. On the other hand much that had appeared to me to be important, and indeed essential, had been omitted. For instance, Faust's conversation with Wagner, defining his attitude towards learning; then the words of the old peasant and what follows, showing Faust as a practising doctor and the scepticism which ensued. And so forth and so on. And then the love-scenes—there they were with the ceaseless bustling to and fro, just as Goethe had arranged them, destroying all possibility of theatrical unity. In a word, nothing had been *done*, nothing undertaken, but cuts; and I was bold enough to say so to His Excellency's face, bluntly and honestly; adding that I considered my version infinitely more dramatic, more concentrated, better and more effective. To which he replied: 'Oh of course, you young people always know better than your elders!' but without rancour, following it up with his stock phrase: 'Well, well, how nice that is!' and smiling amiably.[2]

Many months beforehand, as both he and Goethe knew, Holtei had perpetrated a *Faust* of his own. Blinded by rage and Satan, as he put it, he determined to write one and produce it, after his

---

[1] Holtei, op. cit. Vol. II, pp. 191 f.   [2] Ibid. p. 223.

Goethean version had been rejected by Weimar. Based on the Schütz-Dreher puppet-play, and certainly influenced by Goethe's *Faust I* and his Helena-act, it is an unequal and at times a most tasteless production. To domesticate a domestic in any shape or form may seem to savour of magic in the twentieth century; but to find Gretchen sweeping out Faust's study in Wittenberg in the opening scene of Holtei's drama is nevertheless a most painful experience. We are reminded (to her detriment and her doom) of that virtuous servant-girl in Pfitzer's version of Widman's Faust-book who was at least partly responsible for the flood of seductions which at one time bade fair to swamp Faustian literature altogether. Holtei almost certainly represented his Margareta as a 'hired help' in order to avoid those changes of scene to which, as we have seen, he was a sworn enemy. He explained it ingeniously enough as a scheme engineered by her father Rudolph (a night-watchman), who wished to gain access to Faust and to question that famous scholar about the theological issues raised by the Reformation. This interview adds to the spiritual despair of the hero, who realizes that, despite all his learning, he cannot solve the doubts, difficulties and perplexities of the simple and untutored Rudolph. When the latter retires, Faust is tempted by various phantoms representing the deadly sins, but rejects their unattractive offers and utters a summons obviously aimed at producing another Earth Spirit, who does not manifest. Voland (an *alias* for Mephistopheles, as Voland carefully explains) appears instead and urges Faust to be done with brooding and to live life to the full, for life is short. This platitude has a sensational effect upon the portraits of ancestors and scholars adorning the study-walls, which are transformed into erotic and obscene tableaux; but have the grace to resume their former appearance when Margareta enters the scene. She cannot see Voland, but she smells him, commenting on the oppressive atmosphere, and rejecting Faust's ardent advances, for she is already half betrothed to a worthy young man called Phillip. She appears only moderately fond of him, however, when he comes to court her after Faust has gone off with Voland; but before they have time to come to an understanding good or bad, she is obliged to bundle him into her bedroom owing to the inopportune entry of Wagner, her devoted though elderly slave. Here the wretched Phillip is discovered by Faust (now rejuvenated and splendidly clad) returning with Voland during Margareta's absence. Nothing could be easier than to stab him to death and fling his body into the Elbe; and nothing could be easier either than to seduce Margareta late that night. For she comes sleep-walking into the study and awakes to find herself in the presence and then in the arms of the man whom she had innocently adored from the first, and of whose crime in murdering Phillip she is in blissful ignorance. Voland meanwhile, on a year's trial as Faust's familiar, has taken possession of Margareta's kerchief used to stanch Phillip's blood. This has magically formed into the wording of a pact, complete with the signature of Faust, a theatrical device on the same level as the transformation of the portraits and the hilarious clowning of the skeletons in Faust's study, who make merry with Voland after the seduction-scene.

It will be agreed that, with the possible exception of the conversation between Faust and Rudolph, this act has little to recommend it, being a mixture of the squalid and the grotesque in almost equal proportions. But the second act is on a much higher level. It is a skilful development of the puppet-play scenes at the court of the Duke of Parma, in which Wagner enacts the part of Casper; and it also contains an interesting, original and potentially very poetical idea in Holtei's conception of Helena. As the act progresses it gradually becomes clear that the lovely Countess Helen, with whom Faust is desperately in love, is none other than Helen of Troy. Voland had summoned her up from the shades and given her the semblance of reality in order to corrupt Faust still further and to make him forget Margareta. This she has been successful in doing; but she has fallen in love with Faust in the process, has become aware of her identity too, and is determined to escape with the man she loves from the clutches of Voland back to ancient Greece:

> Then back to ancient Greece we'll wend our way,
> Where in great halls my stored-up wealth is lying,
> Where (no mere dreams) my forebears live undying,
> And the old gods themselves protect my way.
> I see the swan its snow-white wings unfurling,
> I am aware of my immortal birth;
> The new-born joy of ancient myths and mirth,
> I feel it coming: from the trees it's swirling;
> And in the rays of all the suns of old,
> I gaze on thee, I have thee, and I hold![1]

[1] K. von Holtei, *Doktor Johannes Faust*, Wiesbaden, 1832, p. 93.

This development, by which Helen is no mere tool used by the evil spirit, but a being from a different world, striving for and partly achieving independence, so that a conflict between the pagan underworld and the Christian powers of hell is engaged, is undoubtedly original, capable of organic evolution and poetical treatment. Voland at first is contemptuous of Helen and sure of his power over her, describing her as a borrowed shape, uncertain of her identity, swaying reed-like before the breath of reality, a description which shows the influence of Goethe's Helena. Then, realizing that she is breaking away from his control and luring Faust from him, he resorts to a strange but effective device. Faust, aided and abetted by Voland, is performing the obligatory feats of necromancy before the assembled court, Helena too being in the audience. First Alexander the Great and then Aristotle are summoned and appear. Voland now insinuates into the ducal mind the desire to witness an execution, a request which disconcerts Faust, but which he obeys, making the necessary invocation. With indescribable horror he thereupon sees a vision of Margareta mounting the scaffold, an illusion for which of course Voland is responsible, and which strikes dismay into all hearts on account of its gruesome realism. Faust falls from favour at court as one result, for it is only too clear that the devil was involved in the display. More important for the development of the action, Voland has attained his objective, the destruction of Helena's power over the hero. He can only think of Margareta; and when Voland tells him that Helena is a spectre raised to tempt him, he conceives horror and loathing for her; but also for Voland, whom he dismisses from his presence, the year of trial being up. The evil spirit tries to counteract the effect of this boomerang by reminding Faust of Phillip's murder and confronting him with the blood-stained pact. But the purity of Margareta is such that the writing and the signature have disappeared from her kerchief, and only Phillip's blood-stains remain. Voland, like Helena, is therefore compelled to withdraw for the moment, warning Faust to beware how he calls him again, as that will seal his doom.

Both Helena and Voland return to the attack in the third act. Helena tries to induce Margareta to give her the infant begotten by Faust as a means to recapture him; but does not succeed and hardly deserves to, for she speaks and acts like a third-rate courtesan. This is all the more deplorable because, in ensuing soliloquies, she has some better things to say:

> And the chief of the fallen angels,
> Satan,
> He called me up
> To ensnare the soul of Faust,
> Me, a pagan shade.
> But I barely touched the earth,
> Before I felt
> Divine joy, the instinct of yore,
> An eternal myth reborn.
> I am,
> I live. . . .[1]

I have fought my way to freedom. I am no longer a shade. I am a conscious being, and my soul has thoughts. My old gods are young again.[2]

But in vain does she woo Faust with dream-visions of Greece; he rejects her finally, and she dissolves into mist. Meanwhile much of a dreary and squalid nature has been happening to Margareta, leading to infanticide, discovery, imprisonment and her pending execution. Faust, apprised of her fate, is resolved to save her, and Voland is counting gleefully on this to claim him for hell's own. On her way to the gallows, Margareta is intercepted by Faust and forgives him, confident in her own salvation. She takes the now spotless kerchief from him to bind round her eyes at the moment of execution. Faust, in despair, calls upon hell to save her from her fate; and Margareta (Holtei was terribly unlucky with Margareta) bursts out: 'Faust, I abominate you!' Undeterred by this, Faust calls upon the name of Mephistopheles to rescue her in return for his soul, and Voland immediately appears, but Margareta will have none of his aid. Almost up to the last moment Faust is willing to pay the price of her life in the midst of a fearful cataclysm, the collapse of Wittenberg and snakes abounding. Finally he loses his nerve and implores Margareta to pray for him. She is now seen upon the scaffold kneeling in prayer before a fiery cross, whilst Voland is being swallowed up by the abyss:

> *Faust (on his knees; he leaps to his feet, but is struck by lightning in the act)*. Death!—Mercy!—Grace! *(turning to the cross)* Redemption!—*(collapsing)* God!![3]

[1] Holtei, *Doktor Johannes Faust*, p. 151. [2] Ibid. pp. 162 f.
[3] Ibid. p. 174.

Holtei gave a lively description of the first night of his *Faust*, which took place on 10 January 1829, at the Königstädter Theatre in Berlin. He was very much dissatisfied with the collapse of Wittenberg, done in a most paltry manner by the property-man. The reception was not unfriendly, but not enthusiastic either. The only person who had nothing but praise for the play was the pastry-cook who got rid of all his wares, including the stalest, because the performance lasted five hours and the audience was famished. Even Chamisso, delighted with the conversation about the Reformation, did not grasp the underlying idea of the conflict between Voland and Helena, saying that the latter had not really got across to the audience. As for the part about the Reformation, that had to be cut out by order of the authorities, who thought it contained Catholic propaganda, and that the author must be a Jesuit at least. But if the reception as a whole was lukewarm, Holtei's *Faust* procured him personal happiness in the shape of a wife. Stage-struck and impressionable, he had lost one actress from his bed and board, and was now passionately pursuing another, so far without success. She had been cast for the part of Margareta, and perhaps she was gifted enough to throw some glamour over it, for it evidently melted her heart:

While on that first night sets, blocks and properties were collapsing with a frightful din to let the final scene emerge from a thick cloud of dust, I stood in the background and received from Julia's lips the silent assurance that she would not reject me. The much criticised cross of redemption which was to brand me as a Catholic rose flaming above the ruins of Wittenberg. Margareta in her hair-shirt climbed up the swaying ladder guided by me, and looking down from the narrow rungs she gave me the first sign of love granted and returned. A strange union, formed in the oppressive darkness behind the scenes, whilst in front hell railed in impotent fury and Satan cursed and gnashed his teeth![1]

Chamisso's verdict on *Faust* given to the gratified author: 'You have pulled it off'; the happy outcome to Holtei's courtship of Julia; the pastry-cook's tribute: 'Go on writing plays like that, they are excellent'; and an enormous cake presented as a thank-offering were all on the credit side. But the debit side was proportionately heavy. There was one member of the audience on that first night who was going to make trouble for Holtei, much worse trouble

[1] Holtei, *Vierzig Jahre*, Vol. II, pp. 204 f.

than the commotion created by the allegedly Catholic elements. That was Zelter, whom Goethe had sent to spy out the land and make a report. It was excessively pejorative. Zelter condemned the play root and branch as a mere rehash of Goethe's. One can hardly blame him, for the Margareta scenes are extremely derivative and warranted to offend the taste of the least fastidious, being sordid to a degree. As for the rest, Zelter dismissed the whole as a complete vacuum, intolerably boring and as long as to-day and to-morrow. Poor Holtei! He had meanwhile sent a long explanatory and self-justificatory epistle to August *via* his affectionate and motherly friend Johanna Schopenhauer. She wrote to him as follows on 19 February 1829:

I glanced through your letter to August and then passed it on to him. It is another proof of the goodness of your heart that you have taken the trouble to justify the production of your *Faust*. Considering how badly the old gentleman has treated you in the matter [of Holtei's rejected version of *Faust I*], you owe him no apology. Your *Faust* is now an accomplished fact, has given pleasure to many people and achieved its aim in its *own* way. Surely that is enough? But the old gentleman is eighty years old, and so it's hardly surprising that the clouds of incense sometimes go to his head, and that it is then incomprehensible to him how other people can have the nerve to exist at all. * * * was with him when a letter came from Berlin [Zelter's], in which your *Faust* came off very badly. And the old man was delighted. You must be prepared to find him much less approachable than he used to be when next you come here.[1]

However, Holtei braved the old lion during the birthday celebrations in Weimar and had nothing worse to face than a playful growl. Ardent and generous, the younger man organized a wonderful pageant on the occasion of Goethe's death, performed at the Königstädter Theatre, and took the part of Faust himself, the great magician, who had conjured forth immortal works.

Although Holtei's melodrama (as he frankly entitled it) is a downright failure, the second act is well-contrived; and the three-cornered conflict between Voland, Helena and Margareta for the soul of Faust redeems the play from utter futility, and might have done more than that. The conflict between Gretchen and Mephisto in Goethe's *Part I*, the unequal tussle between Kätchen and Helena in Klingemann's tragedy, have merged into a struggle which, had

[1] Holtei, *Vierzig Jahre*, Vol. II, p. 205.

it been executed by Goethe, would have made of his masterpiece an organic whole. His wonderful representation of the unreality of Helena fired Holtei's imagination; and the further step, her striving for and partial achievement of an independent personality, as Undine strove for a soul, has real possibilities. These are also present in the notion of paganism and Christianity at odds in the underworld (Helena and Voland) and in this life (Helena and Margareta). This latter aspect was very badly handled by Holtei, whose human heroine belongs by rights to the scullery, and whose semi-supernatural protagonist becomes a *demi-mondaine* when confronted with her. Much less homogeneous than Klingemann's drama, which is uniformly rhetorical throughout, Holtei's version of the Helena-episode arouses genuine regrets that he was constitutionally incapable of doing justice to an incipiently poetical idea. As Goethe truly said of him, he was an improviser on paper, and a very facile one. Had he taken more trouble with his *Doktor Johannes Faust*, the formidable 'old gentleman' might have been more ruffled than he was.

CHAPTER X

DON JUAN AND FAUST, 1829

In spite of the fact that Vogt's confusion between Faust and Don Juan seemed to emanate from a disordered brain, it was the natural outcome of an element inherent in the legend from the beginning. When the hero of the Urfaustbook became utterly and irretrievably degraded, he turned away from spiritual questionings, voyages of exploration, feats of necromancy and magical pranks to lead that 'swinish and epicurean life' which so much horrified his first biographer. The magi of antiquity, with the exception of Solomon, were indifferent on the whole to the charms of women; but from medieval times onwards love between the sexes gradually assumed overweening importance in Western Europe, as is evident in literature; and sexual immorality became the most heinous of sins, wickedness incarnate. The Faustbooks naturally included it in their catalogue of crimes; but, though not treating it lightly, they did not dwell on it, being more interested in the spiritual ruin of the hero and in his feats of magic than in his love-life. The puppet-plays whittled this down to the Helena-episode, and to advances occasionally made by Faust to the consort of whichever notable he was entertaining with necromantic displays. When domestic tragedy entered the action in the persons of Weidmann's Helen, Schink's Mathilde and Goethe's Gretchen, the breach was widened to allow of a succession of women whose virtue was attempted by Faust. Schink, Klinger and Voss all represented a rake's progress of this kind; when Schöne, Hoffmann and even Grillparzer attempted to continue *Faust I*, they felt impelled to repeat it, that is to say they exhibited another seduction. By this time Mozart's *Don Giovanni* (1787) had brought the irresistible Spaniard well to the forefront in Europe as a whole; and it was only a matter of time before a conscious juxtaposition of Don Juan and Faust should legitimize the half-conscious contamination between the two legends which had prevailed hitherto. This was done by Christian Dietrich Grabbe (1801–1836).

Although he died young in degradation, penury and squalor, never really achieving what it was in him to achieve, there is no question but that Grabbe was a dramatist in whom genius was present. He is very much neglected to-day as a Storm and Stress writer born too late; but this convenient label leaves out of account his remarkable dramatic objectivity, a quality the Storm and Stress hot-heads would have scorned to possess. It also leaves out of account Grabbe's extraordinary development from that wild and monstrous but powerful production, *Duke Theodore of Gothland*, through a satirical comedy as light as love and a series of great histories in the Shakespearean manner, to his last granite-hewn realistic style, which made no welcome concessions to facile emotions. His four-act tragedy *Don Juan and Faust*, 1829, was written under a less exacting dispensation, and might have profited by greater restraint. It remains a most interesting and original land-mark in Faustian literature.

Goethe's Faust, in a famous and much-quoted passage, lamented the presence of two souls in his breast, both insatiable; the one desiring illimitable gratification of the senses, the other of the mind. Grabbe dramatized this dualism by representing Faust contending with Don Juan in a series of dramatic actions, the spiritually aspiring mind at war with the ruthless and passionate lover. Put like this, it would almost seem as if Grabbe had at long last reconciled the irreconcilable legend to the introduction of an extraneous and alien element, by recognizing it frankly as such and incorporating it in its typical representative. It looks like a stroke of genius; for both Faust and Don Juan were heroes of folk-lore with their roots deep down in primitive ritual practices; moreover both were overweening and immoderate; both sinned beyond forgiveness in order to gratify their desires, and both forfeited their souls in consequence. To bring them together under one tragic roof would be to acknowledge their kinship, and at the same time to free Faust from the burden of those perpetual love-affairs which were strangling the magician. For, once Goethe had introduced the Gretchen tragedy into the action, it was almost impossible to think it out again. His *Part I* was a living and vital work of art which had given a new orientation to the legend. It must go forward; it could not go back; but a real object-lesson as to whither it was tending might give future Faustian poets pause; and at the very least, by separating out the love-interest and isolating it in the person of Don Juan, the confusion which had been there ever since *Faust I* might be partially clarified.

But Grabbe was not reasoning things out like this; he was interested in the contrast between two different types of men, and to a certain extent in their racial differences. So that love-interest won yet another victory; for the conflict between the two men rages round Donna Anna, with whom both are violently in love, each according to his nature. Conquering one's disappointment as best one may, it therefore behoves one to determine how far Grabbe succeeded in portraying the two souls of Goethe's Faust at war in this drama. There is an instinctive hostility between them even before they become rivals for the love of Anna; but the action, which takes place in Rome and on Mont Blanc, rarely brings them together. When it does, and indeed throughout the play, Don Juan throws Faust completely into the shade; for oddly enough the dramatist, a brooding, bitter, disillusioned and discontented man, was extraordinarily successful with the Spaniards, Juan and Leporello, whilst the Germans, Faust and the satanic *Ritter*, only rarely rise above the level of bombast and rant. The situation in brief resolves into this: Faust, having spirited Donna Anna away from Don Juan, who is about to elope with her after having slain her bridegroom at the wedding-festival, transports her to a magic palace on the summit of Mont Blanc. (There is probably an echo of Byron's *Manfred* here.) There he vainly courts her; and when she reproaches him with his married state, he conjures up a vision of his wife at home in Wittenberg and slays her before Anna's eyes. Then, becoming aware of Juan's approach to rescue her, he makes off to deal with him. The latter, struggling up the slopes of the mountain with the terrified Leporello, mocks at the man of magic who cannot win Anna's heart, and is whirled away by a terrific storm, the panic-stricken Leporello with him. Back in Rome, Juan issues his fatal invitation to the statue of Anna's father, whom he has slain in a duel; while Faust, maddened by the knowledge that Anna loves Juan and will never surrender herself to him in spite of the power which his diabolic pact has given him, kills her by a death-wish, and then knows real despair:

Faust. Anna!
Noble and lovely, even in her death!
And as I weep these tears, they prove to me
That God lived once and then was sacrificed.

We are His fragments. Our sorrows and our speech,
Our loves and griefs, and our religion too,
These are our dreams of Him.[1]

He is now prepared to die and go to hell after inoculating Don
Juan with his own despair about the death of Anna. But his
adversary refuses to entertain that emotion:

Don Juan. Who says despair? When misery and woe
Storm in upon us, misfortune's towering waves,
And heart's blood raging, then run up the flag
Which flutters boldly on the mast of life!
And on the very verge of the abyss
Fight on for life's fair honour and its fame![2]

Faust now surrenders himself to the *Ritter*, who is lurking to claim
him:

Faust. Defiant still
Into thine arms I cast myself. But know:
If I'm eternal, then I'll war with thee
Through all eternity, and thou—beware,
For I may conquer yet, and trample thee
Beneath my feet, as I did here on earth.

This is a rather more dignified version of the Klingemann finale;
both heroes go down to their doom still titanically unsubdued; but
Don Juan carries off a clearer moral victory. When the statue of
the Governor offers him salvation if he will repent at the eleventh
hour, he elects to remain true to the law of his own inner being:

Don Juan. What
I am I will remain. If I'm Don Juan,
Then no one I, if I become another!
And better be myself in sulphurous hell
Than saint-like hover in the realm of heaven.
With voice of thunder thou hast asked me. Hence
With thunderous voice I give thee answer: *No!* . . .
And still I cry with my last breath on earth:
'My king, my fame, my country and my loves!'[1]

---

[1] C. D. Grabbe, *Werke*, Leipzig and Vienna, n.d., Vol. III, p. 124.
[2] Ibid. p. 135.   [3] Ibid. p. 136.   [4] Ibid. p. 145.

In this last scene, as indeed throughout the play, Don Juan steals Faust's thunder; for, although one has the impression that Grabbe took particular pains with Faust, giving him a tremendous and tremendously long opening monologue and a very portentous invocation, as well as abysmally profound things to say, he never comes alive, and never gains one's sympathy. Whereas Don Juan and to a lesser extent Leporello seem to be bursting with life. Their scenes are really dramatic, full of action, laughter and poetry; and Don Juan himself is a fascinating character: incorrigibly amoral, heartless, cynical and even cruel, he is quick-witted, passionate, gallant and absolutely fearless, like a beautiful beast of prey endowed with imagination and speech. He takes nothing in the world seriously but his own enjoyment, cannot resist a dare, is incapable of recognizing defeat, and reckons danger as one of the highest pleasures life can offer. This is a portrait of irresistibility; Grabbe's Don Juan has that quality, so easy to affirm of a hero, so difficult to exhibit; and Leporello makes an excellent foil to his master, a really comic figure, with many of Don Juan's vices, but also a born coward and a traitor at heart.

That such a Faustian character as Grabbe himself should have failed with Faust and been so brilliantly successful with Don Juan is strange in one way and explicable in another. For, if love was to be the test, then clearly Faust would have to play second fiddle to Don Juan. Wittingly or not, Grabbe's drama shows very clearly what violence had been done to the Faust-legend by turning the hero into a rake. He could not compete with the dazzling Spaniard when it came to the breaking of hearts.

It is only a relative failure, however. Grabbe's Faust towers far above the dim or maudlin, weak-kneed or bellowing heroes who, in this interim period between the two parts of Goethe's dramatic poem, came forward to enact the part of Faust in Germany. One would have to go back to Klinger or Chamisso to find a Faust comparable in stature to Grabbe's outside Goethe's *Faust I*. And the drama itself, though far from perfect, is the most interesting and significant contribution to Faustian literature made by anyone (always with the exception of Goethe) since Marlowe's day. For a striking contrast was made between the two legendary figures who were living such a conspicuous life in literature simultaneously, and between whom there was an elusive resemblance, although they represented opposite poles of the human personality, pure instinct and avid intellect. This symbolized not only something that was happening to the Faust-legend, but a conflict as old as humanity itself. Performed in 1829, again in 1832 and 1835, the drama was revived by Wolzogen in 1877 and acted fairly frequently towards the end of the nineteenth century; and this was undoubtedly because, though the execution is faulty, Grabbe's *Don Juan and Faust* is based on a truly dramatic idea.

CHAPTER XI

THE APOTHEOSIS OF FAUST, 1832

When Goethe died in 1832, bequeathing his *Faust II* to posterity, the uneasy interim period was rung to its grave. The greatest poet of the age, and Germany's greatest poet, had completed his life's work after all; expectation, speculation, anticipation were finally laid to rest. That chapter at least was closed.

To judge by Schöne, Grillparzer, Pfizer, Rosenkranz and Hoffmann, and indeed by one's own knowledge of human nature, everyone will have presumed that at least one scene featuring Faust's remorse and despair on the subject of Gretchen would open the new proceedings. Was it because Schöne and Rosenkranz had overdone the subject so mercilessly that Goethe refused to satisfy those very natural expectations? It is possible at least; for Schöne had imitated Goethe's style so closely in the wild outbursts of horror and grief that he had literally taken the words out of Goethe's mouth; had the latter attempted his own version, it would have read like a plagiarism from Schöne; and in any case would he not instinctively recoil from doing anything that Schöne and Rosenkranz had done before him? Luckily for Goethe and for us, the rest of Schöne's 'continuation' was a mere repetition of the Gretchen tragedy and could have no inhibiting effects; but when one feels inclined to regret the absence of that almost necessary scene, a perusal of Schöne's pseudo-Goethean heart-searchings will reconcile one to the lack.

It is rather ironical therefore to find Goethe avoiding the Scylla of Schöne only to fall into the Charybdis of Pfizer, by representing the curing of Faust's misery and remorse whilst he lies sleeping on a flowery lawn by a chorus of elves conducted by Ariel who sing his grief away. If Goethe saw Pfizer's scene in the *Morgenblatt* after he had composed his own, he must have felt as if a malign fate were dogging his footsteps; for even Faust's determination to live henceforward with a view to achieving the highest possible form of existence corresponded roughly to the aim of Pfizer's hero.

Once this awkward transition from the first part to the second had been negotiated, Goethe must have breathed a sigh of relief at leaving his parasites, plagiarists and other sedulous apes miles away behind him. By committing himself to the Helena-episode, he had on the other hand turned back to the tradition enshrined in the folkbooks and the puppet-plays from which the first part of his poem had been on the whole such a significant departure. His adherence to the legendary pattern and themes and the wonderful way he transmuted them are the outstanding features of *Faust II*, as has already become apparent in the description of the Helena-act. The action now opens at the court of the Emperor Maximilian, where Faust is discovered making his bow (after Mephisto has paved the way for him) in the wake of countless of his predecessors in popular tales, in popular plays and also in literature. Mephisto doubles the parts of his confederate and court jester, wearing the mantle of that engaging and cunning fool, the puppet Casper, with his own inimitable and raffish grace. There was generally a wedding to celebrate in the puppet-plays when the pair of rogues arrived at court; and here it is the carnival which gives Faust and Mephisto an opportunity to display their powers at a masked ball. Faust, attired as Plutus, scatters gold and jewels all around, produces a terrifying but bogus conflagration and manages to obtain the Emperor's signature on a piece of parchment. Its facsimile then appeared on the paper-money whose introduction would (according to Mephisto) set the tottering finances of the realm on a sound footing. Moreover it was perfectly valid since it could be redeemed by the buried treasure scattered broadcast throughout the Empire. Pots of magic but delusory gold figured largely in the puppet-plays; and the Faustian magical rituals were for ever giving instructions as to how to locate and unearth buried treasure. The showers of gold at the carnival and the proposed search for hidden treasure had ample precedent in the tradition. So had the next item on the programme. Whatever royal or ducal person had to be entertained by the magician in story or in play, he always demanded ghosts, and Maximilian was no exception to the rule. He wished to see Helen and Paris, Faust airily promised to produce them and then discovered that Mephisto was inclined to make the same kind of difficulties about summoning them up as he had done about corrupting the mind of Gretchen. He was more justified on this occasion, however, for feats of necromancy, as was always stressed in the Faustbooks, were difficult and dangerous operations. Mephisto objects that pagan shades are outside his province entirely; but he knows exactly what must be done to raise them. Faust must undertake a journey to the Mystic Mothers, the guardians of the eternal, ideal or Platonic shapes and forms of all living things. It is a terribly lonely and unutterably desolate journey to take:

> *Mephisto.* No way!—Where foot-steps tread not,
> And may not tread: where appeals stead not
> And never will stead. Art thou prepared?
> There are no locks and no latches to lift,
> From solitude to solitude onward thou'lt drift;
> Has thy mind through such wastelands and deserts yet
>   fared? . . .
> And hadst thou swum across the boundless ocean
> And there space infinite beheld,
> Thou yet wouldst see wave after wave in motion,
> E'en though impending death thy fear compelled.
> Thou wouldst see something,—in green water dim
> Of peace-lulled seas the wandering dolphins swim;
> Wouldst see the sailing clouds, sun, moon and star;
> Naught shalt thou see in endless void afar,—
> Nor hear thy foot-step fall, nor meet
> One stable spot to rest thy feet.[1]

One catches one's breath; for not only is this a most moving confession of the loneliness of soul of those who go out into homelessness in the search for an inexorable ideal, it is also the transfiguration by a great poet of those supernatural journeys through the firmament and beyond undertaken by Faust in the folkbooks, and indeed by many and many a magician before him; and further than that it reflects the isolation of mind, the danger and the terror to be faced when the spirit of man goes down to meet the spirits of the dead in order to summon them back. The mysterious mythological mothers, about whom much scholarly ink has been spilt, will not see Faust when he comes among them with the key Mephisto has given him, for they can only see the shadows they are guarding; but if he touches the blazing tripod in their midst, it will follow him up to the world we know, and by its means he will be enabled to summon the shades of Helen and Paris to appear. There is probably a complex of alchemical symbolism

---

[1] *Faust II*, ll. 6222 ff.; based on Bayard Taylor, op. cit. p. 187.

underlying these instructions, which are too fantastic to be poetical, for when alchemy comes in at the door, poetry flies out of the window. But the dialogue as a whole is intensely dramatic, full of suspense, eeriness and beauty. It is followed by a highly amusing scene in which Mephisto dispenses various magical remedies to the ladies and gentlemen of the court much as Weidmann's Wagner had done sixty years before; and then Faust returns triumphantly from his perilous voyage and produces Paris and Helen for the assembled court, acting a love-scene in dumb show. Taking a leaf out of Count Hamilton's book,[1] all the ladies carp at Helen and rave about Paris; whilst the men sneer at Paris and are enraptured by the sight of Helen. Faust for his part is so much transported by the sight of her that he forgets the first law of necromancy: never to address, let alone touch, the spirits raised. Distraught by jealousy, he flings himself between the pair of lovers; there is a loud explosion, the spirits vanish and Faust falls senseless to the ground as he had fallen once before, at the court of Queen Elizabeth of England.

But it is not this final incident which engages the attention and occupies the mind; it is the speech which Faust utters when Helena appears. It was perhaps uncritical to compare it with Klingemann's; but it would be even more so to place it beside Marlowe's. Goethe had a forerunner and a rival in the Elizabethan dramatist whom there was no transcending on the subject of Helen. What is more, he had a rival in his earlier self, whose more spontaneous rapture when Faust glimpsed Helen in the magic mirror in the *Witches' Kitchen* throws a rather melancholy light on the whole subject, the light which Goethe turned to such wonderful account in the Helena-act.

A deliberate reference to the vision seen in the *Witches' Kitchen* shows that Goethe was aiming among other things at an organic development of his dramatic poem. Hence the return to the Gothic study at the beginning of the second act. One had almost forgotten its existence; but there it is, absolutely unchanged says the rubric; and yet time has not stood utterly still even in this ancient seat of learning. Only three years have passed since Faust conjured up the Earth Spirit; but a new Famulus has been installed; and the young scholar, who is now a Bachelor of Arts, has profited by Mephisto's counsels and has become a cross between a young

[1] See above, pp. 137f.

blood and a young tough. Bumptious and hard-boiled, he reads Mephisto a lecture on Fichte's philosophy, and in doing so breaks into a speech which is a very close parody of Faust's apostrophe to the setting sun in the scene *Before the Gate* in *Part I*. This is another echo; but would it have taken the form of a parody if Goethe had not been sickened by the ease with which Schöne and Rosenkranz had imitated, emasculated and vulgarized the poetical idiom of *Part I*? To my mind it also appears not unlikely that Goethe deserted reality so completely in the second part of his *Faust* because of Schöne's distressing 'continuation'.

If Schink had anticipated the satire of Fichtean philosophy, and Pfizer had also sketched the brutalizing effect of Mephisto's evil counsels on the student, no one had ever had the 'good idea' of introducing a Homunculus into the action. But then none of Goethe's imitators or predecessors was initiated into the mysteries of alchemy; and (as a forthcoming monograph will abundantly prove) the early studies Goethe had undertaken in that curious branch of learning had gone very deep and had profoundly affected his attitude to science as well as much of the symbolism in his poetical works.[1] It is Wagner who has been devoting himself to the chemical production of organic life in his laboratory; and Mephisto appears in the nick of time to complete the process and animate his tiny 'cousin' still enclosed in the phial. The latter is then able to look into the mind of Faust, still in a paralytic swoon and dreaming of Helen, and to determine that the only way to revive the patient is to take him to Greece. This paves the way for the *Classical Witches' Sabbath*, in itself a pendant to the Northern Sabbath in the first part and therefore organically important for the structure of the poem as a whole. It is a descent into the classical underworld balancing the descent into the Christian underworld in *Faust I*, and both complexes of scenes are therefore comparable to those journeys to hell which Faust undertook in the Urfaustbook in the wake of countless other legendary heroes and gods. The Northern Sabbath tended towards puerility; but this is not a reproach which can be made of its classical counterpart, which (like the masked ball in the first act) goes on far too long and contains so many recondite mythological allusions that one feels bewildered and out of one's depth.

[1] R. D. Gray, *Goethe the Alchemist*. (To be published by Cambridge University Press early in 1952.)

It has, however, an organic function to perform. The Sabbath in the first part led Faust away from Gretchen; the classical Sabbath leads the hero towards Helen. Awakening as soon as he touches Greek soil, he begins at once to seek for her amid the thronging shapes and forms around him. Falling in finally with Chiron, he is taken by the latter towards the abode of Persephone, where he is to plead, as Orpheus and others had done before him, that the beloved woman may be permitted to ascend again to the world of men. Goethe sketched but did not execute this scene, turning away from Faust to follow the fortunes of Mephisto. The Nordic fiend is an uneasy guest at the classical Sabbath, continually befooled by the sirens and their like; but he finally achieves a suitable Greek disguise for the third act by borrowing the monstrous and hideous form of one of the three Phorkyades or Fates. Then the interest shifts to Homunculus, who is aiming at escaping from his phial and becoming a real being. This is brought about when he shatters his crystal prison at the foot of Galatea's sea-borne chariot, and begins a new embryonic but organic existence in the creative element of the sea. Glorious though this triumphant finale is which takes place among the dancing waves and the flying foam, and deeply though the commentators have delved into the subject of Homunculus, he remains an engaging oddity whose progress towards rebirth, even including the splendid immolation, cannot compensate for the lack of the scene in which Faust was to have implored the rebirth of Helen. Both Homunculus and the Earth Spirit derived ultimately from Paracelsus; and the difference in size between them seems to me symbolical of the difference in Goethe's attitude towards magic in 1772 and 1830. In his youth it has been a mighty and terrible power; in his age it had become a subject for playful philosophical fantasies.

The first two acts, however episodic in character, represent a uniform action, beginning when Faust goes down to the Mystic Mothers in search for the eternal idea of Helen, continuing with the catastrophe when he attempts to make it a real part of his life, and concluding with his determination to call her shade up to earth in order to assuage his desire. It is the record of a love and longing so impassioned and incurable as to be extremely moving, for a beauty that never was on sea or land; it can only be evoked in the dream-world of the Helena-act, and not even there for long. Once the dream has vanished, there is no recapturing it in life.

Hence the complete disappearance of Helen and all that she stood for in the final acts of the drama. The cloud-like garments which had upborne Faust dislimn at the beginning of the fourth act, assuming a radiant nebulous form for a moment (Juno, Leda, Helen? asks Faust), and then dissolve into a tender strip of mist rising ever higher into the ether; the sweet young loveliness of Gretchen shines on him and seems to beckon.

In the Urfaustbook the hero became embroiled with the knight on whose head he had maliciously clapped a pair of magic horns and was forced to do battle with him and his numerous adherents. He won his victories by magical means depending largely on illusions; he also later teased his friends or maddened his enemies by producing floods of illusory water and laughing at the antics they then performed. Goethe harked back to this tradition in the fourth act, in which Faust with the help of Mephisto wins an engagement for the Emperor, who is at war with an Anti-Emperor, by magical and delusory means; he routs the army of the adversary by fire and water raining down on them or flooding round them from all sides. Faust modestly and untruthfully attributes his success to the intervention of the Necromant of Norcia whom the Emperor had saved from execution in Rome. This irrelevant personage was borrowed from the *Life of Benvenuto Cellini* translated by Goethe in 1796–7; he was a wizard who produced one of the most sensational magical evocations in all history;[1] and the introduction of his name at this juncture was probably a private joke of Goethe's, one of the many mystifications which he insinuated into this and other works. But, although Faust consented to lend himself to all the martial hocus-pocus produced by Mephisto, ending in victory for the Emperor, it was with serious intent. After a transparent temptation-scene based on the Gospels in which Mephisto offers Faust the glories and riches of the world, the latter defines the aim and states the desire which now obsess him. This new venture was nothing less but also nothing more than to limit the limitless ocean, that is to say to reclaim land from the sea. It was in order to obtain a strip of coast-land from the Emperor for this purpose that he had made a feint of winning the latter's war for him. If it was a truly Faustian task to take up arms against the boundless sea, it was an almost anti-Faustian emotion which made him rage in despair at its infinite, restless

---

[1] See my *Ritual Magic*, pp. 118 ff.

and purposeless motion; for this was in a way to rage against himself and the course of his previous existence. A change of heart was evidently on the way; but at first, that is to say in the fourth act, there is no sign of anything more positive than enmity towards 'the aimless force of elements unruly':

> Let that high joy be mine for evermore,
> To shut the lordly ocean from the shore,
> The watery waste to limit and to bar,
> And push it back upon itself afar!
> From step to step I settled how to fight it:
> Such is my wish: dare thou to expedite it![1]

If Faust is changing in one way, he has so far not changed in another; Mephisto is to accomplish the task for him; and the only real interest in the rather tedious magical battles (whose strategy has been highly commended by professional soldiers) lies in the discomfort, oppression, fear and even outrage they induce in all the participants, including Faust himself. Everyone feels that there is something wrong, wicked and sinister in the means which have secured the victory; and the Church in a highly satirical scene makes a very good thing of the crime committed by the Emperor in allying himself with a black magician. This is another echo from *Part I*, when the Church took possession of the jewels Mephisto had procured for Gretchen; and one is bound to confess that Goethe's restrained but telling irony has gained rather than lost by the passage of the years.

The scheme for the reclamation of land from the sea was a complete departure from Faustian tradition; and even (as far as I know) from magical tradition altogether, although control over the elements figures largely on the list of the presumed powers of both white and black magicians; and the former often made a highly philanthropic and benevolent use of it. But the fifth act, whilst developing the reclamation-*motiv*, came to grips with the main problem presented by the final scenes in the folkbooks and puppet-plays, the question of salvation depending on repentance. Like his predecessors Faust is in a very hardened state of mind when the chance is given. Much land has by now been reclaimed from the sea, but all the hard work (and some of it has been as black as night) has been done by Mephisto and his assistants. It has not

---

[1] *Faust II*, ll. 10,228 ff.; cf. Bayard Taylor, op. cit. p. 284.

cost Faust a single drop of sweat, although we are given to understand that it has cost others rivers of blood. Corrupted by great possessions and power, Faust is now a much more ruthless person than the young ruffian who stabbed Valentine to death and then abandoned Gretchen for the witches on the Brocken. He is eating his heart out (à la Naboth) because a little cottage with an adjacent chapel belonging to an aged couple Philemon and Baucis forms an enclave in his lordly dominions. He wants to displace them; they want to stay where they are; the sight of their little property enrages him, and the chapel-bell drives him to fury; in a word, to quote someone who came after him, his patience is exhausted:

> No sorer plague can us attack
> Than to be rich and know a lack!
> The chiming bell, the lime-trees' breath
> Are symbols of the Church and death.
> And my almighty, potent will
> Is broken by this eyesore still.
> What shall I do to fight this feeling?
> I rage whene'er the bell is pealing![1]

This is a harder and a worser man than the Faust who broke down and abandoned his suicidal resolve when the Easter bells rang out; on a much lower spiritual level, since petulance and greed have replaced divine discontent; and the bells chiming across the gulf which divides his present from his former self underline the tragic difference. Incited by Mephisto, Faust now gives orders to displace those tiresome old people by violence if necessary. The result is violence indeed: forcible entry, a conflagration and a threefold death.

Although blaming Mephisto for the outcome, according to his wont, Faust is profoundly shaken by this catastrophe. As he broods over it on the palace balcony, four grey old women can be seen and heard below seeking an entry: want, debt, carking care and need, those dismal entities all human beings must cope with sooner or later, unless they belong to the privileged classes, such as magicians, who do not know the meaning of want. But no one is immune from anxiety and dread, so that care slips in through the key-hole to tempt the repentant magician. He has come to recognize at last what he had always obscurely known, that his real

---

[1] *Faust II*, ll. 11,251 ff.; cf. Bayard Taylor, op. cit. p. 309.

tragic guilt, from which all his misdeeds and misfortunes spring, lies in his dependence on magic. And the question now arises: can he bring himself to renounce it? In a wonderful monologue, followed by the eerie temptation-scene forced upon him by the presence of care, he makes and subsequently keeps the resolution to be done with magic for good; and, reaffirming his scepticism on the subject of a world beyond and a God above us, he refuses to acknowledge sorrow's might. As the logical result of renouncing magic, those disabilities which belong to his hoary years immediately descend upon him. Blind and dying, but unaware of this, he gives trenchant orders for the continuation of his great work, which he believes to be on the verge of completion.

The tragic irony of this scene has still to find its equal in the literature of the world. Hideous ghouls, summoned by the gleeful Mephisto, are busy digging the grave of Faust, singing snatches of song from the grave-digger's ditty in *Hamlet*; whilst the unconscious victim sees in his mind's eye a future race of free people inhabiting the land his efforts have liberated for them. The trace of his days on earth will thus be secured for aeons to come. In an ecstasy of anticipation, he speaks the fatal words he had been so certain he would never utter when he signed the pact and sinks down lifeless into the grave-diggers' arms. Even Mephisto is moved by such an end to such a life:

Mephisto.	The last sad, empty moment—that
	(Poor soul) he wished to keep for ever,
	He, who withstood me in such gallant wise.
	Well, Time is Lord, and there the old man lies.
	The clock stands still.
Chorus.	Stands still, like midnight dumb.
	The hand has stopped,
Mephisto.	Has stopped, and all is done.[1]

There is a double reminiscence here, an echo of the words of the pact in the first part, and another echo:

Marlowe's	
Faustus.	The stars move still, the clock will strike,
	The devil will come, and Faustus must be damn'd. . . .
	[The clock striketh twelve.][2]

[1] *Faust II*, ll. 11,589 ff.   [2] Marlowe, *Tragical History*, pp. 171, 173.

Goethe's echo of Marlowe is one of the great moments in Faustian literature. One seems to hear the chiming of all those countless clocks which had rung out the fatal hour again and again ever since Elizabethan days as darkness fell over the doomed magician. They have run down at last. Time has stopped for Faust; he is on the threshold of eternity.

One would like to leave him there, as certain of his salvation as one was of Gretchen's before the voice from above announced the self-evident fact in *Faust I*. But Goethe had a tradition to contend with which was not broken yet, in spite of the strenuous efforts of Weidmann, Schink, Schöne, Holtei and their like. He also had a reputation to maintain; and he would surely have been not more but less than human if he had not felt it incumbent on him to do better than they. He must therefore dot the i's and cross the t's of a situation it would not do to leave to his readers' imagination; and moreover since the blatant Schöne had forestalled the obvious ending by his *Epilogue in Heaven*, he must take a different line. After representing Mephisto's defeat by the choir of angels, a highly ironical scene, Goethe therefore sent Faust's immortal soul drifting upwards into Roman Catholic skies to the sound of a tantalizing music, lovely, light, almost playful; charming, melodious, disarming; but not the music of the spheres; chanted by saints, seraphim, cherubim, the Gospel Marys, the Virgin Mary and the penitents, amongst them one who was once called Gretchen:

> Ach neige,
> Du Schmerzenreiche,
> Dein Antlitz gnädig meiner Not!
> Das Schwert im Herzen,
> Mit tausend Schmerzen
> Blickst auf zu deines Sohnes Tod.[1]

So she had prayed in her anguish and despair in *Faust I*.

> Neige, neige,
> Du Ohnegleiche,
> Dein Antlitz gnädig meinem Glück.
> Der früh Geliebte,
> Nicht mehr Getrübte,
> Er kommt zurück.[2]

[1] *Faust I*, ll. 3,587 ff.   [2] *Faust II*, ll. 12,069 ff.

This is now the burden of her song, as she 'clings' (according to the rubric) to the Virgin Mary; and it is an echo from the past which could well be spared; for of all the plagiarisms which Goethe's *Faust I* had to suffer, this seems the worst. It throws stage-lighting where none has the right to be. It might almost have been perpetrated by Schöne.

It had been made tragically clear in the Urfaustbook, in Marlowe's drama and in all subsequent traditional statements of the legend that until the last moment it was not too late for Faust to repent and be saved. Indeed his fearful wrestlings with his own soul for that end are of a poignancy which (even in the puppet-plays, let alone in Marlowe's tragedy) there is no gainsaying and no withstanding. But divine grace could not operate, because Mephisto was ever on the alert to harden the heart of the hero and teach him to despair. The victory went to the powers of evil. Goethe's hero was theologically speaking in a state of invincible ignorance throughout the dramatic poem. He experienced crushing remorse and self-loathing during the Gretchen tragedy and inter-mittent horror at his bondage to Mephisto; but he was not seriously concerned with the welfare of his soul and never really jeopardized it. He abjured magic just before the end, although still completely sceptical and indifferent about the next world. To be active and occupied here and now, striving unremittingly, was to him the sum of man's endeavour. Though not in a state of grace, he was in a state in which divine grace could operate; and all the more so since he had surrendered the fruits of his unholy alliance with Mephisto before he died. This was of the utmost importance in legendary tradition, and in ritual tradition too, where the success-ful repudiation of the pact depended on rigid abstention from further diabolic benefits. It would clearly have been legal quibbling of the most vindictive kind to damn him for words spoken under a cruel misapprehension, defining an essentially noble ideal, especially as most of the speech was in the conditional future.

Happily for Faust and for Goethe there were many precedents for the eleventh-hour salvation of repentant black magicians. There was Cyprian, there was Theophilus, there was Pope Sylvester II, there was Militarius, there was Robert the Devil, there was Roger Bacon. And now at long last Doctor Faustus joined this happy band of sinners; and he joined them naturally and logically under the Catholic dispensation under which they had all obtained pardon and grace, whereas he had been damned under the Lutheran persuasion. But Goethe was not satisfied with mere salvation. There were probably two reasons for that tremendous final scene, and the commotion throughout the heavens as Faust's soul rises upwards. The salvation itself had taken place earlier, when the angels had bemused Mephisto into surrendering what he considered his lawful prey. What followed was rather in the nature of an apotheosis. It achieved something that Lessing, Weidmann, Schink, Lenz, Schreiber, Müller, Schöne, Holtei and Hoffmann had attempted in vain: the transfiguration of the hero, his salvation not in this play or in that, not in one poet's mind or in another's; not temporarily for a certain age and at a certain time; but as a symbolical figure for posterity. From being a mere magician, who might at a pinch escape eternal damnation, he became (the angelic hosts announce it) a symbol for the absolute incorruptibility of man, who can spend a life-time erring but will not finally be false to the light that is in him. Whether one likes it or not, and many who have surrendered to the spell of the Urfaustbook, of Marlowe and of the puppet-plays do not like it at all, this is what Goethe achieved, and partly at least by sparing no poetical device in his power when it came to the final scene. Even the indefinable irony helps.

But it was not only because of the great opportunities for poetry and grace offered by Catholic angelology that the last scene in the dramatic poem took place where and how it did. It was because the Faust-legend went down fighting, defying even Goethe to revoke its decrees on its own religious ground. He gave ground gracefully and reverted to an older and more merciful tradition, transforming the utter spiritual defeat of a mortally misguided man into grace abounding for the striving soul of humanity.

PART IV. POST-GOETHEAN FAUSTS

Chapter XII. NON-GOETHEAN FAUSTS
> (*a*) Ragtag and bobtail Fausts, 1833–1895
> (*b*) An incomprehensible Faust, 1839
> (*c*) An ennobled Faust, 1919

XIII. UN-GOETHEAN FAUSTS
> (*a*) A tragic Faust, 1836
> (*b*) An irreclaimable Faust, 1842

XIV. ANTI-GOETHEAN FAUSTS
> (*a*) *Danse macabre*, 1847
> (*b*) 'Schiller's' Faust, 1859–1869
> (*c*) A parodied Faust, 1862–1886

XV. THE FIRST FAUST REBORN,   47

NON-GOETHEAN FAUSTS

(a) Ragtag and bobtail Fausts, 1833–1895

Many a man will limn me whose clarity's to seek;
They'll paint me in their pictures as if I were a freak;
Neither in love nor hatred, in struggle or defeat
Will they quite comprehend me; our minds will never meet.[1]

Thus spake the hero to Wagner as he neared his end in Ludwig
Bechstein's *Faustus* in 1833. They were prophetic words, although
the author himself was speaking retrospectively in this agreeably
rhymed and attractively illustrated modern version of Pfitzer's
edition of Widman's Faustbook. In order to bring it up to date he
inserted two chapters of 'prophecies' made by Faust on the course
of history down to Bechstein's own day, including the Armada,
the Massacre of St Bartholomew, the French Revolution and
Napoleon. Much more interesting than this transparent device are
the two cantos added at the end. In *The Scorn of Hell* the devils
mock at Faust in the nether regions, and taunt him with the almost
total oblivion which will be his lot on earth:

> Posterity will scarcely the name of Faustus know,
> And you'll be jolly lucky to adorn a puppet-show.[2]

But this is not the last word. The final canto, *Through Night to
Light*, declares on the contrary that poetry will redeem him:

> Oh, blessed whom a ray of light from poetry can save!
> The singer brings redemption to dark Cocytus' wave;
> And in the crown posterity around his brow doth bind:
> *Through night to light!*
> These starry words in flaming script you'll find.[3]

This is the most endearing solution of the Faustian dilemma,
'damnation or salvation?', ever offered; and particularly winning

---

[1] L. Bechstein, *Faustus. Ein Gedicht*, Leipzig, 1833, p. 167.
[2] Ibid. p. 191. [3] Ibid. p. 195.

because it is quite obvious from the context that Bechstein was paying a tribute to Goethe, although he does not mention his name. Quite apart from making Widman readable, an almost impossible feat, Bechstein deserves an honourable mention for this graceful and gracious idea.

Yet the prophecy made about the fortunes of Faust in literature heading this section is also apt, and particularly appropriate to the rank and file of the fifty-odd representatives of post-Goethean *Fausts*. The majority were by men of so little distinction as to be absent from the pages of standard works on German literature; and a sizeable number are vainly to seek in the big libraries, including the British Museum. Research might unearth some of them; and amongst those whose titles or dates suggest that it might be worth while to do so I would mention the following, all of them in German:

C. E. Mölling, *Faust's Death, a tragedy in five acts*, Philadelphia, 1864.

Adolf Müller, *Faust. Tragedy in five acts. A second part to Goethe's Faust*, Leipzig, 1869.

Adolf Müller, *Doctor Faust's End*, 1887.

K. A. Linde, *Faust. Third part to Goethe's Faust*, 1887.

Lorenz Schmitt, *Doktor Johann Faust*, 1926.

The title of Müller's first drama shows that the silly season of second parts to Goethe's *Faust* was still not over; and indeed we shall meet other specimens of this strange phenomenon. Nor was Linde the only one to write a third part. An anonymous author printed some scenes in Duller's *Phönix* in 1838 dealing with Faust's posthumous existence and also with the fortunes of those he had left behind him on earth. To judge by the specimens given, it is no great matter for regret that the author discontinued the series. A notable feature of the post-Goethean period is the spate of parodies, farces, skits, humorous sketches and comic poems written round the person of Faust: *Faust in Auerbach's Cellar; A modern Faust; Faust and Gretchen; Doctor Faust's Cellar Rides; Doctor Faust in Salzburg; Mephistopheles in Rome; Faust, the democrat converted too late. A terrible tragedy in six long acts, contracted for the sake of brevity into three acts. In free imitation of His Excellency Wolfgang von Goethe*—these are some of the ephemeral facetiae the Faustian-minded indulged in. Jens Baggesen's *Completed Faust* (1835) was on a more monumental scale, being a satire on romanticism in general and on the Faust- and Goethe-manias in particular with special reference to the current craze for medievalism. Although Goethe himself, under the pseudonym of Martin Opitz, is one of the *dramatis personae*, the fun is far indeed from being fast and furious; and only a very artless reader would see much wit in such occasional parodies of Goethe's masterpiece as the following imitation of the opening monologue:

> Thank God, I've neither studied philosophy,
> Nor law, nor medicine; and what's more
> Still less have I engaged in theology,
> Or anything else with labour sore;
> And therefore no wretched fool am I
> Whose efforts have left him high and dry.[1]

The serious poems written about Faust are hardly more interesting, even though Gottfried Keller and Emmanuel Geibel grace, if they do not adorn, the list; and the prose tales are not impressive either. In 1833 J. Seidl perpetrated a fantasia about Lessing's lost Faustian manuscripts; D. Schiff contributed his mite to the identification of Fust and Faust in 1835 by a tale in which the hero vainly tries to sell his Bible in Paris; and Adolf Brennglas rewrote Hamilton's story in 1861 under the title *Elizabeth and Faust*.

Negligible though all the ragtag and bobtail Fausts of the nineteenth century and after are, it yet seems necessary to give some idea of their quality by selecting four or five for a cursory examination. The first to strike the eye is Karl Gutzkow's dramatic fantasy *Hamlet in Wittenberg*, which he dated 1832 but probably did not write until 1835:

> Tieck suggested the hypothesis [said Gutzkow in his introductory note] that Hamlet had been in the closest possible relationship with Ophelia before going to Wittenberg. Encouraged by my reading of the Romantic poets, I aimed at depicting a kind of spiritual marriage with Ophelia. In the second part of his *Faust* which was not published until after his death in 1832, Goethe came out with a similar mystical mating between Faust and Helena.[2]

This is disingenuous. By dating his sketch 1832, Gutzkow was claiming independence from Goethe, whose Helena-act had, how-

---

[1] J. Baggesen, *Poetische Werke in deutscher Sprache*, Leipzig, 1836, p. 140.

[2] K. Gutzkow, *Gesamelte Werke*, Jena [1872], Vol. 1, p. 369.

ever, been published in 1827, and had very probably suggested the subject-matter of this sketch. Gutzkow rather ingeniously brought Hamlet and Horatio into contact with Faust and Mephisto (in the guise of the poodle Prästigiar) in a Wittenberg inn. At Hamlet's request the magician, or rather his familiar spirit, conjured up a living likeness of Ophelia, and produced her again for Hamlet in private. But, because the means were evil, she came in the shape of a sensual temptress, sapping the young prince's willpower and making him unfit for the ordeal that lay before him. As a kind of curtain-raiser to Shakespeare's drama, *Hamlet in Wittenberg* betrays the intellectual bent of Gutzkow's mind, but also his lack of poetical gifts.

Slight and almost irrelevant as this Young German glimpse of Faust may be, it arouses retrospective respect when compared with *Faust. A Tragedy*, published by Braun von Braunthal in 1835. He had the modesty to bring it out under his initials; and he had the distinction of being one of Lenau's friends; but his *Faust* would, I believe, carry off the booby-prize even against such formidable competitors as Schreiber, Vogt, Voss and J. D. Hoffmann. Almost entirely independent of tradition and of Goethe, Braunthal at least did not hook his action on to the end of the Gretchen tragedy, for which omission one is duly grateful. Otherwise gratitude is far enough from one's thoughts as one wades through a welter of dreary nonsense comprising love-affairs, betrayals, the Paris underworld and vengeance coming to a head at the monastery of St Just, where Charles V is solemnly retiring from the world. Murder, infanticide, suicide, remorse and despair succeed each other at random; and Faust finally takes his own life with Mephisto prowling in the offing and ready to seize him:

At this moment, the shining figure of Juanito [Faust's illegitimate son] rises at his head holding out a palm-leaf. The strains of an organ are heard in the distance and the shade sinks down.[1]

The organ and the palm-leaf presumably spell salvation; but by the time one has reached the end of this melodramatic rigmarole, one is in no state of mind to care either way; for here once more is a nadir in Faustian literature.

Although Xaver Schmid's *The New Faust* (1851) is not quite so crack-brained as Braunthal's drama, it is more hair-raising in one

---

[1] Braun von Braunthal, *Faust. Eine Tragödie*, Leipzig, 1835, p. 152.

way, because it was obviously written in blissful ignorance of Goethe's *Faust II* thirty years after its publication. This puts Schmid at the bottom of a class of two which J. D. Hoffmann had hitherto occupied in solitary state:

I have often wished [wrote this terrible ignoramus] that Goethe had written a second *Faust*, whose way had led upwards. He represented in a masterly fashion how nature and the devil between them vanquished the doubting hero. But could he not also have shown how a higher redeeming power comes to the rescue of the striving soul and wins a victory with it over nature and the devil? He would then not only have explained the *fall* of man, but also the other cosmic happening, the *redemption*! He only wrote about the dark aspect of life.[1]

Labouring under this curious misapprehension, Schmid flung himself into the breach with the story of a second coming of Faust, who had inhabited an old castle on the Danube in the sixteenth century and had vanished thence mysteriously after performing many evil deeds. He had reappeared in the nineteenth century and had then disappeared again; but this time he had done nothing but good and indeed had left an almost saint-like memory behind him. He did more than that, however, bequeathing to the old caretaker of the castle a bundle of papers which the latter handed over to the author, who faithfully transcribed them. They comprise several scenes written in emasculate verse penetrated with piety, whether Faust is holding monologues, or dialogues with his old friend Augustin, with his former lover Angelica or with Mephisto, that accursed tempter who is put to flight when Faust challenges him to make the sign of the cross. This unintentional reminder of the puppet-plays and ballads only serves to show how much virtue went out of the legend when it fell among the minor *literati*.

Hans Schilf's full-dress tragedy *Faust* (1851) does nothing to redress the balance. In its melodramatic and scenic excesses it recalls Klingemann; in its fearful and wonderful originality it is in line with Hoffmann and Braunthal. The opening act depicts the raging passion Faust is brought by Mephisto to conceive for the virtuous matron and mother Margarita von Esse, and her eventual surrender to him owing to a magic draught and much Mephistophelian hanky-panky. In the second act the lovers are

[1] T. Faber [X. Schmid], *Der neue Faust*, Rastatt, 1851, p. 15.

discovered sleeping it off in a neglected and overgrown but lovely garden, where they have lain wrapped in an enchanted slumber for a whole year. The Sleeping Beauty and the mating between Goethe's Helena and Faust merge in this synthetic situation. The lovers awake, riddled with remorse, to rude tidings, gleefully communicated by Mephisto. Margarita's husband and Faust's Famulus Karolus have slain each other in a duel about the erring wife; the world, execrating the lovers, believes them to be dead; and their only chance of survival is to make off to foreign parts. Margarita implores to be allowed to see her child Marianne just once before departing: and, herself unseen, she is a shattered witness of the innocent infant being rocked in menial arms, to the sound of this agonizing lullaby:

> Oh sleep then, my darling, the wind rages wild
> Whenever a mother forsakes her poor child;
> Oh sleep, little birdie, your nest is forlorn,
> No feather will keep your bed snug from the storm.[1]

Profiting by the paroxysm of maternal anguish which overwhelms Margarita, Mephisto offers to restore the child to her if she will give herself to him; for, shaken by an impure passion for the unfortunate woman, he now hankers after her soul:

> I am a spirit, shrivelled and burnt up;
> Give me your human soul, all fresh with dew![2]

Margarita rejects this notion with contumely and Mephisto poisons her whilst she is in a hypnotic trance of his inducing. When she comes round, he produces an antidote; but she refuses it with virtuous scorn and retires to give up the ghost. Learning of this catastrophe, but unaware of Mephisto's part in it, Faust after much ranting and raving signs a blood-pact with the fiend, whilst the alchemical laboratory and the astrological tower collapse in ruins at his feet. The third act, placed outside the *Tower of Megalomania of Modern Babel*, introduces a phantom Margarita among the ghosts of young maids and matrons still avid for love (a reminiscence of the appearance of the ghost-like Gretchen on the Brocken); and there is a great deal of confusion, turmoil and

---

[1] H. Schilf, *Faust, Tragödie in fünf Aufzügen*, Leipzig and St Petersburg, 1891, p. 49.
[2] Ibid. p. 54.

general revolutionary uproar, in which an infinitely dreary hermit plays the part of *raisonneur*. Nor does the situation improve with the removal to India in the fourth act. In this glamorous land Faust weds the princess Zemire and becomes king; but is dethroned in the fifth act by a band of conspirators led by Mephisto. Zemire poisons herself and then Faust with an asp *à la* Cleopatra; and the hero dies after a solemn farewell speech in which he declares that God will forgive and save him. There seems no valid reason to doubt his words; for it is much more difficult to pardon Schilf than his unfortunate hero.

Hermann Hango's epico-dramatic poem *Faust and Prometheus* (1895) was conceived on much more ambitious lines, being a long-drawn-out transcendental argument between the sublime creator Prometheus, who hymns the greatness, glory and indestructibility of life, and the despairing and sceptical Faust. The latter is a modern descendant of the sixteenth-century Faustus, and he takes the gloomiest possible view of the lot of humanity and the inevitability and finality of death. In a grandiose panoramic vision Prometheus shows Faust how the universe came into being and how the world was created by cosmic processes. This is followed by glimpses of evolutionary progression: geological periods, prehistoric epochs and dissolving anthropological views. The history of civilization is then unrolled; primitive times yield to a golden age; the relapse into barbarousness generates the rise of religions; the figures of Moses, of the Buddha, of Christ and of Mohammed flash past. Roman Catholicism is scourged, Luther introduced with a fanfare of eloquence; but his liberating act is also shown to have produced the scepticism from which the sixteenth-century Faust suffered so acutely. A highly idealized portrait of this 'honest doubter' is shown to his modern descendant; but the latter is not suborned by that. He objects violently to the optimism informing Prometheus' view of the history of mankind, and instances the many dismal failures and fearful unhappiness of the human race. Prometheus counters with the nobility of soul displayed by such heroes as Columbus and such martyrs as Galileo. He concludes by an ecstatic description of the future: the disappearance of wars and disease; the greater longevity of man, and a better world germinating from his dust. Convinced at last, Faust emerges from this glimpse into the past and future restored to light and happiness.

If noble sentiments and great art were synonymous, this watered-down version of Schiller's *Artists* and *Excursion* would rank high among Faustian literature. As it is, whilst sparing a sigh for hopes at the very best indefinitely deferred, one can only accept the verdict of posterity, by whom Hermann Hango (together with nearly everyone else considered in this section) has been totally forgotten.

(b) An incomprehensible Faust, 1839

The same cannot be said quite so emphatically of Ludwig Hermann Wolfram (1807–52), who produced a dramatic poem called *Faust* in 1839; for he at least found a conscientious scholar called Neurath who attempted in 1906 to rescue him from oblivion by re-editing his *Faust*. Unhappily it is one of those ponderous and forbidding editions, provided with an unreadable introduction and indigestible notes, with which many a poor author had been rung to his grave. Wolfram was a poor author in the literal sense. His wretched existence, in which begging-letters, drunkenness, indebtedness and even petty larceny played a dismal part, ended in a prison infirmary. Here he died among wastrels of his own hopeless type, but presumably without his saving grace of poetry. Tedious and tiresome as Wolfram's *Faust* is with its woolly symbolism, allegorical whimsies, topical satire and crack-brained romanticism, it is redeemed here and there throughout by flashes of fascinating poetry. But these spontaneous spurts of loveliness waver and misfire under the weight of the quasi-philosophical burden the poem bears, defined by Neurath with characteristic solemnity as '*an Hegelian-Schellingesque pantheistic-Catholicized Protestantism*'.[1] This is almost enough to discourage one at the outset; nor is the flowery dedication to Wolfram's dead wife Cecilia likely to arouse much enthusiasm; it is followed by a long introductory poem and a preface in prose, both of them bewailing the parlous state of the German genius:

> A *puer dolorosus*,
> A modern Œdipus,
> The age's Son of Sorrows,
> The German Genius. . . .

[1] L. H. Wolfram, *Faust, Ein dramatisches Gedicht in drei Abschnitten*, ed. Neurath, Berlin, 1906, p.E. 263.

'Why dost thou rouse the sleeper
With wailing and with woe,
And knowst not that corruption
Into the earth must go?'

'And knowst not that the Saviour
Suffers and dies for us?
Then rest three days from labour,
Oh German Genius!'[1]

This unexpected identification of the German genius with the saviour of humanity is carried a step further at the close of the poem, when Faust is acclaimed in the following terms:

Ah, could I but this once behold thy face,
Transfigured Sufferer, bearing all the sins of man
And doubters' labyrinthine errors too,
With mind's dread katabasis, for our sakes.[2]

Before this outcome is reached, a great deal has to be gone through, which seems to stand in no organic connection with the saintship attained at the end. There is the recurrent satire, directed with a good deal of venom against the Young German writers; there is the hero-worship for Napoleon and Uhland to contend with, and the strange course the action takes with its tripartite division into *Nature*, *Life* and *Art* and its chronological hay-making. The most recognizably Faustian scene in the drama, and *qua* scene altogether the most successful, occurs at the inception of the poem and takes place in a churchyard on a midsummer night. Faust holds a tremendous opening monologue, chiefly dealing with the anguish and despair caused him by his wife's death:

One moment has transformed thee into dust,
And in the lily's calyx on thy grave
I recognise thy being's particles.
Oh, mystery of nature, cruel-kind,
Sweet smell the flowers! Yet lily-sprites
(Or so croak agèd crones in children's ears)
Excel in mischief; and the devil sports
Midsummer nights, they say, among the flowers.
Worst of them all, these snow-white chalices.
In some old yellowed tome there runs this rede
(By Paracelsus writ or Campanella):

---

[1] Wolfram, op. cit. pp. vi–x.   [2] Ibid. p. 209.

'When lily-white is wedded with moonshine,
And to this moonlit mating of the flowers
A drop of dew is added from the limes,
Thou'lt shortly see'— But soft, the vault's astir.[1]

Three ghosts now rise one after the other. The first is a mocking spirit; the second a satirical portrait of one of Wolfram's many literary bêtes-noires; the third is the ghost of Hamlet, now drawn for the second time into the Faustian sphere of influence. Refusing at first to reveal the secrets of the grave to Faust, Hamlet finally unveils the fearful truth: it contains the mouldering remains of human thought and the corpse of its infant son. An eloquent comparison of this group with Napoleon and the little King of Rome is drawn. Poetry, fair as the moon, lies at their feet, for Uhland, who had immortalized her, is dead. The action of *Nature* now becomes too fantastic, complicated, ironical and allegorical to repay analysis; it is summarized together with the course of Faust's early life in a speech to Heraclitus towards the end of the section, which ends with the curse uttered by Faust when surrendering himself to the god of nature (Dionysos or the devil) and rejecting all other gods:

A curse upon existence, ancient, oh my father, rests upon me:
By night I was conceived and brought to birth
Whilst lightning flashed and thunder-roaring howled the gale;
All nature was in uproar at this crisis of the storm. . . .
And how I lived, oh father, how I grew to be a man,
Reveal I cannot: for eternal dark
Envelops my young days with inky cloak of night.
And yet at times, akin to lightning's flash
From out the mighty womb of yesteryear,
A blessed remembrance pierces to my soul,
Showing a paradise which sinks down into naught,
Showing me heaven, by midnight straight engulfed. . . .
I cursed the heavens wholly, gave myself to gods of death,
Called upon hell and Satan, and then once more sank down,
Broken beneath the burden of my sorrow's crown.[2]

Poor Wolfram! Behind all the preposterous grandiloquence, one is aware of a piteous personal confession.

The second part of the poem, *Life*, depicts a Don Juanesque career for Faust, who is initiated into the mystery of love (equated

---

[1] Wolfram, op. cit. pp. 8f.   [2] Ibid. pp. 81 ff.

with death) by the beautiful vampire Amanda. He then transfers himself to Venice, is called in by the Doge to cure his beautiful young niece Fiordiligi by hypnotic means, seduces her whilst she is in a magnetic trance and is thrown into prison. Fiordiligi, now deeply in love with him, frees him, and they are escaping together across the Lagoon when a sudden storm spells sudden death to both. In order to save Fiordiligi, Faust invokes the aid of Satan at the price of his eternal soul. They are rescued from a watery grave; but Faust's love perishes, and Fiordiligi dies of a broken heart. Removing to Spain, the Teutonic Don Juan lays siege simultaneously to the heart of Doña Clara and a maidservant; he commits a murder, is forced to flee from Granada and falls ever deeper into crime, saying at one point of his downward course:

The spirit of that man pursues me. I slew him by the altar-rails whilst he was praying, and seduced his wife whilst he was bleeding to death before the stone image of the Crucified One. How many murders have I committed now?[1]

One of the bugbears of German Faustian literature puts in his unwelcome appearance at this stage, Ahasuerus, the Wandering Jew; and the action begins to die away of inanition. To cut a very long story short, Faust finally breathes his last in the arms of a pure young peasant girl; and, although his body and soul are doomed to perdition, his spirit is saved, a strange situation and an unexpected *dénouement*, but vouched for by Pontifex Maximus in the third part, called *Art*:

> *Pontifex.* But then because the art of life betrayed him,
> The *holy art of dying* was unfolded
> In its calm inborn greatness of becoming,
> And in the evening darkness of a hut,
> Protected by a maiden's purity,
> Whilst dreamily the wall-clock struck the hour.
> *He left this world in faith and certainty,*
> *Reborn anew to holy godhead's life,*
> *Transported by the rapture of true knowledge. . . .*
> But *Halleluja!* sounds the *Saviour's* voice,
> The saviour's, soldier's, judge's voice of thunder:
> Body and soul are damned—*the spirit's saved!*[2]

---

[1] Wolfram, op. cit. p. 184.   [2] Ibid. pp. 217 f. (Wolfram's italics).

This curious outcome has the sanction of Hegelian dialectic, or so Neurath affirms, and who am I to contradict him? It remains a singularly inept solution of the Faustian problem; nor has the hero done anything during the dramatic poem to justify his final equation with the scapegoat-saviour of mankind. Had Wolfram's symbolism been less nebulous throughout, he might have been more convincing at the end of this strange work, to which I have done only rough justice, but to which I have also shown mercy by passing over many excrescences on the unwieldy and top-heavy structure.

(c) An ennobled Faust, 1919

Wolfram's *Faust* is a tantalizing production; for the lyrical gifts to which it bears witness and a certain cloudy nobility of mind make one regret that the total effect should be so utterly unworthy of its higher moments. A similar feeling of promise unfulfilled assails the reader of *Faust. A Play*, by Ferdinand Avenarius (1856–1920). The student of German literature approaches this work with rising hopes; for (unlike Wolfram) Avenarius' name is fairly well-known as that of a poet and a lover of poetry, sensitive and discriminating, devoting his energies to the task of spreading his own knowledge and appreciation of literature and art among a wide public. Any contribution made by him to Faustian literature should therefore be interesting at least, and possibly more than that. But from Lessing downwards the theme had proved an acid poetical test. Many had felt themselves called; few indeed had been chosen; for, failing the simple directness of mind of the folk-poets, it seemed to demand a greatness of vision beyond the scope of sheep and goats alike. Avenarius at least was not among the goats. Neither glaring lack of taste nor of sense can be laid at his door. Like Grillparzer, Schöne, Pfizer, Rosenkranz and others, he began his drama immediately after the execution of Gretchen, and was therefore attempting to provide Goethe's drama with a second part more to his own individual taste. The scene of the prologue is laid by the gallows; a storm is raging and among the voices which are heard in the wind is that of Gretchen, singing folk-songs and hymns, and addressing Faust much as she had done in the prison-scene. In spite of this deliberate echo from Goethe, there is something weird and genuinely moving too in the high-wrought situation. It induces such unhappiness in Faust that he willingly listens to the counsels of a monk who has befriended him; together they make off on a pilgrimage to Rome to obtain absolution and consolation from the pope. Mephisto, scoffing and gibing, is debarred from following them on account of the cross on the monk's rosary; but consoles himself with the reflection that the potion he has caused Faust to drink will soon wipe out his memories of Gretchen and the consequent remorse. This by no means ineffective prologue is far and away the best of the many and various efforts made by the poets to hitch the wagon of their Faust dramas to Gretchen's beckoning star.

The first act plays in Rome and would appear to have been influenced by Holtei rather than by Goethe. It opens admirably. The Renaissance is at its height; the passion for the art of antiquity at its most intense, when Helen herself is discovered, a transcendently lovely statue in a sarcophagus on the Capitol. The Vatican is determined to do away with this ominous image before the sight of it maddens men's minds; but Mephisto, who has engineered the discovery, is there in the sarcophagus with Helen. Motionless they wait, whilst the Swiss guards force the crowd back and retire, clanging the great doors shut, intending to return and destroy the statue. Then, peerlessly beautiful, she rises from the coffin and breaks into peals of exultant laughter. This stirring, indeed thrilling, resurrection is the prelude to a most disillusioning sequel. Meant to represent irresistible but soulless pagan beauty, a woman without memory, conscience or human emotions, she develops (like Holtei's glamorous phantom) into a mere meretricious courtesan. As such she passes from Faust's embraces to those of dukes, cardinals and the pope himself almost automatically. When *Faust* stabs her to death in his jealousy and rage, she becomes once more the lifeless statue which she had only really ceased to be when she was laughing on the Capitol. A visit to Michelangelo hard at work on his *Moses* brings Faust's Roman adventures to a close, after which he returns to Germany.

The second act gives glimpses of University life in the dark setting of religious intolerance and persecution. Galileo's fate (transparently camouflaged as that of an anonymous professor) illustrates the fearful spiritual tyranny then abroad, but somehow misses fire; and in the third and fourth acts a certain restiveness accompanies the realization that we are once more being asked to participate in the Peasants' Revolt. Into this Scylla the essentially noble or at the very least well-meaning Fausts were all too apt to be swept since the days of Klinger; whilst their less lofty-minded namesakes were sucked into the Juanesque Charybdis. Avenarius' hero, now a reformed character, fights stoutly in the people's cause, but is defeated in his heroic efforts to liberate humanity. In the fifth act, alone, betrayed, abandoned and in despair, he commands Mephisto to reveal to him the whole past history and future fortunes of the human race. Nothing loth, the malicious fiend projects upon the back-cloth a series of pictures showing nature and man evolving from primeval slime by means of bloodshed, lust, cruelty and rapacity. Finally he evokes a fearsome apparition: the Head of Humanity, its features distorted by evil and madness. Faust addresses it in impassioned tones; and love and wrath, good and ill chase each other across the countenance of the being now torn by a dualism in which the desire for peace and virtue gradually predominates. Mephisto, hoist with his own petard, attempts to exorcize the vision, but fails:

> *Faust (exultantly).* Demon! *It stays! It stays!*
> For tis not thou that orderest the ways
> Of earth's progression. Longing divine doth raise
> Desire-racked flesh eternal form to give,
> And God doth live! (*To the vision*):
> Thou art humanity who in seeking errs!

(*Meanwhile the apparition has become a supremely noble head, recalling that of Goethe at the height of his maturity.*)

> *The Vision.* Sire upon sire
> Thought hath hewed,
> Even when, dire,
> It did delude.
> What darkens
> Sinks down to creation's womb;
> What lightens
> Shines upon truth's great loom.
> I am the godhead emerging in man.

(*The apparition sinks slowly back into darkness, and the stars begin to appear in its place.*)

> *Faust (rises ecstatically to his full height with uplifted hands).*
> Godhead emerging too in me!
> How, oh God, I have sought for Thee,
> And that which bid me seek
> Wast Thou in me!

(He now suddenly becomes aware of Mephisto prowling round him like a hyaena round its still living prey. When the demon realizes this he stiffens watchfully, so that for a short space both stand, rigidly regarding each other.)

    Faust. Ho thou! Thou art no more, begone!

(In uncontrolled rage, the now completely devilish demon-shape springs at Faust and strikes him to the heart. Then he burrows hastily down into the earth and disappears. The stars have appeared everywhere in the sky.)

    Faust. That struck the flesh, it did not strike the soul!
        This is my highest moment and my goal.

                    (He sinks down.)

Avenarius should have had the self-restraint to stop there. But he allowed Faust to go on at some length, dying finally amidst an impressive *mise-en-scène*:

(Nothing is to be seen but the wide heavens, solemn and great, the stars are resplendent in the blue night. Deepest calm reigns. After a long pause the curtain falls slowly.)[1]

Avenarius' *Faust* is not without its points. The prologue, if not great imaginative poetry, is an epilogue to the Gretchen tragedy such as no one else (not excluding Goethe) has ever been able to devise. The resuscitation of Helen from the marble sarcophagus is an exciting moment in Faustian literature. The final scene, in conception if not in execution, is more serious and more deeply felt than Goethe's. It is the only one, among rival attempts at salvation, that can bear, if not sustain, a comparison. But the drama as a whole is feeble; its impact is flabby, its hero well-meaning but negligible. One cannot make great drama by tracing the laborious up-hill progress of a self-righteous, rehabilitated and reformed rake. Goethe, who contemplated this course at the beginning of *Part II*, continued in a different vein.

[1] F. Avenarius, *Faust. Ein Spiel*, Munich, 1919, pp. 132f.

CHAPTER XIII

UN-GOETHEAN FAUSTS

(a) A tragic Faust, 1836

Nikolaus Franz Niembsch von Strehlenau (1802–1850), dear to all lovers of poetry under the name of Lenau, said very truly that, although Goethe had written a *Faust*, he had not therefore established a monopoly of the subject from which everyone else was automatically excluded. He spoke not only for his own generation but for posterity too; and it certainly needed saying in his own day when the poets as a whole felt a deep and instinctive dissatisfaction with the conclusion of *Part II*, sometimes with the matter, sometimes with the manner, and often with the action of the second part as such. Braun von Braunthal, Wolfram and Avenarius, by producing variant versions of the salvation of the hero, were indirectly criticizing Goethe's; and Lenau's tragic *Faust* (first edition 1836, slightly revised version 1840) could be interpreted as a reaction against the optimistic philosophy on which Goethe's dramatic poem as a whole was founded. But Lenau's lovely poem is something other and much greater than that. It is an expression of his own deep, incurable melancholy; the confession of a truly Faustian personality: restless, passionate, rudderless, hopeless even when most resigned. His unappeasable desire to penetrate to ultimate 'truth'; his dissatisfaction with philosophy, law and medicine as means to that end; his ever-present sense of frustration and isolation; his profound feeling for nature, ministering to sorrow rather than joy; his failure to find an anchor in any social or even human harbour—he is such a strange commixture of the hero of the Faust-legend and Goethe's Faust that it is almost as if he had been created by Faustian poetry; an impression made more vivid still because the enthusiastic feelings he aroused in his friends were of the kind great poetry inspires. When the light of his beauty-loving mind began to flicker and then went out, poetry itself seemed temporarily extinguished for those who mourned his loss.

From a poet of this nature one would naturally expect a peculiarly Faustian *Faust*. Lenau's is outstandingly beautiful and predominantly lyrical, although cast in an epico-dramatic form. Compared with Marlowe and Goethe, let alone with the vast majority of Faustian poets, he seems nearer to the heart of the ultimate mystery, and far less capable of representing it objectively. Goethe's *Faust*, notoriously subjective too, and much less entangled with the philosophical aspect of the situation than Lenau's, is nevertheless more detached from the main issue in which the hero is involved. This is no doubt partly due to the sixty-odd years of its growth. The distance in time between the beginning and the end entailed a certain intellectual objectivity. This is to seek in Lenau's poem, some have thought to its detriment; for the issues remain obscure and the tormenting doubts in the hero's mind are never subjected to any other standard than Mephisto's searing cynicism. There are signs that Lenau wished to adjudge in the three-cornered conflict between Christianity, paganism and scepticism rending Faust's soul; but his own similar predicament defeated him in view of his essentially lyrical genius. His *Faust* loses in clarity, in spaciousness and in cosmic resonance what it gains in tragic intensity and in human appeal. Except for the Gretchen tragedy, to the height of which it never attains, it is more moving, though less interesting, than Goethe's *Faust*; more melting and much sadder. The greatness, the power and the glory retreat before heart-ache and grief.

But Lenau's *Faust* transcends mere personal sorrow, since it recaptures the shaken mood of a whole disoriented and sceptical generation, and more than that. The hero speaks with the unmistakable accents of all those often tragically gifted men who are also tragically minded; he speaks for a whole category of human beings predestined to spiritual shipwreck; to take instances only from the present study: for the Lenzes, the Grabbes and the Wolframs of this world. The first glimpse of Lenau's Faust shows him courting disaster and refusing consolation. Climbing rashly and recklessly up a mountain-side at sunrise, he feverishly scrutinizes and impatiently rejects the stones, plants and insects he finds along his path, for none of them reveals the secret of its inmost being. He pauses for a breathing-space, and the sound of church-bells and hymns reaches him softly from the valley below. Unlike Goethe's Faust, his spiritual turmoil is increased by the Christian message of faith and joy. He hears in the voices of the worshippers an outcry of bitter anguish from forsaken humanity, imploring their saviour to appear; but they will cry in vain (he calls out savagely), no saviour, no leader will ever come to their aid. This blasphemous outburst does not fall on deaf ears; a dark and ominous being rescues Faust from death when a false step is about to plunge him into the abyss beneath his feet. A strong hand draws him back. The stranger disappears.

Faust is next seen bending over the dissecting-table in his laboratory arguing bitterly with Wagner about the limits of human knowledge; and desperately appealing to Mephisto, who interrupts them, for the solution of his doubts. The latter answers inexorably that the only road to truth leads through guilt; and in the pact-scene, deep in a dark forest, Faust faces this intolerable dilemma:

> A dreadful discord this, bitter as gall,
> When storms of questions rage within and call,
> Whilst outside, unresponsive, death-like, still,
> Inflexible, eternal, reigns the Will.[1]

In vain does a monk plead with him for humility of mind; Faust sends him to the rightabout; and when Mephisto appears, he allows himself to be persuaded to burn the Bible and to sign the pact by which Mephisto is bound on his side to lead him finally to truth. What the latter has in view is to bring about a divorce between Faust and nature, now that he has triumphantly severed him from God; and this has cut him off from all his old associates too, as a subsequent scene with Wagner and his former friend Isenburg makes painfully clear.

It may have been that gay little dance-song with its raffish implications sung under the lime-tree in *Before the Gate* in *Faust I* which inspired the next scene laid in a village inn, where Mephisto seizes the fiddle from the rustic fiddler and plays the famous waltz which Liszt set to music.[2] Few and far between, it must be owned, are the occasions in Faustian literature when any illusion of magic has actually been created. Marlowe's Faustus persuades us of this when addressing the phantom Helen. Goethe's Earth Spirit truly

---

[1] Lenau, *Sämmtliche Werke*, Stuttgart, 1881, Vol. II, p. 101.

[2] Involuntarily, too, one remembers the Viennese ballet, in which Faust danced off with the miller's bride; for the heroine of this scene is also a bride. Cf. above, pp. 84 f.

seems to come by the power of magic. Lenau's waltz conjures up its irresistible effect. The wildness, the sweetness, the intoxicating and insidious glamour are there in the words, in the rhymes, in the headlong and heady rhythm, inciting, urging, compelling Faust to his first ruthless downward step into swirling sensuality. This is the real thing, miles removed from the synthetic magic potion brewed in the *Witches' Kitchen*. Like Faust himself, one watched that unconvincing hocus-pocus with sophisticated scepticism. Lenau presents the cup to the reader's lips, and for the moment he is as lost to everything but what the music intends as Faust and his helpless victim. Those literary critics who speak disparagingly of too great virtuosity in connection with Lenau's waltz are possibly resenting a victorious assault upon their magically unbridled emotions. Be that as it may, no one could expect either Faust or his victim, little Hannchen, to do anything but surrender to the delirium in the music.

The spell dissolved when the fiddle ceased; and almost before the strains died away, Faust was back with the yokels, accompanied by Mephisto, now disguised as the poodle Prästigiar. Folkbook pranks enliven the proceedings here; and another obligation to tradition was fulfilled by a complex of scenes at court, where Mephisto gives evil counsel to one of the ministers; and Faust makes the place too hot to hold him by a savage satire on the royal bride and groom. Riding away alone as evening falls, he comes to a smithy and halts there to have his horse shod. The smith, a simple soul, gay without guile and an ardent though not a servile snob, induces his sombre, laconic and disdainful guest to sup with him and his beautiful wife. The fiery wine and the smith's rollicking toasts move Faust to sardonic mirth; but, Mephisto, appearing half-way through the feast, succeeds in stirring up lustful feelings towards his host's desirable helpmate; and another seduction is imminent. Nemesis intervenes in the shape of Hannchen, reduced to wretchedness and rags, begging alms for herself and her starving child. It sounds melodramatic enough, and in a way it is; but Mephisto saves it from bathos by his gleeful contrast between then and now; quoting Faust's enraptured comments on Hannchen's loveliness at the village dance and pointing to the repulsive squalor of her present appearance. He is Faust's evil conscience personified, but a completely cynical one; and her frantic outcries as Faust rides wildly away are unavailing to soften his hardened yet unhappy heart. This crude but realistic repetition of the Gretchen tragedy paves the way for one of those representations of remorse in which Lenau was a past-master, and in which he transcends Goethe completely. Marlowe's Faustus speaks to our shuddering souls; Lenau's hero speaks straight to our hearts; and it would be an atrophied heart indeed that could remain unresponsive. In the *Midnight Procession* following immediately on the incidents in the smithy, Faust, gloomy and disconsolate, is riding through a wood at night, paying no heed to the soft summer murmuring and fragrance all around him, nor to the wooing of the nightingale's song. Hidden behind a tree, he watches a midnight procession celebrating the festival of the Eve of Saint John appear, pass by and finally vanish: children, young nuns and reverend priests chanting gentle and solemn hymns:

> But when they've all passed by and their clear singing
> Gentler and farther sounds to silence winging;
> And when the torches shed their farewell light
> (Which changed the wood into a magic world),
> Withdrawing from the trembling leaves dew-pearled,
> And Faust was left alone again that night;
> Then to his horse's mane he bowed his head,
> Clutching it fiercely, whilst fast tears did rain,
> Hot tears and bitter in his grief and pain,
> Such as before he never yet had shed.[1]

Unlike the flood of tears which overwhelmed Goethe's Faust when the Easter bells broke in upon his suicidal thoughts, this bitter weeping has no purifying and regenerating effect upon Lenau's hero. On the contrary, *The Lake* shows a further progress in guilt and misery. It lies outside a convent's walls, fringed by whispering rushes and covered with water-lilies. The moonbeams are playing on the surface of this water like children on the surface of the mystery and sorrow of life. Faust and Mephisto are pacing up and down on the edge of the lake and Faust, staring at it hopelessly, is mourning dumbly that ever he was born. Maliciously Mephisto recalls the days when he wooed and won an inmate of the convent under the self-same moon which has now risen on his grief and her despair. Faust gruffly bids him hold his peace; and Mephisto, after a sharp retort, plunges into the lake and reappears

[1] Lenau, op. cit. Vol. II, p. 142.

holding out the shimmering bones of a dead child, a memento, he cynically mocks, of those nights of love. Gruesome and macabre, this unexpected turn of the screw induces greater horror than Gretchen's piteous description of the drowning of her child. And, oddly enough, though he says no word, it induces greater sympathy for Faust. Lenau betrays here and elsewhere an almost Dostoyevskian capacity for kindling pity where reprobation would normally be felt.

The seduction of Hannchen, whose unnerving appearance thwarts the contemplated seduction of the smith's wife, and the seduction of the nun show Lenau's Faust beginning to go the way of those whose increasing moral degradation was represented by borrowings from *Don Juan*. In the complex of scenes grouped round the figure of Maria, Lenau attempted to show the effect of a nobler and more spiritual passion on the mind of Faust; and just because it was so much greater than the lighter loves, it plunged him into irredeemable guilt. Maria is a king's daughter, beauty, charm, grace and innocence personified, though perhaps not very real to the reader. Faust is painting her portrait, a wonderfully imaginative (and symbolical) piece of work, for he is depicting her serene and angelic countenance against the darkly lurid background of a raging sea. His exalted feelings for his lovely model, who shrinks before them, have reached a fever-pitch of passion pouring itself out in a frenzied declaration when Duke Herbert, her betrothed, whose suspicions have been aroused by Mephisto, comes storming into the room, insults Faust mortally and is stabbed to death. Faust now has a murder upon his soul, as was also the case with Goethe's hero after the death of Valentine; but how very differently these two criminals react! Goethe's Faust is hurried away by Mephisto and is next seen at the Witches' Sabbath. Lenau's Faust also allows himself to be spirited away from the scene of the stabbing; but he is next met with alone in the mountains and alone with his crime. It is a beautiful evening, calm and serene; spring is on the way and all nature is smiling; but nature and Faust are now divorced. Every blossom seems to be murmuring: 'Thou shalt not kill'; the freshness of the woods, the green pasturage, the peace of the mountains, the clear red trumpet-tones of the evening sky cut deep into his anguished heart because he has violated the *pax naturalis*. Most poignantly of all, the distant stream far down in the valley with its softly mourning voice seems like his innocence weeping from afar.

Bitter resentment and self-justification follow; for is not murder the world's first law? And is man the only being who commits it? This is the cue for Mephisto's entrance, who continues the heart-hardening process and temporarily dispels Faust's remorse by bumpers of fiery wine. But only temporarily. In the unutterably lovely farewell which Faust takes of his mother's grave before setting off on the sea, love and hopeless sorrow, rending regrets and tearless contrition seem to evoke a mournful murmur from the cross on her tomb. Mephisto intervenes and draws Faust away into the near-by wood. Here, in a conversation added in the second edition, he blames the divorce from nature, not on any individual action of any single man, but on the Jews who drove a wedge between nature and mankind as a whole by creating the conception of a Messiah, and thereby laying waste the inheritance of the Indians and Greeks, who had bequeathed a grandiose pantheistic view of life to humanity. In vain will Spinoza in the future attempt to right this wrong; for the holy covenant has been broken once and for all. These ideas, which Heine was expounding with great eloquence at the time in his accounts of German literature and philosophy, derived from the Saint-Simonians, who, however, were confident that the balance between the soul and the senses could be restored. As for Lenau's Faust, neither pantheism nor monotheism can satisfy him. The existence of a transcendent God would degrade him to the status of a mere sandal on His feet, or a vessel for His grace; whereas if God is immanent in nature, then man is but a thoroughfare and not an end in himself. Mephisto rejoins wittily that it is indeed a vexatious dilemma; since the one would treat him *en canaille* and the other *en canal*. He had better retreat within himself, a temptation to which his prideful and satanically soaring mind is fatally, tragically subject.

Lenau said of his voyage to America that the sea had gone to his heart, and one can well believe it when reading those melodiously murmuring lines which lull Faust to sleep on shipboard at night. Heine's cradle-song entitled *Night in the Cabin* in *North Sea* is wonderfully hypnotic but lacks the simplicity of Lenau's lullaby, whose rhythm, subtly altering throughout the twenty-odd lines, evokes the motion of the sea, the nearness of death and the coming of sleep with unobtrusive but spell-binding mastery. The sleeper dreams and sees from a lovely ocean island his innocent childhood sail past, followed by his murderous manhood, awakening to find that the dream-storm in which it vanished was an illusion and that the sea is utterly peaceful, silent and calm. He and Mephisto in a wild and ominous conversation conjure up a fearful storm which ends in shipwreck, whilst Faust, defying the Creator and exulting in the elemental turmoil, flings the terrified captain overboard, who perishes with a craven priest in the mountainous waves. The sailors, Faust and Mephisto gain the shore and seek shelter in an inn. This penultimate scene forms a pendant to the earlier village gathering at which Hannchen was seduced. It is remarkably vivid, lively and realistic, and the figure of the sensible and sagacious materialist Görg is as successfully drawn as that of the rollicking and jovial smith. Faust, now utterly contemptuous of sensual lures, snubs a would-be light-of-love and enters into an argument with the stolidly rational and serenely epicurean Görg. That sturdy soul snaps his fingers at metaphysics and religion, only believes what he can see and touch, considers Faust's behaviour and conversation devoid of sense, cannot abide Mephisto, and prefers to dance with the girl rejected by Faust rather than to become involved with sombre and sinister strangers. His strength of character, integrity of mind and unruffled independence make a great impression on Faust, pointing as they do to his own chaotic emotions and incoherent thoughts.

The contrast is still painfully vivid to him when he leaves the inn and goes out on to the rocky beach. It is now night, the sea still storms unceasingly; and it seems to him that even the waves, the lightning and the wind are less homeless and restless than his own lonely heart. The feeling of divorce from God and nature is now more than he can bear; yet the dreadful isolation must continue, since his truly satanic pride refuses to acknowledge that he is the creature of either. Absolute and universal knowledge would not satisfy him now. He must be omnipotent or nothing; and this is actually, as he realizes, the desire for annihilation:

> Ha! how the sea skyward doth start,
> And echoes loud in thee, oh heart!
> It is the self-same aspiration
> That here within my breast doth lie
> And hurls the sea up to the sky:
> The longing for annihilation;
> It is the conflict, clamorous, hoarse,

To burst through barriers by main force,
And then in rapturous deathward fall
To perish all together—all![1]

The longing for annihilation is, according to Schopenhauer, the deep, instinctive desire of the Will itself; and when it becomes fully conscious in man it will always engender the conception of nothingness and utter oblivion as the ultimate desirable goal. When humanity as a whole has reached this awareness, the Will, released at last, will sink back into itself, and the world of phenomena will disappear. This is Brahmanical philosophy which has often been mythologically expressed in legend and art. In a small Hindu temple by the sea at Mahabalipuram there is a beautiful marble statue of the great god Vishnu recumbent in deep sleep. He is dreaming, and his dreams create the world which will vanish into nothingness when he awakes, a highly imaginative statement of the illusory nature of reality which made a violent appeal to Heine:

Life is the dream of an intoxicated god, who has taken French leave from his carousing colleagues. He has sunk down to sleep on a lonely star and is unaware himself that he is creating everything he dreams. These visions are often clad in madcap motley, but often too they are harmonious and reasonable. *The Iliad*, Plato, Marathon, Moses, the Venus of Medici, the Strasbourg cathedral, the French Revolution, Hegel and steam-boats are individual good ideas in the dream of this sleeping god. But he will not sleep for ever; and when he awakes and rubs the sleep out of his eyes and smiles, our world will dissolve into nothingness; more than that indeed, it has never existed.[2]

Lenau's Faust in a mood compounded of exaltation and despair comes to the same conclusion. If he and his pact and the devil himself are only a confused and disturbing dream of the divinity, is it not possible (he asks) that his own urgent and impatient desire for truth is a sign and token of the godhead's approaching return to consciousness; and that the desire to awake is masquerading as the desire for knowledge? With the wild hope of rejoining the dreamer, he stabs himself and dies, dreaming (as he puts it) a knife into his heart. Mephisto is gleefully assured that he is wrong and has become the lawful prey of hell; but the evil spirit himself may be but a figment of the dream.

[1] Lenau, op. cit. Vol. II, p. 192.
[2] H. Heine, ed. Elster, Vol. III, p. 136. Chapter 3 of *Ideen oder das Buch Le Grand*, published in 1826.

Lenau's Faust-tower

It is not really possible to put Lenau's *Faust* into other words than his own. His language resists transposition into English verse and prose alike. I have despaired of rendering the impression in the first medium and failed in the other. The episodes sound banal; the grief-laden tale and its woe-stricken hero, wayward and wild, escape analysis and elude literary criticism. This is the reason why the mysteriously lovely poem is almost totally unknown outside Germany and not much regarded there. Yet Lenau's contribution to the Faust-legend is by far the greatest tragic version given in modern times; and its implications are even more ominous now than in his own day. He divined the potential outcome of the insatiable pursuit of knowledge, whose tempo has been increasing so alarmingly since the Renaissance. He saw it as a symptom which might prove to be the cause of the imminent end of humanity. We are now faced with the result. The spiritual guilt seemingly inseparable from the desire for transcendent knowledge, rooted in arrogance and leading to dreams of omnipotence, was revealed by Lenau in a most striking and indeed prophetic manner. And the suggestion that Faust and the Faustian spirit are a symbol of the beginning of the end is not easy to shrug to one side. Whether acceptable or not, it raises Faust once more to the status of a full tragic hero, and a by no means despicable opponent of the optimistic conception embodied in Goethe's protagonist. The absolute incorruptibility of mankind faces its annihilating power. With bated breath the twentieth century awaits the issue.

(b) An irreclaimable Faust, 1842

Kneeling in a chapel by the altar rails, a monk surreptitiously peruses the biography of Faust. The pages have been ruffled by his sighs, and many a cross has defaced the text. Cold with horrified fascination the monk reads on. At times he lifts his eyes from the book and contemplates the image of the crucified Christ, the God whom he has forsworn. Dark shadows steal towards him, long shadows thrown by everything which nature and the world had bestowed upon him: shadows of trees whispering of eternal woe, of leaves brought forth that they may wither and decay; shadows cast by the full moon rising to the summit of the hill, radiating angelic light; magical, languishing, lovely desire; changing to a Medusa mask of sweet and stony grief. These lights and shades play strangely over the wan countenance of the monk ravaged by slow tears. The black leather binding of the book is battered and rubbed, for it has had rough handling. Pacing to the choir at dawn, he may have hidden it in that skull lying in the moonlight under the round window; or, hastening to chapel at midnight with his brethren through vaulted passages and winding stairs, he may have thrust it furtively into the bronze seraph's cup tendered to Christ in His agony. With a reader such as this it is easy to see why many a page is tattered and torn, like ballad-sheets passed round in hostelries. And when Faust's flaming star began to set, the crosses on the leaves were multiplied; tear-stains abounded, pages half torn out, as if a nerve-racked hand had mangled them. Finally only the wood-cuts remained to tell the tale, desperately bold in concept and design, teeming with terror-striking shapes. More lustful too than earlier in the book, with fuller bosoms and with wilder hair, a crowd of lovely women round the Doctor goes.[1]

This remarkable description occurs in the sixteenth canto of Woldemar Nürnberger's *Josephus Faust*, published in 1842 under the pseudonym M. Solitar. Divorced from its context it reads like a highly imaginative evocation of the Urfaustbook, which Nürnberger may well have had in mind. In its context, however, it is steeped in poetical ambiguity, being apparently a commentary on the poem in which it occurs, whilst the anguished yet unregenerate reader devouring the tale by stealth would seem, mysteriously enough, to be Faust. Strange and gruesome as the episode is, it is on a par with the poem as a whole, the product of a darkly original mind, gifted with nightmare vision. His unrelievedly sombre landscapes are penetrated with this quality, which differentiates them from mere Gothic romanticism, for they have a haunting effect. Storm-tossed seas and fathomless lakes; sullen sunsets and menacing moons; no mere catalogue could do justice (and in fact would do a grave injustice) to the dark beauty of the almost sunless world into which the mind of Nürnberger projected the mind of Faust. Between defiance and defeat, a whole gamut of deadly dangerous and desperately sad emotions is played out in this epic poem with its recurrent dramatic moments, clearly inspired by

---

[1] Cf. W. Nürnberger, *Josephus Faust*, 2nd ed., Landsberg, 1847, pp. 151 ff. Curiously enough, Nürnberger's father, Joseph Emil, produced a dramatic sketch, *Faust Junior*, in 1841. This is a mere weak imitation of Goethe's, with a good angel in the place of Mephisto.

Lenau in this and in other ways, and yet entirely independent and unique. One great difference between the two poems is the noticeable lack of beauty in its cathartic aspect of Nürnberger's. Lenau's *Faust* has so many passages of such melting loveliness as to revive and refresh the most deeply shaken reader. Nürnberger never lets go, hardly even allowing eloquence to break in and clear the air. Darkness deepens, and thickens ominously when garish, livid or lurid lights flicker round the downward path of Faust's unblessed career.

Yet it is the ruin of an essentially noble mind which is pitilessly represented in this uncompromising poem. Like Lenau's hero, Nürnberger's Faust is an anatomist, and had hoped to learn the secret of life on the dissecting table; but he had been forced to the conclusion at the opening of the epic that he knew no more about it than the most ignorant medical student, he who had aspired to be the equal of God:

> With Him, sublime, majestic and eternal,
> Fain had I lived in lofty amity;
> To me He should reveal secrets supernal,
> To me alone of all humanity.[1]

This hope is now abandoned, and Faust in despair mounts to the turret to study the heavens. Mephisto slips in after him, lays his arms round the Doctor's shoulders, and begins to whisper in his ear:

> So fast, so fast, he hardly moves his lips,
> And yet no word escaped the listener. . . .
> He whispers on, although the moon is set
> And sombre dawn comes up in veils of mist;
> He whispers still, no end to it as yet.
> At last Faust groans: 'I beg thee, cease from this,
> It is enough for this time; peace, be still.'
> 'But wilt thou then in life and death be mine?'
> And solemnly Faust: 'Here, take my hand, I will;
> Henceforth and ever more, behold I'm thine.'[2]

This sinister whispering-scene is the prelude to a series of episodes, some of them eerie and wicked and wild, few of them (unlike Lenau's) on a consecutive narrative thread; but in their totality depicting the hero's direful downward course. This is done largely

---

[1] Nürnberger, op. cit. pp. 91 f.   [2] Ibid. pp. 15 f.

as Lenau did it too, by representing Faust as a tragic Don Juan, passing from mere ruthlessness at the beginning to the very perversity of passion at the end. But Nürnberger's hero is much more wanton than Lenau's; and he begins where the latter pulled himself up: with the seduction of a nun, who is helpless before his passion:

> Deeply she sighed, her hands in his were lying;
> She speaks not, stirs not, as with kisses dire
> He covers them, aflame with base desire.
> She moans; her tears are endless as her sighing;
> Yet speaks she not, nor wavers though she weep;
> Does not fly back the convent's walls to seek.
> And when he wildly draws her to his breast,
> She weeps, but steps not back; she's silent still
> When kiss on kiss upon her lips is pressed;
> She weeps, she stirs not, she is silent still.[1]

The second mile-stone along the road of sensual depravity is reached when Faust, meeting in Rome with Manto, the last Delphic priestess, still mysteriously alive, persuades her to reveal the future to him and the meaning of the universe. But at the supreme moment, when the seeress is already possessed by the god, Mephisto draws near and Faust's evil passions awake. He ravishes her body instead of reading her mind, and dooms himself to the lower life of ignorance he had hoped to transcend, his soul more strongly enmeshed than ever in its evil envelope of flesh. Finally, on the banks of a dark and sinister lake, materializing in this poem from the submerged regions of folk-lore like a modern Mummelsee, Faust murders the innocent object of his purest and truest feelings for no better reason than because he knows that he will be unfaithful to her and is morally convinced that she will retaliate in kind:

> I would not leave thee, could not at the last,
> Yet irresistibly I'm onward driven;
> No other man but me shall hold thee fast,
> Since I have loved thee above other women.
> I envy all mankind because of thee:
> This is the goad which drives and maddens me![2]

[1] Nürnberger, op. cit. p. 50.   [2] Ibid. pp. 159 f.

Murderous egotism could no further go; and it is unutterably strange that, after a wild effort to justify the deed before the furies of remorse who beset him, he should have a vision of the holy grove at Colonus whither the blind Theban fled in days of yore. But it is not the last glimpse given of Faust. In the final canto he has become a crippled beggar, limping wretchedly away from the portals of a church and sinking down on a stone beneath the gallows in the falling snow:

> 'Mephisto!' he calls out, but calls in vain;
> The whirlwind carries off the cry again,
> And no one comes; he's still alone, alone,
> Upon the ominous and blackened stone.
> 'Mephisto!', once again and yet once more,
> With pounding arteries that throb and roar.
> He rises up, he calls and goes on calling,
> Through desolate firs the storm-wind rages white.
> He moans aloud, back on the cold stone falling.
> And when he tried to lift himself upright
> His crutch slipped down, in snow-drifts deep it lay:
> A sound was heard from where the fir-trees stand,
> The raven croaked, a something leapt his way
> And put the crutch-stick in his withered hand.[1]

Although this is the end of Faust, it would be doing scant justice to Nürnberger to give the impression that a mere Don Juan is reaping in physical wreckage what he had sown in the flesh. There is a spiritual side to his temptations and to the conflict as a whole which is brought out in some very striking passages. There is probably no wilder or more ghastly Witches' Sabbath to be found in literature than the one described in the canto called *Calvari*, held in a ruined convent on a high hill, whilst Faust lies sleeping at the foot and the forces of evil rage all round him. It ends in an orgy of dancing, during which Mephisto climbs on to a ruined pillar, and two other spirits of the night cling to broken columns on the right and the left:

> This trefoil, devilish, gross,
> Mimics the Calvary of the Cross
> And mocks with terror-striking scorn
> The Man of Sorrows, God of woman born.[2]

---

[1] Nürnberger, op. cit. p. 168.   [2] Ibid. p. 26.

Faust has no part in this satanic revelry, nor is his heart shut to
the divine beauty radiating from the figure of Christ. Coming at
nightfall to a monastery, he hears a chorus of monks chanting to
the Paraclete:

> O salve sancte Paraclete!
> O lux beata trinitas,
> Miraculosa unitas!
> Vos dulces angeli salvete![1]

A healing melancholy steals gently over his mind, causing him
to question Mephisto in shaken accents:

Faust.   Now speak and tell me, if thou e'er didst see
Him, whose sweet spirit now envelops me
(As though I'd never heard the song of hell),
Almighty and resistless, ah, 'tis well!
'Tis sorrow's self which promises to save me
And chains me to His side whose blood shall lave me.
How sawst thou Him? As what rejected worm
Didst thou crawl hiding from His voice's storm? . . .

Mephisto. My friend, you're babbling like an insane friar;
No more than yours have these eyes seen the Sire
Of all the universe; for, the truth to speak,
Hell's like the world: enlightenment's to seek.
A chilly legend is the most we know;
We do not much regard it, let it go;
For without power the tale, forgotten long,
An ancient, echoless and worn-out song. . . .
As for the part I'm called upon to play,
I'm often sick to death of the whole thing
And long for that quiescence death would bring.
It's not so easy to be damned and gay,
With spiteful verve my fiendish tricks to play;
And sometimes when the bowl of wine gives out
Like mere mankind I'd like to howl and shout!
Had I the power of Him who made the world,
Were my poor hoof strong as His arm unfurled,
I would not be content with mere erosion,
No, I should engineer a great explosion,
Destroy this worst of worlds at one fell blow,

---

[1] Nürnberger, op. cit. p. 134.

Pleasure and torment, happiness and woe,
All life, all consciousness, all good and ill,
And Him, and myself too, had *I* my will!
For just like you, I also have my hours
When the bleak emptiness my mind o'erpowers;
What kind of life is this, now tell me true,
To keep on harrying a poor wretch like you?
I'd rather far dismiss you in God's name.
The duty's forced on me; am I to blame?
Oh, thrice accursed, the dog's life that I lead,
Would *I* could call the devil in my need!
Call me a bastard base, call me a monster hated,
Whatever else I've done, at least I've not created.[1]

Faust himself in an earlier canto had expressed a very similar denial of the value of existence and the desire for nothingness and death. He makes no answer now, but sinks into the sleep of absolute exhaustion. He awakes to find the abbot of the monastery bending over him with words of comfort and hope, redemption and eternal life, if he will but continue to repent. As an earnest of salvation, he gives Faust a small phial containing the elixir of life. But, in a grim temptation-scene, modelled on the Gospels, Faust surrenders it to Mephisto for a draught of wine in a burning and stony wilderness; and drop by drop the latter pours it at midnight into a wildly storming sea.

If not the most tragic, Nürnberger's *Faust* is the darkest and perhaps the most dreadful of all the *Fausts* of poetry. It cannot compare with Lenau's for sheer beauty; but it is unique in its strangeness, and a very compelling poem. Why it should be almost totally unknown is a question which raises the problem of the even more incomprehensible neglect of Lenau's version. Neither, it seems to me, has deserved the lack of interest posterity has shown in these two tragic Fausts; whereas no one with any critical sense could regret the fact that the contributions of a Schink, a Schöne, a Hoffmann, a Wolfram and even an Avenarius should have failed to survive their age.

[1] Nürnberger, op. cit. pp. 135 ff.

CHAPTER XIV

ANTI-GOETHEAN FAUSTS

(a) Danse macabre, 1847

Although Lenau's *Faust* shows awareness both of the tradition and of Goethe's version, it goes its own way and is not much concerned with either; and this is even truer of Nürnberger's poem, a highly original nightmare vision generated by the legend, but owing no allegiance to it. Un-Goethean in the highest degree, both poets prove Lenau's contention that Goethe had no monopoly of the subject; but they are far too much concentrated on their own conceptions to be anti-Goethean. It was reserved for that born rebel Heinrich Heine (1797–1856) to be the first iconoclast among the post-Goethean Faustian poets. He had begun to contemplate writing a *Faust* in 1824 and there are several allusions to the work in progress between 1824 and 1826, as well as some details communicated to Eduard Wedekind in 1824, which the latter noted down in his diary. At that time Heine had no idea of rivalling Goethe, as he put it; but considered that everyone should write a *Faust* of his own. His version was to be enlivened by tea-parties held by angels up in the stars, at which Mephisto was to be present, and where Faust's fate was to be discussed. God was not to appear at all; and Mephisto was to be represented as half in love with the angels, especially with Gabriel, for whom he was to feel an emotion midway between friendship and passion, the angels themselves being sexless.

As was the case with Gustav Pfizer's chorus of sylphs and elves singing Faust's remorse away, this is one of those startling coincidences between two utterly different minds (and, what is more, occurring almost simultaneously) which take one's breath away. As an idea it is considerably more Heinesque than Goethean; but Goethe made a highly ironical use of it in the fifth act of *Faust II*, written in 1825, where Mephisto's perverse passion for the choir of angels leads to his downfall and the loss of Faust's soul. It is within the bounds of possibility that Heine mentioned his angelic tea-parties to Goethe when he called upon him in 1824. According to the not very reliable testimony of his brother Maximilian Heine, Heinrich had the audacity to tell the great man that he was 'also' writing a *Faust*, whereat Goethe asked him coldly whether he had no other business in Weimar, and Heine hastily took his leave. Perhaps he had sowed his ironical seed in Goethe's mind before the snub was delivered; but if that were so, it seems unlikely that we should not have heard about it from Heine. A coincidence is more probable, though it certainly is the most striking of any in the history of the Faust-legend. As for the snub, Goethe was suffering under Schöne's plagiarisms at the time and therefore in no very receptive mood to listen to confidences about young Heine's *Faust*. It was an unlucky venture altogether; for it has disappeared completely and was probably burnt with other manu-scripts in the great fire in Hamburg which gutted his mother's house.

It was during a very dark period in Heine's unhappy life that the notion of producing a *Faust* of his own once more took hold of his mind. Already more than half-blind and crippled by the stroke which his fearful state of mind about his uncle's will had precipi-tated in March 1845, he was approached by Benjamin Lumley of Her Majesty's Theatre with the request for a ballet-scenario. This was probably in 1846, the same year in which Scheible produced the first three volumes of his *Kloster*, followed in 1847 by volumes iv and v. The second, third and fifth volumes were devoted to Faustiana of all kinds, including a faithful reprint of the Urfaust-book; and Heine devoured them eagerly. Simrock's rhymed version of the puppet-play, also published in 1846, added fuel to the flames. Ever since 1833 when he gave his version of the Flying Dutchman in *Schnabelewopski* which inspired Wagner, Heine had been increasingly absorbed, fascinated, almost obsessed by folk-lore, particularly Nordic and Greek. This preoccupation is revealed in *Salon II*, 1835, *Elemental Spirits*, 1836, in *The Goddess Diana*, 1846, *Doctor Faust*, 1847, *The Gods in Exile*, 1854, and indeed everywhere in his work. Since his own art was based on folk-poetry, this is not in itself surprising; it made the creation of a *Faust* of some kind from his pen almost inevitable. But that it should have taken the form of a 'dance-poem' needs a word of explanation. Lumley's request was the external impulse; but the *motiv* of what one might call dancing Bacchantes had been at work

in Heine's mind since *Florentine Nights* in 1836. It became ever
more compelling as he became increasingly crippled and helpless,
a Dionysiac compensation of the spirit for the creeping paralysis
of the flesh; and not only *Doctor Faust*, but *The Goddess Diana*
too took the form of a 'dance-poem'. Before sketching the scenario
for a Faustian ballet (a break-neck undertaking, as he was careful
to point out) he immersed himself again in Scheible's *Kloster*, and
he would not have been Heine if he had not been caught and held
by the incommunicable spell the old story exercises still. It aroused
in him a passionate loyalty to the legend and this fused with that
resentment against Goethe the Olympian which was one of the
decisive factors in his spiritual make-up. It now joined forces with
the instinctive hostility engendered in lovers of primitive poetry
and folk-lore by modern and sophisticated versions of popular
legends and myths. Far too great a poet himself to have any real
quarrel with *Faust I* or Helen, he was up in arms against *Faust II*
in general and against Goethe's disregard of tradition:

Unfortunately I could not transcend the technical limits of a scenario,
but within those limits I have endeavoured to do my honest best; and
at least I have attempted to acquire one merit which Goethe cannot
claim. There is a sensible lack throughout his *Faust* of faithful adherence
to the real legend, respect for its true spirit, reverence towards its
inmost soul, a reverence which Goethe who remained an eighteenth-
century sceptic until the day of his death could neither feel nor comprehend. In this respect he was guilty of doing a violence to the legend
which is also aesthetically to be condemned and which finally revenged
itself upon the poet, since all the weaknesses of his *Faust* derive from
his offence against tradition. For, having departed from the pious form
in which the legend lives in the hearts of the German people, he proved
incapable of completing the work on the new sceptical plan, and it
remained unfinished; unless indeed that lame and limping second part
of *Faust* which appeared forty years later be taken as the completion
of the poem as a whole. In this second part Goethe frees the necromancer from the devil's clutches and not only does not send him to
hell, but lets him enter heaven in triumph, accompanied by pirouetting
angels and Catholic cupids; so that the fearful pact with the devil which
caused our fathers such hair-raising terror ends like a frivolous farce, I
nearly said like a ballet.[1]

It was not until four decades later, when he wrote the second part
of *Faust*, that he introduced Helena, and he certainly treated her *con*

[1] Heine, ed. Elster, Vol. VI, p. 496.

amore. It is the best thing, or rather the only good thing, in said second part, in that allegorical and labyrinthine wilderness, in which however a wonderfully perfect Greek marble statue suddenly rises up on a lofty pedestal and gazes at us with such divinely pagan and bewitching blank eyes that melancholy overcomes us. It is the most beautiful statue that ever came out of Goethe's studio, and it is almost incredible that it was chiselled by an old man's hand. . . . I have passed a rather ill-tempered judgment on the second part of Goethe's *Faust*; but words really fail me to express my admiration for his treatment of Helena. And here he remained faithful too to the spirit of the legend, which unhappily, as I said before, is so rarely the case with him, a reproach which I cannot repeat too often. In this connection the devil has the most to complain of. Goethe's Mephistopheles has not the slightest spiritual relationship with the true 'Mephostophiles' as the old folkbooks call him, which strengthens my conviction that he did not know those works when he wrote the first part of his *Faust*. Otherwise he would never have permitted Mephisto to appear in such an obscenely comic and cynically ludicrous guise. For Mephistopheles is no common or garden devil; he is a 'subtle spirit', as he says himself, distinguished, aristocratic and occupying a high place in the infernal hierarchy. . . .[1]

These strictures on Goethe's *Faust* occur in the *Commentary* to the 'dance-poem', a racy, stimulating and poetical account of the history of the legend, far the best that has ever been given in so short a compass. It contains some howlers which cause the hair of scholars (when they have any) to rise on their heads; but these can be and have been corrected in horrified footnotes. Far more important than inexactitudes (however glaring) was the poetical publicity he gave to the Urfaustbook, only recently rediscovered, and published as a rediscovery for the first time by Scheible. The researches of scholars are by no means always crowned with acclamation by poets; and in this case it was by a poet who made everything he touched come alive: dry-as-dust theology, arid philosophy, barren politics, long-lost legends—they all displayed remarkable vitality and some of them began to cut capers at Heine's approach.

The original Faust-legend, if not utterly lost and forgotten, had been so much overlaid by modern versions that it was buried beneath them. The interest aroused by Goethe's great dramatic poem set the scholars to work. They unearthed the Urfaustbook, to which Heine paid such a glowing and inspiring tribute in his

[1] Heine, ed. cit. pp. 509f.

commentary to the 'dance-poem', at the same time using it as anti-Goethean propaganda. He felt deeply on the subject; and he is not the only one who has felt a certain discomfort when turning from the Urfaustbook to Goethe's *Faust II*—the one informed with such spiritual intensity; the other, except for some supreme moments, so playfully ironical. But the discomfort experienced when reading Heine's *Faust* is deeper; for his 'break-neck under-taking' has not come off. Far from resuscitating the sixteenth-century legend, his *danse macabre* appears painfully like an experiment in galvanizing a corpse.

Yet there is a poetical and tragic idea behind the strange performance. Heine was representing in a series of actions that dualism between the spirit and the flesh under which he laboured all his life and sometimes agonized. It is a piece of Saint-Simonian doctrine dramatized by a defeated and disillusioned disciple, who despaired of the harmony prophesied by that sect; and it is therefore in some sort a Young German document, although viewing spiritually and despairingly a problem tackled by the school as a social question capable of solution. In Heine's ballet-scenario Faust's damnation is brought about by the spirit of sensuality incarnate in the devil Mephistophela, by which means he expressed his fundamental conviction of the soul-destroying nature of women. It is not nearly such an impressive statement of this belief as the one given with such fearful force in his *Tannhäuser*; but it harmonized with one of the *motivs* of the Urfaustbook in which Mephisto would sometimes disguise himself as a beautiful woman in order to keep Faust's feet on the downward path; and it also lent itself admirably to the technical requirements of the ballet.[1] What is more surprising at first sight in view of the fact that Heine was such a stickler for legendary tradition is his introduction of the element of witchcraft. But he was strongly drawn to that sinister half-sister of magic because it belonged to the whole complex of folk-lore and legend in which he had immersed himself so deeply. The beautiful woman whom Faust sees in the magic mirror in the first act, and for whom he sells his soul to Mephistophela, is a glamorous duchess who is also a witch, and indeed the Domina, or Satan's bride-in-chief. When they meet in the ducal castle in the second act, where the traditional feats of necromancy

[1] The 'Astaroth' Heine saw in the play given near Hanover was also played by a young girl. Cf. above, p. 89.

are represented by the evocation of David dancing before the ark of the covenant, Faust recognizes her for what she is by her golden shoe, and gives her a *rendezvous* for the next Sabbath. Although not so eerie as Nürnberger's, Heine's Witches' Sabbath which takes place in the third act was based on a careful examination of the demonologists and is a not altogether unsuccessful attempt to infuse the proceedings with a dark beauty:

However baroque, bizarre and extravagant many of these figures are, nevertheless they must not outrage the aesthetic sense; and the ugly impression produced by the grotesque must be softened or obliterated by fabulous splendour or positive gruesomeness.[1]

In the background the goat is seen descending from his pedestal, and after a few strange compliments exchanged with the duchess, he dances a minuet with her. Slow, measured, ceremonious steps. His face shows the melancholy of a fallen angel and the deep boredom of a world-weary prince. All the features of her face betray inconsolable despair.[2]

Nevertheless, as the orgy gets wilder and more obscene, both Heine and Faust are revolted:

. . . he gives expression to his disgust at all the grotesque goings on, at all the Gothic obscenity, which is only a vile and gross mockery of Christian asceticism and just as repulsive to him. He experiences an infinite yearning for pure beauty, for Greek harmony, for the disinterested and sublime figures of Homer's spring-time world. Mephistophela understands him and, touching the ground with her magic wand, she conjures up the image of the famous Helen of Sparta, who vanishes at once . . . he is rapt with enthusiasm; Mephistophela makes a gesture and the magic steeds appear again, on which they fly away.[3]

The fourth act plays on an island in the Archipelago, on which Helen and her maidens are living a magical posthumous existence. There is a temple to Aphrodite in the background, and lovely ritual dances are being held:

Everything breathes Greek serenity, divine ambrosial peace, classical calm. There is nothing to remind one of a nebulous other world, of mystical shudders of voluptuousness and fear, nor of the supramundane ecstasies of the spirit emancipating itself from the flesh. It is all real

---

[1] Heine, ed. Elster, Vol. VI, p. 487.   [2] Ibid. pp. 488 f.
[3] Ibid. p. 489.

plastic beauty without retrospective melancholy and without empty longings and forebodings. Faust and Mephistophela break suddenly into this world, flying down on their steeds. It is as if they were liberated from a sombre nightmare, from some vile illness, some doleful madness, and both revive at the sight of perfect beauty and true nobility.[1]

It almost looks as if even Mephistophela might be saved by contact with the world of pagan antiquity. Characteristically enough, she leads the revels in a Bacchic dance whilst Faust and Helen look on. But the beautiful and happy interlude is of short duration. The duchess, whom Faust had finally scorned at the Sabbath, comes flying witch-like on a bat, waves her magic wand and disenchants the island and all its lovely inhabitants:

> Immediately the heavens darken. Thunder and lightning; the sea surges stormily upwards. A most horrible transformation occurs with all the objects and persons on the whole island. It looks as if everything had been struck by a whirlwind and death. The trees are leafless and withered; the temple has collapsed into ruins; the statues lie shattered on the ground; Helena seated beside Faust looks like a corpse, almost emaciated to a skeleton, in a white shroud; the dancing maidens too are nothing now but bony ghosts . . . with the appearance of lamias . . . and they do not seem to have noticed that they have been transformed. . . . The sea meanwhile rages ever higher and gradually submerges monuments and men. The dancing lamias alone go on dancing as if nothing had happened, gaily striking their tambourines, until the last moment when the waves wash over their heads and the whole island sinks down into the sea. High above the storm-tossed waters Faust and Mephistophela are seen racing away on their black steeds.[2]

A fine curtain; and a very effective contrast is made in Acts Three and Four between the Christian and pagan underworlds, ending in the tragic victory of the former. It is the climax of the action, and one could wish that it had been the catastrophe; for the defeat of paganism by Christianity, so often and often so movingly represented by Heine, is indicated here in a striking and imaginative manner, throwing the enchanted island of Voss (which may have inspired him) into the shades of merited oblivion, and dealing with the Helena-*motiv* in a style which arouses genuine admiration, especially when one remembers the efforts of Klingemann, Holtei and Avenarius. Heine's own particular reading of the Faustian situation achieved a symbolical expression in the fourth act. He

---

[1] Heine, ed. Elster, Vol. VI, p. 490.   [2] Ibid. pp. 491 f.

had said all that he had to say when it came to an end; and the fifth act, showing Faust's attempted marriage with a modest young Germanic bride, is a very decided anti-climax. Mephistophela fetches Faust off at the church door, because his hour has struck, and the strange entertainment draws to its traditional close.

Many elements from the Urfaustbook reappear in Heine's ballet. the princes of hell in strange theriomorphic aspects, the episode of the stag's horns, a glimpse of infernal but illusory armies, the inexorable prohibition to marry, as well as other features from the popular stage versions Heine had seen in his youth; but the whole is as unlike the sixteenth-century story as well may be. Nor, except in the fourth act, is it particularly like Heine. His vivid, imaginative and witty prose style, forced into the strait-jacket of a scenario, lost its flexibility and grace. One need only compare the fourth act of *Doctor Faust* with the mythological dream at the end of the biography of Börne to realize how much the poet in Heine was eclipsed by the nature of his task. And, though only a poet could have written his 'dance-poem', he was not the poet Heine when he wrote it; not the visionary whose remarkable renderings of the conflict between paganism and Christianity received their final heart-piercing expression on his death-bed in *For the Mouche*.

Considering the dynamic effect sickness and sorrow had upon Heine's art, it seems unlikely that his *Doctor Faust* suffered under the bodily and mental anguish he was enduring at the time. The technique dictated to him was largely responsible; but the fact that it was written so consciously under the shadow of Goethe was also crucial. It is this perhaps that really blighted the *danse macabre* with its fantastic Witches' Sabbath and its submerged Atlantis, so that the first explicitly anti-Goethean *Faust* has never attained to a higher rank than that of a literary curiosity.

(b) 'Schiller's' Faust, 1859–1869

Fundamentally Heine's opposition to Goethe derived from his outraged feelings on the subject of the untraditional salvation. He also criticized the manner in which this was brought about, disliking the Catholic machinery and the frivolity with which it was used. The vast majority of readers at that time agreed with him there; and even as late as 1919 Avenarius clearly thought likewise. But no one felt it more passionately and proclaimed it more unremittingly and long-windedly than a certain Ferdinand Stolte (1806–74). This humourless specimen of the *genus Teutonicum* seems to have studied as a doctor and then adopted the less exacting professions of singer, actor and dramatic critic. In this latter capacity he brooded over Goethe's *Faust* and mourned over the deplorable lack of a *Faust* by Schiller. Resolved to fill this aching void, he brought out during the years 1859–69 a 'dramatic-didactic' *Faust* in four parts such as, in his opinion, Schiller (if only he had been spared to undertake the task) might well have written, and dedicated it to the shades of that lofty spirit. In the interests of publicity for this epoch-making work, Stolte travelled round Germany giving readings from it. He claimed that they were rapturously received and quoted a very fair number of enthusiastic press-notices. He was therefore obviously supplying a much-felt want, and certainly supplying it generously. In his introduction to the completed product he protested against the prevalent opinion that the Faust-theme had been exhausted by Goethe, and that any new version of it was doomed to come into the world still-born. He also voiced his intense dissatisfaction with *Faust II* as a whole, and especially with the manner in which the salvation was effected. Further than that, he let fly at the critics who made confusion worse confounded by their commentaries and expositions. In fact he represented in a thoroughly philistine way the general consensus of opinion of that age. This, and the fact that he can never have read more than extracts from his own Faustian opus at any one time, may account for the enthusiastic reception he met with.

His monstrous and totally unreadable would-be 'Schillerian' version runs into 1075 by no means small pages. No list of *dramatis personae* is given, an omission all the more irritating because of the fearfully confusing relationships between them. No localities are indicated either; and only once, as one flounders along, is a helping hand held out. This occurs in the third part, at the beginning of three interminable scenes devoted to long-drawn-out political arguments. Naïvely enough, Stolte acknowledged that they held up the 'intensely dramatic' action, but declared that they were of such fundamental importance that they could not be omitted. He therefore counselled his readers to read the first and last pages of each scene in order to see what was happening; and then to go back and profit at their leisure by the political lessons to be learnt from the discussions. It is unlikely that any reader will ever get far enough to-day to follow this well-meant advice. Nothing but an adamantine sense of duty could urge him on through an action in which Ahasuerus (that noted Faustian incubus) plays the portentous part of a virtuous double to Mephisto. The plot is a tissue of noble-minded nonsense. Guttenberg and the Bible, usurpers and rightful pretenders to the throne of England, Lutheran doctrine, unscrupulous cardinals, glamorous females and pure young maidens rise and sink and sink and rise in the glutinous bog of didactic rhetoric. The shades of Schiller must have been in despair. Stolte borrowed a leaf out of Holtei's book by allowing the writing of the pact to fade away gradually as Faust overcomes the successive temptations put in his way. It flames up and then disappears during a final hectic embrace which teaches him the error of his ways, Ahasuerus and Coelesta (the Gretchen of this play) also throwing their weight into the scale of virtue. He now renounces the pact and, like other Fausts before him, loses his youth on the spot:

> *Mephisto.* Therefore, by hell's potent might,
> Creator and destroyer too
> Of splendour and of glamorous light:
> Youth and beauty, fly off too!
> With marrow dried and faded hair,
> A corpse, oh Faust, you'll soon lie there!![1]

There is still a long way to go, however, before Faust finally gives up the ghost, a spate of lofty inanities, in which the human actors join with the hero, and are supported by the Earth Soul, songs by star-spirits, the voice of a flaming star which perorates at inordinate length, the shades of departed philosophers and noble thinkers who have achieved Christianity; whilst poor Mephisto, crushed by all this, gazes in despair at the blank pact and is then annihilated and swallowed up by the dust of the earth. After further immense soliloquies by all and sundry, in which the Earth Soul takes the prize for volubility, Faust expires at last, exclaiming ecstatically:

> Farewell, farewell! now cracks the veil of flesh,
> And shadows flee; now light streams to my eyes![2]

[1] F. Stolte, *Faust. Dramatisch-didaktisches Gedicht in vier Teilen*, Hamburg, 1870, Vol. III, pp. 382f.   [2] Ibid. Vol. IV, p. 219.

(c) *A parodied Faust*, 1862–1886

The high spirits induced by finishing Stolte's *Faust* at last are raised to positive hilarity by Friedrich Theodor Vischer's *Faust. Third part of the tragedy. Written in faithful imitation of the spirit of the second part of Goethe's Faust by Deutobold Symbolizetti Allegoriowitsch Mystifizinsky*. That one and the same work should give rise to anything so heavily solemn on the one hand and so gloriously gay on the other as vehicles of one and the same protest is an amusing situation in itself. For although other parodies and also other third parts had tried conclusions with Goethe, Vischer's parody is the only one deserving of notice. Since Vischer (1807–1887) was professor of aesthetics in Stuttgart and famous at that, he published the first version of his satire pseudonymously in 1862. But as he was also a courageous fighter, he confessed to his authorship in a volume of critical essays the following year, and boldly justified his attitude, condemning the second part of Goethe's poem as 'a bloodless and lifeless structure'. Feelings, of course, were outraged at his audacity, especially in view of his academic status; heads were shaken, riot-acts read. Eventually Vischer, having produced in 1875 his big critical work on *Faust*, revised the parody thoroughly in 1886 and slightly toned it down, giving the part of Gretchen to Lieschen, and adding, among too many other episodes, an epilogue in which the Faustian commentators and finally Goethe himself were introduced. As it now stands, it is rather too long and has too many extraneous elements in it; but take it all in all, it is a brilliant satire, voicing the considered opinion (after more than twenty years of intense preoccupation with the subject) of a highly gifted critic who was also a sensitive and poetically-minded writer with a genius for versification. He had two aims in view: in the first place an attack on *Faust II*, its allegorical nature, its mannered style, its alleged unpoetical effect and its Roman Catholic conclusion; in the second place he wished to hold the critics and commentators up to ridicule with their pretentious obscurities masking abysmal and invincible ignorance.

The situation, rich in comic possibilities, which Vischer imagines is as follows. The powers that be in heaven, unable to turn a totally deaf ear to the outcry raised by the critics (with Mephisto at their head) that Faust had done precious little to merit eternal salvation, have decreed that he should undergo a further series of tests and trials before being granted final entry into the realms above. He is therefore found dreeing his weird in a half-way-house, solaced by the sympathetic companionship of Lieschen of the well, now a reformed character but still undergoing purification for her lack of charity in the past. Valentine, who has married Bärbelchen and made an honest woman of her, he and none other having been her lover, lives close by with his wife in charge of an inn for the refreshment of those who are on their way from this world to the next. Faust meanwhile has been given the task hinted at in the final scene of *Faust II*, when the cherubs chant:

> Early we were removed,
> Ere life could reach us;
> But he hath learned and proved,
> And he will teach us.[1]

Poor Faust; not only is he the school-master of these young limbs of Satan; he has been ordered to instruct them in the meaning of *Faust II*; and, to add to his tribulations, he is on a strict diet (locusts for lunch) and an enforced teetotaller, whilst the most succulent meals and gallons of heartening beer are being dispensed to all comers at Valentine's inn! Lamenting this cruel fate, he suddenly sees the ceiling divide and Mephisto habited as a *chef* directing the operations of hellish spirits who are preparing a meal warranted to bring water to the mouth of the most fastidious gastronome, chanting meanwhile:

> Vanish, ye narrowing
> Monk-like and harrowing
> Dull dreary walls;
> Give place to cosy,
> Firelit, rosy
> Kitchen so snug! . . .
> Look at the dainty
> Cook who is turning,
> Keeping from burning,
> Roasting and basting,
> Flav'ring and tasting
> Saliva inducing,

---

[1] Goethe, *Faust II*, ll. 12,080 ff.; cf. Bayard Taylor, op. cit. p. 329. Taylor translates *Selige Knaben* by Blessed Boys. I prefer Cherubs, although it may be theologically less accurate.

> Aroma producing,
> Golden-brown shimmering,
> Gleaming and glimmering
> Corpulent goose.[1]

The spell-binding rhythm to which the spirits had sung Faust to sleep in the first part of Goethe's poem so that Mephisto might vanish is equally potent now. The languishing listener falls into a trance; and when Lieschen rouses him, he is like one possessed, absolutely determined, at whatever cost, to fight his way to Valentine's inn and assuage his ravenous hunger, plagiarizing wildly from his own outburst in *Woodland Cavern* as he does so:

> A starveling wretch am I, rottenly housed,
> A ruffian, champing by this dismal stove,
> Gnawed at by hunger, longing to be soused!
> And thou, detached, thy senses well-controlled,
> Midst this mean hovel's chairs and table bare,
> Thy simple, homely life thou dost not scold?
> The ill-stocked kitchen has thy loving care?
> Thee and thy peace I now must undermine,
> Thou, beer-house, claimst this sacrifice as thine!
> Help, devil! make my torments' time to fleet,
> What must be let it happen here and now!
> Fain would I taste of life's delights so sweet,
> And then, for all I care, be damned and how![2]

Mephisto raises no objections and is ready to claim him on the spot; but Lieschen summons Valentine, who gets the better of the evil spirit; whilst the wildly struggling Faust is brought back to his senses by a bucket of cold water from the well. The victory is thereupon celebrated by a choir of invisible good spirits, who on this as on all subsequent occasions break in *à la* Easter Chorus to congratulate the hero; although they never fail to point out at the end (in this instance in prose) that it was a near thing and due to causes other than his own merit. These choruses always open with the words '*Glücklich erstanden!*' parodying '*Christ ist erstanden!*', and as the verb means both to rise again and to pass a test, Vischer has an unfair advantage here over any would-be translator. But he has an unfair advantage in any case; for his close imitation of

---

[1] F. T. Vischer, *Faust, Der Tragödie dritter Theil*, in Geissler, op. cit. Vol. III, pp. 386 f.   [2] Ibid. p. 389.

Goethe's metres, whether taken from the first or the second part of the poem, is positively uncanny in its brilliance, ease, exuberance and inexhaustible verve. His occasional straight quotations from famous and crucial passages in Goethe's drama are also chosen and applied with such aptness and art that criticism is disarmed. Even when the situations depicted are not outstandingly comic (and in one or two instances hardly comic at all), the language continues to delight and amuse all those who know Goethe's text, with its staggering verbal felicities and reminiscences.

In the scene just described, the situation itself, once Lieschen has delivered her exposition, would be humorous only in a very mild degree, were it not for the rhythmical and linguistic echoes from *Faust I* which make of the whole a positive fountain of wit. The second test embodies a gloriously comic notion: the hero of *Faust II* attempting to interpret the poem to a class of (un)holy little brats, with the added handicap that he must spare the rod if he would save his soul. Brimful of mischief, the cherubs have already prepared a hot reception for him in the shape of parched peas strewn on the floor and pitch smeared on his chair, when Mephisto slips in with a box of cockchafers to be released at some suitable moment. To make assurance doubly sure, he also cuts deep incisions into the rod, so that if and when Faust has recourse to it, it will fly in his face and sap his self-control altogether. The stage being now set, Mephisto makes off and Faust enters, noticing (as Gretchen had done on a similar occasion) that the atmosphere seems very close, but attributing this not unnaturally to the colony of cherubs. He takes a nasty toss by slipping on the parched peas, but restrains himself in the nick of time from using the cane and begins to tackle the task of clarifying the cherubs' ideas on the subject of Homunculus. As his own are extremely nebulous, he sits down and reads some fascinating nonsense from a manuscript authority; then, rising to question the unruly class, he finds that he is stuck fast to his chair. In struggling to free himself he tears his trousers, and loses his temper, though not so completely as to preclude a Shakespearean monologue:

> If it were done when 'tis done, then 'twere well
> It were done quickly: if the bastinado
> Could trammel up the consequence, and catch
> With its surcease, success; that but these blows
> Might be the be-all and the end-all here,

But here, upon this school-bench here and now,
The life to come I'd jeopardize for that.[1]

At this point in his reflections Lieschen half-opens the door and whispers to him to desist and to leave well alone, acting (as she does not fail to point out) in a fashion diametrically opposite to Lady Macbeth. Her intervention has the desired effect. Faust returns to the exegesis of Homunculus, only to be interrupted by the swarm of cockchafers. This is the last straw; he seizes the ringleader and swings the cane. But, owing to Mephisto's surgical interference, it breaks in his hand and saves him from irretrievable disaster. Mephisto in the background realizes ruefully that he has once more shown himself to be:

> a part of that same might
> That wills the evil course and furthers right.

> Happily passed! [exult the invisible spirits]
> Hail to the mortal
> Who through the portal—
> Poem explaining,
> Children restraining,
> From caning refraining,
> With beetles a-humming,
> Like pastoral mumming,
> Through the air winging,
> Squeaking and singing,
> Round his nose ringing,
> Grabblingly
> Scrabblingly
> Dabblingly
> Gabblingly—
> Has issued out.
> Though there's some doubt
> Whether with credit;
> Still, let us not medit
> The part in the scandal
> Of the whip's handle,
> But let's light a candle,
> And call it a day.[2]

Amusing and even exciting as the Homunculus scene is, it depends for its full effect on an intimate knowledge of *Faust I*; only a poet

---

[1] Vischer, *Faust*, ed. cit. p. 399.   [2] Ibid. pp. 402 f.

who loved it and knew it inside out could have handled the rhythms and *motivs* with such absolute mastery, endearing one to the original more than ever, as one realizes with mounting admiration that what it gives it gains. In this respect it is like a well-known and expressive face made more remarkable and compelling by a sympathetic caricature.

But the descent to the Mothers, which takes place in the second act, is a descent indeed. Vischer's uncompromising hostility to *Faust II* affected the tone of his treatment, which, instead of riotous and hair-raising fun, degenerated into strident satire. But it is also true that the first part of Goethe's poem is, aesthetically speaking, strong enough to nourish the parody and thrive on it; whereas the second part is on the whole much more vulnerable; and (granted Vischer's point of view) easy game. His purpose, in the fantastic regions now entered for further tests, is to show up the essential unreality of the Mothers, Helen and Euphorion. But, as Goethe had deliberately aimed at that effect, one feels that Vischer is beating the air; and that to exhibit them as puppets of calico and tow was puerile and pointless. Faust comes through the test of meeting Helen again with flying colours; he realizes that she is bogus and declares that she bores him; he also looks on unmoved while Valentine gives Euphorion a good whacking; and when these two personages disintegrate into rags and tatters, he is more than resigned to the *dénouement*:

> Stamp on the remnants, and remove the junk,
> The cult of humanism is unmanly bunk.[1]

The Mystic Mothers and Mephisto thereupon engineer more formidable temptations; the Emperor of a foreign power makes menacing advances to Faust, and these are followed by overtures from Rome. Unluckily these additions to the first version were inserted to give an opportunity for the display of windy patriotism and Lutheran hot air combined with rabid anti-Catholicism. They ring very hollow, and it is difficult to see why Faust needs so much external spiritual aid as well as the assistance of the trusty Valentine to withstand them. But actually this accorded well enough with one of the salient points Vischer was intent on driving home throughout the whole parody: his contention that Faust was a weak-kneed, almost a knock-kneed, hero, who could never by any

[1] Vischer, *Faust*, ed. cit. p. 429.

chance have saved himself by his own endeavours. This is stated categorically by Mephisto at the beginning of the third act in a dialogue held with the Lord, who speaks from behind a cloud. With some show of reason the evil spirit accuses the Almighty of cheating in this respect, a reproach levelled not only against the happenings in the parody, but also against the conclusion of Goethe's poem:

> Mephisto. Thou spakst of instincts, potent if obscure,
> That would direct to clarity his ways;
> No word was said of outside props and stays,
> Thou wert so certain of him, so secure.
> Thou madst a show of handing him to me
> To catch him with my arts if that might be,
> Relying on his innate spiritual merits.
> And now, forsooth, thou'rt helping him with spirits. . . .
> The final outcome is, and that's a fact,
> To save him is an arbitrary act.[1]

In order to placate Mephisto, it is now further decreed that Faust shall undergo a very severe ordeal by caning, administered by Valentine under the supervision of the evil spirit; and that he shall also pass through the trials by water and fire in the course of a mock initiation-ceremony presided over by Doctor Marianus, Pater Ecstaticus, Pater Profundus and Pater Seraphicus. Although carried through with Vischer's inimitable high spirits and metrical ingenuity, this degenerates into rather tiresome foolery; and one is the readier to welcome the apotheosis of Faust and Lieschen and the comment of the Chorus Mysticus:

> The greatest of tastelessness
> Was tasted here;
> The height of preposterousness
> Here it doth jeer:
> The quite unforgivable,
> Pardon it, pray!
> The utterly boring
> Led us astray.[2]

But Vischer had not done yet. In a well-conceived epilogue he introduced the departed spirits of the Faustian commentators,

---

[1] Vischer, *Faust*, ed. cit. pp. 454f.   [2] Ibid. p. 497.

dividing them into two camps, those grubbing for facts and those madly searching for an inner meaning:

Was it seven or six o'clock
When he brought this line to dock?
Or was half-past seven striking
When at last to his own liking
He wrote down this witty notion?

Was it colder, was it hotter
When he sat and talked to Lotte?
And was her little brother Fred,
Instead of being tucked in bed,
A witness of their joint emotion?[1]

Hail, profound interpretations!
Facts exact are often funny ones,
Give us mystic explanations
Peeling layers from poetry's onions!

Nothing here is done by halves:
Men and women, act and fact,
Lions, oxen, dogs and calves,
They're conceptions and abstract.[2]

These two schools of thought now come to loggerheads in a very cathartic fashion for those who have ever ploughed dutifully through their various lucubrations. From words the incensed critics came to blows, and Valentine performs the well-merited function of chucker-out to the great delight of Goethe, who has been eavesdropping at an open window. He is trying to put *Faust* across to Valentine when Vischer enters and confesses to the authorship of the parody. A grand *explication* between the two ensues, during which Vischer pours out everything in his heart on the subject of the allegorical nature and the Catholic flummery of *Faust II*, as well as the style and metres employed, which (he maintained) positively asked to be parodied. But he acknowledged that his dissatisfaction and, more than that, his wrath derived from the enthusiasm, indeed the adoration, inspired in him by Goethe's early works, especially the *Urfaust*:

Let everything else go up in flames
Created by this master's hand;
Let even his name forgotten be,

---

[1] Vischer, *Faust*, ed. cit. p. 502. [2] Ibid. p. 504.

Let but this manuscript be saved,
These pages few that tale unfolding:
'What?' our great-grandchildren will question then;
'Whose is this mind, this nameless spirit,
That with such sure unfaltering hand
Plumbed to the depths of the soul and life?
Who had the power to seize and to shake
Every heart to its very marrow
With a vision so stark and yet so true?'[1]

This I believe to be the crux of the situation, the ultimate reason why the second part of Goethe's *Faust* has had such a rough passage among the poets and poetry-lovers. Heine, Grillparzer, Lenau, Mörike, Vischer, Hebbel, Hehn, Strauss, Gottfried Keller, Conrad Ferdinand Meyer, Paul Heyse and Nietzsche—none of them liked it. For some, if not for all, *Faust I* barred the way to an appreciation of *Faust II*; for others it was the tragic situation depicted in the Urfaustbook; for all it was the change-over from the direct to the symbolical treatment of the subject, that treatment which contemporaneously and subsequently found such ardent enthusiasts among the critics. C. P. Snow said very pertinently in the *Sunday Times* of 27 November 1949 that symbolical work is usually overestimated by aspirants to the intellectual life, a contention with which Vischer would obviously have been in complete agreement. It remained for Nietzsche, however, to express the deep religious dissatisfaction aroused in many by the ultra-symbolical final scene. He based his uncompromising attack against Goethe on Plato's reproach that the poets tell deliberate untruths about the gods:

But suppose that someone said in all seriousness that poets lie too much: he would be right; we do lie too much. For we know too little and we don't learn well; so we have to lie.

And who amongst us poets has not adulterated his wine? Many a poisonous hotchpotch has been brewed in our cellars. Much that is 'indescribable', there it was done.

And because we know so little, the poor in spirit are very dear to our hearts, especially young females!

And we even hanker after the kind of thing old women gossip about in the evenings. And we call that being 'eternally feminine'. . . .

[1] Vischer, *Faust*, ed. cit. p. 545.

Alas! and there are so many things between heaven and earth which only the poets have permitted themselves to conceive!

And *above* the skies in particular: for all gods are poets' 'parables', poets' perfidy.

Truly we are always 'drawn upwards' into the clouds; and we place our gaily coloured puppets on the clouds, and then we call them gods and supermen.

And they are just light enough for these stools, all these gods and supermen.

Oh, how tired I am of all this 'inadequacy' which is determined at all costs to become an 'event'! Oh, how mortally tired I am of the poets![1]

The tragic nihilism of the late nineteenth century countered the enlightened optimism of the eighteenth century in this passage. It is like the crossing of two swords. Lenau, Nürnberger, Heine and Nietzsche, implicitly or explicitly, refused metaphysical reconciliation. As for Vischer, he was carried off to hell for his daring; but Goethe promised to plead for him with posterity, and see to it that he was released fairly soon.

[1] F. Nietzsche, *Also Sprach Zarathustra*, ii, *Von den Dichtern*. I have put in inverted commas the direct quotations from the final verse in *Faust II*.

CHAPTER XV

THE FIRST FAUST REBORN, 1947

What might be called the Faustian comment on world events produced in 1919 Avenarius' repetition of the Goethean message of hope and light; whereas the much more powerful statement made by Thomas Mann in 1947 in the long novel *Doctor Faustus. The life of the German composer Adrian Leverkühn told by a friend* can only be compared with Klinger's formidable and sobering indictment of the extreme social and spiritual peril menacing miserable mankind. Although by no means so profound a metaphysical interpretation of the Faustian problem as Lenau's, it is nevertheless the first serious attempt made since then to put the case not only tragically (which both Nürnberger and Heine had also done) but to underline its wider implications. Mann limited his purview to the fate of Germany during the two World Wars; Lenau represented a universal aspect fraught with danger for humanity. A comparison between the two exemplifies Aristotle's contention that 'Poetry is something more philosophic and of graver import than history, since its statements are of the nature rather of universals, whereas those of history are singulars'.[1] There is another fundamental difference. Lenau kept to the spirit but neglected the letter of the legend; Thomas Mann adhered firmly and faithfully to both, basing himself as regards the pattern of events and in certain central situations also linguistically on the Urfaustbook of 1587.

The hero, Adrian Leverkühn, bedevilled from birth by a restless, scornful, enquiring mind and a dangerous passion for music, is helped through his schooling by an uncle, studies theology at the university, becomes dissatisfied with it and abandons divinity for music, thus becoming an apostate from God. He is ensnared by the wiles of the devil, enters into and ratifies a pact with him, holds a colloquy with him in which he questions him about hell and its torments and later undertakes supernatural journeys with

[1] Aristotle, *On the Art of Poetry*, tr. Bywater, Oxford, 1929, p. 43.

him. He is granted magical powers as a composer of music, but human love has been prohibited, and his attempts to break through this prohibition by marriage and by other means are cruelly punished. In later life he enters into a strange spiritual connection with a mysterious woman whom he never sees (Helen) and his little nephew Nepomuk is a reminder of the sprite Justus Faustus. As Leverkühn feels his end draw near, he summons all his friends together, intending to play to them passages from his masterpiece *D. Fausti Lament*. He introduces it by a plenary confession of his pact and an account of his past life; he then collapses into insanity. This outline will show that Mann was almost as faithful to his original as Marlowe had been when dramatizing the English Faustbook. But no bare analysis can do justice to the extraordinary skill with which he has handled the archaic mythological machinery as a means of conveying the stark emotional truth of the situation.

Since the days of Klinger and the Storm and Stress, none of the tragically-minded Faustian poets had managed (and few of them had even tried) to make anything of hell and its torments. But when Mann was writing his *Doctor Faustus* the powers of evil and destruction were raging fiercely in a war-riven world; and if the days of black magicians, black sabbaths and Black Books were gone, so too were the days of enlightened optimism, of tolerant humanism and even of grand romantic pessimism. Tragic nihilism was literally on the war-path; a whole great nation had (in Mann's view) succumbed to the lures of the devil; the emotional climate of the legend had recurred; the scapegoat-hero must suffer the traditional fate. It remained to make it convincing in the atomic age.

Mann's theoretically satisfactory solution was to transpose the events of the Urfaustbook into the mental sphere, where all our aspirations, fears, despairs, torments and terrors do in fact reside. Adrian Leverkühn is convinced of the reality of his infernal pact; the reader, aware that this is the delusion of a mind diseased, is conscious at the same time of something uncanny in the hero and of something sinister in the succession of events which are driving him mad. This highly ambiguous situation loses some of its fearful fascination, however, by the deliberate parallel drawn between Leverkühn and Nietzsche, from whose life several episodes are taken, two at least transcribed almost *verbatim* from Deussen's *Recollections*. Although contemporaries of the author's also figure in the tale, thus turning it partly into a *roman à clef*, this seems fundamentally less deleterious to it as a work of art (since such personages will finally be forgotten) than the intrusion of factual details about Nietzsche into an otherwise imaginary biography. It may have been done to suggest that the madness of Nietzsche was a symptom as well as a cause of the contemporary madness of Germany; but it is a questionable expedient; one can much more readily accept the manner in which Thomas Mann laid Dostoyevsky under contribution.

The conversation which Leverkühn recorded in writing that he had held with the devil is very closely modelled on Ivan Karamazov's dialogue with his *alter ego* projected during an hour of delirium into a shabby, sinister and demonic personage, whom he half-recognizes for the delusion it is, the shadow of looming insanity. In his wonderful rendering of this spiritual and psychological crisis, Dostoyevsky interpreted Satanism unforgettably as a dark force lurking in the subconscious human soul. Mann followed in his footsteps and placed his hero in an exactly similar situation. Like Ivan, Adrian describes his visitor as a hateful and sordid person; he begins by doubting his reality, being half aware at first that it is a case of split personality; but, like Ivan, he is finally convinced of the contrary. Both are holding a monologue and mistake it for a dialogue; for both are trembling on the brink of madness. In both cases material objects (Ivan's handkerchief and glass of tea and Adrian's coat and rug) prove that there was no reality in the apparition; but both men are too far gone in delusion by then to believe the testimony of their own eyes. The parallel could hardly be closer; the debt is not concealed; the inevitable comparison is not shirked. Thomas Mann only sustains it owing to the timely help of the Urfaustbook rendered at crucial moments in the dialogue with great force and effect. Otherwise this over-long and over-intellectualized interview between the two souls in Leverkühn's breast reads like a Teutonic anticlimax to an awe-inspiring Slavonic catastrophe. It is none the less a remarkable achievement to have created a modern Faustus by combining the terrible realism of the legend with the psychological mysticism which the great Russian reader of souls infused into medieval demonology. If Leverkühn's surname is in reality Nietzsche, Adrian stands for Ivan, the Russian for Johannes.

The three overriding influences—the Urfaustbook, Nietzsche

and Dostoyevsky—would seem at first sight to exclude Goethe altogether and utterly to eliminate his humane and hopeful interpretation, to sweep it away with the rest of the ruins of an ineffectual, effete and now shattered civilization. It is true that Mann does not accept Goethe's optimistic premises nor agree with his conclusions; but he is far too intimately acquainted with that master's masterpiece not to have been affected by it when composing *Doctor Faustus*. In the first place one cannot but recognize Goethe's Wagner in Serenus Zeitblom, Leverkühn's fictitious biographer; Wagner, reconditioned and brought up to date, wrapped (if one wishes to be fanciful) in the mantle of Eckermann; but Wagner all the same. This simple, subtle and endearing device not only allowed Mann to make full use of his famous 'irony'; it also supplied an object for purely human sympathy otherwise sadly to seek. For Leverkühn himself, kept carefully in the background, has the 'infinite capacity for giving pain' of the full-blown genius; but in other respects is more subhuman than superhuman. The numerous other characters in the book, many of them taken from life and most painstakingly described, have the slightly grotesque unreality of two-dimensional caricatures. This is markedly the case with the brilliantly executed *impresario-entrepreneur* Fitelberg, who makes one unforgettable and dazzling appearance. Amongst all these shadows, Serenus Zeitblom is a solid creature of flesh and blood, an ordinary human being to whom one becomes excessively attached as the story grinds slowly and sombrely on towards its dismal close; and the distressing fate lying in store for the hero and claiming him in the end assumes tragic proportions, not only because the Urfaustbook comes to the rescue again, but also because of the agony of sorrow which overwhelms Zeitblom.

This rather pedantic and pedestrian pedagogue gradually transcends the sphere of his innate faculties and possibilities by his devotion to Adrian, whom he has idolized as a boy and almost worships as a man. He comes to comprehend both the musician and his wonderful music, not through his head but through his heart. Throughout he looks up to Adrian and the latter looks down on him in a manner irresistibly recalling Goethe's Faust when conversing with Wagner. When Leverkühn sets off on a cultural expedition to Italy with a more acceptable companion, one's mind harks back to Wagner left alone in his laboratory what time

Mephisto and Homunculus made gaily off for Greece. Zeitblom is often left in the lurch like this, and suffers greatly as Adrian's friend; and since it is his lot to experience the fearful events in Germany between 1943 and 1945 subsequent to the break-down and death of Leverkühn, he finally and fittingly reveals himself as the real tragic hero of the tale. As a biographer he is not without blemish, recounting everything he remembers with remorseless thoroughness and sometimes almost crushing the reader beneath the combined weight of his own and his hero's knowledge on a vast number of subjects, especially on matters musical. This may be meant as irony, in which case it is mercilessly laboured irony; but beneath the mask of Zeitblom, which wears increasingly thin, one seems to discern the features of that overpoweringly well-informed writer, Thomas Mann, who with all his sophistication has so often fallen short of those specifically civilized virtues, selection and restraint.

In spite of this overloading by learning, the first influence of Goethe is benign. It introduces that atmosphere of humanism and humanity which the greatest of German poets is seen dispensing here at second-hand through the agency of Faust's one-time Famulus. The other influence was malign, for it led the novelist to flounder in a quagmire which he might otherwise have avoided, the quagmire of witchcraft. Only Nürnberger and Heine had so far followed Goethe on to that treacherous ground. Mann went in far deeper and stuck much faster than they; and his reasons for venturing in were diametrically opposite to Goethe's. It was to represent the essential impotence of evil that the Olympian poet held it up to ridicule in its most grotesque and repellent aspect. It was in order to emphasize its sinister power that Mann gave so central and significant a position to witchcraft in his *Doctor Faustus*. Subtly but inexorably he brought it into the picture from the very beginning: in the curious speculations and experiments of Adrian's father; in the miasma of medievalism lingering in the buildings and producing the neuroses of the inhabitants of Kaisersaschern, where the boy spent his school-days. He then expounded the subject of demonology, which he introduced into the curriculum of the theological faculty at Halle. One of the lecturers, an eccentric called Kumpf, fancied himself as a twentieth-century Luther, and reproduced the Reformer's habits of mind and speech, in particular his obsession with the devil and hell, against which

Kumpf was continually animadverting in good round sixteenth-century terms, often lifted bodily from the Urfaustbook. In spite of being a half-ludicrous figure, his lectures were popular in the extreme, and he somehow put his diabolism across.

The other lecturer, a much more insidious and sinister personage, was a true *advocatus diaboli*, a Mephistopheles in modern dress. Schleppfuss (a name economically suggesting both the devil and Goebbels in one breath) concentrated his intellectual resources on creating considerable confusion in the minds of his youthful audience on the subject of good and evil, corrupting them as Goethe's Mephisto had corrupted the young freshman, but in a subtler and deadlier way. In particular he spoke about good being generated by evil and evil by good, and also pointed out that freedom implies (indeed almost demands) the freedom to do evil. Ivan's Grand Inquisitor combined cynicism with human kindness, totally to seek in Schleppfuss; but there is a strong family likeness between their paradoxes and sophistries. Schleppfuss further regaled his audience, in order to make confusion worse confounded, with tales of black magic and witchcraft, of pacts with the devil and burnings at the stake, with which the *Malleus Maleficarum* and kindred demonologies abound. With his tongue in his cheek he spoke throughout as a supporter of the 'mercy' of the Inquisition in saving the souls of witches and sorcerers by condemning their bodies to the flames. As a peculiarly telling instance of this clemency he recounted the story of a young man who delivered up the girl he loved to torture and death because she had used a salve obtained from a witch in order to ensure his fidelity. For Schleppfuss was never tired of voicing the rabid hostility shown to women as the agents and instruments of sex, the focal point of diabolic temptation; and although he made a great parade of merely quoting the ideas animating the Inquisition, he seemed to be propagating them personally. Later events were to show that Leverkühn was profoundly affected by all this; and well he might be. The lectures given by Mephisto in his academic incarnation form one of the many *bravura* passages in the book, and are a speaking witness to the range and depth of the author's reading.

With the subtle poison distilled by Schleppfuss working in his veins, Adrian left Halle and decided to follow the advice of his former music-master Wendell Kretzschmar and abandon theology for music. He did this only after much hesitation, as he confessed in an interminable letter to Kretzschmar; for he felt the choice to be ominous and tantamount to apostasy, using many phrases taken from the Urfaustbook in order to underline the dangerous, alluring, magical and indeed demonic nature of the art to which he was about to commit himself: 'Throwing the scriptures from me . . . apostasy . . . O Homo fuge . . . desperate heart'—these are some of the echoes from the sixteenth-century text which arrest attention in the letter. Mann has used great eloquence in the effort to equate magic and music; but there is a great difference between magic in the metaphorical sense and the Black Art; and unless one is willing to identify music with witchcraft and sorcery it is impossible to shudder at the enormity of the spiritual sin involved in abandoning theology for music. This attitude is, however, completely in line with the theme of the questionable nature of art and of artists as such on which Thomas Mann has played so many variations, an elaboration of Kierkegaard's notion that genius is *ipso facto* sinful. This striking sweeping statement has had a great effect in Germany; and Mann combined it here with Schopenhauer's definition of music as the direct expression of the urgent and irresistible but fundamentally tragic and guilty Will.

His brilliant special pleading on behalf of this conception is dazzling rather than convincing; and yet music has from the earliest times been closely connected with magic. Orpheus and the songs the sirens sang made way for the medieval conception of music as one of the lures and snares of the devil. In the year 1433 during the Council of Basel a party of prelates, priests and monks were walking and talking about matters ecclesiastical in a grove. Suddenly they paused, arrested by the song of a nightingale sobbing its heart out in a lovely lime-tree. Surrendering to the spell, their minds were turned from godly things to beauty and love and the lusts of the flesh, until one of them pointed out that the nightingale was probably the devil and proceeded to exorcize it. Thereupon the little creature confessed that it was an evil spirit and flew away laughing. On the same day those who had listened to its sweet music sickened and soon after died. This story struck Heine's imagination vividly as symbolical of an age in which all beautiful things were thought to be evil. It harmonizes with the fact that seemingly heavenly music was a constant feature of those magical banquets with which the hero of the Urfaustbook so often regaled his friends. Moreover Mephisto was skilled in the art and had a devilish orchestra at his beck and call:

Lastly, was heard by *Faustus* all maner Instruments of musick, as Organs, Clarigolds, Lutes, Viols, Citerns, Waights, Hornepipes, Fluites, Anomes, Harpes, and all maner of other Instruments, the which so rauished his minde, that hee thought hee had been in heauen, whereas the deuill was by his side.[1]

This and other passages much perplexed poor Widman; after quoting Scripture to show that music was of divine origin, he came to the soothing and satisfactory conclusion that the music made by or for Faust was in all probability dance-music—an artless simplification of the problem, but one which Lenau's bewitching waltz makes more acceptable than all the profundities uttered by Thomas Mann about the daimonic element in music. Nevertheless by transforming the sixteenth-century magician into a twentieth-century musician he surmounted one of the worst obstacles to the credibility of the tale he was telling; and moreover replaced the rather jaded miracles and paltry tricks by fascinating accounts of the works Adrian composed under diabolical inspiration. It is true that there are too many of these, just as there is far too much tomfoolery in the Urfaustbook; it is also true that one's interest flags at times beneath the wealth of technical instruction given, much as it sags beneath the load of learning purveyed by Widman. But even imaginary works of genius have more genuine appeal (when described by Zeitblom-Mann) than the utmost the Urfaustbook could do in the way of representing magic. And although the desire for absolute knowledge is perhaps the greatest and the most perilous desire known to man, yet it is perfectly comprehensible that a musician, in despair of creating anything significant or new, should surrender his eternal soul in exchange for the power to produce immortal and peerless works of art.

But unhappily Thomas Mann saw fit to complicate the issue with witchcraft. Having already sold the spiritual pass by abandoning theology for music, Adrian, arriving in Leipzig as 'a stranger in these parts', was manoeuvred into a brothel instead of a restaurant by a scoundrelly porter, whose marked resemblance to Schleppfuss added to the sinister significance of the event. The

---

[1] Cf. Scheible, op. cit. Vol. II, p. 953, and English Faustbook, p. 144. The last sentence is inaccurately translated, and I have amended it.

hero recoiled in horror at finding himself in the modern equivalent of a witches' kitchen and made off with all speed after striking a few chords on the piano. His horror is shared by the reader; for this is almost word for word the story told by Deussen of Nietzsche's similar misadventure in Cologne.[1] The parallelism goes further and the reader fares worse. The soul-searing experience was to have disastrous physical results. Before Adrian could get away, one of the girls, by caressing his cheek with her arm, had much the same effect on him as the vision in the magic mirror had upon Goethe's Faust. He pursued the little brown 'witch' Esmeralda and metaphorically speaking drank the fatal magic potion, which he interpreted subconsciously as signing a pact with the devil. Schleppfuss had artfully prepared the ground for such an extreme and morbid reaction. Meanwhile the real poison with which the girl infected him, acting on an inherited cerebral weakness, accelerated his latent disease.

This is a crying witness to the kind of injury done to magic by inoculating it with the virus of witchcraft as expounded by the demonologists. Goethe could not bring himself to face it squarely; Nürnberger transformed it into a nightmare vision; Heine achieved a legitimate aesthetic effect by contrasting it with Greek beauty at its most radiant and serene; Shakespeare, Middleton and Ben Jonson transmuted it into eerie and sinister poetry. But, as Dryden put it:

> ... SHAKESPEAR's Magick cou'd not copy'd be,
> Within that Circle none durst Walk but He.

Far from copying Shakespeare, Mann was chiefly intent on medical details and psychological motivation. A good many regrettable incidents occur in German literature owing to this passion for careful exposition of character and behaviour. Hebbel was a prime offender; Goethe confessed that he suffered under a kind of compulsion to find a motive for everything and anything. It was this (aesthetically speaking) utilitarian consideration which forced his

[1] Cf. Thomas Mann, *Die Entstehung des Doktor Faustus*, Amsterdam, 1949, pp. 33ff., for the author's own views on the use he has made of Nietzsche; the book as a whole is interesting from a self-revelatory point of view; but not really very helpful, except perhaps on the subject of the use made of Schönberg's music and for some factual details about his literary and personal models.

hero to pass through the ordeal of the *Witches' Kitchen*, in order to account for his subsequent behaviour with Gretchen. Adrian Leverkühn, almost pathologically puritanical, had to be convicted in his own eyes of an unforgivable sin which his disordered mind could plausibly construe into a satanic pact. Objectively considered, it was a delusion; subjectively considered, it was a fact; physically considered, it was to spell his ruin. Like Goethe's *Witches' Kitchen*, the Esmeralda episode represents a triumph of ingenuity; but the fever of excitement about the sexual lapse sets one's teeth on edge.

It was therefore in a shaken and unstable mind that the dialogue between the musician and his diabolical double took place, which was based on Ivan Karamazov's. It is a central and crucial moment in Adrian's life; for the pact, which he believes to have been implicit in his moral downfall, is now ratified in the manner and in the very words of the Urfaustbook:

In a word [the evil spirit announces] there is no need of cross-roads in the Spesser wood between you and me, nor of magic circles. We are in the business together and in accord. You have attested it with your blood, and my present visit is a confirmatory one merely. . . . We for our part will be subject to you in the meantime in all things, and hell shall profit you greatly, if you but renounce all living creatures, and the whole heavenly host and all human beings, for so it must be. . . . But when the sands have run out I shall have full power to deal with you as I think fit and at my pleasure: to rule, command, govern, and lead all that you have and are, whether body or soul, flesh or blood, goods or chattels, to all eternity.[1]

Adrian faints whilst the terms of the contract signed by his predecessor nearly four hundred years earlier ring in his ears; and one feels that he has reason for it; they still have a sinister power. But even more dreadful is the description of hell and its torments, in which the fearful imaginings of the sixteenth century and the concentration-camps of the twentieth meet at the world's end.[2] This is one of those passages which at intervals throughout an extraordinarily unequal work testify to the greatness of the writer. Yet the dialogue as a whole is not impressive. A pale reflection of Dostoyevsky's, it wearies by its length; and whether as an expert

[1] Thomas Mann, *Doktor Faustus. Das Leben des deutschen Tonsetzers Adrian Leverkühn, erzählt von einem Freunde*, Stockholm, 1947, pp. 383f., 386; cf. Scheible, op. cit. Vol. II, pp. 950f.
[2] Cf. Mann, op. cit. pp. 378ff., and Scheible, op. cit. Vol. II, pp. 965ff.

on the subject of venereal disease or as a musical critic, the devil can hardly be said to shine. His seedy appearance, continually changing, arouses little interest; even when he manifests as Schleppfuss during part of the *séance*, he is not at the height of his former academic incarnation, not really in good form.

This interview took place in Italy in 1911 or 1912. Leverkühn spent those years in the land where the lemon-trees blow with the friend called Schildknapp, who had the invaluable gift of making the sardonic hero laugh, although the jokes which are given as specimens of his wit suggest that this was no great feat; and indeed saturnine, scornful and sometimes sniggering laughter was a stock response of the hero to persons and events. Zeitblom greatly deprecated Schildknapp, who was certainly no purveyor of moral uplift, but seems to have done little or no harm to his musical friend.[1] At some period subsequent to the ratification of the pact Adrian undertook, or believed that he undertook, or tried to make Zeitblom believe that he had undertaken, a series of supernatural or semi-supernatural journeys in the good old traditional style. Scrapping the dream-journey to the nether regions described in the Urfaustbook in favour of a submarine exploration and retaining the voyage through the firmament, Mann described both in the light of modern scientific knowledge and theory. This is another *bravura* passage, which almost takes one's breath away by its dazzling display of learning lightened by brilliant irony anent the wonders of the deep, astronomical calculations and the expanding universe. The unhappy Zeitblom hardly knows whether his friend is pulling his leg or not, whilst Adrian, smiling sardonically, hints and then almost states that he has been down to the bottom of the ocean in a diving-bell and has been shot through space in a rocket. With great skill Mann develops the theme in a manner which gives full value to his dislike and distrust of modern science; so that in a restricted sense he is in harmony here with the attitude of the Urfaustbook towards forbidden knowledge. It is a striking performance, not unlike a stupendous exhibition of fireworks, in which a succession of shooting stars illuminate the circumambient darkness and then disappear. Goethe's Faust, complying with the tradition of supernatural journeys, went down through terrible desolation and loneliness in search of the Mystic Mothers; and in

[1] Cf. Mann's *Entstehung des Doktor Faustus*, pp. 79f., for the interesting *apologia* given on the subject of the living model for Schildknapp.

the wonderful description of the emptiness and isolation awaiting him, Mephisto warns the magician:

Naught shalt thou see in endless void afar.[1]

This one line says more to the imagination than all Thomas Mann's astronomical figures about space; but a deliberate verbal reminiscence seems to hint that he was challenging the comparison.[2]

Adrian Leverkühn now retired to a village in the hills outside Munich called Pfeiffering. This was the name of the hamlet in the Urfaustbook where the magician deceived the horse-coper with a bundle of straw, one of a number of clues scattered with increasing liberality as the story goes on. He settled down in a farm-house and began to compose those masterpieces of musical inspiration for which he had jeopardized his soul. They became steadily more disturbing, visionary, apocalyptic and spiritually perverted as time went on. Meanwhile the terrible recurrent headaches which he had inherited from his father and to which he had been subject since childhood increased alarmingly in frequency and intensity with the progress of his disease. Otherwise nothing of any moment happened to him for a considerable time, although much of a distressing nature was happening in the corrupt and deadly dreary society of Munich, symptomatic of times tragically out of joint. Adrian held himself apart from all this in his country asylum, well looked after by the farmer's wife; solitary, remote and undisturbed from 1912 onwards, except for occasional visits from friends and trips to Munich. Exempt from military service during 1914-18, he suffered little or no inconvenience from the war, nor from the attendant and subsequent food-shortage, since he was living on the land and devoted if eccentric female friends supplied him with extra delicacies. He was therefore enjoying that immunity from material hazards which is the traditional prerogative of magicians. But, being in reality a mortally sick man, he suffered greatly and we are spared none of the painful medical details of his cruel disease. Happily there were alleviations, among which must be

---

[1] Goethe, Faust II, l. 6246; cf. Bayard Taylor, op. cit. p. 187.

[2] Cf. Goethe: 'Ins Unbetretene, Nicht zu Betretende' (Faust II, ll. 6222f.), with Mann: 'das Unerschaute, nicht zu Erschauende' (Doktor Faustus, p. 412).

counted the strange relationship with the mysterious Frau von Tolna, who affected Adrian's life beneficently whilst remaining invisible to him. She wrote highly perceptive letters about his music, and sent him a ring with a pagan inscription which he always wore when he was composing. Being a great lady and a plutocrat into the bargain, she brought his name to the notice of those who mattered in the world of art and established his reputation. But they never met, although Adrian stayed for a time in one of her castles during her absence. Zeitblom was tremulously delighted about this connection, which brought, he said, an element into Adrian's life:

. . . from a sphere high above all learning, from the sphere of love and faith, of the eternal feminine in a word. . . . What name belonged to her by right in her relationship with Adrian Leverkühn? To what name did she lay claim? To that of a tutelary goddess, of an Egeria, of a ghostly beloved?[1]

Although her real name was (as Mann admits) Frau von Meck, the invisible friend of Tschaikovsky, her functional name is Helen, a ghost-like lover, playing a ghostly and mysterious part in the musician's life and for ever problematical. This was as near as the twentieth-century writer could well get to the wraith of the folkbook; and though she is rather too distant and dim, he was right not to venture closer. She seems to have entered the hero's orbit in the early nineteen-twenties, whereas his abortive attempt at marriage came several years later.

Love had been expressly forbidden to Leverkühn in the contract. He broke through this prohibition by a passionate friendship with a gifted young violinist Rudi Schwerdtfeger and then fell in love (save the mark) with a charming, black-eyed French girl called Marie Godeau. He first employed Zeitblom to arrange one of those *Ausflugs* or excursions into the country so favourable to courtship that one can hardly imagine a German betrothal taking place without one; and he then sent the devoted Rudi (now also in love with Marie) to propose marriage for him. Thomas Mann declared that this was a Shakespearean reminiscence, based on the *Sonnets, As you Like It, Much Ado about Nothing* and *The Two Gentlemen of Verona*, and substantiated this by showing how he

[1] Mann, *Doktor Faustus*, pp. 594, 598.

had smuggled quotations from these works into his text. But the similarity between the Adrian-Rudi-Marie situation and the Nietzsche-Rée-Lou combination is more obvious; and a contemporary imbroglio was also behind the episode. Whatever its source, it is an unpleasing episode. Adrian's lack of heart and decency met with its just reward. Marie preferred Rudi and accepted his hand; but the feather-headed young flirt was thereupon shot dead by a discarded mistress; and Adrian attributed this catastrophe to his disobedience to the diabolic command against love. This incident is not exactly calculated to arouse sympathy for the hero, whose actions are those of a mental and moral imbecile.

But indubitably of a genius too, since he began to compose the oratorio entitled *D. Fausti Lament* immediately afterwards. Inspiration was rudely checked by another irruption of tragedy into his hitherto sheltered life. It came in the shape of a long visit from his little nephew Nepomuk to recuperate from the measles. Justus Faustus has on the whole been very unlucky in literature, since he has been crowded off the stage again and again by 'real' if illegitimate sons of Faust either suffering infanticide, or miraculously escaping that doom and acting as instruments in the final salvation of their fathers. Only Goethe made poetical use of a highly poetical idea, transforming the strange little sprite of the folkbooks into Euphorion; and then, identifying Euphorion with Byron, singing that wonderful lament on a daimonic spirit that had been too soon eclipsed. Thomas Mann (devotedly attached to his little grandson Frido) represented Adrian's nephew as being so endearing, unearthly, elfin and angelic that all hearts melt in the presence of 'Echo' as he whimsically calls himself, including the hitherto stony and atrophied organ of Leverkühn. The almost explicit intention was to represent him as a 'Christ-child'; but (as was also the case with Esmeralda) a fog of sentimentality blurs the picture. It was not altogether Mann's fault. Shades of all the 'innocent' children of domestic drama, from Arabella in *Miss Sara Sampson* downwards through the mute little victim Edward in Weidmann's *Faust* and the fearful little prigs who people the Storm and Stress tragedies and later melodrama, have gathered together round Nepomuk and helped to make him what he is: an insufferable little Simon Pure. Even so, he hardly deserved the fate meted out to him; for he contracted meningitis and died in agony, none of which the reader is spared. It is one of Mann's most excruciating death-bed scenes, which is saying a good deal.

The terrible effect upon Adrian is admirably described. Convinced that 'Echo' suffered these torments and died because he loved the child and that the curse he labours under has operated again, he closes his mind to comfort and completes *D. Fausti Lament*. Mann's rendering of this oratorio, based on the two like-named chapters in the Urfaustbook, represents a climax in the novel and one of the high-lights in Faustian literature. It is not only extremely moving in itself, it is the most profound and imaginative commentary and interpretation the first Faustbook has ever received, the most sensitive piece of creative criticism it has ever evoked. The transposition into musical terms of the laments of the folkbook will be memorable in many minds long after the story of Leverkühn himself has faded away.

The last chapter is on an equally high level; and again this is because it is based on the Urfaustbook. Adrian's final speech to his assembled friends, recapitulating the facts of his life as seen through the delusion that has haunted him for so long, is given in the language and sometimes in the very words of his sixteenth-century predecessor. And when he breaks down with a fearful wailing cry before he can play to the stricken company (or what is left of it) that strange and terrifying masterpiece which somehow glorifies his fate, the tragic sympathy hitherto withheld overwhelms one at last. This would rank high among the tragic conclusions to the fate of Faust which have been represented since the days of Marlowe, if the tale had ended there. But the Postscript giving the lamentable course of a typical paranoical case, and once more dragging Nietzsche in *via* Deussen, considerably diminishes the total effect.

Adrian Leverkühn was born in 1885; he became incurably insane in 1930 and died on 25 August 1940. Serenus Zeitblom began his biography on 27 May 1943, and wrote the penultimate chapter on 15 April 1945. From time to time he paused in the tale he was unfolding to reflect upon the terrible events taking place in the 'recounting time', which nearly always betrayed a certain affinity with those occurring in the 'recounted time'. This device served to emphasize the fact that the twentieth-century 'Doctor Faustus' was a symbol or a symptom of the Germany of his day; and it certainly must be allowed that the periodic irruption of the Second World War gives greater proportions to the whole and a far deeper emotional value to the work than either the hero or his fate could possibly have aroused by themselves. But the parallel is shaky, and the symbolism is intellectual, almost a contradiction in terms. It was by a gradual and inevitable process of organic growth that Goethe's Faust finally came to shed his individual nature and stood revealed as personified mankind. It was by a blinding flash of revelation that Lenau's Faust saw just before he died that his desperate desire for ultimate truth might have cosmic implications. But Thomas Mann deliberately and of set purpose fabricated his hero for the part he was to play; piecing him together from the protagonist of the Urfaustbook, from Ivan Karamazov and from Nietzsche, and then transforming this composite figure into a mad musician. The devil says that the artist is the brother of the criminal and the madman, and Thomas Mann seems to be roughly of the same opinion; but this is one of the many sweeping statements which lack the sanction of universal truth, a rule of thumb with so many and such important exceptions as to be invalid. And even if it were true, where is the parallel with Germany? Leverkühn and Germany are very strikingly represented as victims of dark and demonic forces; but an artist's fate is something much too individual to symbolize a nation's destiny. The attempt to do so here would result in laying the blame for the tragedy Germany brought about and suffered at the door of her musical gifts, or in regarding her as in some special sense the artist among nations. The cap does not fit; and ruthless political ambitions are in a different category from the *hubris* of genius. The symbolical validity of Mann's *Doctor Faustus* is questionable in the extreme.

It achieves an emotional value, however, towards the end in the glimmering of hope born of utter despair, which is also to be discerned in Faust's last speech to his friends in the Urfaustbook:

Lastly . . . this is my friendly request, that you would rest, & let nothing trouble you: also if you chance to heare any noise, or rumbling about the house, be not therwith afrayd, for there shal no euil happen vnto you: also I pray you arise not out of your beds. But aboue all things I intreate you, if you hereafter finde my dead carkasse, conuay it vnto the earth, for I dye both a good and bad Christian; a good Christian, for that I am heartely sorry, and in my heart alwayes praye for mercy, that my soule may be deliuered: a bad Christian, for that I know the Diuell will haue my bodie, and that wil I willingly giue him so that he . . . leaue my soule in quiet: wherefore I pray you that you would depart to bed, and so I wish you a quiet night . . . and let mine be horrible and fearful.[1]

The ambiguity in these last words was not the theme of Thomas Mann's extraordinarily impressive interpretation of the speech. Zeitblom describes this portion of his friend's cantata as:

. . . a proud and bitter perversion of the scriptures . . . in the 'friendly request' made by Faustus to his comrades in that last hour, to go to bed, *to sleep now and take their rest* and not to let any fears assail them. It is hardly possible in the framework of the cantata not to recognize in this advice the conscious and deliberate antithesis to the 'Watch with me' of Gethsemane. And again this 'last supper' has a consciously ritual stamp; with it is combined the converse of the notion of tempta- tion: Faust rejects as a temptation the possibility of salvation. . . . This is brought out much more clearly and strongly in the scene with the good old man who invites Faust into his house in order to undertake a pious attempt to convert him and who is represented in the cantata quite clearly as a tempter. The temptation of Christ by Satan is obviously the model for this; and obviously too the *Apage!* has been transformed into a proud and desperate *No!* directed against false and flabby piety.[2]

Adrian's version differs from the original in the immeasurably greater spiritual pride and perverted heroism shown at the end. The hero of the Urfaustbook was in no such exalted and obdurate state of mind; the loop-hole left open in the sixteenth century was stopped up, it would seem, in the twentieth. But the idea that the body might redeem the soul by its agony took root in Mann's mind: salvation by suffering, extended in the Rilkean sense of utmost defeat producing victory, informed the final passage of the description of *D. Fausti Lament*, and a faint almost transcendental hope trembled in the air:

But what if the aesthetic paradox . . . were but a form of the religious paradox: that from the deepest depths of hopelessness hope is born, even if only in the shape of an almost inaudible question? That would be hope beyond hopelessness, the transcending of despair; not the

---

[1] English Faustbook, p. 228. I use the English version for the sake of the prose. I have altered 'would' to 'wil' and slightly emended the end, which P.F. did not translate accurately. Cf. Scheible, op. cit. Vol. II, pp. 1065 f.

[2] Mann, *Doktor Faustus*, pp. 743 f.

betrayal of it, but a miracle beyond all belief. Listen to the end. Listen with me. One group of instruments after another falls silent, and what remains is the high G of a cello, the last word, the last lingering note, slowly dissolving in *pianissimo-fermate*. Then all is over: silence and night. But the note that remains still vibrating in the silence, the note that is no longer there, that only the soul can hear, the dying fall of lament, is no longer that; it changes its meaning and stands like a light in the dark.[1]

One is almost forced, when faced with Thomas Mann's *Doctor Faustus*, to ponder the relative poetical value of the sixteenth- and twentieth-century versions. To begin with a truism: had it not been for the Urfaustbook there would have been no *Doctor Faustus*. There would also have been no heart-shaking description of hell and its torments, no tragic pact, no wonderful musical rendering of the final laments, no last speech of Leverkühn to his friends. In a word, all the most moving and poetical passages in Thomas Mann's novel derive directly from the Urfaustbook and are closely modelled on it textually. The greatness of the total impression is at least three parts due to the anonymous sixteenth-century author. This is an extraordinary case of dynamic inspiration, surely unparalleled in the history of literature: that a long-forgotten archaic text should force itself into the work of a highly sophisticated and gifted writer such as Thomas Mann, and carry all before it. What can the twentieth-century author offer to counterbalance that? He has certainly done a real service to the legend by bringing the Urfaustbook into circulation again enshrined in the pages of a strange and challenging novel; and he has further enriched it by re-creating the spiritual situation in penetrating words and phrases. There will always be those who, like Herder and like Heine, prefer primitive poetry to literary reconditioning; and for these Mann's utmost eloquence will never compensate for the directness and immediacy of the original version. But others will find greater beauty and depth in Leverkühn's *Lament* than in the text underlying it. There is and there can be no final verdict in a matter of this kind. Yet when all is said and done, one may take leave to doubt that three hundred years hence Mann's *Doctor Faustus* will have the mighty inspirational power which the Urfaustbook has had on him.

[1] Mann, *Doktor Faustus*, pp. 744f.

338

CONCLUSION

The sudden irruption of the Urfaustbook into modern times, its powers undiminished and its sombre lustre undimmed, may give some notion of the overwhelming effect it produced upon readers of the sixteenth century. Its compelling quality can be gauged by the fact that it forced itself upon Marlowe, insisting upon dramatization; and its tragic afflatus was such that it bent the literature of ceremonial magic to its purposes, transforming puerile invocations into a satanic performance entailing irremediable spiritual ruin. This highly imaginative intensification of the legendary data stamped it so indelibly as to resist the utmost in farcification, sensationalization, sophistication and contamination to which the Faustian organism was subjected during the sixteenth, seventeenth and eighteenth centuries; so that the lowest and the last of the traditional puppet-plays is still instinct with tragic life. To judge by the humdrum career of the Urfaustbook in Germany, where it ran through successive editions peaceably enough until Widman manhandled it to its doom, English prose and Elizabethan tragic vision were the decisive factors in releasing the dynamic element latent in the Faust-legend. But violence was also done to magical ritual in achieving this result. During the whole complex of Faustian events which ran their erratic course from 1587 to 1759, tragic mythology lorded it over ritual optimism and imposed its inexorable law upon it.

Yet ritual did not take this lying down. It can be seen fighting back in the comic scenes on the popular stage and in the puppet-plays, where Casper, by means of Faust's Black Book, brings the devils to heel. This is orthodox magical doctrine and did a good deal to lighten the gloom surrounding the figure of the doomed magician. Moreover legend made some concessions to humour too, and a close alliance occurred between both in the famous scene in which Faust chose his familiar spirit from a number of applicants for his superior speed. *The Black Raven*, claiming to be a Faustian ritual text, borrowed this notion from legend; the stage and puppet-play versions adopted it too; folkbook humour and ritual cocksureness collaborated to make a very good thing of it. Always

339

and inexorably defeated in the last scenes, ritual optimism never quite gave up.

It was not ritualism, however, but rationalism which, in the person of Lessing, brought up the big guns to vanquish tragedy. Poetically speaking, this was a complete failure, and it was not until Goethe in the wake of Schink fell back upon magical texts, invoking a tradition perennially hostile to tragedy, that the power of the pact was broken. It is therefore admissible to say that in Goethe's *Faust* ritual optimism at long last conquered the Faustian territory. But this is far indeed from being the whole story. Lessing and enlightenment were at least equally responsible for the altered religious attitude and a host of minor combatants contributed to the final victory.

For Goethe's *Faust* differs radically from Marlowe's (which was directly and simply inspired by P.F.'s translation of 'Spiess') in being the meeting-ground of so many Faustian and non-Faustian influences and sources as to be a supreme example of the assimi-lative powers of creative genius. His poem had deep roots in traditional soil, so deep as to draw up into itself many cognate themes of folk-poetry. But he also soaked up like a sponge notions, scenes and *motivs* originating in other minds and transformed them by that spiritual alchemy which is the fascinating function of poetry. Inspired, indeed beglamoured, by the puppet-plays, he did not neglect the more prosaic folkbooks; grandiose dreams dreamt by Paracelsus were merged with the stuff and nonsense found in magical texts; hints from *Macbeth* and a snatch of song from Ophelia fused with the grotesqueness of a Löwe and the tuneful-ness of a Schink. Hans Sachsian humour enlivened his scene; domestic tragedy and fallen females melted into ballad-poetry and ended with echoes from medieval *aubades*. It was in this fashion that *Part I* came into being. The pattern of the puppet-plays reinforced by the Faustbooks underlies *Part II*. The scenes at court with their magical displays, the feat of necromancy, the super-natural journey, Helen of Troy, the *katabasis* in the *Classical Witches' Sabbath*, the mating between Faust and Helen, their strange little offspring, the magical battles, the final remorse; it is all on lines long since laid down. But Weidmann was probably behind Mephisto's court-quackery; Hamilton certainly conditioned the scene of invocation; Marlowe and Klingemann had both greeted Helen earlier; Schink had satirized Fichtean philosophy and had made a young girl beloved by Faust one of the agents of his final redemption. Paracelsus had created Homunculus, and Byron had died at Missolonghi. Last but not least, the ghouls sang a song from *Hamlet*, and Marlowe's clock ran down. Added to all this, part of the material assimilated in *Faust II* was Goethe's *Faust I*. That he did not assimilate more may well have been due to the fact that Schöne and Rosenkranz had been beforehand with him here, so that he had recourse to a parody of his earlier style in Act II in order to even things up. But he fell into the same trap himself when he allowed Gretchen in heaven to plagiarize from Gretchen on earth.

Otherwise none of all this is plagiarism. Sometimes deliberately, sometimes unconsciously, Goethe wove his web from legends, folk-poetry, occult tradition, Elizabethan drama and contemporary collaborators. It was all grist to his mill; everything was trans-figured and became his, even the shoddiest material. The shoddiest of all were the disreputable Black Books, so completely transformed as to be totally unrecognizable. Nevertheless they played a sub-terranean part in exploding the tragic tradition associated with the name of Faust. When enumerating the sources and influences which helped to shape Goethe's world-renowned masterpiece, the Christianized and Faustianized ritual text called *Magia Naturalis et Innaturalis* ought to be given a place; an ambiguous, shadowy, ghostlike place perhaps; for Goethe himself dismissed it con-temptuously as 'full of the most reasoned nonsense'. This is a mild judgment, since it is an illiterate production; blighted by the basest utilitarianism, grotesque, greedy and utterly devoid of poetical imagination. But it appealed throughout to divine grace, and particularly in the matter of the making and breaking of pacts.

Both Marlowe and Goethe irrigated their Faust dramas with ceremonial magic. The Elizabethan dramatist satanized the sub-ject; the German poet disinfected it; and, except for Schink (who may have owed his conditional pact to the gipsy puppet-play) there is no other trace of this element in the literary *Fausts*. The tragic poets could well spare it in view of its childish optimism; but its absence from 'salvationist' productions probably contributed to their poverty-stricken effect. It is a rather remarkable fact that Goethe's is the only name which can be put forward with any conviction when considering the salvation of Faust. Lessing's Berlin Scenario, the wistful fragment bequeathed by Lenz and

Müller's unpublished Roman *Faust* evade critical judgment. We are left contemplating Weidmann, Schreiber, Schink, Schöne's second drama, Holtei, Pfizer, Rosenkranz, Hoffmann, Braunthal, Wolfram, Schmid, Stolte, Schilf, Hango and Avenarius. And what, with the best will in the world, can be said in their favour? A consolation prize might be awarded to Pfizer and Wolfram for flashes of poetry; an honourable mention made of the lofty sentiments uttered by Hango and Avenarius; Schink had some respectable passages and a host of 'good ideas'; and Holtei a memorable moment with Helena. But otherwise they are all negligible; and though (with the exception of Stolte) they have proved not unentertaining in a way, I fear that, having lived their little hour again in this book, they will sink back into the oblivion they so richly deserve. The tragic writers on the other hand cannot be dismissed so lightly. They include Müller, Klinger, Soden, Benkowitz, Chamisso, Schöne's first drama, Grillparzer, Klingemann, Voss, Grabbe, Lenau, Nürnberger, Heine and Thomas Mann. Relegating Benkowitz, Schöne and Voss to the waste-paper basket containing Weidmann and his consorts and putting Soden and Klingemann in the same category as Holtei slightly below Avenarius, we are left with two powerful Storm and Stress writers, one gifted and two very great poets; one dramatist of outstanding renown and another of unequal but arresting power; a justly famous contemporary novelist and an unjustly forgotten, uniquely original poem.

Broadly speaking, these writers were carrying on the Marlovian tradition; but for the most part quite unconsciously; for it is a strange feature of the fortunes of Faust in Germany that Marlowe seems to have been almost totally disregarded by the Faustian poets. Goethe did not read him until 1818, ten years after Part I was published, when Achim von Arnim sent him Wilhelm Müller's translation made in 1815, with an introduction by Arnim himself. This had been written contemporaneously with his Faustian episode in *The Guardians of the Crown*, which was certainly innocent of Marlovian influence. Scheible printed Müller's translation with Arnim's introduction in the fifth volume of *Das Kloster* in 1847, where Heine saw it. But he was much more interested in the Urfaustbook and Simrock's version of the puppet-play than in Marlowe; and although other translations of *The Tragical History of Doctor Faustus* appeared subsequently (1856 and 1870), their effect upon the German Faustian writers is to seek. Nevertheless the Urfaustbook and Marlowe through the medium of the puppet-plays were indirectly responsible for Lessing, Goethe and their innumerable successors.

It is possible to distinguish four main trends in the entangled situation which developed after Lessing. His influence on the 'salvationists' was decisive; but, had Goethe not adopted his reorientation of the legend, it could only have been described as singularly unfortunate. Klinger represents an impressive pessimistic reaction, introducing a vast historical background and the workings of an inexorable nemesis. But those who imitated him, a Soden, a Schöne and a Voss, debased his conception. It was the same story with Goethe's *Part I*; largely owing to the Gretchen tragedy, this produced havoc in the shape of unwitting parodies, admittedly the sincerest form of flattery, but nothing else. Nor did the reaction against *Part II*, in so far as it was a deliberate reaction, prove fruitful; for the variant versions of the salvation, aiming at the sublime achieved the ridiculous; Heine failed, though in a fascinating manner, to wed the traditional tragedy with the requirements of Her Majesty's Theatre; and Vischer's brilliant parody of Goethe, effective enough as a protest, cannot compete with the poem.

Meanwhile another influence, combined of two elements, had been discernible in Grabbe's tragedy: Byronism and Don Juanism. In a much more intangible way it almost seemed as if the history of the Urfaustbook, P.F., Marlowe and the German stage were repeating itself. Goethe's *Part I*, creatively speaking still-born in the land of its birth, fired the mind of Shelley, who brought it to the notice of Byron; but it seems to have been an oral translation made by Monk Lewis when he visited Byron in Italy which inspired the notion of a 'witch-drama' materializing as *Manfred*. This clearly affected the Alpine scenes in Grabbe's Faustian drama; but Byronism rather than Manfredism wedded to Mozart's *Don Giovanni* was at work in Lenau's mind when he composed his *Faust*, and is accountable for the melancholy, the music and the despair. Not, however, for the tragic vision; that was Lenau's own; and at this distance of time it can be seen to mark a turning-point in the history of the legend.

It was the unquestioning belief in its fearful assumptions that made the Urfaustbook such a dynamic force and Marlowe's poetical statement such an enduring factor in its survival. That faith was shattered by the age of reason. Satan, eternal damnation and hell lost their foothold in reality and have so far not regained the ground given up. But there can be no salvation where no damnation looms. Symbolism was called in to mediate between a tragic myth and a noble, humane and enlightened ethic from Lessing onwards down through Goethe and beyond. Symbolism proved strangely recalcitrant; but, mated with irony, finally did Goethe's bidding and seemed to explode the myth in a manner possibly partaking of mirage, but at least devoid of the bogus element manifest in Ithuriel, Earth Souls, Star Spirits, Wandering Jews and the Head of Humanity.

Yet, if it was hard enough in all conscience to save Faust from a non-existent peril, it was even harder to commit him to the flames of a non-existent hell, and only Klinger and Grabbe can be compared (at a respectful distance) to the puppet-plays in this respect. They do not come within sight or sound of Marlowe; whereas Thomas Mann, by representing the hero's fate as subjectively but not objectively real, intensified the effect of the Urfaustbook in some passages, but restricted it considerably on the whole by introducing the *motiv* of madness. Chamisso, Lenau and Nürnberger avoided the traditional ending, to the great advantage of their poems; but only Lenau, instinctively reacting against Goethe, saw the tragic truth behind the mythological symbolism. His interpretation of the doom lying in wait for the Faustian spirit is a great answer to Goethe's apotheosis of the striving soul of humanity, the only one of its kind made in Germany; and for over a hundred years the only one made at all.

The challenge has now been carried a step further in the land of intellectual lucidity and icy moral courage by Paul Valéry in his unfinished Faustian comedy *Lust*, which goes straight as a die to the fallacy underlying symbolical lip-service to the power and prestige of Satan to-day:

Faust. Écoute. Je ne puis te cacher que tu ne tiens plus dans le monde la grande situation que tu occupais jadis.

Méphistophélès. Penses-tu? . . . [. . .]

Faust. Tu ne fais guère peur. L'Enfer n'apparaît plus qu'au dernier acte. Tu ne hantes plus les esprits des hommes de ce temps. Il y a bien quelques petits groupes d'amateurs et des populations arriérées. . . . Mais tes méthodes sont surannées, ta physique ridicule. . . .[1]

And then comes the fearful comment on whither the Faustian spirit has led humanity, in which the prophecy made by Lenau is seen to be coming true in the atomic age:

Faust. [. . .] Pendant que tu te reposais ainsi dans la paresse de ton éternité, sur tes procédés de l'An I, l'esprit de l'homme, déniaisé par toi-même! . . . a fini par s'attaquer aux dessous de la Création. . . . Figure-toi qu'ils ont retrouvé dans l'intime des corps, et comme en deçà de leur réalité, le vieux CHAOS . . .

Méphistophélès. Le CHAOS. . . . Celui que j'ai connu? Ce n'est pas possible . . .

Faust. On pourra te montrer ceci . . .

Méphistophélès. Le CHAOS . . .

Faust. Oui. Le Chaos, le vieux Chaos, ce désordre premier dans les contradictions ineffables duquel espace, temps, lumière, possibilités, virtualités étaient à l'état futur . . .

Méphistophélès. Ils ont retrouvé le CHAOS. . . . J'étais Archange![. . .]

Faust. [. . .] Songe, songe, Satan, que ce changement extraordinaire peut t'atteindre toi-même, dans ta redoutable Personne. . . . C'est le sort même du Mal qui est en jeu. . . . Sais-tu que c'est peut-être la fin de l'âme? Cette âme qui s'imposait à chacun comme le sentiment tout-puissant d'une valeur incomparable et indestructible, désir inépuisable et pouvoir de jouir, de souffrir, d'être soi, que rien ne pouvait altérer, elle est une valeur dépréciée. L'individu se meurt. Il se noie dans le nombre. Les différences s'évanouissent devant l'accumulation des êtres. Le vice et la vertu ne sont plus que des distinctions imperceptibles, qui se fondent dans la masse de ce qu'ils appellent 'Le matériel humain'. La mort n'est plus qu'une des propriétés statistiques de cette affreuse matière vivante. Elle y perd sa dignité et sa signification . . . classique. Mais l'immortalité des âmes suit nécessairement le sort même de la mort, qui la définissait et lui donnait son sens et son prix infini.[. . .]

Tout le système dont tu étais l'une des pièces essentielles n'est plus que ruine et dissolution. Tu dois avouer toi-même que tu te sens égaré, et comme dessaisi, parmi tous ces gens nouveaux qui pèchent sans le savoir, sans y attacher d'importance, qui n'ont aucune idée de l'Eternité, qui risquent leurs vies dix fois par jour,

[1] P. Valéry, '*Mon Faust*' (*Ebauches*), Paris, 1946, pp. 44ff. Omission marks are the author's, except those in square brackets, which are mine.

pour jouir de leurs neuves machines, qui font mille prestiges que
ta magie n'a jamais rêvé d'accomplir, et qui sont mis à la portée
des enfants, des idiots. . . . Et qui font produire à ces miracles un
mouvement d'affaires inconcevable. . . .[1]

'Un mouvement d'affaires inconcevable'; perhaps only a French-
man could say so much in five words and say it with such austerity
and restraint; nor did Valéry develop the theme, swerving off in
Gallic vein to depict in his comedy the machinations of Mephisto
against the virtue of Faust's innocent young secretary, Lust. But
he had said enough to indicate a crisis in the dramatic history of
Faust in literature, if this history is interpreted (and I think it
must be) as a conflict between religion and rationalism as to the
ultimate fate of the Faustian spirit, the desire for infinite knowledge. Religion won a signal victory with Marlowe; rationalism,
mythologically disguised, triumphed with Goethe; Lenau foresaw
and Valéry noted whither that triumph was tending. The deep
superstitious fear felt by 'Spiess' for uncompromising intellectual-
ism is now seen to have been, if not justified, then at least based
on a highly prophetic instinct. This conflict is not yet resolved;
the two forces are still engaged in what appears to be a life-and-
death struggle.

Let us return from such sobering speculations to the more
pleasing regions of literature and the fortunes of Faust over a
period of 360 years. The detailed study of this development has
not impaired Goethe's unique position as the outstanding saviour
of Faust, nor detracted one iota from the beauty of his masterpiece.
But it has shown how much he was conditioned by his age, how
much of the spade-work involved in saving his hero was done for
him by others and what a wealth of stimulating notions he owed to
his predecessors and contemporaries, those numerous now forgotten tributaries to his mighty stream. It flowed on majestically,
fertilizing the land of poetry but not much enriching the Faustian
territory stretching beyond it into the future. Where Goethe has
so far failed, Marlowe most signally triumphed, being prepotent
and pre-eminent as far as creative inspiration goes and moreover
the master of accents so sublimely tragic as to transcend in his
great moments Goethe and everyone else. After Goethe came
Lenau, whose vision of life, let alone his wonderful lyrical genius,

---

[1] Valéry, op. cit. pp. 54 ff.

should ensure him a conspicuous position on the Faustian roll of honour, as a foeman worthy of Goethe's steel.

There are others who, like Lenau himself, have suffered undue neglect because they were within the orbit of radiance shed by Goethe and have therefore been overlooked by those who are blinded by his light. But the manifest imperfections of all the *Fausts* produced from Marlowe down to Thomas Mann are also accountable for this state of affairs. Rough justice has on the whole been done to everyone but Lenau. Yet should a tragic writer of genius arise and journey along the road to Faust as Goethe did before, what a wonderful use he might make of those striking or interesting and often beautiful moments and scenes scattered on the way. Basing himself on tradition, but leaving Marlowe, Goethe and Lenau intact in their poetical integrity and for obvious reasons Grabbe too, he would still have an almost embarrassing choice of fruitful moments and ideas at his disposal. He might consider beginning with a pandemonium; and he could find no better model than Schink's (with Ithuriel's part cut out). Müller's sky-larking undergraduates, if kept within due bounds, make a telling contrast with the desperate hero and the eerie devils invoked in that wild scene in the gambling-den. And surely the notion of testing the devils by their speed (as long as Lessing was short-circuited) would appeal to a lover of tradition, who might also wish to include as comic relief the inimitable magic circle in which Casper summoned and dismissed the flustered fiends with such lightning quickness. Ah, he would need to be a genius indeed to mix comedy and tragedy with that deep simplicity the puppet-showmen possessed. It would be considerably easier to make use of Wolfram's invocation of the dead; and perhaps the weird dialogue between Aristotle and Faust, so laconically sketched by Lessing, might come into its own at last. And if, after all, the tragic writer felt that he could not ignore the Gretchen-*motiv*, he could choose between a scene on the lines of Avenarius and the strangely sinister parting which Grillparzer described. And should Goethe and Heine between them have bedevilled him with witch-craft, then Nürnberger's ghostly and ghastly Sabbath should be made the basis of his. Would he dare to give us a glimpse of Mephisto taking a dish of tea with the angels on the stars? Perhaps only a Heine could safely be trusted with that; but the enchanted Greek island and the terrible transformation it underwent are there, waiting for a tragic genius to immortalize them in verse. With infinite caution he might make something of Holtei's Helen; but he would shun Klingemann's and Avenarius' like the plague. Whatever else he discarded, however, Leviathan's great speech of indictment at the end of Klinger's novel would almost certainly not be passed by. Then Chamisso's last words might be heard together with the traditional striking of the clock; the forlorn voice of Lenz's Faust drifting up from the underworld; and the faint and far-away message of hope uttered by Thomas Mann.

The last sound dies away; the vision fades; from across the gulf of centuries Mephisto speaks the epilogue:

Ah, Faustus, if there were a ladder stretching from earth to heaven, made of swords instead of rungs, so that I should be cut into a thousand pieces with every step I took, yet would I still strive to reach the summit, so that I might behold the face of God but once more, after which I would willingly be damned again to all eternity.

BIBLIOGRAPHY

It would need a volume to list the critical studies written around and about Goethe's *Faust*. I have therefore restricted the bibliography almost entirely to historical and other sources and the texts themselves, as the present book is largely based on these. References to other works consulted will be found in the footnotes.

SOURCES

Bianquis, G., *Faust à travers quatre siècles*, Paris, 1935.

Engel, K., *Zusammenstellung der Faust-Schriften vom 16. Jahrhundert bis Mitte 1884*, Oldenburg, 1885.

Geissler, H. W., *Gestaltungen des Faust*, 3 vols., München, 1927.

Kiesewetter, K., *Faust in der Geschichte und Tradition*, Leipzig, 1893.

Palmer, P. M., and More, R. P., *The Sources of the Faust Tradition from Simon Magus to Lessing*, New York, 1936.

Peter, F., *Die Literatur der Faustsage bis Ende des Jahres 1848*, Leipzig, 1849.

Petsch, R., *Lessings Faustdichtung*, Heidelberg, 1911.

Scheible, J., *Das Kloster*, 12 vols., Stuttgart, 1846–9.

Theens, K., *Doktor Johann Faust, Geschichte der Faustgestalt vom 16. Jahrhundert bis zur Gegenwart*, Meisenheim am Glan, 1948.

Tille, A., *Die Faustsplitter in der Literatur des 16. bis 18. Jahrhunderts*, Berlin, 1900.

Warkentin, R., *Nachlänge der Sturm- und Drangperiode in Faustdichtungen*, München, 1896.

Wendriner, K. G., *Die Faustdichtung vor, neben und nach Goethe*, 4 vols., Berlin, 1914.

GERMAN FAUSTBOOKS IN CHRONOLOGICAL ORDER

Historia von D. Johann Fausten, dem weitbeschreyten Zauberer und Schwarzkünstler . . . Gedruckt zu Franckfurt am Mayn, durch Johann Spiess, 1587; 2nd ed., 1588; other editions down to 1598.

Ein wahrhaffte und erschröckliche Geschicht von D. Johann Fausten, dem weitbeschreiten Zauberer und Schwarzkünstler . . . Getruckt zu Tübingen, bey Alexander Hock, 1588; rhymed version.

Des durch seine Zauber-kunst bekannten Christoph Wagner's (Weyland gewesenen Famuli des Weltberuffenen Ertz-Zauberers D. Johann Faustens) Leben und Thaten . . . Weyland von Friderich Schotus Tolet, in Teutscher Sprache beschrieben, Berlin, 1714; first edition, 1594; purporting to be a translation from the Spanish.

Wahrhafftige Historia von den grewlichen vnd abschewlichen Sünden vnd Lastern, auch von vielen wunderbarlichen vnd seltzamen ebentheuren: So D. JOHANNES FAUSTUS Ein weitberuffener Schwartzkünstler vnd Ertz-Zaüberer, durch seine Schwartzkunst, biss an seinen erschrecklichen end hat getrieben . . . durch Georg Rudolff Widman, Hamburg, 1599.

J. N. Pfitzer's version of Widman, Nürnberg, 1674.

Des durch die gantze Welt beruffenen Ertz-Schwartz-Künstlers und Zauberers Doctor Johann Fausts mit dem Teufel aufgerichteten Bündniss . . . Druck befördert von einem Christlich Meynenden, Franckfurt und Leipzig, 1728.

Doctor Faust, Fliegendes Blatt aus Köln: a ballad, first published 1818.

FAUST IN ENGLAND IN CHRONOLOGICAL ORDER

A Ballad of the life and deathe of Doctor Faustus, the great Cunngerer, London, February, 1588–9.

The Historie of the damnable life, and deserued death of Doctor Iohn Faustus . . . translated into English by P. F. Gent., London, 1592.

Marlowe, C., *The Tragical History of Doctor Faustus* (? 1592); first quarto 1604; then 1616, 1624, 1631, 1663.

The Second Report of Doctor John Faustus, containing his appearances and the deeds of Wagner . . . London, 1594; 2nd ed., 1680.

The Judgment of God Shewed Upon one John Faustus, Doctor in Divinity, London, 1675, a ballad.

Mountfort, W., *The Life and Death of Doctor Faustus, made into a Farce* (1684); ed. Francke, Heilbronn, 1886.

Thurmond, J., *Harlequin Doctor Faustus,* London, 1724; a ballet-pantomime.

Thurmond, J., *The Miser: or Wagner and Abericock,* London, 1727; a ballet-pantomime.

A dramatical entertainment, called the Necromancers, or Harlequin Doctor Faustus, London, 1768; a satire on Thurmond.

Logemann, H., *The English Faustbook of 1592,* Gand, 1900.

Rohde, R., *Das englische Faustbuch und Marlowe's Tragödie,* Halle, 1910.

POPULAR DRAMA AND PUPPET-PLAYS

A. *Historical*

Beaumont, C. W., *Puppets and the Puppet Stage*, London, 1938.

Bittner, K., *Beiträge zur Geschichte des Volksschauspiels vom Doctor Faust*, Reichenberg in Bresgau, 1922. (Prager deutsche Studien, Heft 27.)

Bruinier, J. W., *Faust vor Goethe*, Halle, Vol. i, 1894; Vol. ii, 1910.

[Collier, J. P.] *Punch and Judy*, 2nd ed., London, 1828.

Creizenach, W., *Versuch einer Geschichte des Volksschauspiels vom Doctor Faust*, Halle, 1878.

Schade, O., *Faust vom Ursprung bis zur Verklärung durch Goethe*, Berlin, 1912.

Tille, A., *Das katholische Fauststück, die Faustkomödien-ballade und das Zillerthaler Doctor-Faustspiel*. (Zeitschrift für Bücherfreunde, 1906–1907.)

Tille, A., *Moderne Faustspiele*. (Zeitschrift für vergleichende Literaturgeschichte, Weimar, 1896.)

B. *Texts*

ed. Bielschofsky, *Das Schwierlingsche Puppenspiel*. (Bericht über die königliche Gewerbsschule in Brieg, 1881–2.)

ed. Engel, *Das Volksschauspiel Doctor Johann Faust*, Oldenburg, 1874. (Proved by Bruinier to be spurious.)

ed. Engel, *Doctor Faust. Schauspiel in drei Akten*. (Deutsche Puppenkomödien, VIII. The showman was Wiepking.)

ed. Hagen, *Das Berliner Puppenspiel*. (Germania, 1841. The showmen were Schütz and Dreher.)

ed. Hamm, *Das Puppenspiel vom Doctor Faust*, Leipzig, 1850. (The showman was Bonneschky.)

ed. Hein, *Das Prettauer Puppenspiel*. (Das Wissen für Alle, 1901.)

ed. Kossmann, *Das niederländische Faustspiel des 17. Jahrhunderts*, Haag, 1900.

ed. Kralik and Winter, *Das niederösterreichische Puppenspiel*. (Deutsche Puppenspiele, Wien, 1885.)

ed. Kraus, *Das böhmische Puppenspiel vom Doctor Faust*, Breslau, 1892.

ed. Lübke, *Die Berliner Fassung des Puppenspiels vom Doctor Faust*. (Zeitschrift für deutsches Altertum, 1886. Based on the texts of the showmen Linde, Wolfram and Schlüssel.)

ed. Petsch, *Das fränkische Puppenspiel vom Doctor Faust*. (Zeitschrift des Vereins für Volkskunde, 1905. The showman was Ludwig Schmidt.)

ed. Schade, *Doctor Faust. Ein Puppenspiel.* (Weimarisches Jahrbuch für deutsche Sprache, Literatur und Kunst, 1856. Based on two texts, one *c.* 1810, the other 1824.)

ed. Scheible, (1) *Johann Faust. Ein Trauerspiel in 3 Theilen und 9 Aufzügen.* (In *Das Kloster*, v, 1847. Augsburg version; possibly from Burkhart's puppet-theatre in the 1840s.)

ed. Scheible, (2) *Johann Faust oder der gefoppte Doctor. Ein Lustspiel mit Arien.* (*Das Kloster*, v. This is almost identical with J. F. Schink, *Der neue Faust*, 1778: Augsburg version.)

ed. Scheible, (3) *Faust. Eine Geschichte der Vorzeit. Zu einem Schauspiele in drei Akten bearbeitet von Christoph Winters für das Puppentheater in Cöln.* (*Das Kloster*, v.)

ed. Scheible, (4) *Doctor Faust oder der grosse Negromantist. Schauspiel mit Gesang in fünf Aufzügen.* (*Das Kloster*, v. First published by von Below in 1832. The showman was Geisselbrecht.)

ed. Scheible, (5) *Der weltberühmte Doctor Faust. Schauspiel in fünf Auf zügen.* (*Das Kloster*, v. Strasbourg version.)

ed. Scheible, (6) *Doctor Johann Faust. Schauspiel in zwei Theilen.* (*Das Kloster*, v. Ulm version.)

ed. Tille, *Der Plagwitzer Faust.* (Deutsche Puppenkomödien, x.)

[Simrock, K.] *Doktor Johannes Faust. Puppenspiel in vier Aufzügen*, Bonn, 1846. (A rhymed synthetic version.)

Literary Fausts

I give the first editions throughout unless they are undiscoverable. Where no place of publication is given, I have been unable to procure the text.

Anon., *Faust der grosse Mann oder seine Wanderungen durch die Welt mit dem Teufel bis in die Hölle*, 2 vols., Wien und Prag, 1798.

Anon., *Dr. Faust im Reiche der Todten. Ein recht romantisches Nachspiel zu allen romantischen Tragödieen des Namens. Von einem Sachwalter der abgedienten Seelen*, Berlin, 1817. (16 pages.)

Anon., *Der dritte Theil des Faust.* (Phönix, ed. Duller, Frankfurt am Main, 1838.)

Arnim, A. v., *Die Kronenwächter*, Berlin, 1817. (Book 2, 1.)

Avenarius, F., *Faust. Ein Spiel*, München, 1919.

Baggesen, J., *Der vollendete Faust.* (*Poetische Werke in deutscher Sprache*, III, Leipzig, 1836.)

Baumbach, R., *Der Adept.* (*Neue Lieder eines fahrenden Gesellen*, Leipzig, 1880.)

Bechstein, L., *Faustus. Ein Gedicht*, Leipzig, 1833.

[Benkowitz, K. F.] *Die Jubelfeier der Hölle, oder Faust der jüngere. Ein Drama zum Ende des achtzehnten Jahrhunderts*, Berlin, 1801.

B.[raun] von B.[raunthal], *Faust. Eine Tragödie*, Leipzig, 1835.

[Brennglas, A.] Glassbrenner, *pseud.*, *Elisabeth und Faust.* (Lustiger Volkskalender für 1861, Leipzig, 1861.)

Chamisso, A. v., *Faust. Ein Versuch.* (Musenalmanach, Berlin, ed. Chamisso and Varnhagen, 1804.)

Czilski, C. St., *Faust. Ein dramatisches Gedicht*, Halle, 1843.

Dammas, K. H., *Faust*, 1865.

Dehnike, R., *Der neue Faust.* (*Gedichte*, Berlin, 1866.)

[Engel, J. J.] *Der travestierte Dr. Faust*, Berlin, 1806.

F. G., *Doctor Faust. Ein Schattenriss*, Danzig, 1797.

Fellner, F., *Der neue Faust*, 1902.

Fitger, A., *Fausts Schatten. An Charles Darwin, 12. Februar*, 1879. (*Winternächte. Gedichte*, Berlin, 1881.)

Geibel, E., *Fausts Jugendgesang.* (*Neue Gedichte*, 8th ed., Stuttgart, 1865.)

Geibel, E., *Historische Studien.* (*Neue Gedichte*, 8th ed., Stuttgart, 1865.)

Goethe, J. W. v., *Urfaust*, 1775; ed. E. Schmidt, Weimar, 1887.

Goethe, J. W. v., *Faust. Ein Fragment*, Weimar, 1790.

Goethe, J. W. v., *Faust, der Tragödie erster Theil*, Weimar, 1808.

Goethe, J. W. v., *Helena. Klassisch-romantische Phantasmagorie*, Weimar, 1827.

Goethe, J. W. v., *Faust, der Tragödie zweiter Theil*, Weimar, 1832.

Grabbe, C. D., *Don Juan und Faust. Eine Tragödie*, Frankfurt am Main, 1829.

Grillparzer, F., *Faust. Ein dramatisches Fragment.* (*Nachgelassene Schriften*, Leipzig, 1855.)

Gutzkow, C., *Hamlet in Wittenberg. Dramatische Phantasie.* (Allgemeine Theaterrevue, Stuttgart, 1835.)

Hamilton, A., *L'enchanteur Faustus.* (*Oeuvres*, Paris, 1771.)

Hango, H., *Faust und Prometheus*, Wien, 1895.

Harring, H. P., *Faust im Gewande der Zeit. Ein Schattenriss mit Lichte.* (Literarisches Museum, Leipzig, 1831.)

Heine, H., *Doktor Faust. Ein Tanzpoem*, Hamburg, 1851.

Hoffmann, J. D., *Faust. Eine Tragödie von Goethe. Fortgesetzt von J. D. Hoffmann*, Leipzig, 1833.

Holtei, K. v., *Doktor Johannes Faust. Melodrama in drei Akten.* (Beiträge für das Königstädter Theater, Vol. 2, Wiesbaden, 1832.)

Jacobsen, E., *Faust und Gretchen*, Berlin, 1858.

Jahn, H. E., *Faust. Eine Satire*, Rostock, 1880.

[Kalisch, D.] *Faust, der zu spät bekehrte Demokrat. Furchtbare Tragödie in 6 langen Abtheilungen, der Kurze wegen in 3 Akte zusammengezogen. Frei nach Sr. Excellenz Herrn Wolfgang von Goethe, von D.K.*, Berlin, 1853.

Keim, F., *Mephistopheles in Rom*, 1890.

Keller, G., *Modernster Faust um 1845. (Sämtliche Werke*, Bern, Vol. 14, 1936.)

Klingemann, E. A. F., *Faust. Ein Trauerspiel in fünf Akten*, Leipzig und Altenburg, 1815.

[Klinger, F. M.] *Fausts Leben, Thaten und Höllenfahrt*, St Petersburg, 1791.

Komareck, J. N., *Faust von Mainz. Ein Gemälde aus der Mitte des fünfzehnten Jahrhunderts, in vier Aufzügen*, Leipzig, 1794.

Kotzebue, A. v., *Die redenden Taschen.* (Die Grille, Königsberg, 1811.)

Lenau, N., *Faust. Ein Gedicht*, Stuttgart und Tübingen, 1836. Revised version, 1840.

Lenz, J. M. R., *Die Höllenrichter.* (Deutsches Museum, Leipzig, 1777.)

Lessing, G. E., *Szene aus Faust.* (Siebzehnter Literaturbrief, Berlin, 1759.)

Lessing, G. E., *Berliner Szenario. (Theatralischer Nachlass 2*, Berlin, 1786.)

Leuburg, A., *Faust. Ein dramatisches Gedicht*, Berlin, 1860.

Linde, K. A., *Faust. Dritter Theil zu Goethes Faust*, 1887.

Löwe, J. F., *Die Walpurgis Nacht*, Hamburg und Leipzig, 1756.

Lutze, A., *Faust in Auerbachs Keller. Lustige dramatische Szene*, Berlin, 1839. Fifteen pages.

Manitius, K., *Ueber Göthes Faust.* (Gedichte, Dresden, 1856.)

Mann, T., *Doktor Faustus. Das Leben des deutschen Tonsetzers Adrian Leverkühn, erzählt von einem Freunde*, Stockholm, 1947.

Mann, T., *Die Entstehung des Doktor Faustus, Roman eines Romans*, Amsterdam, 1949.

Mecklenburg, A., *Faust*, 1860.

Mölling, C. E., *Fausts Tod. Eine Tragödie in fünf Aufzügen*, Philadelphia, 1864.

Moeser, A., *Doktor Faust in Salzburg*, 1864.

Müller, A., *Faust. Tragödie in fünf Acten. Als zweiter Theil zu Göthes Faust*, Leipzig, 1869.

Müller, A., *Doktor Fausts Ende*, 1887.

Müller, J. F., *Situation aus Fausts Leben*, Mannheim, 1776.

Müller, J. F., *Fausts Leben dramatisiert. Erster Theil*, Mannheim, 1778.

Nürnberger, J. E., *Faust junior. Dramatische Skizze. (Ernste Dichtungen*, Kempten, 1841.)

[Nürnberger, W.] Solitar, M., *pseud.*, *Faust. Ein Gedicht*, Berlin, 1842. Second edition called *Josephus Faustus* and brought out under author's name, Landsberg, 1847.

Pfizer, G., *Faustische Scenen.* (Morgenblatt für gebildete Stände, Tübingen, 1831.)

Platen, A. v., *Fausts Gebet*, 1820. (*Gesammelte Werke*, Stuttgart und Tübingen, 1839.)

Rosenkranz, K., *Geistlich Nachspiel zur Tragödie Faust*, Leipzig, 1831.

Scheerer, Th., *Stauf. Eine Dichtung*, Berlin, 1839.

Schiff, D., *Johann Faust in Paris, 1463.* (*Novellen und nicht Novellen*, Berlin, 1835.)

Schilf, H., *Faust. Tragödie in fünf Acten*, Leipzig und St Petersburg, 1891.

Schink, J. F., *Doktor Faust. Ein komisches Duodrama.* (Reichard's Theaterjournal für Deutschland, Gotha, 1778.)

Schink, J. F., *Der neue Doktor Faust, eine Plaisanterie mit Gesang in zwei Aufzügen.* (Zum Behuf des neuen Theaters, Salzburg, 1782.)

Schink, J. F., *Prolog zu einem dramatischen Gedicht Doktor Faust.* (Berlinisches Archiv der Zeit und ihres Geschmacks, Berlin, 1795.)

Schink, J. F., *Doktor Fausts Bund mit der Hölle.* (Berlinisches Archiv der Zeit und ihres Geschmacks, Berlin, 1796.)

Schink, J. F., *Doktor Faust. Romanze aus einer noch ungedruckten Oper.* (Becker's Almanach und Taschenbuch, Leipzig, 1800.)

Schink, J. F., *Johann Faust, Dramatische Phantasie, nach einer Sage des sechzehnten Jahrhunderts*, 2 vols., Berlin und Züllichau, 1804.

Schmid, U. A., *Faust.* (*Blüthen einer Weltenschauung*, Jena, 1874.)

[Schmid, X.] Faber, Tertullian, *pseud.*, *Der neue Faust*, Rastatt, 1851.

Schmitt, L., *Doktor Johann Faust*, 1926.

Schöne, C. C. L., *Faust, eine romantische Tragödie*, Berlin, 1809.

Schöne, C. C. L., *Fortsetzung des Faust von Goethe. Der Tragödie zweiter Theil*, Berlin, 1823.

[Schreiber, A. W.] *Scenen aus Fausts Leben*, Offenbach, 1792.

Seidel, J. G., *Dr. Faust am Riederberge.* (Gedenke mein! Wien, 1833.)

Seybold, W., *Der umgekehrte Faust oder Frosch's Jugendjahre. Fragment*, Reutlingen, 1816.

Soden, J. H. v., *Doktor Faust. Volksschauspiel in 5 Akten*, Hamburg, 1797.

Stolte, F. L., *Faust. Dramatisch-didaktisches Gedicht in vier Theilen*, Hamburg, 1870.

Tieck, L., *Anti-Faust oder Geschichte eines dummen Teufels. Ein Lustspiel in fünf Aufzügen mit einem Prologe und Epiloge*. 1801. (*Nachgelassene Schriften*, Leipzig, 1855.)

Trautmann, P. F., *Ein moderner Faust. Zauberposse mit Gesang und Tanz*, Berlin, 1854.

Valéry, P., *Mon Faust.* (*Ébauches*), Paris, 1946.

[Vischer, F. T.] *Faust. Der Tragödie dritter Theil. Treu im Geiste des zweiten Theils des Goetheschen Faust gedichtet von Deutobold Symbolizetti Allegoriowitsch Mystifizinsky*, Tübingen, 1862. Revised version 1886 with author's name.

Vogl, J. N., *Doctor Fausts Kellerfahrten*. (Schenken- und Kellersagen. Altes und Neues. Wien, 1860.)

Vogt, N., *Der Färberhof oder die Buchdruckerei in Mainz*. (Die Ruinen am Rhein, Frankfurt am Main, 1809.)

Voss, J. v., *Faust. Trauerspiel mit Gesang und Tanz*, Berlin, 1823.

[Weidmann, P.] *Johann Faust. Ein allegorisches Drama in 5 Aufzügen*, München, 1775.

[Wolfram, L. H.] Marlow, F., *pseud.*, *Faust. Ein dramatisches Gedicht in drei Abschnitten*, Leipzig, 1839.

Zapf, G., *Fausts Jugend und Ahasvers Tod*, 1888.

INDEX

Characters in the works discussed are printed in italics.

A

Aaron, 7
Abericock, Akercocke, 61
Aciel, 134
Actaeon, 23
Aeschylus, 124
'Agrippa', 183
Agrippa, C., 7, 221
Ahasuerus, 143, 227, 279, 310
Aicher, A., 95 f.
Albertus Magus, 7
Alexander the Great, 46, 76, 102 f.,
    138, 242
Alexander VI, Pope, 27, 165
Alexander VI, Pope, 168
Alexo, 95, 98
Amanda, 279
Angelica (Klinger), 164
Angelica (Schmid), 273
Anhalt, Duke of, 46
Anna, 187
Anna, Donna, 249 f.
Anton, 213
Antonius Morus, 24
Apono, Peter of, 24
Arabella, 127, 334
Ariel, 253
Ariosto, 8
Aristophanes, 153
Aristotle, 23, 321
Aristotle, 120 f., 133, 172, 242, 347
Arnim, A. von, 212 f., 227, 342
Asmodeus, 55
Astaroth, 87 ff.
Auerhahn, 176
Augustin, 273
Aurelia, 214
Avenarius, F., xi, 280 ff., 284, 300,
    307, 308, 321, 342, 347 f.

B

Babes in the Wood, The, 64
Bacchus, 153 f.
Bacon, Roger, 7, 54, 56, 64, 66, 264
Baggesen, J., 270 f.
Baian, Prince (the Bulgar), 7, 24
Baines, R., 43
Balhorn, J., 21
Ballardites, The, x
Bar, Johannes von, 24
Bärbelchen, 135, 312
Bateman's Ghost, 67
Baucis, 261
Baudelaire, C., 90
Beaumarchais, P.-A. C. de, 215
Beautymad, 130
Bechstein, L., 269 f.
Beelzebub, 120
Benedict IX, Pope, 26
Bennett, Arnold, xi, xii, xvii
Benkowitz, K. F., 174 f., 183, 211,
    342
Benno, Cardinal, 27
Benvolio, 47
Berlioz, H., xi
Berthold, 213
Birde, W., 52, 56
Bittner, K., 69
Black Raven, The, 73, 87 f., 102,
    183, 339
Blankenburg, F. von, 122, 124 f.
Boas, F. S., 42
Boccaccio, G., 8
Bodin, J., 7
Bonneschky (puppet showman), 92,
    94
Borgias, The, 165, 214
Börne, L., 308
Braunthal, B. von, 272 f., 284, 342

Brennglas, A., 271
Brentano, C., 232
Browne, R., 70
Bruiner, J. W., 69
Bruno, G., 133
Bruno, Saxon, 46, 53
Brunswick, Carl Wilhelm Ferdinand of, 73
Burton, R., *Anatomy of Melancholy*, 23
Byron, Lord, xiff., 236, 249, 334, 341, 343

C

Cain, 6, 10
Cain, 143
Camerarius, P., 18
Campoamor, xi
Casper, 65, 104ff., 186f., 241, 254, 339, 347
Cato, 172
Cayet, V. P., 21
Chamisso, A., 177, **191**ff., 200, 214, 227, 244, 251, 342, 344, 348
Charlemagne, 74
Charles V, Emperor, 46, 138, 272
Charon, 71
Chehov, A., 154
Cherubin, 215
Chiron, 258
Cholmeley, R., 43
Christlich Meynender, The, 29, 96, 132
Cigognini, G. A., xi
Cinthio, 214
Circe, 24, 27
Clara (Hoffmann), 226
Clara (Voss), 214
Clara, Doña (Wolfram), 279
Clement II, Pope, 26
Cleopatra, 88
Cleopatra, 137
Cockayn, Sir A., xi
Coelesta, 310
Columbine, 84
Columbus, 275
Congreve, W., 61
Corneille, T., xi

Cornelius, 48
Corvinus, G. S., 70
Creizenach, W., 69, 70, 107
Crispin, 76, 104
Cyprian, 4, 264

D

Damasus II, Pope, 27
Dante Alighieri, 49, 122
Da Ponte, xi
David, 76, 102
Dee, John, 32
Deininger, J., 96
Delilah, 76, 102
Democritus, 23
Deussen, P., *Recollections of Nietzsche*, 322, 329, 335
Devils appearing in speed-scene, 99, 115ff., 148
Dibdin, xi
Dick, 47
Dick Whittington, 64
Dickers, T., 52
Diebler, A., 85
Diether, 229
Dionysius Areopagita, 23
Dorinde (Rosalinde), 139, 155, 178
Dormion, xi
Dostoyevsky, F., 323f., 330
Dryden, J., 61, 329
Duller, E., ed. *Phönix*, 270
Dumas, A., père, xi, xii, xvii
Dummling, 176

E

Eckard, 179f., 186ff., 213
Eckermann, J. P., 238, 324
Eckius, 146
Ecstaticus, Pater, 317
Edward, 126f., 334
Egeria, 7
Eichendorff, J. von, 232
Elizabeth, 126f., 129
Elizabeth, Queen, 137f., 154, 256
Endor, Witch of, 7, 180
Engel, C., 92, 125, 127
Engel, J. J., 122, 124f., 179
Epicurus, 23

Erloffus, Abbot of Fulda, 24
Esmeralda, 329f., 334
Espronceda y Delgado, J. de, xi, xiii
Esse, Margarita Von, 273f.
Essex, Earl of, 137f.
Euphorion, 236, 316, 334
Euripides, 123f., 234
Eve, 129

F

Fair Rosamond, 137f.
Faustbooks, 3–30 (German), 31–41 (English), 46, 50, 52, 61, 104, 126, 138, 146, 160, 204, 232, 236, 247, 255, 321ff.
Faustin, 188
Faustina, 218
Faustus, Justus, 23, 27, 127, 236, 322, 334
Fichte, J. G., 187, 257
Fiordiligi, 279
Flecker, J. E., xi, xii, xvii
Fortunatus, 192
Frederick III, Emperor, 212
Frederike, 153
Full-of-Care, 130
Fust, J., 161, 172, 211, 213, 271

G

Gabriel, 128, 301
Galatea, 258
Galileo, 275, 281
Galotti, Emilia, 179
Geibel, E., 271
Geisselbrecht (puppet showman), 90, 92, 94, 96, 99, 102, 105f., 109f., 231
Gerstenberg, H. W. von, 142f.
Gesta Romanorum, The, 8
Gilberti, O., xi
Gluck, C. W. von, xi
Godeau, Marie, 333
Goebbels, J., 326
Goethe, A. von, 238, 245
Goethe, J. W. von, xiff., 8, 13, 21, 28, 82, 101, 104, 108, 121, 125, **131**ff., 139ff., 141ff.,

146ff., 152f., **154**ff., 159f., 163f., 167, 169, 175, 177ff., 182, 185ff., 191, 194, **195**ff., 215, 217ff., 228ff., **232**ff., 238ff., 245f., 247f., 251, 253f., **253**ff., 270ff., 280ff., 284ff., 288, 294, 301ff., 308f., 311ff., 324ff., 334, 336, 340ff.
Golden Legend, The, 8
Goldoni, C., xii
Goliath, 76, 81, 102
Görg, 291
Gormo of Denmark, 24
Gotthard, 187
Gottsched, J. C., 118f.
Gounod, C., xi
Grabbe, C. D., xiff., 215, **247**ff., 285, 342ff., 347
Grand Grimoire, 183f., 205
Greene (actor), 69
Greene, R., 44, 47
Gregory XI, Pope, 26
Gregory VII, Pope, 26
Gretchen, xii, 8, 29, 131f., **131**ff., 148, 151, 153, 155ff., 164, 170, 172, 178, 186, 187, 188, **197**ff., 216ff., 223, 225, 228, 232, 239f., 247f., 253f., 258ff., 263f., 280f., 283, 285, 288f., 311, 314, 330, 341, 343, 347
Grillparzer, F., **215**ff., 227, 247, 253, 280, 319, 342, 347
Grimmelshausen, J. J. von, 70, 160
Gryphius, A., 77ff., 80, 83, 119
Guastalla, Prince of, 179, 214
Gürgel, 173
Gutzkow, K., 271f.

H

Haggard, Rider, 87
Hagen, F. H. von der, 90, 92
Hamilton, A., 137f., 256, 271, 340
Hamlet, 271f.
Hamm., W., 92, 94ff., 104
Hamann, J. G., 141ff.
Handt (puppet showman), 93
Hango, H., 275f., 342
Hannchen, 287, 289, 291

Hans Wurst, 75, 81, 83, 94, 96, 104f., 107
Harlequin, 57ff., 61
Harring, H. P., 221f., 224, 227, 237
Harriott, T., 43
Hebbel, C. F., 319, 329
Hehn, V., 319
Heine, H., xi, xvii, 8, 71, 86ff., 150, 215, 220, 232, 290, 301ff., 319, 320, 321, 325, 327, 338, 342f., 347
Heine, M., 302
Helen of Troy, 5, 8, 15, 16, 23, 27, 28, 50f., 74, 81, 88f., 103f., 110, 126, 132, 137ff., 146, 173, 226, 228ff., 247, 254ff., 271, 274, 281, 283, 286, 303f., 306f., 316, 232, 340, 348
Helena (Weidmann), 126ff.
Helim, 170f.
Heliogabalus, 24
Henslowe, P., 54
Herbert, Duke, 289
Herder, J. F., 114, 141f., 338
Hermogene, 24
Herz, 146, 148, 202
Heyse, P., 319
Hoffmann, E. T. A., 171
Hoffmann, J. D., 220, 224ff., 227, 237, 247, 253, 265, 272f., 300, 342
Hogarth, W., 61
Holofernes, 76, 102
Holtei, K. von, 237ff., 263, 265, 281, 307, 310, 342, 348
Homer, 21, 142, 225, 306
Homunculus, 257f., 314f., 325, 341
Honorius III, Pope, 27
Horatio, 272
Horn, F., 90
Hugo, 226
Hungary, King of, 138

I

Inez, Doña, xiv
Isabella, 186f., 190, 214
Isenburg, 286

Ithuriel, 127ff., 155, 172, 174, 178, 180, 188f., 228, 232, 347

J

Jack Daw, 59
Jambres, 7
James I, *Daemonologie*, 4, 203
James, Henry, 233
Jamnes, 7
Job, 160, 196
John XII, Pope, 26
John XIX, Pope, 26
John XX, Pope, 26
John XXI, Pope, 26
Jonson, Ben, 61, 157, 329
Juan, Don, de Tenorio, xv
Juan, Don, xff., 100, 164, 211, 215, 247ff., 297f.
Juanito, 272
Judas Iscariot, 6, 129
Judith, 76, 81, 102
Judith, 88
Julius Caesar, 143

K

Karamazov, I., 323, 330, 336
Kallista (puppet showman), 93
Kant, I., 192f.
Karolus, 274
Käthe (Kätchen), 229, 232, 245
Keats, J., 232
Keller, A., 70
Keller, G., 271, 319
Kelley, E., 32
Kierkegaard, S., 327
Kleist, H. von, 95, 192
Klinge, Doctor, 21
Klingemann, E. A. F., xi, 185, 228ff., 233, 238f., 245f., 250, 256, 273, 307, 340, 342, 348
Klinger, F. M. von, xi, 96, 101, 132, 141ff., 159ff., 169, 172f., 174f., 177f., 183, 191, 195, 196, 200, 211ff., 218, 232, 247, 251, 282, 321f., 342ff., 348
Klopstock, F. G., 122, 128f.
Knellius, Magister, 146ff.

Kölbel, 146ff.
Komareck, J. N., 211
Kotzebue, A. F. F. von, 212f., 227
Kretzschmar, W., 326f.
Krummschal, 115
Kurz, J. F. von, 71, 79, 81, 84f., 87, 197
Kumpf, 325f.

L

Laurentius, 24
Lavater, G. K., 142
Lazarus, 81
Leisewitz, J. A., 142f.
Leitner, K. C. F., 90
Lenau, N., xiff., 272, 284ff., 296f., 300f., 319ff., 328, 336, 342ff.
Lenchen, 151, 152, 178, 188
Lenz, J. M. R., 132, 141f., 152ff., 159, 175, 183, 191, 200, 265, 285, 341, 348
Leo IX, Pope, 27
Leporello, 211, 249, 251
Lercheimer, A., 7, 18ff.
Lessing, G. E., xi, xiv, 80f., 83, 96, 98f., 113ff., 124f, 126, 127, 130, 131, 132f., 139f., 143, 148, 152, 154f., 157, 159, 171f., 174f., 177, 178, 179, 182, 191, 196, 211, 228, 265, 280, 340f., 343f., 347
Leutbecher, J., 92
Leverkühn, A., 321ff.
Lévi, E., 5
Leviathan, 161ff., 212ff., 348
Lewis, Monk, 343
Lieschen, 135, 311ff.
Liese, 172f.
Linde, K. A., 92f., 270
Liszt, F., 286
Lorgée (puppet showman), 94
Louis XI of France, 164
Lowes, J. L., 24
Löwe, J. F., 120, 197, 340
Lübke, H., 92ff.
Lucifer, 32, 36, 56, 82f., 144f.
Lucifuge, 184, 205
Lucretia, 102

Lucretia, Signora, 86f., 100, 150
Lumley, B., 302
Luna, Johannes de, 22
Luther, M., 9, 11, 13, 26, 27, 28, 34, 106, 275, 325
Lynceus, 235

M

Macarius the Hermit, 24
Machiavelli, 214
Magia Naturalis et Innaturalis, 183f., 189, 203f., 341
Mann, T., xi, xvii, 321ff., 342, 344, 347f.
Margareta, 240ff.
Maria, 289
Marianne (Hamilton), 137
—— (Schilf), 274
Marianus, Doctor, 317
Marlowe, C., xiff., 8, 13 ,26, 41ff., 52ff., 69, 72, 74ff., 80, 83, 90, 99, 103f., 107, 113, 123f., 126f., 130, 134, 183, 194, 196, 205, 233, 251, 256, 262f., 264f., 285f., 288, 322, 339ff.
Marthe, Frau, 134f., 187, 199, 218
Marwood, 127
Mary (Virgin), 82, 151, 186f., 263f.
Mathilde, 178, 180, 186ff., 201, 247
Maximilian, Emperor, 225, 254
Mazzini, G., 221
Meck, Frau von (Fon-Mekk), N. F., 333
Medea, 127
Medici, The, 214
Melanchthon, P., 125
Mellefont, 127
Melton, J., 54
Melusine, 192
Mendelssohn, M., 120
Menelaos, 235f.
Mephistophela, 305ff.
Meretrix, 81ff., 127
Merimée, P., xi, xii, xvii
Merlin, 7, 24, 27, 54
Metrodorus, 23
Metternich, Prince, 211

Meyer, C. F., 319
Michelangelo, 281
Middleton, T., 67, 157, 329
Miles, 47
Militarius, 264
Milton, J., 49, 72, 128f., 196
Mohammed, 143
Molière, J.-B. P., **xi**ff.
Molina, Tirso de, xiff.
Mölling, C. E., 270
Moncrieff, W. T. T., xi
Montaldo, Count of, 188f.
Mörike, E., 319
Mosca, 24
Moses, 7, 43
Mother Goose, 64
Mother Shipton, 64, 67
Mountfort, W., xi, 57ff., 63, 84
Mozart, W. A., xiff., 211, 216, 247,
    343
Müller, A., 270
Müller, J. F. (Maler), xi, 96, 122,
    139, 142, **143**ff., 153, 155, 159,
    163, 172, 174f., 178, 182, 188,
    195, 196, 202f., 213, 265, 342,
    347
Müller, W. 342
Mylius, C., 137

N

Napoleon, 269, 277f.
Nathan the Wise, 121
Nepomuk, 322, 334
Neumann, J. G., 30, 70
Neurath, O., 276, 280
Nicodemus, 129
Nietzsche, F., 319f., 322f., 329,
    335f.
Nose-to-the-Ground, 130
Nostradamus, 203f.
Numa Pompilius, 7, 24
Nürnberger, W., xi, xii, **204**ff.,
    301, 306, 320f., 325, 329, 342,
    344, 347

O

Ophelia (Shakespeare), 136, 340

Ophelia (Gutzkow), 271f.
Opitz, M., 271
Orestes, 124
Origen, 23, 189
Orkanus, 81
Orpheus, 23, 258, 327
Othin (Odin), 7
Ovid, 23

P

P. F., *Gent.*, 21, **31**ff., 40f., 44ff.,
    50, 52, 340
Padamera, 102
Paletes, 24
Paracelsus, 7, **132**f., 157, 258, 340f.
Paracelsus, 179f.
Paris (son of Priam), 138, 254ff.
Parma, Duke of, 74, 76, 81, 102,
    138, 241
Parsons, R., 43
Paul II, Pope, 27
Pepys, S., 56
Percy, T., 114
Persephone, 258
Petsch, R., 92
Pfitzer, J. N., 28ff., 84, 131, 269
Pfizer, G., **220**f., 227, 237, 253,
    257, 280, 301, 342
Philemon, 261
Phillip, 240ff.
Phillips, E., 63
Phorkyas, 180, 233ff.
Pickelhäring, 75, 104
Pierrot, 61
Platen, A. von, 227
Plato, 23, 192, 319
Plautus, 21
Pluto, 71, 73, 82, 101
Pompey, 74
Pope, A., 63
Powell, R., 64
Prästigiar (the poodle), 272, 287
Profundus, Pater, 317
Prometheus, 143
Prometheus, 275
Prospero, 66
Punch, 61, 64, 65, 104
Pythagoras, 23

R

Raleigh, Sir Walter, 42 f.
Ralph, 47, 58, 76
Ralph, J., 66
Randolph, T., 54, 55
Raphael, 82
Raphaele, 188 f.
Recha, 121
Regnini, xi
Richard III of England, 164
Richardson, S., Clarissa Harlowe, xi.
Richter, J. P. F. (Jean Paul), 167
Rilke, R. M., 95
Robert the Devil, 24, 27, 264
Robertus (Klinger), 163, 165
Robertus (Voss), 213 f.
Robin, 47, 58, 76
Robin Hood, 64
Rohde, R., 32 f.
Romeo, 216
Rosenkranz, K., 222 ff., 227, 237, 253, 257, 280, 341 f.
Rosimond (actor), xi
Rousseau, J. J., 142, 167
Rowe, N., xi
Rowland, The Imposter or tis the Humer of the age, a Farce, 59 f.
Rowley, S., 48, 52, 56
Rudolph, 240 f.

S

Sachs, Hans, 11, 14, 17, 135, 196, 340
St. Dunstan, 54
St. John, 82, 203 f.
St. Michael, 224, 227
St. Peter, 129, 226
Sara Sampson, 127
Satan, 4, 5, 27, 49, 106
Satan, 128 f., 166, 176, 345
Saul, 7
Scaramouche, 57 f., 61
Schade, O., 92
Schedel, H., Nürnberger Chronik, 36
Scheible, J., 84, 92, 109, 302 f., 304, 342

Schildknapp, 331
Schilf, H., 273 ff., 342
Schiller, J. F. von, 142, 150, 167, 173, 192, 225, 233, 236, 276, 309 f.
Schink, J. F., 137, 139 f., 151 f., 154 f., 177 ff., 191, 196 f., 201 f., 206, 213, 214, 215, 221, 226, 247, 257, 263, 265, 300, 340 ff., 347
Schirin, 188, 228
Schlüssel (puppet showman), 93
Schmid, X., 272 f., 342
Schmitt, L., 270
Schiff, D., 271
Schleppfuss, 326, 328 ff.
Schöne, C. C. L., 212, 215, 217 ff., 222 ff., 226 f., 247, 253, 257, 263 f., 280, 300, 302, 341 ff.
Schopenhauer, A., 292, 327
Schopenhauer, Johanna, 245
Schreiber, A. W., 169 ff., 174 f., 183, 265, 272, 342
Schröder, G., 71, 72, 75
Schütz-Dreher (puppet showmen), 90, 92, 94, 96 f., 240
Schütze, J. F., 90
Schwerdtfeger, R., 333
Scio, Sebastian de, 70
Scot, Reginald, 7, 45
Scotus, 24
Seidl, J., 271
Seraphicus, Pater, 317
Seraphine, 214 f.
Seuffert, B., 150
Shadwell, C., xi
Shakespeare, W., 53, 58, 61, 136, 142, 157, 329, 333, 340 f.
Shallow, Sir Credulous, 59
Shaw, G. B., xi, xii, xvii
Sheba, Queen of, 102
Shelley, P. B., 343
Sidney, Sir Philip, 137 f.
Silvergrub, 130
Simon Magus, 4, 7, 24, 27
Simrock, K., 302, 342
Sisyphus, 74
Snow, C. P., 319

Socrates, 143, 172, 200
Soden, F. J. H. von, 171 ff., 175, 183, 211, 213, 228, 231 f., 342 f.
Solitar, M., *see* Nürnberger, W.
Solomon, 204, 207
Solomon, 102
Solon, 172
Sommer, E., 90
Spiess, 'Spiess', *see* Urfaustbook
Spinoza, B., 290
Spohr, L., xi, 95
Stolte, J., 308 ff., 342
Stranitzky, J. A., 74, 75
Strauss, D. F., 319
Strauss, J., xi
Strehlenau, N. F. N. von, *see* Lenau, N.
Susanna, 187
Swedenborg, E., 133
Swift, J., 64, 66, 104
Sylvester II (Gerbert), Pope, 11, 26, 186, 264

T

Tamburlaine, 41
Tannenbaum, 42
Tantalus, 74
Terence, 21
Teridates, 7
Teutonicus, J., Canon of Halberstadt, 7, 24
Thales, 23, 24
Theodo, Magister, 7
Theodore, 126 f., 129
Theophilus, 4, 264
Therese (Hoffmann), 226
Therese (Schreiber), 170 f.
Thoms, W. J., 52
Thunderclap, 130
Thurmond, J., 60 f., 63, 67, 84
Tieck, L., 175 ff., 238, 271
Tityos, 74, 76
Tolna, Frau von, 333
Torquemada, 164
Tritheim, J., 7, 18, 24
Tschaikovsky, 333
Twardowski, 186

U

Uhland, J. L., 277 f.
Undine, 192, 246
Urfaustbook, ed. Spiess, 3 ff., 13–41 *passim*, 45, 72, 83, 85, 99, 119, 127, 134, 149, 151, 164 ff., 181 f., 192, 213, 257, 259, 264 f., 295, 302 ff., 308, 319, 321 ff., 330 ff., 334, 336, 338 f., 343 f.

V

Valdes, 48
Valentine, 135, 199, 261, 289, 312 f., 316 ff.
Valéry, P., xi, xii, 344 ff.
Victor II, Pope, 27
Victoria, 81
Villiers, J. de, xi
Virgil, 7, 24, 27, 49
Vischer, F. T., xi, xvii, 311 ff., 343
Vizibuzli, 115
Vogt, N., 211, 215, 227, 247, 272
Voland, 240 ff.
Voltaire, F.-M. A., 73, 165
Voss, J. von, 87, 213 ff., 227, 247, 272, 342 f.

W

Wagner (Faust's Famulus), 9, 11, 22, 24, 27, 38, 47, 52, 58, 61, 75, 105, 107, 109, 126, 129 f., 133, 146, 155, 170, 200, 202 f., 221, 223, 229, 238, 240 f., 256 f., 269, 286, 324
Wagner, H. L., 132, 137, 142
Wagner, R., 302
Wagnerbook, 22 ff., 28, 52
Wallerotti (actor), 71
Warner, S. T., xi
Wedekind, E., 301
Weidmann, P., 83, 124 ff., 132, 137, 140, 143, 146, 152, 154, 168, 172 f., 174 f., 178, 182, 191, 226, 228, 231 f., 247, 256, 263, 265, 334, 340, 342
Weimar, Duke of, 131

Welsh Book, The, 68

Widman, G. R., **22**ff., 31, 33, 41, 84, 113, 131, 165, 182, 240, 269f., 328, 339

Wierus, J., 7, 18

Wiese, S., xi

Wildfire, 7, 24

Wolfe, H., xi

Wolfram (puppet showman), 93

Wolfram, L. H., **276**ff., 284f., 300, 342, 347

Wolzogen, E. von, 252

Z

Zamora, A. de, xi, xiv

Zarmocenide the Assyrian, 24

Zedechias, 7

Zeitblom, S., 324f., 331, 333, 335, 337

Zelter, K. F., 220, 245

Zemire, 275

Zephon, 128

Zingerle, I. V., 71, 80, 83

Zoroaster, 24, 27

Zorilla, J., xiff.

Zyto, 7

THE MAGIC IN HISTORY SERIES

FORBIDDEN RITES
A Necromancer's Manual of the Fifteenth Century
Richard Kieckhefer

CONJURING SPIRITS
Texts and Traditions of Medieval Ritual Magic
Claire Fanger

RITUAL MAGIC
Elizabeth M. Butler

The MAGIC IN HISTORY series explores the role magic and the occult have played in European culture, religion, science and politics. Titles in the series will bring the resources of cultural, literary and social history to bear on the history of the magic arts, and will contribute towards an understanding of why the theory and practice of magic have elicited fascination at every level of European society. Volumes will include both editions of important texts and significant new research in the field.